THE COMPLETE IDIOT'S GUIDE® TO

Paganism

by Carl McColman

ALPHA

A member of Penguin Group (USA) Inc.

To Don and Julie

ALPHA BOOKS

Published by the Penguin Group

Penguin Group (USA) Inc., 375 Hudson Street, New York, New York 10014, U.S.A.

Penguin Group (Canada), 10 Alcorn Avenue, Toronto, Ontario, Canada M4V 3B2 (a division of Pearson Penguin Canada Inc.)

Penguin Books Ltd, 80 Strand, London WC2R 0RL, England

Penguin Ireland, 25 St Stephen's Green, Dublin 2, Ireland (a division of Penguin Books Ltd)

Penguin Group (Australia), 250 Camberwell Road, Camberwell, Victoria 3124, Australia (a division of Pearson Australia Group Pty Ltd)

Penguin Books India Pvt Ltd, 11 Community Centre, Panchsheel Park, New Delhi—110 017, India

Penguin Group (NZ), cnr Airborne and Rosedale Roads, Albany, Auckland 1310, New Zealand (a division of Pearson New Zealand Ltd)

Penguin Books (South Africa) (Pty) Ltd, 24 Sturdee Avenue, Rosebank, Johannesburg 2196, South Africa

Penguin Books Ltd, Registered Offices: 80 Strand, London WC2R 0RL, England

Copyright © 2002 by Carl McColman

International Standard Book Number: 0-02-864266-X
Library of Congress Catalog Card Number: 2002102228

08   07   8

Interpretation of the printing code: The rightmost number of the first series of numbers is the year of the book's printing; the rightmost number of the second series of numbers is the number of the book's printing. For example, a printing code of 02-1 shows that the first printing occurred in 2002.

Printed in the United States of America

Publisher: *Marie Butler-Knight*
Product Manager: *Phil Kitchel*
Managing Editor: *Jennifer Chisholm*
Senior Acquisitions Editor: *Randy Ladenheim-Gil*
Development Editor: *Jennifer Moore*
Production Editor: *Katherin Bidwell*

Copy Editor: *Amy Lepore*
Illustrator: *Jody Schaeffer*
Cover/Book Designer: *Trina Wurst*
Indexer: *Amy Lawrence*
Layout/Proofreading: *Brad Lenser, Mary Hunt*

Contents at a Glance

Contents

Foreword

How fortunate we are to live in an age when so many pagans are not only "out of the broom-closet" but are also writing books like this one. Twenty-five years ago, this book would not have been published. Twenty-five years ago, the majority seemed to believe that

Pagans were wild men who hugged trees and indulged in polymorphously perverse orgies with wild women

Witches were evil, wicked, mean, bad, and nasty, and they had green skin, too

Druids were kooks who worshipped trees and big, tall rocks and dressed like shepherds

Shamans were con artists who sold weekend enlightenment for a high price.

Today we know better. Today most people understand that paganism is a genuine religion. Although it's based on the "elder wisdom" of the pre-Christian tribes of Europe, it is a new religion that we recreate every time we cast a circle or invoke a goddess or a god.

And this new religion is growing. Because there's no pagan census bureau, we don't know precisely how many of us there are, but just look at the Web—at www.witchvox.com, for example—or at the shelves at your local bookstores. You'll see pages and pages of pagan writing. Someone's got to be reading all those pages.

That would be you and me. I'm a Witch and a writer. I assure you that I do not have green skin. Although I don't like to get the outdoors on me, I worship the ground I walk on, which is our precious Mother Earth. Like thousands of other pagans, I also worship the Goddess Who Is All That Is. (And I drive a Toyota, not a broomstick.)

And you? Perhaps you're already a pagan and have already brought our ethical principles of tolerance and doing harm to none into your life. Perhaps you already realize that when we worship the old gods and goddesses we do so with joy and creativity.

More likely, you already know pagans. They probably sit in the cubicles and offices all around you, doing their jobs, raising their kids, living more or less normal lives. You see them at the grocery store, in line at the post office, at Little League games, at the movies. That's a funny thing about us pagans: We look just like you. Well, sometimes we dress up, and then we look fantastic.

It's been said that pagans are becoming mainstream. Well, this is partly true. I think it's truer, however, that the mainstream is going pagan. No matter where they worship, people are learning to love, respect, and take care of our beautiful, blessed planet. We're learning that we all are kin and that some of our cousins walk on four feet, fly, swim, or have roots in the ground. Many of the standard-brand churches are coming to realize that their lonely god does not appeal to half of the population (the female half). Some standard-brand churches are coming to acknowledge that the Goddess may well indeed be the grandmother of God. (The first man known to have talked to God was Abraham, who lived ca. 1900 B.C.E. We have goddess figures like the Willendorf Mother that are at least 35,000 years old.)

So, dear Reader, I'm glad that you picked up this book. It's interesting, it's funny, it's useful. My friend, Carl McColman, gives us "the big picture" about paganism. A respected pagan and scholar himself, he knows from his own experience how to balance our spiritual devotion with a candid presentation of the facts of who pagans are and what we believe. And you can tell from the table of contents that he has a wicked sense of humor. Whether you're exploring new spiritual paths or deeply in love with the old gods and goddesses, you'll find Carl's writing both interesting and entertaining. What more could a reader ask?

Bright blessings to you!

—Barbara Ardinger

Ostara, 2002

Barbara Ardinger, Ph.D., www.visionaryfiction.com/bawriting, is the author of *Goddess Meditations, Practicing the Presence of the Goddess,* and the forthcoming *Finding New Goddesses: Reclaiming Playfulness in Our Spiritual Lives.*

Introduction

Paganism is a topic filled with mystery, romance, and spiritual adventure. Many vivid images come to mind when you think about pagans: witches stirring their cauldrons as they brew their magic potions … druids chanting their ancient runes as they prepare to perform their primitive sacrifices in a grove of oak trees … tribal medicine men, beating their drums as a ritual of healing begins. These images may have more to do with Hollywood than with authentic paganism in the twenty-first century, but for increasing numbers of people, paganism has emerged as a thoroughly modern spirituality centered on love for nature, personal growth, and approaching Spirit as both Goddess and God. These modern pagans have a distinctive way of expressing spirituality and enjoying the pleasures of life. For pagans, life is not a burden to be endured while waiting for a pie in the sky; it's a wonderful and marvelous opportunity to experience love, joy, and growth in a world given to us as a gift from the Divine Mother and her Sacred Consort.

Perhaps you are thinking about embracing the pagan path for yourself, or maybe you are just curious about this rapidly growing alternative spiritual path. Either way, this book can help you understand the basics and appreciate the special perspective of the pagan world.

How to Use This Book

Paganism is a broad subject with many unique subcategories, so this book aims to give you an overview to help you understand the big picture. In the pages to come, you'll get a taste of how pagans view the world, the pagan perspective on history, and—most interesting of all—what pagans actually do as they practice their unique spirituality today. Hopefully, you'll be inspired to try some of the rituals and meditative exercises yourself and take a hands-on approach to learning about the beautiful world of nature spirituality.

This book is divided into five parts:

Part 1, "Pagan Basics," introduces you to the modern expression of nature spirituality and Goddess worship. You'll meet three major types of pagans: witches, druids, and shamans.

Part 2, "How to Think Like a Pagan," surveys the key points of pagan beliefs and the pagan world view. From cosmology to the cycles of life, this section discusses the basic principles of the pagan path.

Part 3, "Ritual," provides you with everything you'll need to begin honoring nature and the Goddess yourself. Ritual tools, holidays and festivals, and a sample ritual script will help you on your way.

Part 4, "Magic," uncovers the myths and realities behind the quest for spiritual power. You'll learn the important roles of meditation, divination, and healing in magical spirituality.

Part 5, "Living the Pagan Life," shows you what you'll need to incorporate earth spirituality into your daily routine. The ethics of paganism, pagan communities, and paganism in popular culture round out this section.

Extras

You'll find boxes in every chapter that provide helpful definitions, tips, cautions, and intriguing factoids to help you learn and understand more about the world of paganism.

> ### Drumbeats
>
> In these boxes, you'll find a variety of interesting pagan tidbits.

> ### ⚠ CAUTION Taboo
>
> These boxes provide cautionary notes to help you avoid pitfalls in the pagan world.

> ### Oracle
>
> These tips will increase your understanding of nature spirituality and will help you along the pagan path.

> ### EarthWords
>
> Here you'll find definitions of words associated with paganism or with spirituality in general.

Acknowledgments

Many people have contributed in both large and small ways to helping make this book a reality.

Love and thanks to Lady Galadriel and Lord Athanor, Lady Devayana Augusta, Anne Newkirk Niven, Sylvia Sultenfuss, Cindy Snowball, and the employees of New Leaf Distributing Company and the Phoenix and Dragon Bookstore for providing moral support as this book was being written. Special thanks to John Beasley, Linda J. Sherer, J. M. (Cernunnos), and Numina for reading sections of the manuscript and providing helpful suggestions. Deep appreciation goes to Fox Gradin, photographer extraordinaire; Olaf, her trusty assistant; and members of the Earth Mystic Circle who posed, including Selene-Ka, Lisa L., William Morris, Numina, and Melody Pettus. Thanks also to the members of Emerald Rose for permission to use a group publicity photo and to Rikki Osborne and Peter Manzi for help at the eleventh hour.

Linda Roghaar and Randy Ladenheim-Gil worked the initial magic to make this book happen, while Jennifer Moore has been the most understanding of editors. ("Yes, Jennifer, I promise I'll have that chapter to you today!") I appreciate everyone else at Alpha who contributed to making this book a reality.

Finally, heartfelt thanks to everyone associated with the various pagan communities and groups I have had the honor to study with and/or participate in over the years: Earthstar; The Mill House and the Rock; Starbridge Sanctuary; Peachtree Grove, ADF; Circle of the Sacred

Hoop; Ravenwood Church and Seminary of the Old Religion; Dogwood Local Council of the Covenant of the Goddess; House of Oakspring; Grove of the Unicorn; and the Earth Mystic Circle. Because of the diversity of the pagan community, the leaders and members of these groups may not necessarily agree with or endorse all the views expressed in this book. (Since pagans value diversity, they acknowledge that it's okay to disagree with one another.) Still, each of these communities played a pivotal role in my own spiritual journey, and for that I remain profoundly grateful.

Special Thanks to the Technical Reviewer

The Complete Idiot's Guide to Paganism was reviewed by an expert who double-checked the accuracy of what you'll learn here. This helps us ensure that this book will give you everything you need to know about the world of paganism. Special thanks are extended to Barbara Ardinger, Ph.D., for taking on this essential task.

In addition to being a superb editor, Barbara is a scholar/priestess of the Goddess who has written several wonderful books, including *Goddess Meditations, Practicing the Presence of the Goddess*, and the forthcoming *Finding New Goddesses*.

Trademarks

All terms mentioned in this book that are known to be or are suspected of being trademarks or service marks have been appropriately capitalized. Alpha Books and Penguin Group (USA) Inc. cannot attest to the accuracy of this information. Use of a term in this book should not be regarded as affecting the validity of any trademark or service mark.

Part 1

Pagan Basics

Witches. Druids. Shamans. Magicians. Not so long ago, these words had little bearing on modern religion and spirituality. They merely described figures from ancient history, primitive cultures, or characters from myths and legends of yore.

Today all that has changed. A vibrant and diverse spiritual community has emerged throughout the world, grounded in respect for ancient mysticism, reverence for nature, openness to magic, and devotion to the many Goddesses and Gods of old. The proper name for this multifaceted movement is neo-paganism (in other words, the new paganism), but it is popularly known simply as paganism.

Untying the pagan knot is no easy feat, for one of the chief characteristics of this movement is its diversity. Pagans have no ultimate leader or sacred text; instead, they rely on inner guidance, personal conscience, and a wide variety of traditions to shape their spirituality. The first step to understanding paganism is recognizing its many faces. Thus, in this part of the book, you'll discover the pagan path not only in general terms, but also through learning about several major types of paganism.

Chapter 1

Welcome to the Pagan Path

In This Chapter

- What makes a pagan tick?
- The strange history of the word "pagan"
- Stereotypes and misconceptions, be gone!
- Different kinds of pagans
- Getting started on your own pagan adventure

Do you love nature, so much so that spending time in the great outdoors fills you with an almost spiritual sense of wonder and joy? Are you drawn to the great Gods and Goddesses of ancient mythology? Do the ceremonies and spiritual practices of Native Americans appeal to you—or, for that matter, the mysterious, unexplained stone circles of England and Ireland and the *druids* whom some believe worshiped there? Are you interested in witchcraft, the use of magic power to achieve your goals and to bring health and happiness to you and your loved ones? Do you believe that science and spirituality should not be at odds, but rather should work together for the common benefit of humankind?

Perhaps you are interested in alchemy or the occult—ancient traditions of hidden wisdom and spiritual philosophy used to transform the human soul into a higher state. Or your interests may lie more in the direction of primitive, nature-based, spiritual practices in which ritual contact with spirit guides

EarthWords

One of the most common forms of modern paganism is the revival of **druid** spirituality. The druids were the philosopher/priests of the ancient Celts. Very little is known about them, but by studying Celtic mythology and the pagan practices of other ancient cultures, modern druids have fashioned a new version of a venerable old wisdom tradition.

Oracle

To appreciate the pagan path, set aside regular time for enjoying the natural world. If you live in the city, find a garden or a park where you can sit quietly; suburban or rural folks might enjoy a forest, some farmland, or even the remote wilderness. Take the time to be silent and listen to your heart's wisdom while enjoying the beauty of the earth.

and power animals can lead to prophecy and healing. Or maybe you don't care for supernatural gobbledy-gook and simply think it's a good thing to try to live an ethical life in harmony with the laws of nature.

If your interests lie in any of these areas, you could be someone who finds meaning and joy in the pagan path.

Telltale Signs of a Pagan Personality

Like many pagans, I believe that just about anyone can enjoy and benefit from the unique perspective of nature spirituality. But also like most pagans, I don't believe in trying to convert others to my way of seeing things. So, if paganism is the right path for you, I hope you'll explore it further. I also want to state right up front that I believe it's okay that some people are pagans and others aren't. Whether because of personality type, beliefs, or mere preference, not everyone will choose to explore the pagan path. And that's fine. But you may be wondering, "Is paganism for *me?*" Well, here's a quick checklist to see if you might have some of the common characteristics of the pagan mindset (if there is such a thing). One of the wonderful things about paganism is that it appeals to a wide variety of people with many different backgrounds and ways of seeing the world. It may be difficult to nail down once and for all what the "typical" pagan is like, but this list can still help you learn a little about paganism in general:

◆ Most pagans love nature, whether that means a city park or a remote wilderness area. Weather permitting, the average pagan would much rather be outdoors.

◆ Pagans tend to be open-minded and curious people. They are not necessarily antireligious, although many tend to find that traditional religions leave them cold. Before they discover paganism, many will say, "I'm spiritual, but I'm not religious." Heck, they might say that even after embracing paganism because many pagans do not consider the pagan path to be a "religion" but simply a way of life.

◆ Pagans come in all political shapes and stripes, but most have a basic sense of fairness and justice. For this reason, pagans generally think that the traditional idea of

God as father—without a corresponding concept of Goddess as mother—is, well, out of balance and probably deeply unfair to women.

♦ Pagans prefer thinking for themselves to being told what to think. They love to ask questions, and they believe it is a good thing to question authority and challenge *dogma*. The average pagan would much rather learn by experience than simply accept something on faith.

♦ Pagans love life! They don't consider life on Earth to be some sort of painful trek through a vale of tears; rather, they have an honest and realistic assessment of life as containing both pleasure and pain, joy and sorrow, happiness and disappointment. To pagans, the point of spirituality is not to escape life but to learn ways to maximize its joy and minimize its sorrow.

♦ Many pagans get a kick out of studying ancient mythology and learning about Gods, Goddesses, and spiritual practices of long ago. For some pagans, this is a way of connecting with their ancestors, but for many others, it's simply for the joy of it.

♦ Pagans often have some sort of natural bent toward spirituality and mysticism. Gazing into the night sky will fill many a pagan with a sense of wonder and awe, while others simply approach spirituality out of a belief that there are latent powers in the human mind and body that can be used to make life better. For lack of a better word, these powers may be called "magic."

EarthWords

Dogma refers to beliefs or opinions held as truth simply because some authority said so. Most religious groups have dogmas that shape what their members are expected to believe. While there's nothing wrong with an organization having rules or regulations, many people chafe against religious dogma because it can be based on superstition or outmoded theories or, worse yet, can be used to control people's thoughts and behaviors.

EarthWords

Ritual originally meant simply a religious rite, but it can have a much broader meaning, including any behavior or action performed in a customary or ceremonial way with some sort of spiritual meaning. Lighting a candle to meditate can be a very simple, beautiful ritual, as can an elaborate and complex ceremony performed by Buddhist monks, complete with chanting, incense, and bells.

♦ Pagans like to use *ritual* to mark the passage of time, whether that means the normal progression of months and years (as seen in the movement of the moon around the earth and the earth around the sun) or the significant transitions in life, including birth, coming of age, marriage, entry into old age, and death. What these rituals are like—whether simple or elaborate, whether done in solitude or in a large group—varies from pagan to pagan.

◆ Nearly all pagans have strong ethical and moral beliefs. Many believe in such principles as freedom and love. Some insist that "harming none" is an important moral concept, while others adopt traditional values like honor and hospitality. Given their love for nature, many pagans are strong environmentalists. Although there are as many different kinds of pagan ethical codes as there are types of paganism, they all share in common a belief that ethical codes are important and are meant to be taken seriously.

Do you see echoes of yourself in some, most, or even all of these? If so, then welcome home to the pagan path!

What's in a Name?

Paganism is probably the only spiritual path in the world whose name originally was a derogatory term. In fact, the words "pagan" and "paganism" have been used for years to say not what something *is* but what it *is not*. Let me explain.

The original meaning of the word "pagan" comes from the Latin word for "civilian" or "rustic." Probably the modern equivalent would be "redneck" or "country bumpkin." Originally, a pagan was someone who didn't live in the city. But then, when Romans and inhabitants of other major cities began to convert to Christianity, all the rustics and country bumpkins held on to their traditional forms of spirituality and religion. That's when pagan came to mean "non-Christian." Over the centuries, the meaning of the word expanded to mean "primitive," "savage," "amoral," and all sorts of other unsavory connotations, but the main sense of the word was simply non-Christian.

The only problem with this definition is that it says what paganism isn't, not what it is! Sure, paganism as it is practiced in modern times is an alternative to religions like Christianity and Islam, but it's much, much more than that. So, what's a handy definition? Well, going back to the concept of "rustic" can be helpful since pagan spirituality almost always involves reverence for nature. But people who live in cities or suburbs can be just as pagan as rural folk, so I'd like to propose a new definition of pagan, which is based on an anagram of the word itself:

People **A**doring **G**oddess **A**nd **N**ature

Even this definition is imperfect. For every pagan who mainly worships the Goddess, there are other pagans who worship a God and Goddess in equilibrium, or who revere a variety of different Gods and Goddesses from ancient cultures. Likewise, many pagans worship the ground they walk on, while to some, nature is far less interesting than a room full of books. But since *most* pagans have some degree of reverence for nature and *most* have some sort of devotion to the Goddess, this definition works as well as any.

> **Drumbeats**
>
> Some pagans actually prefer the term "neopagan" to describe themselves. They look at it this way: The earliest and original pagans were the folks who practiced some form of Goddess-oriented, nature-based spirituality from ancient times until the European renaissance prior to and during the early years of the Christian era. These pagans, therefore, are the paleopagans (*paleo-* means "old"). The neopagans, or "new pagans," are those who, beginning around the middle of the twentieth century, have been dedicated to reviving what they regard as ancient religious traditions, whether through witchcraft, druidism, or some other form of nature reverence. To complicate matters even further, some writers point out that people in the eighteenth and nineteenth centuries made attempts (usually quite inaccurate) to revive practices like druidism, but these attempts often ended up looking more like Christianity in a funny robe than anything else. Such quasi-pagan movements are referred to as the mesopagan (or "middle pagan") era.

What Pagans Are *Not*

Perhaps you're saying to yourself, "When I think of pagans, I think of primitive savages who perform human sacrifices and have giant sex orgies to please their angry Gods!" Hold on. Before going any further, let's take a minute to banish a few common misunderstandings about the pagan path.

The Devil Doesn't Live Here Anymore (In Fact, He Never Did!)

First and foremost, *pagans are not devil worshipers.* They never were, and they never will be. Why would the members of one religion worship the bad guy of another religion? Anthropologists have seen how, when a culture changes religions, the Gods (and Goddesses) of the old religion come to be regarded as devils or evil spirits in the new faith. This is what happened when Christianity came to Europe. The Christian way of seeing the universe (as some sort of battlefield where a single good God and a single bad devil are duking it out) was completely foreign to the pagan mind. As Christianity became dominant, most of the old pagan Gods and Goddesses came to be regarded as demons, while the popular horned Gods, such as Pan in the Greek world or Cernunnos in the Celtic, came to be identified with the Big Baddy himself. This was essentially a smear job done to make the old religion look bad, thereby encouraging people to submit to the new religious regime.

Modern pagans try to take a balanced view of history. Without meaning to gratuitously slam the Christian faith (Christians are human beings who make mistakes like everyone else), pagans reject the propaganda that seeks to link the old Gods with the Christian devil. In doing so, pagans are free to accept, learn about, and revere the old Gods on their own terms.

No Blood Sacrifice, Please

Modern pagans also renounce the practice of human and animal sacrifice. They reject the idea that their Gods require blood sacrifice just as much as modern Jews and Christians reject the notion. Granted, there is real evidence that ancient pagans performed human and animal sacrifice—just as in ancient Biblical times, human and animal sacrifice was performed (Remember the story about Abraham almost killing his son Isaac? The angel stopped him at the last minute, providing a ram for him to kill instead. The point of the story, which many people conveniently overlook, is that Abraham thought sacrificing his son was a perfectly respectable thing to do until the angel told him otherwise.) But just as it wouldn't be fair to judge modern Christians and Jews on the practices of their spiritual ancestors, it's also not fair to judge modern pagans on the pagan deeds of ancient times.

Drumbeats
A 1973 horror movie, *The Wicker Man,* is something of a cult classic among pagans. Set on a remote island in modern-day Scotland, the movie follows the investigations of a police officer who discovers a thriving pagan community, complete with human sacrifice. Modern pagans disavow the shedding of blood in their rites, of course. But for those who enjoy an offbeat, spooky movie and who keep in mind that this depiction of modern paganism is not entirely accurate, it's an entertaining film.

Now, many modern pagans do believe that there are still appropriate ways to make sacrifices, which can be defined as "offerings to the Gods." But instead of shedding blood, modern pagan sacrifice usually involves offering prayers, songs, words of praise or thanksgiving, flowers, oil, or a token food offering such as pouring some wine on sacred ground or leaving a small meal for wild animals. Even giving up a bad habit can be a sacrifice to the Gods, if done in a spiritually intentional manner.

The Naked Truth About Pagans and Sex

Another common misconception about pagans is that their worship always involves a hot, sweaty orgy. Some people may secretly wish that this stereotype were true! But seriously, if all you're interested in is group sex, you'll have better luck at a swinger's club than at your typical pagan ritual.

While pagan *beliefs* about sex tend to be more liberal than some people's, their sexual *behavior* is pretty much in line with mainstream society. Many pagan groups and gatherings actually have fairly strict standards of sexual behavior. Pagans are just like everyone else in their opposition to adultery, rape, and child molestation. When it comes to such things as gay and lesbian sexuality, bisexuality, and sex between unmarried people, however, pagans are probably more liberal than most, but that's simply because pagans believe sex is natural and therefore good.

A small minority of pagans believe in such things as free love and open marriages, but that's also true of society as a whole. Still, most pagans live very ordinary lives in which they fall in love with one other person and either get married or live in some form of committed relationship.

Some pagans, especially those who practice *Wicca*, sometimes perform rituals in the nude, a practice known as going "skyclad." This is not true of all Wiccans and certainly not of all pagans, but it does seem to get a lot of press. I guess society just loves the idea of naked people dancing around a bonfire, eh? But even those Wiccans who practice skyclad rituals tend to be as middle-of-the-road in their sexuality as most pagans. In other words: They think sex is great with an appropriate partner, but an orgy? No thanks!

For more about pagan views on sexual morality, see Chapter 21, "Pagan Ethics: How to Behave Like an Earthkeeper."

Diversity, Diversity, Diversity

So now that I've dispelled some of the more notorious misconceptions surrounding pagan spirituality, it's time to look at paganism from a more positive angle. You've already seen how pagans tend to look to nature as the main source of their spiritual and/or religious inspiration; I've also touched briefly on how pagans tend to revere Spirit in feminine as well as masculine ways, as Goddess as well as God. What else is there to say about the pagan path?

Probably the most important characteristic to look at now is simply how diverse the pagan community is. Words like "conformity" and "uniformity" don't seem to apply very well in the pagan world. Pagans do not come out of a mold or a cookie cutter. There are three reasons why this is so:

Taboo!

Some individuals and groups describe themselves as pagans but seem more interested in throwing wild parties with drug use and even group sex. A true pagan will never ask you to do anything you're uncomfortable doing (sexually or otherwise). If a person or group strikes you as being focused more on sex than on spirituality, don't waste your time with them.

EarthWords

Wicca is a pagan religion inspired by traditional forms of witchcraft. It's a modern religion, established primarily by Gerald Gardner and his followers during the 1940s and '50s. The word comes from the Middle English word for witch, *wicce*. People who practice Wicca are called Wiccans as well as witches. Pagan witchcraft and Wicca, incidentally, will be examined in greater detail in Chapter 4, "Wicked Good!"

EarthWords

A **shaman** is someone who practices a primal spirituality based on the wisdom of indigenous people. The word originally came from a Siberian culture, but it has become a common term for describing medicine men and women, witchdoctors, and other kinds of spiritual priests/healers. Nowadays, many people in urban cultures study shamanic practices from a wide variety of indigenous cultures and incorporate these practices into their spiritual life.

EarthWords

A **sigil** is an image or sign used in magical spirituality. It is seen as embodying spiritual or mystical power.

1. Paganism is a broad and universal concept. There is room in the pagan community for Wiccans, witches, druids, *shamans*, miscellaneous Goddess worshipers and nature mystics, and plenty of people who refuse to wear any kind of label at all.

2. Because paganism is a spirituality of experience rather than belief, there is no requirement that everyone must think the same way or believe the same things. On the contrary, most pagans consider it a point of honor that they think for themselves.

3. People who embrace paganism may have ancestral links to a wide variety of cultures, including Egyptian, Celtic, Greek, Italian, Norse, Baltic, Native American, or many other heritages. Even if a person isn't related to a particular culture by blood ancestry, many pagans believe it's okay to respectfully embrace an ancient tradition (or traditions) simply because you're interested in it. Thus, different pagan groups and individuals may have different spiritual practices with any of a variety of cultural "flavors."

Even in their symbolism, witches and druids and shamans differ. The most common symbol used by Wiccans is the pentacle, a five-armed star enclosed in a circle. For many shamans, the Medicine Wheel, an equal-armed cross enclosed in a circle, represents an image of the cosmos. Druids also have their own *sigils*, or symbols of their path, such as a circle intersected by two upright parallel lines—the sigil of modern American druids.

Left: The witches' pentacle.
Center: The druids' sigil.
Right: A shaman's depiction
of the cosmos.

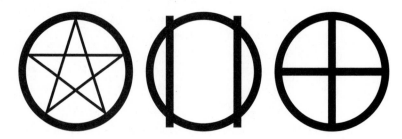

Glinda and Merlin, Meet the Medicine Man

The three main groups of pagans that this book will look at in greater depth are the Wiccans, the shamans, and the druids. Imagine what would happen if Glinda, the Good Witch of the North from the Land of Oz, Merlin the druidic magician from the Court of Camelot, and Kicking Bird, the medicine man (shaman) in the movie *Dances With Wolves* all got together to try to figure out what their spirituality had in common. The common vision they would come up with would embody the core principles of paganism that more and more people every day are practicing—and it would be very similar to the principles and exercises you'll find in this book.

You Can't Fool Mother Nature

Whatever style of paganism you choose—from Wiccan to druidic, from shamanic to magical, from Norse to Egyptian, or even an eclectic blending of all of these—the one characteristic you share with all your pagan sisters and brothers is a connection to Mother Earth. If pagans adore nature, then by doing so, pagans equally revere the entire planet on which our natural world exists. Some pagans even believe that Mother Earth is a conscious being, an idea I'll look at more closely in the next chapter.

Oracle

When you're just beginning to explore the pagan path, take your time. Try to learn all you can about Wicca, druidism, shamanism, and other forms of nature spirituality. Don't commit to the first style of paganism that catches your eye; another branch of the pagan path may end up suiting your personality better.

Pagans Believe In What They Experience

Some pagans like to think of Spirit as a single, unified force, almost like "The Force" from *Star Wars*. Many others prefer the male-female polarity implied in a single God and Goddess. Others, especially those who have studied the ancient myths of pre-Christian cultures, prefer to see Spirit in a variety of ways. In the pagan world, there is room for each of these positions. Why? Because paganism is primarily a religion of experience, not of dogma. If you most clearly experience Spirit through many different Gods or Goddesses, then that is the right path for you. The same is true if you find Spirit best through the experience of an all-encompassing Lady and Lord. And so forth.

CAUTION

Taboo!

So you've decided that you're a pagan. Great! But avoid using labels like "witch" or "druid" or "shaman" to describe yourself. Among nonpagans, such words can be confusing or even threatening. Among many pagans, such terms are often titles of respect that must be earned after years of study and spiritual practice.

Glinda and Merlin and Kicking Bird might disagree heartily on many details of their unique spiritual perspectives. That's perfectly okay. But in recognizing that they all share a common reverence for Mother Earth and a similar devotion to Spirit, even though they experience Spirit in different ways, they would be able to affirm a fundamental unity.

Welcome to the Pagan Adventure

One way to practice paganism would be to learn about shamanism, study Wicca, find out all you can about druidism and other ancient wisdom traditions, and then blend them all together into a smooth eclectic mix. Indeed, that's pretty much what you'll find in the pages to come. But you might discover that you feel a special tug toward the magic of witchcraft, toward the primal healing practices of shamanism, or toward the elegant myth and mystery of the druids or a similar ancient priesthood. If so, follow your heart. By reading this book, you are now on the pagan path!

Don't worry. There's no paperwork to sign, no pledge cards to fill out, and you don't even have to say you believe a certain way. Nor do you have to renounce any other beliefs or ideas that have been meaningful to you.

The Ultimate Authority: You!

What's great about the pagan path is that the power stays totally with you. To be a pagan, you don't have to obey a bishop or follow a guru or comply with the rules of this or that religion. Sure, some pagan groups are very structured, and if you choose to study and learn within these groups, you might have to toe their line. But you can also follow the pagan path without joining any sort of group; instead, you can just relying on your own knowledge, intuition, and (most important of all) experience.

In the pagan way of seeing things, you are your own ultimate authority. You decide what you believe, how you behave, and what spiritual practices you observe. Interested in magic? Go for it. Want to learn a form of psychic healing? No one will stop you. You'd rather learn about the universe by studying quantum physics instead of the Greek Gods? It's perfectly appropriate, if it's appropriate for you.

> **CAUTION**
>
> **Taboo!**
>
> Most pagans believe no one has the right to dictate to others what to believe. But this doesn't mean pagans get to ignore tradition, defy common sense, or reject the wisdom of elders. Most pagans believe it's important to respect our human limitations and humbly learn from those who have knowledge to share.

Two Ways to Learn the Pagan Path

If you really want to learn pagan ways, I recommend that you do two things: First, study what you can. This involves not only reading this book but also doing further study. (See Appendix A, "Recommended Reading," for a wide variety of recommended books on pagan topics.) Gaining knowledge also can be facilitated by studying with a pagan teacher or joining a pagan group. I'll talk more about this later. While participating in a pagan group may not be for everyone, it can be a great way to expand your pagan know-how. But amassing knowledge is only one of the ways to learn the pagan path.

The other way is (you guessed it) through experience. This means not only reading about rituals but either participating in a ritual put on by a pagan group or even trying your own hand at a ritual you can do yourself. It means not only learning about the many Gods and Goddesses of world mythology but actually setting up a shrine and meditating on the God(s) and Goddess(es) who appeal to you. It means not only thinking about taking care of the earth but actually making changes in your life so that you live more in harmony with nature.

When you put together these two ways of learning, the knowledge based and the experiential, you have a thorough plan for getting to know the ways of paganism, inside and out. Before you know it, you'll be a seasoned practitioner of the *old ways!*

Why You Can't Stereotype a Pagan

With so much variety under the umbrella of paganism, it's easy to see that pagans, as a group, defy easy classification. Maybe you can try to stereotype pagans, but almost anything you say about many or most pagans simply will not hold true for all of them.

Don't worry. One of my goals in writing this book is to introduce you to the many varieties of paganism, and I will do this in greater depth in the chapters to come. Even so, I'll just be scratching the surface—I only have room to talk about a few of the many different kinds of pagan spirituality. If all this seems a bit overwhelming, take heart. There are plenty of basic principles that most pagans embrace. These core ideas will form the basis of this book's exploration of the nuts and bolts of pagan spirituality. Reading this book not only will teach you about paganism, but if you are interested in becoming a pagan, I'll provide basic instructions for what to do, step by step, to incorporate the Goddess and nature into your own spiritual life, beginning today!

> **EarthWords**
>
> Many different synonyms for paganism exist. Some people refer to paganism (especially Wicca) as "the Old Religion." A lovely name for witchcraft is the "Craft of the Wise." The **old ways** is another such way of talking about the spirituality of Goddess and nature.

The Least You Need to Know

- ◆ Pagans follow a variety of spiritual philosophies and paths.
- ◆ Pagans don't worship the devil or perform blood sacrifice.
- ◆ Almost all pagans revere nature and the earth as sacred.
- ◆ Pagans usually believe in a Goddess or a God or many Goddesses and Gods.
- ◆ The best way to learn the pagan path is by combining knowledge with experience.

2

All-Natural Ingredients

In This Chapter

◆ Tree huggers—and proud of it!

◆ Mother Earth = the Goddess

◆ How to get to know nature better

◆ Mom says, "Clean up your mess"

◆ The inner wilderness

Almost without exception, pagans are nature lovers. This is true whether a pagan lives in the middle of the city, in the suburbs, or in a remote rural setting. It's true whether the pagan is a student, a sales clerk, a computer programmer, or a physician. It's true for pagans who think of themselves as witches, as druids, as shamans, or as just plain old pagans.

Pagans Love Nature

Of course, you don't have to be a pagan to love nature. Most people of just about any spiritual persuasion find pleasure in spending time outdoors, whether in the mountains, at the beach, or in a colorful flower garden. And lots of people, again regardless of their religion or philosophy of life, will acknowledge that nature has a spiritual quality. To some people, getting outdoors seems like getting closer to God. Indeed, the famous architect Frank Lloyd Wright was quoted as saying, "I believe in God, only I spell it 'Nature.'"

I don't know if Frank Lloyd Wright would have considered himself a pagan or not, but his perspective is certainly one that most pagans would agree with. Paganism is first and foremost a nature spirituality because pagans regard nature as a *manifestation* of Spirit.

This is not to say that pagans see the Goddess as nothing but the natural world or universe. Many followers of the old ways understand Spirit as having both a physical and a spiritual dimension, just like human beings have both a body and a soul. Well, just as the body of a human being is his or her physical form, so too do pagans regard nature as the physical form of the Goddess.

Four Out of Four Spiritual Leaders Agree!

If you study many of the ancient stories associated with the founders of the world's great religions, you'll see that, almost without exception, all of the important action took place outdoors. When the Buddha achieved total enlightenment, he was meditating under a tree. When Moses heard the God of his people speak, he was standing by a burning bush. Jesus preached his most famous sermon while sitting on the side of a mountain. Mohammed, likewise, underwent his most profound mystical experience while sleeping in a cave.

Nowadays, it seems like most religions are stuck inside of churches, synagogues, mosques, and temples. Well, to each his own, but pagans tend to be more like the founders of the world's great religions. In other words, pagans go outdoors to feel closer to Spirit and to seek out mystical wisdom and experience.

The Whisper of the Wind

So is paganism just some sort of recreational activity? Hardly! Of course, like anyone else, pagans enjoy outdoor activities ranging from camping to hiking to backpacking to cross-country skiing. But the pagan path is far more than an outing club. Most people go out into the woods to "get away from it all," but to pagans, that's only half the reason. When a pagan gets close to nature—whether that means going out into the Montana wilderness or visiting the corner park—he or she is not just getting away from the distractions of modern life; he or she is also getting close to the Goddess.

Mother Nature Is a Real Goddess!

We live in a society heavily slanted toward seeing the spiritual world in terms of just one male God. All of our money says "In God We Trust," and even our swear words get their wallop from the idea of a single God whose name can be used in vain.

But humankind did not always see the world in terms of being created by this one old fellow in the sky. Archaeology has shown that ancient religions often put more effort into worshipping a mother Goddess than a father God. In early written histories, mythologies, and legends, you can see that pagan cultures viewed Spirit not as a unified man-God but as a community of Gods and Goddesses. In many, but not all, myths of ancient cultures, the earth and the natural world were seen as a Goddess. Often the sky was seen as a God. This made for a nice match, as the Earth Mother and Sky Father would get together and fertilize the universe.

It was a nice way of seeing things, but then with the rise of religions based on worshiping only a single male God, the Earth Goddess fell out of favor. There's no "In Goddess We Trust" on our money. But the irony is, even after thousands of years of *patriarchal* religion, the Goddess of the earth still lives on in the concepts of "Mother Earth" and "Mother Nature."

To most people, these are quaint images of a feminine personification of nature, kind of like how Santa Claus is a personification of Christmas. But pagans see deeper than that. They realize that Mother Earth/Nature is the ghostly survival of the great Goddess whom our ancestors revered as Earth herself. For pagans, reviving Goddess worship and rejuvenating our understanding of nature as the Goddess is a central part of spirituality.

If paganism is an alternative to *patriarchal* religion, does that make pagans *matriarchal?* Actually, nearly all pagans would describe their spirituality as either matrifocal or gender-balanced. A matrifocal spirituality (such as many forms of Wicca) place particular honor on the Goddess, but don't see her as a dominating or ruling deity. She is a loving mother, not an autocratic queen. Other pagans prefer to see the Goddess and the God as balanced in their role as divine figures, as a spiritual symbol of true equality between mortal men and women.

> **EarthWords**
>
> The word **patriarch** literally means "the father who rules." Therefore, a **patriarchal** religion is a religion ruled by fathers—either the ultimate father (God) or his masculine representatives here on Earth (such as priests, bishops, rabbis, or popes). Incidentally, a **matriarch** is a mother who rules, so a **matriarchal** religion is oriented toward the authority of a Goddess and her priestesses.

Drumbeats

As you begin to walk the pagan path, I recommend that you think of the Earth Mother as simply "Mother Earth" or "Mother Nature." Eventually, though, you'll want to learn about how Mother Earth has been depicted in various mythologies from around the world. In Greek mythology, she is Gaia. In Irish tradition, she is Anu, the ancestral mother. In Germanic myth, she is Nerthus; and in Phoenician myth, she is Beruth. Of course, each of these Goddesses has a slightly different personality based on the culture she comes from, but they all are manifestations of the earth in divine form. One of the most fun parts of pagan spirituality is learning about different Goddesses (and Gods) from world mythology and seeing which ones are most appropriate for your spiritual observance.

The Gaia Hypothesis: There Really *Is* a Mother Nature!

For some pagans, Mother Earth might only be a symbol of nature. But many others really do believe that nature has consciousness, just as you and I do. Our bodies consist of billions and billions of cells, all pulling together to form the physical setting in which human consciousness exists. Well, why wouldn't all the plants, animals, and other natural elements of the earth pull together to create a planetary mind—the consciousness of the Goddess?

If this seems just a little too woo-woo for you, rest assured that this idea has even been explored by scientists. Back in the 1970s, two British scientists, Dr. James Lovelock and Dr. Sidney Epton, outlined a hypothesis that the earth regulates its own conditions to make itself more conducive to life. They called this "the Gaia hypothesis," after the Greek name for the Earth Goddess. According to the Gaia hypothesis, because a number of factors on earth, such as the salinity of the ocean and the mean temperature of the planet's surface, have remained pretty much constant over time, it appears that the earth is herself making choices to keep her system biofriendly. This implies that the earth is behaving as a single organism: Mother Nature, the Goddess.

Of course, a hypothesis is not proven scientific fact. But the fact that scientists would even consider such a notion points to the pagan idea of nature-as-a-Goddess as a reasonable spiritual principle.

Communing with Nature

So, if pagans see nature as a manifestation of the Goddess, what does this mean? How does this idea make a difference in the life of a pagan?

Of course, on one level, this just means that when a pagan enjoys nature—from tending a garden to backpacking in a remote wilderness—he or she can find spiritual meaning in the activity. On another level, pagans seek not only to enjoy nature but to commune with nature as well. This means doing a variety of things in relation to the natural, all for the purpose of growing spiritually.

How to Commune with Mother Earth

If you're interested in becoming a pagan, the best way to get started is to find your own way of communing with nature. There is no one right way to do this. I'll give you a few ideas for how to get to know the natural world better that will work whether you live in the middle of a concrete city or in a remote log cabin deep in the woods.

Oracle

One way to understand the concept of communing with nature is to look at an example from another religion. Some forms of Christianity have a ritual called Holy Communion, in which Christians eat bread and wine as a way of communing, or feeling the presence of, Jesus in their lives. In a similar way, pagans spend time in nature as a way to find and appreciate the presence of the Goddess in their lives.

Take Time to Get to Know Your Mother (Nature)

If you want to get to know someone, the first thing you have to do is spend time together. This is just as true when you want to get to know Mother Nature. Spending time in nature may not seem very "religious" or "spiritual" at first, but if you make the effort to enjoy nature on a regular basis, you will soon discover just how spiritually nurturing it can be.

What are the best ways to spend time in nature? It depends on your circumstances. If you are a physically challenged person living in an urban apartment, you may find that the best way to connect with nature is to cultivate houseplants. Or you may enjoy occasional strolls through a local park. Suburban and rural folks can encounter the natural world in their backyard, and if you have a taste for adventure, you might find striking off for a trek through the forest to be the best way for you to commune with Mother Nature. Fortunately, Mother Earth is just as present in a simple potted African violet as in a vast mountain range. Sure, maybe it's easier to notice the spiritual dimension of nature in a breathtaking vista, but if you take your time, you'll connect with the spiritual element of nature in even a city park or a family pet.

Here are some other ideas of how to connect with nature:

◆ Don't have time to maintain your own garden? Why not offer to help out a friend with his or hers once in a (regular) while?

◆ Put a birdhouse and/or feeder in your backyard, close enough to be able to watch it from in the house.

◆ Live too far from a body of water? Why not get an aquarium to enjoy the beauty of aquatic life in your own home.

◆ Get to know the unique characteristics of the region where you live. Whether you live in the Arizona desert, the rain forests of Washington, an island off of Georgia, or the Minnesota prairie, your local environment will have treasures to be found nowhere else. Get to know what makes your neck of the woods so special.

◆ If all else fails, plan your next vacation with a nature theme. Even just spending a weekend camping in a state park can be a great way to spend time with Mother Nature.

Oracle

Find at least one way to commune with nature on a regular basis. If possible, this should be an outdoor spot that you visit on an ongoing basis. But even if it's caring for an indoor plant or pet, that's okay. You'll want to pick a spot where you can spend time sitting in silent reflection, just getting to know nature better and listening with your inner ear to the wisdom you might find in this setting. Doing this not only will be rewarding in itself, it will help you develop meditative skills that will benefit you as you learn more about pagan ritual.

Listen and Learn

Once you have found a way to spend time with nature on a regular basis, you may wonder, "Okay, now what do I do?" The next step on the way to communing with nature on a regular basis may be the most important step.

Think of what it takes to get to know a new friend. Obviously, spending time together is an important first step. While you're together, though, you have to do more than just sit and watch TV. To truly get to know someone, you have to listen, learn, and ask questions about him or her.

Relating to nature requires the same things as relating to another human being. To get to know Mother Nature, you need to listen for her voice and learn as much as you can about her. You can do this in two ways: through direct observation and interaction with nature and through learning as much as you can about nature, whether from a teacher, books, or even videos.

Drumbeats
Does the idea of "listening to" or "asking questions of" Mother Nature seem odd to you? Depending on your personality type, you might feel comfortable with the idea that the Goddess has a real personality with whom you can interact on a spiritual level, or you might prefer to think of the Goddess as an abstract symbol that helps you think about nature in a positive way. Either approach is okay. Remember, pagans have no dogma, so there's no one "right" way to think about the spirituality of nature, or of the Goddess.

Learning from Nature

For the purposes of pagan spirituality, the single best way to learn the ways of nature is to spend time with her. When you do this on a regular basis, you'll learn not only about the world but, even more importantly, about yourself. That makes sense; after all, you are a part of nature, too! To help you get started on your quest to learn all you can about nature, here are a few of the lessons I've learned over the years. You'll see that I've mentioned not only the lesson itself but also how this point has made a difference in my spiritual life. You might find it helpful to write down the lessons of nature that you discover.

Oracle

Do you keep a journal? If not, now's a great time to start. Whenever you sit in nature, meditate, perform a ritual, or do any of the other spiritual activities explored in future chapters, take time to write about your experience. Keeping your own journal makes it easier to remember your spiritual experiences and to record your progress as a pagan.

- ◆ **Silence is powerful.** I love to get away from it all, to leave the city behind and really immerse myself in the wilderness. Among other reasons, I love going where it is truly and deeply silent. I've found the silence of nature to be a great place where I can really get in touch with what's going on in my head—and even let go of some of the chitchat in my brain. Nature's silence makes me calm and centered.

- ◆ **The earth is abundant.** Where I live (north Georgia), this is especially true with the lush mountain vegetation, but there's abundance even in the deserts of Arizona, if only an abundance of sand and sky. Nature's abundance manifests in big ways, too—a big sky, big oceans, big mountains, big trees. Nature is plentiful, too. When I think about how abundant nature is, I become less worried about all the material possessions I don't have. Nature reminds me that I already have plenty of what really matters.

◆ **Everything moves in a cycle.** Day and night … high tide and low tide … summer and winter … Just about every part of the natural world has some sort of rhythm to it. Think about your own body, with the beating of your heart or the cycles of your breathing. Nature's cycles remind me that life doesn't move in a straight line; it moves in a circle.

◆ **Diversity is healthy.** Imagine a forest where all the trees are the same or a garden where every flower is identical. Not only would something like that be boring, it wouldn't really be sustainable. An ecosystem needs a wide variety of plants, animals, weather patterns, and soil conditions to remain vibrant and healthy. Nature's diversity reminds me that not only is it okay to live in a diverse world, it's actually a good thing. So all the diversity in the human family (different ethnicities, different religions, different philosophies of life) is better than if we all looked and thought alike.

◆ **Things always change.** Nothing stands still in the natural world. Plants grow, animals reproduce, and that which has died slowly decays and breaks down. The changes in nature are part of the cycles and diversity found in the environment. So not only are things always changing, there's a deep level at which change is a good thing. I try to remember this when things are changing in my life, especially if it's not a change I would have chosen for myself.

◆ **Beauty matters.** Sometimes we get so focused on what's practical or useful that we lose sight of simple beauty, but any flower can tell you that its beautiful colors and aroma are necessary to attract a bee. In the wild, beauty is practical, color is useful, and it all blends together into a pleasing array of sensuality. The more I realize what an important role beauty plays in the natural world, the more I realize that we humans (since we're part of nature) need to cultivate beauty in our lives—whether that means taking care of our appearance and physical fitness or developing our natural talents at painting, writing, music, or some other art form.

◆ **There is a wilderness inside each of us.** This lesson comes not only from spending time with nature but also from recognizing that humankind is just as much a part of nature as everything else. Over the years, I've grown to love nature because it has a wild, untamed, primal quality about it. Well, guess what? Each and every one of us has a wild, untamed, primal dimension to our inner selves. Sometimes we keep that part of ourselves well hidden—almost like how our culture tries really hard to keep nature under control by paving the ground and building environmentally controlled buildings. But just as beneath and beyond our cities the wilderness is still out there, so each of us has a wild place "in there."

Drumbeats

Many works of literature explore the tension between civilization and wildness in the heart of humanity. Modern novels like Jack London's *The Call of the Wild* or Ernest Hemingway's *The Old Man and the Sea* explore this theme. Some, like William Golding's *The Lord of the Flies*, suggest that wildness is dangerous. But others, such as Margaret Atwood's *Surfacing*, examine the wildness in the human heart from an almost pagan position of reverence. Pagans don't advocate rejecting civilization, but most do believe that the wilderness (whether inside us or in our environment) ought to be respected rather than feared, honored rather than denigrated.

Learning About Nature

Spending time getting to know nature—and discovering ways in which Mother Nature can teach us more about spirituality and about life—is something every pagan will enjoy doing. It's not enough to just hang out with the trees and the animals, however, important though that may be. Thoughtful pagans also take the time to learn more about nature from a scientific and ecological perspective as well as from an inner, spiritual perspective. This doesn't mean you have to go back to college and get a Ph.D. in biology (although if you want to do it, go for it).

Becoming more knowledgeable about nature can be as simple as regularly watching a science program on public television or reading a new book each month that deals with environmental issues. Remember, the point behind this is not to win a ribbon or earn a grade, but simply to increase your understanding of, and relationship with, Mother Earth.

Environmental Awareness Quiz

Here's an excellent tool to start you on your journey of learning about nature. If you're like me, the first time you look at this quiz you might feel intimidated. That's because, as a society, we tend to be so ignorant of nature that even the simple questions on this quiz can leave us feeling, well, ignorant. But don't give up. See this quiz as a challenge. Try every month to find out the answer to just one of the questions on this quiz. Before you know it, you'll be one of the most knowledgeable nature-lovers around!

This quiz is excerpted from "Where You At—A Bioregional Quiz" by Leonard Charles, Jim Dodge, Lynn Milliman, and Victoria Stockley, from *Home: A Bioregional Reader* (New Society Publishers, 1990).

- ◆ Trace the water you drink from precipitation to tap.
- ◆ How many days till the moon is full?

- What was the total rainfall in your area last year?
- Name five native edible plants in your region and their season(s) of availability.
- From what direction do winter storms generally come in your region?
- Where does your garbage go?
- How long is the growing season where you live?
- On what day of the year are the shadows the shortest where you live?
- Name five grasses in your area. Are any of them native?
- Name five resident and five migratory birds in your area.
- What species have become extinct in your area?
- From where you're reading this, point north.
- What spring wildflower is consistently among the first to bloom where you live?

Establish a Ritual Way of Nurturing Your Relationship with Mother Earth

As you spend more time with nature and make the effort to learn its ways both through your personal experience and through research and reading, remember to keep Mother Nature in mind. For pagans, nature is not some inert stage on which people live their lives; rather, it is the manifestation of the Divine Spirit that creates us, loves us, and cares for us. At first it might be hard to think of nature in this way, but the more energy you put into seeing Mother Nature as a true Goddess, the easier it becomes to recognize her as such.

One way to become accustomed to seeing the divinity in nature is to create a simple ritual you can perform on a regular basis—perhaps even once a day—to strengthen your ties to Mother Nature. Think of a ritual as a way of phoning home and talking to your mother. To get you started, here is a very simple little ritual that you can perform in five minutes.

To perform the ritual, either go to your favorite spot in nature (such as your backyard) or find a place in your home where you can keep a plant or some other symbol of the natural world. This can be performed in front of your altar. (See Chapter 14, "Tools for Ritual," for more information about altars).

1. Sit in a comfortable position with your spine upright and your body relaxed. Take at least three deep breaths, allowing your body to relax more deeply with each breath and allowing your mind to slow the busy chitchat of your thoughts.

2. When you feel sufficiently relaxed, in your mind's eye, envision the earth. See her as a blue/white/green disc in space, as she would appear if you were looking at her from the moon. Take a moment to appreciate her beauty.

*For pagans, Earth is our
mother and our Goddess.*

3. Say the following words aloud (or to yourself if you are in a public place or otherwise not alone):

> As a drop of water is part of the ocean,
> So I am part of the earth, my Mother.
> She created me, she nurtures me,
> and she will receive me when I die.
> In gratitude I honor her at this time.

4. Now do a simple act to honor Mother Earth. You might light a candle; you might simply make a deep, reverent bow; or you might sing a song that expresses your love for her.

5. Sit quietly for at least a minute or two (up to 15 minutes is okay), reflecting on your connection with your mother, the earth.

If you want to adapt this ritual in some way to make it more truly your own act of devotion, be my guest. Just remember to keep in mind the purpose of the ritual: to strengthen your sense of being connected to nature as your mother and to feel love and gratitude for her in how she cares for you.

Taking Care of Mother Earth

One of the most important issues facing the earth today is the impact of modern technology and human population growth on the natural environment. A staggering number of problems—from air and water pollution to destruction of the rain forests to excessive production of garbage resulting in overflowing landfills—all add up to a planetary *ecosystem* under excessive stress. Since we human beings are responsible for these environmental problems, it is up to us to fix them. Pagans, as a community of people who love and revere the earth as our mother, are in a unique position to stand up for environmental responsibility.

You don't have to be a powerful politician or a leading businessman to be able to make a positive difference for the environment. Indeed, the actions of ordinary people like you and me are ultimately just as important as the policy decisions made in places like London, Moscow, and Washington, DC. As pagans, if we believe that Mother Earth takes care of us, it's common sense to see it as our duty to return the favor and take better care of her.

> **EarthWords**
>
> The earth's **ecosystem** involves all the processes in place on our planet that support life, including the various life forms (both animal and plant) as well as inanimate elements such as the atmosphere, water supply, soil, and energy from the sun. When one part of the system is damaged (say, for example, polluted water), it has an effect on all the other parts of the system.

> **Taboo!**
>
> When looking at all the problems facing the environment—from global warming to overpopulation, from nuclear waste to the endless generation of plastics and other forms of trash—it's easy to feel hopeless and helpless and even to give up. Don't do it! Your Mother Earth needs you, no matter how small your efforts may be to heal the problems facing the earth.

Forget About the Joneses

One of the biggest problems facing the environment is the amount of "stuff" we consume, from buying disposable products like cameras and ballpoint pens to the endless amount of plastic packaging that seems to come with every new item purchased. One of the easiest ways to make a positive impact on the environment is to stop trying to keep up with the Joneses. How many times have you bought something, whether it's an item of clothing or a toy or a new piece of electronic equipment, only to find that you hardly use it at all? Meanwhile, the credit card bills keep piling up, and it's one more thing thrown away. Stop this vicious cycle before it starts. That way, you can keep your money in the bank, keep your life simpler, and make a positive impact on the environment—all at once!

I'm not saying you should be so strict and austere that you never get to buy something that's fun or convenient. But I believe if we all thought twice (or thrice) about the things we purchase, we could make a real difference in the world.

Here's a good rule of thumb: If you're about to make an impulse purchase, stop and wait three days. If after three days you still really want the item, go buy it. If not, congratulate yourself on the money (and landfill) you've saved.

Oracle

Are you having difficulty curbing your shopping habit? Cut up your credit cards. When you can only spend what you have, you learn to think twice about what you buy. If you already have large balances on your credit cards, you'll pay them off faster once you stop adding new balances to your account.

The Three R's

No, not reading, writing, and 'rithmatic—reducing, reusing, and recycling. I already touched on reducing in the last section; if you reduce the amount of stuff you use, you help the environment. Next comes reusing. As much as possible, if you can reuse boxes, padded mailers, clothing, toys, and whatever else you might have, it makes a positive difference. Finally, there's recycling. From paper to plastics to glass to cardboard, there are plenty of household materials you can take to the recycling center and thereby keep them from going into the dump.

All this talk about protecting the environment may not seem very "spiritual" on the surface, but in reality, it's deeply spiritual. Why? Because it's more than just cleaning up a mess—it's showing our Mother Earth how much we love her. Sure, spending time in nature, learning about nature, and performing rituals are all ways to love your Mother Earth. But when you roll up your sleeves and get to work, that's *really* making a statement!

Warriors for the Wilderness

As a pagan, you can see yourself as a warrior for the wilderness. Now, I don't mean "warrior" in the sense of someone who commits acts of aggression. Rather, I mean it in terms of defense—someone who does what it takes to protect what he or she loves. As a warrior for the wilderness, you'll not only think about saving the environment, you'll commit to doing something, no matter how small, to make a difference in your world. You can even make a promise to Mother Earth as part of your getting-to-know-nature-better ritual.

The Wilderness Within

Earlier in this chapter, I mentioned that nature can teach us to recognize that there is a wild, untamed place inside each of us. Along with taking the time to get to know nature as it exists outside of us, you'll also want to get to know the wild places inside yourself better. You can do this through ritual, through spending time in silent meditation (see Chapter 17, "Meditation: Welcome to Magical Boot Camp!" for more on this subject), or through noticing how your heart and mind connect with external nature—all these can be a clue to your inner wilderness.

Do you love waterfalls, springs, and the ocean? Perhaps you have a watery personality. Do you feel drawn to deserts and to the languid days of summer at its hottest? Then you could be a fiery type. Perhaps you're a bird person, with a real fondness for hawks, eagles, and crows. Or you might be more of an earth type, feeling drawn toward deer and bears or to the tall trees of the forest. Whatever your inclination toward nature, notice it and make notes of your interest in your journal. Connecting to the wilderness within you can be an important first step on your ongoing pagan journey.

Now that you've begun to explore the pagan path by becoming more closely connected to nature, I want to introduce you to three of the largest varieties of paganism: shamanism, witchcraft, and druidry. You'll look at each in turn over the next three chapters.

The Least You Need to Know

◆ Pagans revere Mother Earth as an aspect of the Goddess manifest in nature.

◆ The Gaia hypothesis suggests that the earth may be seen as a single, unified organism.

◆ Spending time in nature and learning about the natural world are excellent ways for pagans to put their spirituality into practice.

◆ For pagans, protecting the environment—even in small ways—is practically a sacred duty.

◆ Just as there is a natural wilderness outside of us, pagan spirituality invites you to recognize the "wilderness within."

Please Don't Squeeze the Shaman!

In This Chapter

- ◆ Tribal spirituality from around the world
- ◆ Meet the world's first guides to the spirit realm
- ◆ The shamanic trance
- ◆ Core shamanism
- ◆ Why shamanism matters to pagans

One of the most important lessons of nature spirituality is also very simple. We human beings are part of the physical world. We do not exist "above" or "outside" of nature but are an integral part of the earth's ecology. Therefore, meaningful nature spirituality not only will look to the rest of nature for wisdom and purpose, it will also look within at the wisdom to be found within the human family.

But where will you find this sacred wisdom? For many people, the most powerful collection of teachings about the spirituality of Mother Earth comes from the most ancient of magical and religious traditions—the tradition of shamanism.

Welcome to the World's Oldest Spiritual Path

As you learned in Chapter 1, "Welcome to the Pagan Path," a shaman practices a primal spirituality based on the wisdom of *indigenous* people. In its original and most accurate meaning, the word "shaman" refers to a specific kind of spiritual healer found in Siberia. In our time, however, it has become a catch-all term for just about any kind of spiritual practice from a culture without modern technology—in other words, a culture that lives closer to the rhythms of nature than the people of modern urban societies do.

EarthWords

Indigenous cultures are native to a region; in other words, they've existed there since time immemorial. The aborigines in Australia, the Maori in New Zealand, and the Zulu people of South Africa are a few examples of the world's many indigenous peoples.

Obviously, since shamanism covers a wide array of sacred practices from pretechnological cultures, it also goes back—way back—to the dawn of human history. Even before the written word, evidence that suggests shamanic spirituality has been found in cave paintings and religious statues made thousands of years ago. From this ancient evidence, we not only see that shamanism is the world's oldest spiritual tradition, but we also learn some basic spiritual truths that can be applied to our modern-day pagan practice.

The First Shamans

In this day and age, people tend to think of shamans as basically medicine men or witch-doctors—in other words, as functioning primarily as healers. The first shamans, however, may have had a different function. Cave paintings, like the image of a man wearing an animal's head and antlers found in Les Trois Fréres cave in France, suggest that ancient people relied on spiritual ceremonies and magic to help ensure success in hunting. Could this primal figure, half-man and half-animal, be one of the earliest shamans, dancing in a ceremony to call on the animal spirits to secure enough food for the coming winter? Or could this figure represent the spirit of different animals on whom the people called for guidance?

Although we may never know the exact nature of the earliest shamans or the true purpose of the ancient art that is the only evidence we have of spiritual practices from prehistory, we do know that shamanic practices occur in primal societies on earth today and are gaining popularity even in the more "advanced" civilized cultures.

When Is a Shaman Not a Shaman?

When is a shaman not really a shaman? Actually, most of the time. You see, the word "shaman," technically speaking, only refers to a specific kind of spiritual figure from an indigenous culture in Siberia. In recent years, however, many spiritual teachers and writers have used the word "shaman" to mean almost any kind of tribal, indigenous, or primal spiritual practice from all around the world. So you'll hear of Celtic shamanism, Native American shamanism, African shamanism, and the like. In actuality, there's no such thing as Celtic or Native American shamanism. Although it is true that various primal cultures from the Celtic lands, Africa, and other parts of the world certainly had their ancient spiritual traditions, it's technically incorrect to call them shamans.

So here I am, perpetuating the error. That's because the word "shaman" has practically become synonymous with "primal spirituality"—and so that's the sense in which I use the word. It's important, however, to remember the original, more technically precise meaning of the word.

The Elements of Shamanism

Like paganism, shamanism (in the popular meaning of the word) is an umbrella term. It refers to many different kinds of spiritual practice from many different cultures. There's no such thing as a shamanic religion; there's no church or organization one joins to become a shaman. On the contrary, most shamans in traditional cultures pass on their wisdom from master to apprentice, sometimes with the younger shaman actually coming from the same family as the elder or being chosen because the apprentice exhibits an aptitude toward psychic ability or has undergone some sort of spiritual crisis in his or her life.

Even in its modern, New Age-ified form, shamanism is not a religion but a spiritual practice. Some individuals and organizations do exist to provide training to those who feel called to the shamanic way of life. (See Appendix B, "Resources," for information on shamanic training centers.)

The World Through a Shaman's Eyes

So how does a shaman think? What does a shaman do? And what does any of this have to do with paganism?

Well, since paganism is a spiritual path of reconnecting with nature and shamanism has its roots in the most ancient of cultures, the way shamans see the world can help a pagan to have a deeper relationship with Mother Earth. The first important quality is that most shaman traditions are *animistic*. In other words, shamanism recognizes the universe we live in not as some mechanistic world devoid of

EarthWords

Animism is a way of approaching life that recognizes that all things have a spirit—from plants and animals to inanimate objects such as crystals, stones, mountains, rivers, and so forth.

spiritual consciousness but as a cosmos teeming with spirits, both large and small. In the animistic approach to reality, everything has its own spirit (kind of reminds you of the Gaia hypothesis). Beyond the physical world of the senses, there are wonderful, magical (and sometimes terrifying) realms where spirits dwell—variously called the otherworld, the underworld, or simply the spirit realm.

Some folks see this as "primitive" spirituality since more "advanced" civilizations tended to see a split between God and nature. But the skeptical, scientific, modern way of seeing things has resulted in a world in which runaway materialism and dependence on technology have filled the environment with toxins and pollutants, meanwhile adding stress to people's lives as they struggle to keep up with the demands of a computerized, mechanized lifestyle. Maybe if more people learned to revere the spirits in nature, like shamans do, we'd find a way out of the environmental mess we've gotten ourselves into.

The Shaman's Initiation

How does a person become a shaman? It's not a club or a church you join, nor is it achieved by going to school and earning a degree. Becoming a shaman requires undergoing a powerful spiritual process of *initiation*.

In many cultures, the shaman's initiation can be a frightening and even dangerous experience. Many shamans undergo an experience of death and rebirth in which spirits usher them through a process of not only dying but even bodily dismemberment, leading to a time of profound enlightenment before culminating in the body being reborn, only now with shamanic powers. These experiences reveal to the shaman the deep mysteries of life and death, of the spirit world and the wisdom to be found there. After the initiation, a shaman is truly a new person: one ready to serve the community as a healer and sage.

EarthWords

An **initiation** is a sacred ritual, ceremony, or event that marks the beginning of a new phase in one's spiritual life. A true spiritual initiation creates a profound and lasting change in the initiate.

In different shamanic cultures from around the world, there are many different styles and forms of initiation. Some are grueling ordeals; others involve the shaman experiencing life-threatening bodily illness. On the other hand, some shamans inherit their office from an ancestor. Again and again, however, some sort of initiatory ritual or ordeal marks the transition from being an ordinary person to becoming a shaman with magical powers and the ability to heal. As you shall see in upcoming chapters, this is a practice that many pagans have adopted into their spiritual lives as well.

Talk to the Spirits

Remember Dr. Dolittle, the veterinarian who could talk to animals? Well, a shaman is one up on him because the typical shaman has the ability to communicate with spirits (and since many spirits are connected to animals or plants, that means a shaman can talk to the animals and beyond!).

When shamans go into a trance or perform a healing ritual, they travel to the spirit realm, where they seek alliance with friendly or powerful spirits and if necessary do battle with malevolent spirits to subdue them and achieve their goals. As expected, the spirits that a shaman encounters can take many forms and have many types of personalities. The world of spirits that a shaman encounters is not like the black-and-white world of popular religion in America, where there are only two kinds of spirits: good ones (angels) and bad ones (devils). The shamanic way of seeing things is much more realistic: Spirits can be friendly or hostile, powerful or weak, trustworthy or treacherous, indifferent or passionate, and on and on. Some spirits are very helpful to the shaman, and these often become a shaman's allies (more on this later in the chapter). Other spirits are enemies, and still others are more or less neutral. It's the shaman's job to figure out which spirits can help him achieve his healing goals and which spirits to ignore (or to keep an eye on).

> **Drumbeats**
>
> In different primal cultures, sometimes only men were shamans, sometimes only women, and sometimes both men and women could practice. Thus, for modern pagans interested in following a shamanic path, it is open to both women and men.

Shamanic Trance and Shamanic Journeying

How does a shaman encounter the spirits? Typically, shamans employ a variety of ritual techniques to enter into a trance or some other altered state of consciousness. In many indigenous cultures, especially in South America, shamans use hallucinogenic plants to assist them in attaining the trance state. Other shamanic cultures use other techniques to enter the trance state. One of the most popular ways to induce a trance is through the hypnotic steady beating of a drum or some other rhythmic musical instrument.

> **CAUTION** **Taboo!**
>
> Although some researchers (notably Carlos Castaneda and Terence McKenna) have documented the use of psychoactive and hallucinogenic plants in some tribal cultures, modern shamans need to stay away from such practices. Not only are most hallucinogenic plants illegal, but many are dangerous if not used in precisely the correct way. Furthermore, traditional shamans receive elaborate training before they ever use drugs in their ceremonies. With drumming and meditation, we have plenty of effective ways to enter altered states of consciousness without psychoactive plants!

When a shaman goes into a trance, a number of things may happen. The shaman may take on the properties of a *power animal* and fly, swim, or run to the spirit realm. Or he may climb up and down a tree seen to connect the world of ordinary reality with the spirit worlds above and below. Or he may simply experience a powerful inner transformation that puts him in direct contact with his *spirit guides* and allies.

EarthWords

A **power animal** is a helpful or guiding spirit that comes to the shaman in a form of an animal. Such a spirit may provide wisdom, guidance, instruction, or even criticism to the shaman, all to help the shaman be more effective. The "power" in the name refers to spiritual power, not just physical power; thus, a turtle or a field mouse can be a power animal just as easily as a bear or a wolf can.

As the name implies, **spirit guides** are nonphysical beings who provide guidance and support from their vantage point in the spiritual realm. Spirit guides come in all shapes and sizes; a person might have allies (guides who remain loyal for years and years) or a series of guides who come and go, each with a different lesson to teach or wisdom to impart.

When the shaman is in a trance state, spirits can speak through him, giving wisdom to those who attend to him during the trance. Or he may simply appear to lose consciousness altogether, but when he returns from his journey, he brings healing knowledge to benefit the sick. Sometimes, a shaman may not remember the circumstances of the trance at all. The experience of shamanic trance and journeying differs from culture to culture or from shaman to shaman. The common elements of the shamanic experience usually involve some form of journeying to the realm of spirits to subdue unfriendly spirits and to appeal to helpful ones for guidance and aid.

Healing Through Spirit, Plant, and Animal Allies

When a shaman does his spiritual work, he knows he will face deep forces in the form of neutral, unfriendly, or possibly even downright hostile spirits. He also knows he can't do this alone. I've already talked about how a shaman seeks friendly spirits to be his guides and allies. These spirits often are related to the "real-world" animals and plants in the shaman's environment. Just as the shaman might find support in a power animal that teaches him or gives him extraordinary powers, on a much more down-to-earth level, shamans make it part of their practice to be knowledgeable in the medicinal qualities of herbs so that the spirit of the plant can be applied to the healing of the client in a very practical way.

Similarly, shamans in hunting societies learn all they can about the animals they typically hunt so that the shaman can divine important information about the movement of the herd and can appeal to the spirits for help to make the hunt successful.

Another service many shamans perform is "soul retrieval." The way shamans see it, sickness can be caused by situations in which a person's soul (or part of the soul) has been stolen or kidnapped by an unfriendly spirit. The shaman will go into a trance, hunt down the offending spirit, and take back the piece of his client's soul that is missing. When the retrieved soul is reunited with the client's body, healing follows.

Drumbeats

Some psychologists speculate that the spirits a shaman encounters are actually powerful subconscious forces in the shaman and/or in his clients. The powerful journey to the spirit realm where the shaman does battle with unfriendly spirits can be seen as a metaphor for helping the client find psychological wholeness and integration, which in turn can lead to physical healing.

The Shaman's Drum

Here's one more characteristic of shamanism that deserves mentioning: In nearly all traditional shamanic cultures, the shamans use some form of music, sound, or percussion to help them enter into a trance. The most common instrument used is the drum. Indeed, modern research confirms that steady rhythms can help induce altered states of consciousness such as the alpha state (the brainwaves that a person achieves when meditating). Drumming can be a powerful shortcut to meditative—or more profound—states of consciousness. The shaman's drum has become one of the most recognizable elements of shamanism, and even in modern cultures in which people are attempting to create a neoshamanic spirituality, the drum is almost universally used as the single best tool for going within and encountering the spirit world.

Oracle

The ideal way to experience shamanic drumming is with a frame drum, which one person plays steadily while others go on their inner journeys. If you don't have access to a drum (or to a friend to play it), the Foundation for Shamanic Studies (www. shamanism.org) has produced a series of recordings ideal for shamanic use.

The Teachings of Black Elk

One of the most famous of Native American shamans is the Lakota medicine man, Black Elk, who lived from about 1862 to 1950. Two books that record his teachings, *Black Elk Speaks* and *The Sacred Pipe*, have become modern classics of Native American spirituality. In *The Sacred Pipe*, Black Elk talks about seven important rites that the Lakota people performed to practice their spirituality. Learning about these rites not only can teach us about the shamanic dimension of Native American spirituality, it can also provide important background information for pagans who wish to incorporate shamanic practices into their spirituality.

> **CAUTION**
>
> **Taboo!**
>
> Many people, especially of European descent, become interested in the spirituality of cultures other than their own and started practicing that "borrowed" spirituality, almost as if they were learning a new hobby. To many indigenous people, this is disrespectful behavior. So always be respectful when learning about traditions of people different than you. Before you start practicing a borrowed religion, try learning more about the ways of your ancestors first (and if you're of European descent, see Chapter 4, "Wicked Good!" and Chapter 5, "The Philosophical Pagans: Druids and Other Revivalist Groups," for some ideas where to begin).

The Sacred Pipe

Black Elk told Joseph Epes Brown (the researcher who compiled *The Sacred Pipe*) the powerful legend of the White Buffalo Calf Woman, who gave the sacred pipe to the Lakota people. According to the legend, many years ago a wonderful, radiant, and very holy woman came to the people, dressed all in white and calling herself White Buffalo Calf Woman. She instructed the chief to gather all the people together, and once the tribe had gathered, she presented a gift to the chief: a sacred pipe made of stone, with a stem made of wood and 12 feathers attached to it. She instructed the chief that this was a sacred tool that must be treated with reverence and respect. The stone pipe represented Mother Earth. The wooden stem represented the trees and plants and all things that grow from the earth. The feathers represented the birds of the air. With the pipe, the people made prayers, and the smoke that rose from the pipe carried their prayers to *Wakan-Tanka*—the great, holy, powerful Spirit of the heavens.

The sacred pipe represented the interconnection of the cosmos. The earth, the heavens, and all living things were connected together in this holy object. After White Buffalo Calf Woman finished explaining her gift to the chief, she walked slowly away; as she left them, she turned into a buffalo that magically changed colors—first red, then white, then black—before finally disappearing over the horizon.

The Sweat Lodge

During her talk to the people, White Buffalo Calf Woman promised the Lakotas that they would receive a number of sacred rituals to help them honor the spirits, their ancestors, and the natural world. One of these rituals involved a powerful purification rite using a *sweat lodge*. A sweat lodge ceremony combined using heat and steam to cleanse the body (sweating removes toxins from the bloodstream) with prayers and chants to perform a similar purification for the soul.

A typical sweat lodge uses the energies of the four elements: air, fire, water, and earth in the ritual. (These will be discussed in detail in Chapter 11, "Elementary, My Dear Pagan!") Earth is represented by the stones that are heated in fire. Water is poured over the heated stones, transforming the air inside the lodge to steam. Perhaps it is the primal encounter with the combined powers of the elements that makes a sweat lodge such a powerful spiritual experience.

EarthWords

Sweat lodges are small chambers made of stone, dug into the earth, or even made of branches covered with blankets or skins. Participants in a sweat lodge ceremony enter the small, dark chamber, taking along stones heated by a fire. Water is poured on the stones to create heat and steam, causing the participants to sweat profusely, thereby experiencing a physical (and spiritual) cleansing.

Crying for a Vision

Black Elk also spoke about the ritual of "crying for a vision," or Vision Quest. This powerful experience entailed an individual going through rigorous spiritual preparation, culminating in a retreat into the wilderness for several days of solitude and fasting, seeking a vision or encounter with spirit allies or power animals. Such a ceremony has elements of initiation about it and can be compared to other shamanic initiations from different cultures. What was remarkable about the Lakota Vision Quest was that it wasn't only for shamans—any man or woman could cry for his or her vision.

Black Elk spoke of other ceremonies related to the Lakota way of life—a total of seven. Each ritual combined a deep reverence for Wakan-Tanka with a similar honoring of the natural world. Like shamanic practices from other parts of the world, the spirituality of the Lakota made a proper relationship to the earth a central part of life.

Core Shamanism

Since shamanism originated in pretechnological cultures ranging from Siberia to the Arctic Circle to the Amazon Rainforest, those of us who live in a highly technological, urban society don't have access to shamanism except perhaps through books and films. How can the wisdom of these ancient traditions be brought to bear on the pressing problems of modern life? After all, just about everyone recognizes that our relationship with nature has become totally out of balance. Perhaps the wisdom of the shamans can help us reconnect with the natural world. But how, when shamans live in such remote areas and serve cultures so totally different from technological society?

One answer to these questions is a movement begun by Michael Harner, an expert on shamanism and author of *The Way of the Shaman*. Harner proposed a concept called "core shamanism," which is based on the most universal of shamanic practices from around the world, adapted and integrated for urban dwellers. Today, Harner (and others like him) provide training in core shamanism in major urban centers in North America and other parts of the world.

Shamanic Basics for the Urban Seeker

What does core shamanism entail? Well, to pursue it fully, you need to find a qualified shamanic practitioner who can teach you the ins and outs of trancework, soul journeying, and connecting to power animals and other spirit allies. Inner journeying can be a beautiful experience, but it can also be scary and unsettling. If you think you would like to study shamanism seriously, think of it on a par with becoming a lawyer or a doctor. Reading a book or two is not enough.

If you simply want a taste of shamanic spirituality as part of your journey to paganism or to help you decide if studying shamanism in depth is the right path for you, here are a few suggestions for opening yourself up to a shamanic way of life (even if you live in the city or the suburbs):

◆ Learn all you can about shamanism in its natural habitat. Remember, core shamanism is derived from the real thing, which existed (and still exists) among indigenous peoples. This can include not only reading and research but also visiting sites that were sacred to Native Americans or indigenous peoples. Just remember to be respectful whenever learning about spirituality from a culture other than your own.

◆ Try to connect with your own power animals. Do you feel a special affinity to a particular animal, say, an eagle, or bear, or elk? Do people tell you that you look like a raccoon or act like a ferret? Do you love to dress all in black (you raven, you), red (cardinal), or blue (jay)? Do you dream about dolphins or manatees? Pay attention to the animals that show up in your life again and again. What lessons for living might you learn from these beings? Do they bring any particular message to you during meditation?

Oracle

Are you interested in learning the shamanic ways of a particular people—say, the Lakota Indians, the Australian aborigines, or the Yoruba people of Africa? If so, make this part of your learning process: Get to know the economic and political circumstances of that group of people in today's world. Many indigenous people live in extreme poverty and often are in danger of their culture being totally wiped out as modern technology affects every corner of the world. See if there's anything you can do to help the people of that culture, as a way of showing respect and saying thanks for the wisdom you've received.

Once you've made contact with your power animal(s), you'll want to learn more and more about the animal and the wisdom it has to share with you. One way to keep your power animal in mind is to have physical reminders of the animal in your living space. A painting of the animal, a small statue of it, or even a tooth, bone, or feather found in the wild—all of these can be wonderful objects to help you connect with the energies and consciousness of your guide.

◆ Deepen your meditation with drumming. Either use a drum that you and a friend take turns beating in a steady rhythm or get a drumming CD or tape made specifically for shamanic practitioners. Don't use such a recording while driving! It's best to do drumming meditations in a safe, quiet, comfortable place with no bright lights or distractions. Be prepared to take your meditation experience to a deep level. Keep a journal handy to record any experience you may have with power animals or helpful spirits. Don't, however, do this for long periods of time without the guidance of a qualified teacher.

Technoshamanism: Spirituality at 180 Beats per Minute

Finally, I should mention the concept of "technoshamanism," which has become popular in the rave community. Since drumming can induce states of relaxation and mild trance, people realized that the rapid beats of modern techno dance music can also lead to altered states of consciousness. Of course, the dance scene is also a place where some people use illegal drugs to enhance their experience (a practice I don't recommend). Truly profound meditative states can be attained while dancing to techno music—even without drugs.

If you're into that scene, you'll enhance your appreciation of shamanism by supplementing your experience with knowledge of traditional shamanism and by learning how shamanic practice can be used as a healing tool to make the world a better place.

Shamanism and Paganism

Okay, so what does all of this have to do with paganism?

Well, shamanism, like druidism and Wicca (the subjects of the next two chapters), is one of the most popular forms of paganism. Some pagans follow an almost purely shamanic style of spirituality, studying indigenous shamanism and learning the techniques of core shamanism. Indeed, these folks would probably rather be called shamans than pagans. But since shamanism is such an earth- and nature-oriented spirituality, many urban shamans also think of themselves as pagans (and vice versa).

European Shamanism: The Roots of Wicca and Druidism

Even those pagans who practice Wicca, druidism, or one of the many other varieties of paganism can benefit from learning about the ways of the shaman. This is because the ancient, primal spirituality of Europe (the homeland of Wicca and the druids) has a distinctively shamanic flavor. Researchers like Carlo Ginzburg and John Matthews have pointed out that ancient druidism and medieval witchcraft show links to primal shamanism. Like shamans from other cultures, the pre-Christian Europeans practiced a nature-based spirituality that involved interaction with the spirit world. Like other shamans, the European shamans believed that animals and plants had magical and healing wisdom to share. There even are similarities in cosmology—the mythologies of pagan Europe often spoke of a great world tree that connected the underworld, the heavens, and the world of the senses, just like the cosmologies of other shamanic cultures.

So, even if you're interested in paganism because you want to be a druid or a witch, take the time to become familiar with shamanism, the world's oldest wisdom tradition. It's a foundation that will serve you well, no matter what pagan path you follow. If you're like many pagans, you'll eventually be blending elements of shamanism, Wicca, druidism, and other traditions to form your own eclectic style of spirituality.

Go Honor Your Own Ancestors

Here's an interesting insight into the relationship between shamanism and the new paganism. These days, many people of European ancestry study with Native American elders. But many Native American elders have this to say to the Europeans who study their ways: "We are flattered that you want to come and honor the ways of our ancestors, but we wonder when you're going to go honor the ways of your own ancestors?" This comment is not meant as an insult or a putdown, but it speaks to a simple truth: Deep, earth-centered wisdom can be found in every culture and every tradition, even the tradition of your own heritage. This doesn't mean it's wrong for Europeans to practice Native American spirituality, for Africans to practice Celtic spirituality, or whatever. It does mean that, whatever spiritual lineage you adopt as your own, you'll also benefit from discovering the rich tradition of your own forebears. Go back far enough, and you'll find a tradition that honors the earth. That's part of who you are.

The Least You Need to Know

- ◆ Shamanism is a catch-all term to describe a variety of spiritual practices from indigenous cultures. The word "shaman" comes from a particular Siberian word for a spiritual healer.
- ◆ Shamans see spirits in all things—plants, animals, even rocks and minerals—and interact with the spirits to gain wisdom, knowledge, and healing power.
- ◆ Shamans form alliances with spirits to gain particular benefits. Some of these spirits are associated with animals and are known as power animals.
- ◆ Most shamans use drumming to induce a trance (an altered state of consciousness).
- ◆ Almost all varieties of modern paganism can be traced back to a form of shamanic spirituality.

Chapter 4

Wicked Good!

In This Chapter

- The history of the craft
- Basic principles of Wicca
- What witches do
- Why Wicca is growing so fast
- The relationship between Wicca and paganism

For many people, the modern pagan revival and witchcraft are practically synonymous. This is because Wicca (as the pagan religion inspired by witchcraft is known) is the largest single variety of paganism. Not all pagans are witches, of course. But even for pagans who aren't interested in Wicca, it's important to know the ins and outs of the "Craft of the Wise" since it plays such an important role in the pagan world.

Wicca, the Middle English word for "witch," has several shades of meaning. Its original meaning is unclear; some experts think it means "wise," while others think it means "to bend" (like the bent strips in a wicker basket). Whatever its actual etymology, many modern witches like it because it's not loaded with misconceptions like the words "witch" and "witchcraft." Yet other witches prefer the word "witch" as a way of reclaiming a word that for too long was used to attack or oppress women. Still other witches don't like the term because they think it has been overused by New Agers who don't truly understand the mysteries of real witchcraft.

To some witches, Wicca is a lovely name for the religious dimension to their spirituality, while other witches insist witchcraft is not a religion. As you explore the pagan path, you'll find many different opinions over something as simple as what labels people wear.

To summarize: While Wicca is a pagan religion based on traditional witchcraft, not all pagans are witches, not all witches like to be called Wiccan, and then there are even some Wiccans who don't like to be called a witch.

A Brief History of Wicca

Once upon a time, in the minds of most people, the word "witch" meant something frightening and fearful. Many people thought of a witch as an evil hag, a woman with dark and terrible supernatural powers who was not above using those powers for her own personal gain—and to get rid of anybody in her way. On top of all this, witches were believed to be worshippers of the Christian devil who would gather at night in secret, infernal meetings to perform lewd and blasphemous acts.

Thanks to this stereotype of evil-doing witches, thousands of innocent people—mostly women—were killed during an approximately 200-year period of European history known as "the Burning Times" (because many of those who were killed were burned at the stake). This hysterical persecution of witches also touched North America, most famously in Salem Village, Massachusetts, in 1692.

With the rise of modern science and philosophy, however, religious and legal authorities began to reject the idea of witches as only superstition. Eventually, the persecution of alleged witches died out, and the laws banning such practices were seen as quaint leftovers of an irrational earlier age.

Then, in the nineteenth and early twentieth centuries, a new idea arose: that maybe the "witches" were not sorcerers and devil-worshipers at all but actually adherents of the long-suppressed ancient, pre-Christian religion of Europe. In the early years of the twentieth century, an English scholar named Margaret Murray published two books, *The Witch-Cult in Western Europe* and *The God of the Witches*, both of which asserted that witchcraft had nothing to do with the Christian devil and was in fact the last remnants of the old pagan religion.

Even though nowadays many scholars question the details of Murray's scholarship, her basic idea—that witchcraft should be regarded as a pagan religion instead of devil worship—has revolutionized the way we think about both witches and pagans. In 1954, however, a book was published that sparked a spiritual revolution. It was called *Witchcraft Today* and was written by an eccentric old Englishman named Gerald Gardner, who presented himself as an actual practicing witch.

Drumbeats

In her day, Margaret Murray's theories of witchcraft were widely accepted by both scholars and the general public. In more recent years, however, many aspects of her theories have been questioned by academic experts. For one thing, Murray (who as far as anyone knows was not a witch) insisted that witchcraft was an organized religion, but there's no evidence to support such a claim. She also insisted that witches universally worshipped a great mother Goddess and a horned God—again, with no hard evidence to back up her claims. Although many modern scholars still accept the idea that witchcraft is a form of paganism, most now prefer to think of witches as more like shamans (who basically work independently without any organized religion) than like priests (who get their power from being authorized by an institution). And just as shamans all over the world practice their spirituality in a wide variety of ways, so probably did the ancient pagans of Europe worship many different kinds of Gods and Goddesses.

Gerry's Kids

Gerald Gardner wrote that witchcraft had continued to exist, although largely in secret, over the centuries since the persecutions. He himself had been initiated into a witch coven in the late 1930s, and although the other members of his group preferred to keep it a secret, Gardner was worried that the old religion was dying out. He saw himself as a man on a mission: to teach the world about the Craft of the Wise, thereby encouraging other witches to come forward while also encouraging nonwitches to consider taking up this ancient and venerable practice.

Well, whether Gardner was actually saving a dying religion, or just making up a new one based on his romantic conception of witchcraft, is up for debate. One thing is for sure: He sparked a spiritual revolution that is still going strong 50 years later.

The Growth of Wicca

In the years after Gardner, many other people came into the public eye as witches. Some of them (like Doreen Valiente and Patricia Crowther) were actually initiated by Gardner, but others (like Sybil Leek and Robert Cochrane) claimed they had been members of other Wiccan *lineages* that existed before Gardner's books were published.

EarthWords

A **lineage,** in Wicca, refers to a specific tradition of Wicca and the history of how that tradition was passed down over the years. All lineaged priestesses and priests can trace their tradition back through the witch who initiated them, the elder who initiated their initiator, and so on. Some traditions trace back to a famous witch like Gardner or Leek, while others claim to trace back even further.

During the 1960s and 1970s, young people in America and some other parts of the world took up a variety of social and political causes: protesting the war in Vietnam, fighting the oppression of African Americans or of women, working to save the environment from runaway pollution and development, and so on. In many cases, the counterculture (as it was called) rejected the social and spiritual values of mainstream society.

Wicca, with its deep love for the earth, devotion to the Goddess, and empowering of women as priestesses and high priestesses, seemed to be a wonderful spiritual path for many young people. Thus, Wicca exploded in popularity during this time, and because so many of the new, young witches brought a heightened political and social sensibility to the craft, many Wiccans came to see that feminism, environmentalism, and Wicca fit together beautifully. Finally, in 1979, two major books were published that celebrated this marriage of pagan spirituality and progressive social values: Starhawk's *The Spiral Dance* and Margot Adler's *Drawing Down the Moon*. Among the newer, or "feminist" witches, lineage and tradition wasn't as important as simply honoring the earth and the Goddess. Of course, many witches remained very traditionalist in their approach. Between these two main types of Wicca, the craft continued to grow in popularity with no sign of slowing down, even today.

The Elements of Wicca

So, what makes Wicca tick? Why is it more popular than ever before, appealing to a wide variety of people, from teenagers who want to learn how to do spells to 40-year-olds who want a spirituality in which it's okay to be a feminist?

Well, much of the appeal of Wicca lies in the central values of paganism: Goddess worship and nature reverence. But let's look at some of the unique qualities of the craft and see what makes this path so attractive to so many.

The Lord and the Lady

Actually, when I say that Wicca is a Goddess tradition, I'm really only telling half of the story. Nearly all traditions of Wicca see Spirit as male and female, as a God as well as a Goddess. Incidentally, one of the biggest differences between Wicca and other forms of paganism is that Wiccans tend to see God and Goddess as unified entities, whereas folks like the pagan druids tend to think in terms of many unique Gods and Goddesses rather than just one Great Lord and Lady. Wiccans love to learn the mythologies of cultures from around the world and try to learn about as many different Gods and Goddesses as they can, but consider the different names and personalities of the various Gods and Goddesses as different facets of the same, single jewel. In fact, some Wiccans even teach that the God and the Goddess are merely two sides to the same coin—meaning, in effect, that they are monotheistic.

Oracle _____

Many Wiccans use the phrase "All Gods are one God, and all Goddesses are one Goddess" as a way of explaining their understanding of deity. Wiccans love the many faces of Gods and Goddesses from throughout world mythology and will call on many different Goddesses and Gods in their rituals. However, they see the many Gods and Goddesses as aspects of a unified Spirit.

Some witches use a triangle to explain their concept of deity. The top point of the triangle represents pure Spirit, which exists without form. The bottom two points signify the forms that Spirit takes when relating to humans: a masculine form (or the God) and a feminine form (or the Goddess).

Spirit

Goddess   God

The Goddess and the God can be understood as manifestations of pure Spirit.

The Charge of the Goddess and the Wiccan Rede

Many people think of Wicca as little more than a philosophy for working *magic* or casting spells. If this were true, Wicca would not even qualify as a religion; it would merely be a tool that a person uses, like psychology or aerobics, to make his or her life better. In truth, Wicca is much more than just magic. Like other religions, Wicca involves belief in deity, ethical rules that Wiccans are expected to follow, and beliefs about the way the universe works and even what happens after you die. So part of Wicca's appeal lies in how it speaks to people's spiritual needs, no matter what their age and life circumstances.

EarthWords _____

Magic is a process of ritual, visualization, affirmation, and meditation designed to change consciousness and harness spiritual energies to bring about real changes in life. Some pagans spell it with a k (magick) to distinguish it from stage magic or sleight-of-hand.

Like other religions, Wicca has developed a wonderful collection of poems and prayers that people can use to express their devotion to the Lord and the Lady. One of the most famous, the Charge of the Goddess, expresses what many witches believe is expected of people who follow the old religion. Many different versions of the charge exist; here is an excerpt from the version found in *A Witches' Bible* by Janet and Stewart Farrar.

> *I who am the beauty of the green earth, and the white Moon among the stars, and the mystery of the waters, and the desire of the heart of man, call unto thy soul. Arise, and come unto me. For I am the soul of nature, who gives life to the universe. From me all things proceed, and unto me all things must return; and before my face, beloved of Gods and of men, let thine innermost divine self be enfolded in the rapture of the infinite. Let my worship be within the heart that rejoiceth; for behold, all acts of love and pleasure are my rituals. And therefore let there be beauty and strength, power and compassion, honour and humility, mirth and reverence within you. And thou who thinkest to seek for me, know thy seeking and yearning shall avail thee not unless thou knowest the mystery; that if that which thou seekest thou findest not within thee, thou wilt never find it without thee. For behold, I have been with thee from the beginning; and I am that which is attained at the end of desire.*

Drumbeats

The Charge of the Goddess is one of the most-loved elements of modern Wiccan ritual. But where does it come from? In his book *The Triumph of the Moon: A History of Modern Pagan Witchcraft*, British scholar Ronald Hutton points out that parts of the charge can be traced to a number of different sources. However, Doreen Valiente, who was a priestess in Gerald Gardner's coven and went on to write several books on Wicca, rewrote the charge in the mid 1950s, and subsequent versions (like Starhawk's version reprinted here) are only slightly different. As a priestess of the old religion, Valiente no doubt revised the charge simply as an act of love, without seeking fame or money; even so, it's important that we acknowledge her contribution.

The Charge of the Goddess is important because it emphasizes the spiritual aspect of Wicca. Notice the spirit of love and joy that fills these words. Wicca is not a gloomy religion of repenting from your sins and constant self-discipline. On the contrary, Wicca emphasizes celebration, joy, love unto all beings, and a heart that rejoices.

Another important part of Wicca is a deceptively simple little saying, called the Wiccan Rede:

> *An' it harm none, do what ye will.*

The word "An'" basically means "As long as." So, as long as you harm no one, in Wicca, you are ethically free to exercise your will and seek what you desire. This may look very simple, but it's actually one of the most demanding of ethical principles one could ever imagine. Exercising your freedom cannot infringe on the rights of others—or even on your own best interests. In Wicca, there's no rule against alcoholic beverages, but since alcoholism or even excessive drunkenness is harmful to yourself, it's against the Wiccan Rede. Some people think the Wiccan Rede permits sexual freedom, and indeed, Wiccans like other pagans often are pretty liberal in their attitudes toward lovemaking. But irresponsible sex resulting in an unwanted pregnancy is harmful, as is spreading sexually transmitted disease; such things as rape and infidelity are certainly harmful as well. So when you really stop and think about it, the Wiccan Rede is a fairly strict rule. It's strict, but in a common-sense way that also encourages personal freedom and responsibility.

Of Solitaries and Covens: How Wicca Is Organized

In addition to its spiritual and ethical dimensions, Wicca also appeals to people because of the way it is organized. Most religions tend to organize around large communities, whether churches or synagogues or mosques, that require membership, financial support, and (if you really get involved) endless participation in committees. Wiccans have two choices for how they express their spirituality, both of which (at least to Wiccans) seem much more appealing. These choices are membership in a coven or solitary practice.

◆ Covens are groups of three to thirteen people that usually gather around one or more elders (high priestesses or high priests) who teach younger Wiccans the ways of the craft. Wicca, like shamanism and other forms of paganism, has many variations, and so there are many different ways in which covens are organized. Most covens gather on the full moons and on eight important holidays called the Sabbats. (See Chapter 13, "The Wheel of the Year," for more on these holidays.) When they gather, they not only teach the ways of the craft, they perform rituals, work magic, and perform initiations.

Most covens are intentionally small; when a coven gets too big, it will often split into two groups. This process is called hiving, and it's the process by which the old religion grows. Once a coven hives off, its new high priest or priestess is the authority for that group and does not have to answer to anyone else (except to the Gods, of course). Most responsible priests and priestesses will continue to seek guidance from their elders, however, even after they have hived off.

Not all gatherings of Wiccans or witches call themselves covens. Some groups may prefer to call themselves groves or circles.

♦ Even though the coven, which is small enough to fit in most people's living rooms, is much more attractive to most Wiccans than a large, impersonal religious institution, for some witches, even 13 can feel like a crowd. These are witches who are temperamentally best suited to practice their spirituality all alone or maybe with just one other person. These Wiccans are known as *solitaries*. In the old days, solitaries would learn the craft from an elder, often someone in their own family. Nowadays, most solitaries probably learn either from studying in a coven or from reading a book written especially for solitaries (like *The Complete Idiot's Guide to Wicca and Witchcraft*). Like coven members, solitaries observe the moons and the Sabbats and perform rituals and magical work. They are responsible for their own education, however, and instead of initiation, they simply go through a personal process of self-dedication to the Lord and the Lady.

Climbing the Wiccan Ladder

Many Wiccan covens and groups have a structured program for training members in the ways of Wicca. This process involves earning a series of degrees, usually three. When a person first becomes interested in Wicca and approaches a coven, he or she can become a student or a neophyte ("beginner"). After a period of study (which usually lasts at least a year and a day), the student can, if prepared and spiritually ready, receive the first degree, which involves a special ritual of initiation. First-degree Wiccans can usually participate in, and sometimes even lead, the rituals of the coven. After further study for at least a year and a day, the initiate might be ready to progress to a second-degree initiation; usually at this point, the Wiccan is authorized to teach newcomers. After additional preparation, the individual may finally pursue third-degree initiation. Having reached this level, he or she can go and start a new coven (although, in some traditions, only women can start new groups).

Some Wiccan groups have various other initiation stages, and some groups think the degree system is hierarchical and don't do that at all. Wicca is a multifaceted religion with many different variations.

Oracle

In many covens, members of the group are referred to as "firsts," "seconds," and "thirds." This is common shorthand for a person's degree. Also, most covens wear robes during their rituals, and even if the robes are all the same color, members will wear different-colored cingulums (cords tied around the waist); the different colors signify the different levels of initiation.

What Do Wiccans Do?

Okay, so Wiccans (and other witches) can be solitaries or members of covens, and they (like almost all pagans) love the earth and the Goddess. But aside from that, what exactly do they do?

The stereotypes we debunked in Chapter 1, "Welcome to the Pagan Path," for pagans in general all apply to the various forms of the craft. In other words, Wiccans don't worship the devil, engage in orgies, or perform bloody rituals of human sacrifice. That kind of stuff only happens in B-grade movies. Witches honor a beautiful and kind spirituality that is centered on three activities: magic, ritual, and healing. Pretty much everyone you meet who calls him- or herself a witch will be dedicated to these three endeavors.

Drumbeats

When people think of witches, they often think of an old hag dressed all in black, with a pointy hat, warts on her nose, and a broom as her favored method of transportation. Straight out of *The Wizard of Oz*, huh? One of the most significant, if not the single most important, characteristics associated with a witch is her gender. In short, only women are witches. Men might be wizards, warlocks, or magicians but not witches. This may be so in the world of stereotypes, but in the real world of Wicca, this gender bias doesn't hold. Men as well as women can practice witchcraft and are known as "witches." Words like "wizard" or "magician" aren't used and especially not "warlock." (Some witches teach that a warlock is actually a witch who was banished from a coven for unethical behavior.) So when you meet a witch, don't be surprised if she's a he!

Ritual

I've already talked about the role that ritual plays in paganism (and I'll go into greater depth about this in Part 3, "Ritual"). This is especially true of Wicca, which in some forms is among the most ceremonial of pagan traditions. Witches create elaborate rituals in which they magically create a "world between the worlds" of mortals and of the gods. Once in this sacred space, the witches (whether as solitaries or in covens) honor the Goddess and the God, do healing or divination work, and simply enjoy the pleasures of their religion. Remember from the Charge of the Goddess, "all acts of love and pleasure are my rituals."

Healing

If you ever attend a gathering of witches, you'll probably see more than one car with a bumper sticker that says "Witches heal." (The other most popular bumper sticker among Wiccans says "My other car is a broom!") Practitioners of the craft take the healing aspect of the old religion very seriously; they are proud of how, in ages past, the village wise woman was a midwife, herbalist, and healer. (And often it was these very women who then got persecuted for being "devil worshippers." Ironic, isn't it?) Today's witches try to live up to the healing traditions of their craft by becoming master herbalists or specialists in psychic healing traditions like *reiki*. Of course, witches always use their skill and knowledge, whether magical or mundane, to heal, never to harm.

> **EarthWords**
>
> **Reiki** is a Japanese method of psychic healing. The word means "universal life force energy." Reiki practitioners have been specially trained to access this energy and channel it through their hands to help bring healing to themselves and others.

To learn more about healing as a pagan practice, see Chapter 20, "The Pagan as Healer: From Medicine Men to Reiki Masters."

Divination

Witches and Wiccans are curious folks. They have a natural desire to figure out what their soul's purpose or mission in life is; they also are curious about the wisdom of the Lord and the Lady and how such wisdom can help them live better lives. They even are fascinated by the future and believe that glimpses into the future are possible (understanding, of course, that human free will means the future is never cast in stone but is a field of possibilities).

Each of these natural curiosities can be explored by the means of divination. Divination involves using a tool (like astrology or tarot) or simply accessing your own deep inner wisdom (through meditation or a trance) to tap into divine wisdom and knowledge—that is to say, the wisdom of the God and the Goddess. This wisdom can teach us our soul purpose, provide direction for life from the viewpoint of the highest good, or even sneak a peek into what is yet to come. Some of the most popular forms of divination are as follows:

- **The Tarot**   A set of 78 lavishly illustrated cards, each of which has an esoteric meaning. In the hands of a knowledgeable or psychically-gifted reader, the Tarot is uncanny in its ability to both predict the future and reveal the secrets of the soul.

- **Astrology**   This uses the position of the sun and the planets to discern powerful dynamics in a person's soul and life. By looking at future positioning of the planets, future influences can be understood and planned for.

♦ **Runes**   An ancient alphabet from northern Europe. Like the Tarot, each symbol has a specific set of meanings.

♦ **I Ching**   A Chinese system based on tossing coins or sticks a set number of times.

♦ **Numerology**   This uses information like your birth date and a numerical value based on the letters in your name to reveal important energies at work in your life.

> CAUTION
>
> **Taboo!**
>
> Divination can be fascinating and fun and, when used properly, can be an effective tool for spiritual growth. But be careful not to get caught up in using divination obsessively or compulsively. Remember that tools such as astrology and the Tarot are meant to help you grow spiritually. Don't let them run your life.

Many other forms of divination exist. The tool used for divination is not as important as the intuition that the tool supports. Most witches and Wiccans believe that every human being has profound psychic and intuitive ability; a divination tool merely helps a person get in touch with his or her own spiritual power. It is that power that leads us to wisdom, both the wisdom of our own souls and the wisdom of the Lord and the Lady.

I'll take a closer look at divination in Chapter 19, "Divination and Omens: Listening for the Divine Whisper."

The Romance of Wicca

Wicca is the largest form of neopaganism and is also one of the fastest growing religions in North America today. Indeed, the Ontario Consultants on Religious Tolerance, a group dedicated to studying the different religions in society and promoting understanding between them, speculates that there could be about 750,000 Wiccans in the United States today—and that number is growing rapidly (see www.religioustolerance.org/wic_nbr.htm). Of course, actual numbers are hard to come by because so many Wiccans tend to keep their spirituality a secret. But this figure is based on how many Wiccan books sell, the attendance of large Wiccan festivals, and similar data.

Many factors contribute to this phenomenal growth of the Wiccan community. Two of the most important factors are that Wicca strives for equality between men and women, and Wicca is a mysterious, romantic spirituality.

A Balanced Faith: Wicca as a Woman-Friendly Religion

I'm not a woman, so I can't speak from personal experience on this issue. But even as a man, I find that the way traditional religions worship a God, but no Goddess, feels lopsided and out of balance. In fact, it seems unfair. Men get to worship a God who is like them, but women don't get a similar feminine face for a deity. Of course, some religions say that God is neither male nor female, but that abstract way of seeing things makes deity even less familiar for both genders.

Drumbeats

Among the many traditions of witchcraft, one form—Dianic Wicca—is known especially for its feminist orientation. Named after the Greek Goddess of the hunt, this tradition was founded by Z. Budapest, author of *Summoning the Fates*, as a way of integrating spiritual feminism and political feminism. Most forms of Dianic Wicca clearly emphasize the Goddess above the God, or omit the God altogether. Also, most Dianic groups allow only women to join or to participate in their rites. Even though some traditions of Wicca emphasize balance between masculine and feminine energy, the Dianic tradition holds an important place in a religion that exists as an alternative to the overly male focus of most of the world's major faiths.

In contrast to traditional religions, not only does Wicca celebrate deity as both Lord and Lady, but most Wiccan traditions consider the priestess as more important than the priest in the function of Wiccan ritual. For many women, this is a wonderful alternative to the sexism in many other religions. Even men find this attractive; for although the priestess is "first among equals," the equality of men and women is still stressed, and most Wiccans try to foster a spirit of partnership and balance between the sexes. That's a good deal, no matter what your gender is.

The Mystery of Midnight: Wicca's Allure

Another reason why Wicca is so popular has to do with its romance. No, I don't mean that Wicca is full of lovebirds (although that's a nice thought). By romance, I mean Wicca is a spirituality that celebrates the mysteries of nature, uses poetry in its rituals, and balances intellectual belief with the pursuit of intuitive wisdom, all in a spirit of devotion to nature and the Gods.

The world we live in is so hypertechnological that it's truly magical to go outside under the full moon, light a candle, and recite a poem of love for the Lord and the Lady. It's an experience that sings to the deepest parts of the soul. It can't be understood but can only be experienced. For many people, experiencing the mystique of Wiccan rituals, even just once, is all it takes to embrace this peaceful, benevolent, life-affirming path.

Wicca as a Form of Paganism

As I've already said, Wicca is the largest form of paganism. For this reason, some people use words like "Wiccan" and "pagan" almost interchangeably. When they say one, they mean the other.

It's important to point out, however, that not all pagans consider themselves Wiccan and vice versa. I know one Wiccan priestess who says, quite sensibly, "I'm not a pagan. I'm an urban." What she means is that she doesn't live in the country but in the city. (Remember from Chapter 1 that the original meaning of pagan is "country-dweller.") For her and some other Wiccans, paganism is such a large, vague term that it's not helpful to explain who they are. Many Wiccans and witches see the craft as a rigorous program of magical and spiritual development that many people will not pursue because of how demanding it is. Many forms of paganism tend to be very relaxed and easygoing in the demands made on people; traditional witches, who take pride in their hard work, may not like to be lumped in with these less-challenging types of nature spirituality.

 Taboo!

Don't call a pagan a witch, or a witch a pagan, unless the person uses these terms him- or herself. The same goes with calling a witch a Wiccan, or vice versa. Many wouldn't mind, but some would be offended by using any of these labels indiscriminately.

On the other hand, since paganism encompasses shamanism, druidism, and other kinds of nature spirituality aside from Wicca, it's important to remember that not all pagans like being lumped in with Wicca. In fact, as you will see in the next chapter, some pagans regard Wicca as very much a product of modern times, while they seek to revive ancient practices from thousands of years ago.

I don't want to overstate this case. For many pagans and Wiccans, there's little difference between the two terms. But for others, there's plenty of difference.

The Least You Need to Know

- Wicca is a modern expression of ancient European paganism, hence its nickname "the old religion." It is based on witchcraft; many (but not all) modern witches practice Wicca.
- Witches and Wiccans adhere to an ethical precept: "An' it harm none, do what ye will."
- Nearly all witches and Wiccans practice some form of ritual, spiritual healing, and divination.

◆ Exact numbers are hard to come by, but experts believe that Wicca is one of the fastest growing religions in America today.

◆ Although Wicca is the largest form of paganism, it's important to remember that many non-Wiccan forms of nature spirituality exist.

Chapter 5

The Philosophical Pagans: Druids and Other Revivalist Groups

In This Chapter

◆ The three ages of druidism

◆ The three types of druids

◆ How folklore and archaeology reveal the secrets of the Celts

◆ The sacred trees of the druids

◆ Other pagan revivals similar to druidism

Next to witches and shamans, the third most enduring symbol of nature spirituality, at least in English-speaking culture, is the druids. Probably the single-most-famous druid is Merlin the magician, but the druids were far more than mere court magicians to the kings. Originally, druids were highly respected philosopher/priests, holding an important social role in the society of the ancient Celts. Imagine blending a lawyer, a scientist, a philosopher, a college professor, and a religious leader together. Then you'd have a person whose function in society approximated that of the ancient druids.

Also like witches and shamans, druids have captured the modern imagination. For several centuries now, various groups have existed, both in Europe and America, that call themselves druids. Some of these groups are little more than fraternal organizations like the Elks Club or the Moose Club. Others are dedicated to preserving Celtic culture and identity. But many of these "druid" groups would not be comfortable wearing the label "pagan." Meanwhile, in the latter half of the twentieth century, newer groups formed that are more firmly committed to reviving the pagan spirituality of the ancient Celts.

Popular Conceptions (and Misconceptions) of the Druids

Before you think about what modern druidism is, let's set the record straight on a few of the more common erroneous assumptions people make about this ancient spiritual community.

Stonehenge—Not!

First and foremost: The ancient druids did not build Stonehenge. Stonehenge, along with the many other stone circles found in the British Isles and Western Europe, predates the coming of the Celtic people by approximately a thousand years. Does this mean the Celts didn't even use Stonehenge? That's a question we can't answer. For one thing, we're still not completely sure what Stonehenge was originally intended for. We know it marks significant dates in the astronomical calendar (like the sunrise on the day of the summer solstice), but as for any possible ritual or religious use, those functions are lost in the mist of time. Of course, many modern druids have gravitated to Stonehenge and have made it a symbol of their spirituality. That's fine as far as it goes, but we need to remember just how little we know for certain regarding that ancient monument.

Drumbeats

Archaeologists have identified four different periods in the history of Stonehenge. Stonehenge I, existing from 2800 to 2100 B.C.E., consisted of a large circular earthwork enclosure with only a few standing stones (and several wooden posts). Stonehenge II, from 2100 to 2000 B.C.E., was marked by the addition of an avenue leading from the circle to the sunrise point of the midsummer sun, along with the addition of two partial, concentric circles of bluestones. The builders of Stonehenge III (2000 to 1500 B.C.E.) erected an outer circle of 30 upright stones that supported a ring of lintel stones. Within this circle stood a horseshoe of five trilithons—two standing stones each supporting a horizontal lintel. Still other alterations were made to the site during what archaeologists label the "IIIB" and "IIIC" periods. Finally came the period of Stonehenge IV, around 1100 B.C.E., when the avenue built during Stonehenge II was lengthened. It's an impressive history, and it all took place centuries before the druids.

Stonehenge, contrary to popular belief, was not built by druids but by pre-Celtic people.

(© 1990 Carl McColman)

More Than Just Tree-Huggers

Another common stereotype about the druids is that they were tree worshippers. This probably comes from the fact that the druids did indeed venerate sacred trees and conducted their ceremonies in a special grove of trees known as a *nemeton.* But the most likely explanation of the druidic veneration of trees comes from our friends, the shamans. In many ways, the druids were the shamans of Celtic culture: They were the healers, the ritualists, the spiritual counselors. We know from Celtic mythology that the ancient Celts saw

EarthWords

Nemeton literally means "sacred grove" or "sanctuary." Incidentally, one of the Goddesses of the Celts was Nemetona, whose name means "Goddess of the sacred grove."

the presence of Spirit in the natural world, from animals to rivers to wells and springs. Obviously, trees were equally imbued with a spiritual essence, and it was the druid's job to honor these powerful beings. Reverence for the trees, however, was only a small part of the druid's spiritual world view.

Shaman in a Kilt

To understand the ancient druids (and the work that modern druids are doing to revive the ancient Celtic ways), it's helpful to think in terms of shamanism. Although the word "shaman" technically does not apply to the Celts, many elements of world shamanism—from the animistic reverence for all things (and especially all living beings) to the

EarthWords

The **faeries** (or fairies) are the nature spirits of Celtic lore. According to Irish myth, the faeries are the Gods and Goddesses who inhabited Ireland prior to the coming of the Celts, and who now dwell in a mystical underground faery-land (the otherworld).

recognition of a spirit realm that exists alongside the material universe—have parallels within the culture of the Celts. Shamans may have contacted spirit guides, whereas the Celts had dealing with the *faeries*, but beneath the semantic differences, the spirituality of shaman and druid are quite similar. One way to think of a druid is as a shaman in a kilt!

If you haven't yet read Chapter 3, "Please Don't Squeeze the Shaman!" I suggest that you take a minute to go through it now. By understanding shamanism better, you will more easily grasp the beauty and wonder of the druid path.

The Three Ages of Druidry

I've been talking about ancient druids as well as today's druids, people dedicated to reviving the old ways of the Celts. But there are actually three eras associated with druidism. In Chapter 1, "Welcome to the Pagan Path," I mentioned the three eras of paganism: ancient or paleopaganism, modern or neopaganism, and the mesopagans of the seventeenth through nineteenth centuries. These divisions apply especially well to the history of the druids.

The first age of the druids involved the ancient Celts who served as the philosopher/priests (and priestesses) of their people prior to the Roman conquest. These druids never committed their wisdom to writing, preferring instead to pass their knowledge down orally from master to student. This means that we've lost their wisdom, for when the druids were wiped out by the Romans, their lore went with them. We do have some written records concerning the druids, but only by Greek or Roman writers, most of whom considered the Celts (and therefore, the druids) as barbarians or enemies. So what little information we have is, unfortunately, slanted.

When the Romans invaded Great Britain, one of the atrocities they committed was the slaughter of the druids at their college on an island in Wales now known as Anglesey. At that time (approximately 55 C.E.), druidism was, in effect, destroyed as an ancient wisdom tradition. That's not to say that all druidic knowledge vanished. But it became hidden in the folklore, mythology, and commonsense wisdom of the Celtic people.

The Druid Revival (Part One)

The second era of druidism began during the Renaissance, when the French and the British began to think of druids as great thinkers from their distant past. By the sixteenth and seventeenth centuries, writers were extolling the virtues of these great philosophers of antiquity. The British writer and antiquarian John Aubrey (1626–1697) was the first person to suggest that the druids built Stonehenge, an idea embraced by William Stukeley, an eighteenth-century clergyman who not only speculated on the Stonehenge-druid connection but fancied himself a druid as well. In 1717, a legendary (but unproven) ceremony is said to have taken place in London, forming a new order of druids; in 1781, an organization called the Ancient Order of Druids was founded in London. The druid revival was underway.

Taboo!

Many writers, from the eighteenth century to the present day, have put forth all sorts of speculations and theories about the ancient druids and their teachings. Some writers even have published outright forgeries, claiming works were of ancient origin when they really weren't. Many of these books are still in print, and the ideas in them are just as bogus today as they were when they were first published. If you are serious about studying druidism, approach the topic with a critical mind and examine each author's research and bibliography to make sure the work is based on real, legitimate information. If you'd like a few suggestions on some of the more reputable books on this topic, see Appendix A, "Recommended Reading."

For most of these druid groups, the emphasis was not on pagan spirituality (Stukely was not the only Christian minister to embrace modern druidism.) but on universal values like brotherhood and national pride. Some of these druid groups have continued to the present; the famous druids who wear white robes and conduct summer solstice ceremonies at Stonehenge and other sacred sites around England come from this eighteenth-century lineage.

The Druid Revival (Part Two)

If the druids of the seventeenth- and eighteenth-century revivals represented a blend of Christian, civic, and pagan values, it was not until the twentieth century that druids became serious about reviving a purely pagan form of druidism. Ironically, the beginning of neopagan druidism began as … a joke. In 1963, a group of students at Carleton College in Minnesota formed a group called the Reformed Druids of North America (RDNA). They did this to get out of having to attend chapel. The college required students to attend chapel on a regular basis, and the only way to get out of it was if you were a member of a different religion; then you had to attend services provided by your religion.

So a group of students formed their "druid" grove and held "services" out in nature as an alternative to having to sit in the boring old chapel services. It was a clever ploy, but the following year the college dropped the chapel requirements—yet the druids kept on going (much to the dismay of the group's founders). At first, RDNA espoused rather vague ideas of nature worship; the movement spread, and different groves took on different identities. Eventually, one member of RDNA, Isaac Bonewits, founded a druid group called Ár nDraíocht Féin: A Druid Fellowship, based specifically on the revival of ancient pagan practices. The modern Celtic pagan movement was underway.

How to Revive an Ancient Religion

What separates neopagan druids from the eighteenth-century variety is that the pagans specifically aim to revive ancient spiritual practices and make them relevant for today, whereas the more "fraternal" orders of druids tend to focus more on social or charitable activities. But how does an ancient religion get revived? Whereas shamanism and witchcraft both had living traditions to draw from, the druids were trying to reignite a fire that had been for all practical purposes extinguished nearly two thousand years ago. What would it take to create a modern druidism that was not just a wild speculation about the past?

The Raw Material for the Druid Revival

Since the ancient druids never wrote down their wisdom, reviving the druid path today requires imaginative detective work, scholarly research, and familiarity with archaeology, mythology, folklore, and even religious practices from other cultures besides the Celts. I've already mentioned how shamanism can be helpful in understanding Celtic spirituality. Many druids look to pagan practices from other parts of Europe, believing that, since the Celts were members of the Indo-European family of languages and cultures, it's reasonable to assume that similarities in religious observance existed among the various branches of Indo-Europeans. Each of these sources of knowledge is like a piece of a large and intricate puzzle. For modern druids, seeing how mythology can shed light on folklore, or how folklore shed light on archaeology, is half the fun of following this spiritual path.

Myth and Folklore

Thankfully, after the Romans conquered nearly all of the Celtic lands and Christianity came to the British Isles and other traditionally Celtic regions, monks in the dark ages set about the task of preserving the ancient myths of the Celts, especially in Ireland and Wales. Tales of great heroes, Gods, Goddesses, and their larger-than-life exploits finally were written down. Of course, being Christians, these monastic scribes often reinterpreted many of the myths in a way that fit in with the Bible's view of things, and often the ancient Gods and Goddesses were demoted to be mere heroes of these tales. Still, even in a corrupt state, the myths provide us with incredible amounts of information, not only about the deities the Celts worshipped but about insights into how the Celts understood the world and the ways in which mortals and Gods ought to interact.

EarthWords

The **otherworld** is the Celtic name for the spiritual realm. It is also known as the underworld or by various names in Irish or Welsh. One of the most wonderful names for the otherworld is *Tir na n'Og*, an Irish term that means "the land of the young."

Through these myths, we've learned the names of the many different Gods and Goddesses the druids revered, as well as their personalities and attributes. We've learned about the holy days of the Celtic year, and most important of all, we've learned about the nature of the *otherworld* and how to properly interact with those spiritual beings who reside there.

Drumbeats

As just one example of how Celtic myth can provide glimpses into Celtic spirituality, consider the story of Pwyll, from the Welsh anthology of myths called *The Mabinogion*. Pwyll was a Welsh prince who, without realizing it, insulted a king of the otherworld, Arawn. To make amends for his insult, Pwyll agreed to spend a year in the otherworld, disguised as the king. He eventually fought and defeated a rival king, thereby securing the entire realm for Arawn. After doing this, Pwyll and Arawn returned to their rightful homes and remained fast friends. The myth concludes by noting that the two continually exchanged gifts. This is a hint to the reader about the proper way humans and spiritual beings ought to relate: by exchanging gifts. Thus, in a ritual, humans might make offerings to the spirits and in turn ask the spirits for favors such as healing or blessings.

Celtic Culture, Archaeology, and Other Religious Traditions: Fragments of a Puzzle

There's more to the druid puzzle than just ancient writings. Some folk practices that have survived into modern times might be clues to the spirituality of the ancient Celts. For example, in Ireland, there are many natural wells that to this day are considered holy by the people. Of course, with the coming of Christianity, many of these wells have been dedicated to the Blessed Virgin Mary. Others are dedicated to Saint Bridget, a Christian saint who has many characteristics in common with an old Celtic Goddess, Brighid. At many wells, people come and tie colorful pieces of cloth to branches of a tree near the well.

EarthWords

The word **votive** comes from the same root as the word "vote" or "vow." A votive offering is something offered to the Gods as part of a prayer or request. When a person makes a votive offering, he or she gives the votive item to deity as part of a request for such things as healing or prosperity.

Taboo!

Some people do a bit of research into this or that theory about ancient religion and then decide that there is "one right way" to be a druid (or whatever the ancient culture is they're studying). While it can be spiritually meaningful to learn as much as you can about ancient practices, don't become self-righteous or snobby toward others. Paganism is based on experience, not dogma.

From folk customs such as these, we can speculate that the ancients considered wells and trees to be holy, their locations suitable sites for making prayers and supplications to the Gods. Indeed, the veneration of wells and trees harks back to the spirituality of the shaman, which is based on recognizing spirits in all things, animate as well as inanimate.

Archaeology is another tool for learning what little we can about the original druids. Of course, excavating ancient homes, graves, or ritual sites can be a matter of interpretation since there's no guidebook to explain what this or that object was used for, but even so, archaeologists have been able to piece together a tremendous amount of information about our ancestors. One interesting practice among the Celts involved making sacrificial offerings to rivers. These offerings often included costly items (such as silver ornaments) or weapons (such as swords). Some rivers and lakes have huge deposits of such *votive* offerings. From this archaeological data, we can theorize that the Celts revered water and believed in making offerings or sacrifices to their deities.

Here's an important point to remember when thinking about all of this spiritual detective work: Much of the speculation surrounding the spiritual practices of the ancient Celts (indeed, of most ancient peoples) is just that—speculation. Folklore, mythology, and archaeology can give us clues into the religious practices of the distant past, and comparing the practices of different cultures can help shed light on this mystery as well. But we need to be realistically humble in acknowledging what we do or don't know. No matter how much neopaganism is based on ancient spiritual practices, what really matters is if a way of honoring the Goddess or nature is helpful and meaningful to us today. All religions and spiritualities grow and evolve over time.

The Elements of Druidism

Between the reports of the classical writers, the ancient myths, folklore, folk customs, and archaeology, what can we say about the druids? How can we synthesize all this information into a spirituality that makes sense for today? Well, many people are doing just that.

And even though there aren't nearly as many pagan druids as there are pagan witches, the ones who have chosen this path have found many beautiful and meaningful ways to express their particular version of nature spirituality.

The Three Kinds of Druids

We know from written sources that druids consisted of three orders: bards, seers (also called ovates), and druids. One of the largest modern druid groups, the Order of Bards, Ovates, and Druids, actually has three grades (similar to Wiccan degrees) that a student must pass through, and the grades correspond to these ancient categories. Other groups, like Ár nDraíocht Féin, encourage people to pursue whichever of the three categories most appeals to them. So one person might want to dedicate his or her entire life to learning the bardic mysteries, while another might want to master the skills necessary to be a true seer.

We've already talked about the druids: they were the priests, scientists, and wisdom-keepers of the ancient Celts. We know they performed a spiritual function because Caesar notes that they presided over the sacrificial rituals of the Celts. Among today's neopagan druids, a person who wishes to become a full-fledged druid needs to master ritual skills, needs to be learned and wise in both science and spirituality, and should have administrative skills for leading the *grove*.

EarthWords

A **grove** is a community of druids. Many nondruidic pagan groups use this term as well. In some Wiccan traditions, groups of 13 and under are known as covens, but once the group grows beyond 13 members, it's called a grove.

Big Bad Bards

The bards are the artists of the druid world. Historically, a bard was a poet/musician who memorized the genealogies, histories, and lore of his people. The bard would entertain his audience by singing of the heroic deeds of Gods, Goddesses, and ancestors, as well as of the chieftain or king whom the bard served. But don't think that a bard was a mere entertainer. A true bard worked magic with his poetry and song, transporting the listeners to a timeless state of reverie.

Bards did more than just praise those who deserved acclaim. A talented bard also was skilled in the art of satire. According to Celtic myth, the satire of a skilled bard was so devastating that it could actually kill the person being satirized. Talk about dying from embarrassment!

Oracle

Of the druidic functions, the bardic tradition survived the longest. In the eighteenth century, a blind Irish harper named Turlough O'Carolan was said to have gotten the inspiration for his music from the faeries. Meanwhile, modern Celtic folk music often features energetic melodies performed on violin, bagpipes, flute, harp, and drums. Much of this music has a hypnotic effect on its listeners. Perhaps the bardic tradition is still alive in the work of these musicians! If you'd like to explore some of the more visionary Celtic performers, check out the Irish group Altan, the Scottish group the Tannahill Weavers, or the Celtic-American bands Cherish the Ladies and Emerald Rose.

Among neopagan druids, bardic skills can cover a variety of artistic endeavors. Naturally, music, poetry, and song are still the primary skills of an accomplished bard. These are wonderful elements to incorporate into ritual and spiritual observance, so a talented bard is a welcome addition to any grove. But even if a person's talents lie in other areas (such as art, drama, writing, or dance), he or she may still rightly be considered a bard. If a druid brings philosophy and leadership to spirituality, a bard brings talent, beauty, and aesthetics.

Keepers of the Second Sight

The final category of the druid world is that of the seer, or ovate. (Ovate literally means "prophet.") These were basically the psychics, the visionaries, and the oracles who had the extraordinary ability to discern information from spiritual sources and bring that information back to the druids for consideration. A seer might be able to simply utilize innate psychic abilities to gather knowledge, but he or she also could be adept at using a system of divination.

Today's seers function pretty much the same way as the seers of old. In a ritual, it is the seer's job to listen for any sign that the Gods may be communicating with the grove. When the seer has a sense of what communication may be coming from the deities, the seer presents that information to the gathering.

The interrelation between bards, seers, and druids shows how effective this division of labor can be. In a ritual, a druid presides, serving as master of ceremonies. The bard sings and offers his or her talents to the Gods. Then the seer reports on whatever message the Gods may have for the people.

Drumbeats

In Arthurian legend, Merlin was King Arthur's druid. Arthurian myth tells of bards and seers in the court of Camelot as well. Arthur's bard was Taliesin, and his half-sister Morgan Le Fay has often been depicted as a wicked enchantress, but in Marion Zimmer Bradley's *The Mists of Avalon*, she is portrayed more compellingly (and sympathetically) as a seer.

Celtic Shamanism: The Lore of the Sacred Trees

Earlier in this chapter, I called the druids the shamans of the Celtic people. One of the most obvious ways in which druids functioned like shamans was in their veneration of trees. We know about the lore of trees sacred to the druids from mythology and also from an alphabet used in some of the Celtic lands known as the ogham. Although the druids never committed their wisdom to writing, the ancient Celts still used script for mundane matters like business transactions or marking property lines. Ogham contained of 20 letters, consisting of lines intersecting a central line (see illustration). Each of the ogham letters corresponded to a tree or other plant native to the Celtic lands.

The Ogham

Character	Name in Gaelic	Name in English	English Equivalent
⊣	Beith	Birch	B
⊣	Luis	Rowan	L
⊣	Fearn	Alder	F
⊣	Saille	Willow	S
⊣	Nuin	Ash	N
⊢	Huathe	Hawthorn	H
⊢	Duin	Oak	D
⊢	Tinne	Holly	T
⊢	Coll	Hazel	C
⊢	Quert	Apple	Q
✚	Muin	Vine	M
✚	Gort	Ivy	G
✚	Ngetal	Reed	NG
✚	Straif	Blackthorn	STR
✚	Ruis	Elder	R
✚	Ailim	Fir	A
✚	Ohn	Gorse	O
✚	Ur	Heather	U
✚	Eadha	Aspen	E
✚	Ioho	Yew	I

The Ogham alphabet is based on the names of trees and plants native to the Celtic lands.

Each tree or plant has numerous spiritual and magical associations with it. Here are some of the trees sacred to the druids and a magical significance for each tree:

- Birch: New beginnings
- Rowan: Protection
- Willow: Intuition
- Ash: Interconnection
- Oak: Strength
- Holly: Balance
- Hazel: Wisdom
- Apple: Abundance
- Yew: Transformation

As a shaman, a druid could meditate under a tree or seek psychic contact with the spirit of the tree to bring the energies that the tree represented into his or her own life. Thus, if a druid were seeking abundance, eating apples, using an apple wand in ritual, and meditating beneath an apple tree were all ways to call the desired abundance into manifestation.

The Power of Three

Notice that there are three types of druids: bards, ovates, and druids. This is but one example of a characteristic common to the ancient Celts: They loved the number three. Indeed, the Welsh bards used to memorize nuggets of information in triads, short poems that expressed a fact or truth in a threefold way. Here are a couple simple examples of what triads are like.

Three sources of modern paganism:

> *The shamans*

> *The witches*

> *And the druids*

Three sorrows in the Celtic soul:

> *The troubles in Northern Ireland*

> *The endangered status of Celtic languages*

> *And the devastation of Mother Earth*

Again and again, the Celts organized their knowledge, their wisdom, and their spirituality in terms of three. In addition to bards, ovates, and druids, the Celts also saw many of their Gods and Goddesses as embodying three personalities and having three names. To the Celts, the earth consisted of three sacred realms: the land, the sea, and the sky. The spirit world was inhabited by three types of beings: nature spirits, ancestors, and the Gods/Goddesses. There were three "doorways" through which to reach the otherworld: a holy well, a sacred fire, or the shaman's world tree.

The Druid Contribution

Druidism brings a unique perspective to the neopagan community. Just as not all neopagans are witches or shamans, not all accept all aspects of druid spirituality. Still, anyone who is exploring the pagan path will benefit from knowing the basics of the druid way.

Why Not Excellence?

Ár nDraíocht Féin (AFD) has two mottos, both of which encapsulate the contribution of druids to the larger pagan community. The first is, "Why not excellence?" Many modern druids, while quite dedicated to spirituality and sometimes even magic, also feel that a revived pagan spirituality needs to be intellectually honest and based on scholarship. Some segments of the pagan community base their spirituality more on fantasy than on fact. This is nothing new; indeed, many druids from the eighteenth century onward loved to speculate on ideas such as the druids originally coming from Atlantis. Whether there's any truth to that or not, it certainly can't be proven. Meanwhile, there's so much exciting information to be gleaned from archaeology, folklore, and mythology that most neopagan druids would rather focus on that material than on speculation that, in their minds, seems silly.

 Oracle

While many pagans form groups, groves, or other communities, it's okay to practice pagan spirituality all by yourself. Just as Wicca and shamanism both have a solitary dimension to their tradition, it's also perfectly fine to be a solitary druid. If you practice any kind of pagan spirituality all by yourself, you might enjoy connecting with others of a like mind through the Internet.

ADF's other motto is, "As fast as a speeding oak tree!" This rather goofy saying reminds us that pagan spirituality is nothing if not based in nature, and there's wisdom in being patient (just like a majestic old oak tree).

Paganism for the Rest of Us

With their emphasis on initiation and intense spiritual experience, shamans and witches follow a path that is, by nature, only for a small percentage of people. Few people have the time or the energy to undergo the training necessary to be a shaman or a priestess of the old religion. Nothing wrong with that: In mainstream religions, only about 1 percent of the membership becomes ministers or rabbis. But if not everyone is going to become a master shaman or a Wiccan elder, what path is there to follow?

Druidism offers a glimpse into what could be called "paganism for the rest of us." The concept of bards and seers, as well as druids, reminds us that different people have different gifts and different ways of practicing their spirituality. Furthermore, the grove, as a larger community than the coven, is naturally more accessible to a larger number of people. Groups like ADF have publicly stated that their rituals are open to the general public: a far cry from Wicca, where secrecy and hiddenness remain the norm, partially because witchcraft is so misunderstood and partially because many witches find that their rituals are more effective when performed in private.

So if you're interested in pagan spirituality but don't think you want to put out the effort necessary to be initiated as a witch or a shaman, the path of the druid may be the right one for you.

Other Pagan Paths with an Ethnic Orientation

Just because this chapter has focused mainly on the druids, don't assume that Celtic culture is the only ancient form of paganism being revived today. Indeed, in the pagan community, many groups are actively striving to breathe new life into the Gods and rituals of ancient times. Here are a few other pagan groups that, like druids, are dedicated to a particular brand of paganism.

CAUTION

Taboo!

Racists like Adolf Hitler have appealed to pagan spirituality to justify their extremist positions. But such an interpretation of ancient religion is a perversion of the true spirit of the Gods and Goddesses. Pagan values like tribal loyalty and honoring of one's ancestry are no excuse for racism or any other form of prejudice.

Asatru: The Way of Valhalla

The people of northern Europe, including the Germanic and Norse cultures, have a vibrant indigenous tradition of Gods and Goddesses as majestic and beautiful as any in Europe. Like the Celts, the Norse are part of the Indo-European family of cultures, so many of their Gods and rites are similar to those of the druids. Modern practitioners of Norse paganism often go by the name of Asatru, meaning belief in or loyalty to the Aesir (Norse Gods). Much of the mythology of this proud culture is steeped in the ethics of the warrior, so Asatru has a more martial feel than many forms of paganism. Thanks to the fact that figures like Richard Wagner and Adolf Hitler had an interest in Norse paganism, Asatru suffers from an unfortunate stereotype of being patriarchal and racist. In its purest form, however, veneration of the Aesir is based on self-empowerment and tribal loyalty, with respect for all races and for women as well as men.

Baltic and Lithuanian Paganism: A Tradition That Never Fully Died

Lithuania (formerly part of the Soviet Union) has become well known in the West because of an odd match: In recent years, the rock band the Grateful Dead has supported their Olympic basketball team. But if your knowledge of Lithuania is limited to tie-dye on the court, here's another interesting fact: Of all the countries in Europe, Lithuania was the last to become Christianized, an event that only occurred around the year 1400 C.E. (By comparison, England was Christianized before 700 C.E., and most other parts of Europe converted to the new religion well before the year 1000 C.E.) Because of the late arrival of Christianity in Lithuania, traditional religion has survived in a much more intact fashion; indeed, to this day, a vibrant pagan community called Romuva (taking its name from one of the last of the ancient European pagan temples) exists there, one that has undergone a renaissance since the demise of the Soviet Union.

Other lands near the Baltic Sea, like Estonia and Latvia, also have their own pagan traditions.

Greek, Roman, Egyptian: Varieties of Pagan Reconstruction

Lest you think all the pagan action is centered in northern Europe, other groups have dedicated themselves to reviving Greek or Roman traditions as well as the religion of ancient Egypt. In some cases, communities may be dedicated to a particular deity (like Isis, one of the greatest of the Egyptian Goddesses, or Athena, Greek Goddess of Wisdom). Other communities, like Nova Roma or the Societas Hellenica Antiquariorum, are dedicated to the revival of their culture's traditions, just like druidic or Asatru organizations commit to reviving Celtic or Norse paganism.

Many pagan organizations have websites or e-mail lists online that are dedicated to helping individuals practice a pagan spirituality consistent with their ancestral or chosen culture, even if no community of such pagans exists nearby. If there is a traditional culture whose religion you're interested in practicing, check out Appendix B, "Resources." There you'll find websites for a variety of different pagan groups.

The Least You Need to Know

◆ Druids have been the subject of much romantic speculation.

◆ Serious attempts to revive ancient Celtic religion rely on archaeology, folklore, mythology, and studying the spiritual practices of other cultures.

◆ In addition to druids, the ancient Celts looked to bards (poet/musicians) and ovates (psychics) for spiritual guidance.

◆ In many ways, druids can be thought of as the shamans of the Celtic people.

◆ Many other cultures throughout Europe and the Mediterranean are experiencing their own pagan revivals.

Chapter 6

Other Pieces of the Pagan Puzzle

In This Chapter

- The Tao of paganism
- The good, the bad, and the karma
- The hidden secrets of Western magic
- The science fiction connection
- Bringing it all together

Wicca, shamanism, and druidism are each important parts of the neopagan world, and each one is important to understand the totality of modern nature spirituality. But paganism is a many-colored beast. There are other influences and sources that have helped shape this rapidly growing spirituality. In this chapter, you'll learn about how paganism has been influenced by Eastern mysticism (especially Taoism and Hinduism) and by some of the *esoteric* systems of the West (like ceremonial magic and the Tarot). Even a famous science-fiction novel has its place in the history of modern paganism. Finally, you'll look at how to piece it all together so that you can begin to explore the pagan path in the most important way possible—the way that works for you.

Welcome to "The Way"

This exploration of other influences on modern paganism will begin in the Far East. Just as shamanism developed into religious or spiritual paths like druidism or witchcraft in the West, in China, a religious system with strong shamanic roots is Taoism. Although Taoism officially dates back primarily to the sixth century B.C.E. when Lao-Tze wrote the masterpiece *Tao Te Ching*, many elements of Taoism actually have deeper links to the ancient shamanic past. Among pagans, Taoism is especially well liked because of its simple yet powerful depiction of spiritual reality in the form of the Tao.

> ### EarthWords
>
> **Esoteric** (or "inner circle") knowledge or information is hidden, confidential, or available only to a chosen few. Much magical or mystical wisdom is considered to be esoteric in that only someone with proper training or wisdom can understand or appreciate such information. Incidentally, the word **exoteric** means "outer circle" and refers to knowledge that is generally or widely available.

The Tao

The Tao is a concept too abstract and mystical to adequately be put into words. The word itself means "way" or "course" and basically refers to the ultimate reality—what we in the West might call Spirit, deity, God/Goddess, or even great mystery. Of course, as soon as you try to put the Tao into words, you've distorted the true Tao, which is beyond the limitations of human language and thought.

How, then, can the Tao be understood? Taoists have developed a beautiful and disarmingly simple depiction of the Tao in a symbol commonly known as the Tao or as the yin-yang symbol. The symbol consists of a circle divided into two paisley shapes: one white, the other black. At the center of each shape is a dot in the opposite color.

The yin-yang symbol depicts the mystery of the Tao.

Yin and Yang

What the yin-yang symbol represents is the basic unity of polarity within the universe. Okay, to put that into English: Think about how a magnet has both a north and a south pole, but it's just one magnet. For that matter, the earth functions the same way, as a huge magnet with north and south poles. A coin has two sides, but it's just one coin. The Tao teaches us that this is a natural part of the way the universe works: two aspects of a single unity. And in the Tao, those two aspects are known as yin and yang.

Yin is the receptive principle within the Tao. Yin is black, dark, passive, encompassing, and traditionally seen as feminine.

Yang is the active principle within the Tao. Yang is white, light, forceful, penetrating, and traditionally seen as masculine.

> CAUTION
>
> **Taboo!**
>
> People who grow up in monotheistic religions often harbor the unconscious notion that "white" and "light" equal goodness and God, whereas "black" and "darkness" equal evil and the devil. These concepts have nothing to do with pagan spirituality. Paganism teaches that both light and dark, both black and white, exist within the spiritual realm of Goddess and God. Neither yin nor yang is better than the other.

Of course, every element of the Tao is symbolically important. The entire yin-yang symbol is contained within a black circle, pointing to how yin is the form in which all things resides. Both the yin and the yang aspects have, at their center, the essence of the other. So it's impossible to separate yin and yang into some sort of dualistic set of opposites. On the contrary, yin and yang require each other to exist.

Here, in this most basic of symbols, we have a powerful template for understanding Spirit in a pagan context. Spirit can be seen as the all-encompassing all—the ultimate reality. Yet when we approach this ultimate reality, we immediately encounter a basic polarity. Masculine and feminine. Yang and yin. God and Goddess.

Baby, You Can Drive My Karma

Another important source for many modern pagans is the majestic tradition of Hinduism, the spirituality and religion of India. This influence can be felt on many levels.

For many Wiccans and other pagans, the Hindu pantheon of Gods and Goddesses is as important and meaningful as the various European pantheons. Indian deities like Ganesha (the elephant-headed remover of obstacles) or Kali (the fearsome Goddess of eternal destruction) have found popularity among Western pagans.

Oracle

Two of Hinduism's most popular deities are Shiva (the God of the eternal dance and destruction/renewal) and Shakti (his female consort who represents his energy; without her, he would be passive and inert). Shiva and Shakti are often portrayed in statues and paintings as making love in a passionate, erotic embrace. They symbolize the universal loving union of the Goddess and the God.

But Hinduism's contribution to the pagan revival goes beyond merely lending a God or Goddess to the West. Because so much of the ancient spirituality of Europe came from the Indo-Europeans—the same people who settled in India about the time that Hinduism was born—many druids or others interested in ancient paganism look to Hinduism for hints about Europe's past. And on another level, Hinduism has been an influence to paganism through the concepts of reincarnation and especially karma.

Reincarnation: From India to Ireland

The Hindus were by no means the only people in ancient times to espouse belief in reincarnation. It is known from the writings of Julius Caesar that the druids likewise acknowledged the transmigration (recycling) of souls. So when pagans talk about reincarnation, they're not just mimicking the wisdom traditions of the East; they're actually reconnecting with their own ancient roots.

The Eternal Wheel

Closely connected to reincarnation is the concept of karma. This Sanskrit word means "work" or "destiny" and refers to a principle of balance and cause and effect at work in the universe. According to karma, every thought, word, and deed we say or do will have an impact on our future destiny. Loving, compassionate, and healing actions create good karma, which leads to blessings or benefits in the future. Likewise, harmful or negative actions lead to similarly unpleasant karma. Karma can shape the future of our current lives, but it can just as easily impact future incarnations.

Karma is a mysterious and profound spiritual principle that cannot be easily explained or understood. For many people, the most important aspect of karma is its inherent justice. Karma reminds us that we are 100-percent responsible for our life, both present and future. The principle of karma maintains that our present circumstances were shaped by our past deeds. If you're unhappy with your current lot in life, karma assures you that, with the right choices, your future will improve. Karma also assures us that people who do bad things and get away with them will eventually pay the price.

CAUTION

Taboo!

The law of karma can make it seem as if people who are poor, sick, or suffering in an oppressive society have just gotten their karmic rewards—in other words, they deserve the crummy conditions of their lives. Well, that may be. But don't use karma as an excuse for blaming people who are less fortunate than yourself; instead, do what you can to make the world a better and more just place. By doing things to help others, from volunteering in a soup kitchen to supporting political reform that benefits the poorest members of society, you create good karma for yourself.

Part of the beauty of karma is how it affirms that the universe we live in is ultimately fair and just, while making unnecessary the sense of foreboding that is part of some other religions. With karma, you don't have to worry about making a blunder for which you will have to spend an eternity in hell. On the contrary, karma maintains that if you make more good choices than bad, you will experience gradual improvement of your life circumstances, incarnation after incarnation. Karma also gives us a chance to right our wrongs. If we blow it this lifetime, we'll have another chance (albeit in a less comfortable life) to make up for it later.

How Pagan Karma Differs from Eastern Karma

Most Eastern philosophy, especially as found within Hinduism and Buddhism, maintains that the endless cycle of incarnation after incarnation is a drag and that karma is almost like a prison. The goal behind religion is to become so spiritually pure that your soul gets liberated from the endless wheel of rebirth. This way of seeing things assumes that the world we live in is bad and that the best thing to do is to try to escape it.

Pagans see things differently. Remember that, to pagans, the world isn't bad but is the physical manifestation of the Goddess. So the eternal wheel of birth, death, and rebirth can be a joyful and wonderful journey. Pagans try not so much to escape karma as to shape it in positive ways. Building up good karma lifetime after lifetime does not lead to some sort of nirvana but simply to evolutionary growth, where each new incarnation is better than the one before. That makes for a fascinating way to spend eternity!

Oracle

According to some Wiccan traditions, witches are governed by the Law of Three, which is a variation on karma. According to the Law of Three, any energy you put forth in your life, whether positive or negative, will come back to you magnified three times.

Spinning Wheels of Light

Another concept from the rich culture of India that has influenced many pagans (indeed, many spiritually minded people of all paths) involves the chakras. Chakra is a Sanskrit word that means "wheel of light," and according to esoteric wisdom, the human body has numerous chakras throughout it. The chakras exist not so much in the physical body as in the aura or psychic body (the soul). Psychics and spiritual healers work with the chakras to ensure that the energy within them is flowing properly.

These are the seven main chakras:

- The root chakra, located at the very base of the spine, governs the soul's relationship to the body and indeed to all of material existence.
- The sacral chakra, located just above the genitals, governs pleasure, social and intimate relationships, sexuality, and reproduction.
- The solar plexus chakra, located above the navel, governs our personal power (the ability to make choices).
- The heart chakra, located at the heart, governs not only love and compassion, but our breathing patterns as well.
- The throat chakra, located at the throat, governs our ability to communicate, our creativity, and our magical ability.
- The third-eye chakra, located at the middle of the forehead, governs our mental ability and our wisdom.
- The crown chakra, located at the top of the soul (above the roof of your head) governs our relationship with Spirit and the otherworld.

Although belief in, or working with, the chakras is not required to be a pagan, most pagans find that the chakras are essential to understanding the spiritual nature of the human body/soul, and working with them is a central part of any kind of spiritual healing activity.

The Way of the Western Mysteries

Alongside the ancient wisdom of shamans and witches and the rather intellectual approach of druidism, another important source in Western Europe has helped shape modern paganism. This is known variously as the occult, hermetic, esoteric, or mystery tradition. This is the tradition of ceremonial magic. Unlike witches (who were usually common people who used herbs and folk cures to perform their magical healing), ceremonial magicians studied the arcane knowledge of ancient societies and combined that knowledge with disciplines such as astrology and *alchemy* to develop a spiritual approach to life mastery.

Ceremonial magic involves finding ritual ways to summon and control spirits or to purify the soul to make it more pleasing to God. Unlike witchcraft and shamanism, which tend to be very much based on the forces of nature, the roots of ceremonial magic come out of the Christian, Jewish, and Islamic worlds. Even so, much of the imagery and wisdom of the occult tradition has roots in ancient paganism and uses rich symbolism that has been incorporated into modern pagan rituals.

The traditions of alchemical and magical research found a home in the modern world with the formation of the Order of the Golden Dawn, a magical society founded in England in the late nineteenth century. The Golden Dawn incorporated wisdom from a variety of sources, including Freemasonry, ancient Egyptian religion, the Kabbalah (a Jewish mystical tradition), the Rosicrucians (a long-standing European esoteric order), as well as ancient writings from alchemists like Paracelsus (1493–1541) or magicians like John Dee (1527–1608).

Much of the ritual and wisdom of the Golden Dawn and other magical societies from modern times has directly inspired modern pagans like Gerald Gardner. Indeed, one of the most notorious members of the Golden Dawn, a magician named Aleister Crowley, helped Gardner rewrite the rituals of his Wiccan coven. Today, some segments of the pagan community revere Crowley as one of the twentieth century's most accomplished magicians.

> **EarthWords**
>
> **Alchemy** is the forerunner of modern chemistry and modern magic. Alchemy literally means the art of alloying metals and refers to ancient efforts to transmute base metals into gold to find a formula of eternal youth or other such early chemical quests. Spiritual alchemy seeks to transmute the "lead" of human existence into a higher, mystically pure ("gold") life.

Drumbeats

Aleister Crowley is the pagan community's weird uncle. He wasn't exactly a pagan himself, having died in 1947 well before the modern neopagan movement was underway. He certainly didn't consider himself a witch or a druid. Crowley was a magician and a famous one at that; he combined a brilliant mind with an excessive personality and seemed to revel in controversy and notoriety. When he was a boy, his strict Christian mother nicknamed him "the Beast," a moniker that apparently pleased him. As an adult, he pursued ceremonial magic with vigor and wrote numerous books about his occult adventures. Much of his writing is pompous and overblown, but he remains one of the most important, if misunderstood, occultists in modern times. Some pagans don't care for his melodramatic style, but others see in him a powerful intellect that contributed much to the study of magic.

Modern pagan concepts, such as the magic circle, the powers of the four directions, and the symbolism of the four elements, all have been richly influenced by the occult tradition. Don't worry if these words are confusing to you now—they will be explained in greater depth in Chapter 11, "Elementary, My Dear Pagan!" Chapter 14, "Tools for Ritual," and Chapter 15, "A Basic Ritual."

Science Fiction Paganism

To this point, all the various elements of pagan spirituality that you've looked at, from shamanism to Wicca to the Golden Dawn, have been traditions from yesteryear. This is perfectly normal because spirituality always has some sort of root in the past, but paganism is a unique spiritual path in that you can find inspiration not only in the wisdom of your ancestors but indeed in almost any way imaginable. As an illustration of this, let's look at the Church of All Worlds, a pagan group that was originally inspired by a science-fiction novel.

Do You Grok the Pagan Path?

In 1961, legendary science-fiction writer Robert Heinlein's masterpiece, *Stranger in a Strange Land* (G. P. Putnam), was published. This story told the bizarre and at times unsettling story of Valentine Michael Smith, a human child who was raised by aliens on Mars. As an adult, Smith returns to earth, but it's not very clear whether he's more human or Martian in his outlook. He exhibits extremely advanced psychic abilities, including a form of mental communion called "grokking." He is totally sexually liberated and takes numerous lovers. (Remember that this book came out during the swinging sixties!) He ultimately becomes the founder of a new religion based on his Martian knowledge, called the Church of All Worlds.

Before the 1960s were over, a small group of science-fiction lovers in the St. Louis area began their own version of the Church of All Worlds. This group combined science fiction, the philosophy of free love, and pagan reverence for nature and the Goddess into a unique new group. Two generations later, the Church of All Worlds is still going strong. Now headquartered in California, it has members throughout the United States as well as in other parts of the world. For many years it published *Green Egg*, a pagan magazine respected throughout the nature spirituality community.

Although some aspects of the Church of All Worlds (such as its support of *polyamory*) are not exactly consistent with the pagan mainstream, the fact that a novel set in the future could inspire one of the most successful of pagan groups shows just how diverse the pagan community is.

Putting It All Together

There are so many different ways to find inspiration as a pagan, what's a new pagan to do? Become a witch? Study shamanism? Learn about the druids or about ceremonial magic? Read science fiction? All of the above?

I've intentionally tried to present information about the many different kinds of pagan spirituality to make the point that there's no such thing as "one right way" to be a pagan. Remember that paganism is a path of experience, not of dogma. If you decide you would like to explore nature spirituality, you may find the total freedom (in other words, the lack of structure) to be a bit disorienting. The world we live in tends to be pretty structured, whether you are following a curriculum at college, working the system at a corporation, or following the teachings of a church or other religious group. In a way, our society is so structured that a lot of people go through life almost like they're on automatic pilot, never really needing to think for themselves or make their own decisions, on a spiritual level or in any other way.

Pagan spirituality, therefore, is a more challenging alternative for many people. Sure, you can join a Wiccan coven or a shamanic training curriculum, and you'll be expected to follow the program just like in any other area of life. But even if you choose such a relatively structured pagan path, first you need to decide what is right for you. Many people follow a pagan path without ever studying with an established group or teacher. This is a path of great freedom.

But with this freedom comes responsibility, for you'll need to choose for yourself what your spirituality looks like. Are you more interested in magic or mysticism? Do you like performing rituals, or is simply meditating enough for you? Would you rather practice your paganism alone, with just one or two trusted friends, or in a group? Do you want to hone your psychic powers, or are you more interested in doing academic research into the wisdom of ancient cultures? And on and on these kinds of questions go.

EarthWords

Polyamory means "many loves." Only a small minority of pagans are polyamorists, but the ones who are believe that it's okay to have a sexual relationship with more than one partner simultaneously, as long as it's done with honesty, integrity, and fairness. If you ever wondered what happened to the free love movement of the 1960s, it lives on today among polyamorists.

Know Yourself!

Some pagan groups teach "Know yourself" as a foundational principle of the neopagan path. Instead of trying to remake yourself into what some priest or pastor thinks a "good" person ought to be, paganism asks of you only that you be true to yourself. Now, this is

Oracle

Not sure what pagan path to follow? You can always ask for help. Before going to sleep at night, ask your spirit guides to help you identify which path is best for you. See if an answer comes to you in your dreams. Guidance can also come through the words of a friend or through coincidences in your life.

not as easy as it looks on the surface. Paganism asks you to be true to your best and highest self, to those parts of yourself that are the most loving, the most trusting, the most free, and the most compassionate. In other words, rise to fullest potential of your nature as a human being (which seems an appropriate thing to say for a nature religion).

If you're reading this book just to learn about paganism, read on. Understand, however, that all I can ultimately provide is one person's perspective on this large and diverse spiritual path. Still, I've tried to present a perspective that embodies the mainstream of pagan thought and practice.

If you're reading this book because you want to explore the pagan way as your own spiritual path, I hope all this talk about taking responsibility for finding your own way as a pagan isn't overwhelming or intimidating. If you're an absolute beginner, keep on reading—the chapters to come will orient you as to many of the basic principles of nature spirituality, including ritual, magic, the holidays of the year, and how to live a day-to-day pagan life. Remember, however, that my perspective is only one of many possible ways to express paganism. If something you read in this book (or in any other book you may study on paganism) doesn't ring true, honor your own intuition. It could be signaling to you that your path is somewhat different from my path or the path of some other author.

Perfect Love and Perfect Trust

"Perfect love and perfect trust" is a password many traditionalist witches use to gain entry into their circles. It's a great phrase for all pagans to keep in mind because it is the clue to developing your own intuition, an important quality that will help you along the path of the Goddess. Take time in your life to love yourself and take some quiet time every day to listen to the stirrings of your heart. Learn to trust your own inner guidance. This, in the end, will help you become a far better pagan than any book or teacher ever could.

To finish this chapter, the next section contains a brief meditation you can do to formally embrace the pagan path as your own. If you don't want to formally embrace pagan spirituality at this time, feel free to read the ritual without actually doing it. But if you feel ready to embrace paganism as your own, this can be a way to announce to your own heart (as well as to the God and the Goddess) that you have chosen the path of nature spirituality.

A Ritual for Embarking on the Pagan Path

To do this ritual, you'll need a quiet place where you can be undisturbed for 10 to 20 minutes. If you're at home, turn off the computer, TV, and stereo and unplug the telephone. Or you may decide to perform this ceremony outdoors, perhaps in the same place where you performed the strengthening-your-ties-to-nature ritual from Chapter 2, "All-Natural Ingredients."

The supplies you need are as follows: a candle, a stick of incense, a small amount of salt, and a small bowl of water from nature (either rain water or spring water). A candle snuffer and incense holder are optional but would be useful. You can perform this ritual standing or sitting, indoors or out. You can perform it on the ground, or on the floor, or at a table.

1. Begin by holding the unlit (!) candle and incense in your hands (or hold your hands over them). Say this brief prayer: "In the name of Mother Nature and of the Spirit who gives life to all, I ask that this candle and incense be blessed as symbols of my spiritual path."

2. Light the candle. Close your eyes and take a deep breath. The candle symbolizes the presence of Spirit. (Note: If you're outdoors and it's breezy, the candle may not stay lit. In this case, simply close your eyes and feel the breeze on your face; it also can remind us of Spirit's presence.)

3. Light the incense from the candle. Put it in an incense holder; if you're outside, you can stick it directly into the soil. Notice the smoke of the incense and think of it as a symbol of your thoughts and prayers being offered to the God and the Goddess(Safety note: whether indoors or out, never leave candles or incense unattended and always make sure no flammable materials, like dry leaves, are near your flame).

4. Hold your hands over the salt and the water. Say this brief prayer: "In the name of the Mother Nature and of the Spirit who gives life to all, I ask that this water and this salt be blessed as symbols of my new spiritual path."

5. Take a few moments to breathe deeply. Relax and feel your body resting either on the chair or on the ground, depending on where you are.

6. Now take three pinches of salt and drop them into the bowl of water, saying this brief prayer: "Salt is of the earth, and water is of water. With these elements I bless myself."

Oracle

The four elements of this ritual—the candle, the incense, the water, and the salt—correspond to the four elements used in nearly all pagan rituals. The candle symbolizes fire, the incense symbolizes air, the salt symbolizes earth, and the water (of course) symbolizes water. Working with these four elements is basic to nearly all pagan ritual and magical effort.

7. Dip your forefinger and middle finger in the salt water (use your right hand if right-handed, left if left-handed). Touch the wet fingers to your forehead lightly, saying, "I bless my mind, so that my spiritual path is always in accord with what I know to be true."

8. Again dip your fingers and now touch your lips. Say, "I bless my voice, that I may only speak words of love, wisdom, and trust."

9. Dip again and now touch your chest at your heart. Say, "I bless my heart, that I may truly love the ways of the Goddess and the God."

10. Dip again and now touch just below your navel. Say, "I bless my power, that all my actions be in accordance with the highest good."

11. Dip again and now touch both feet. Say, "I bless my feet, that I may always walk in harmony with nature."

12. Take a few minutes for silence. In your own words, either spoken aloud, silently, or in writing, declare yourself to be a pagan. If you're having difficulty finding the words, you can say something like this. "I now choose to walk the pagan path. I choose of my own free will, and I make this choice in love and trust. I choose to the best of my ability to harm none. I choose to honor and love Mother Nature, my own nature, and the nature of all my relations. This I declare before the Goddess and the God. May it be so." (If you want, you can end with "So mote it be," which is a fancy way of saying "May it be so.")

13. Remain quiet for as long as feels right. When you feel ready, extinguish the candle. Do not blow it out; instead, snuff it out with a snuffer or your fingertips. If indoors, you can let the incense burn down. Make sure all flames are extinguished before you leave the ritual site, and be sure to leave the place as clean as you found it.

Congratulations! May you find joy and happiness along the pagan path. Read on to learn more.

The Least You Need to Know

- Neopaganism has been shaped and influenced by many cultures and traditions, even Eastern spirituality and science fiction.
- The Tao—the central concept of Taoism—can be helpful in understanding the relationship between Spirit, Goddess, and God.
- Hindu concepts like karma and the chakras have become a part of the spirituality of many, perhaps even most, pagans.
- Because there are so many different ways to be a pagan, you are ultimately responsible for your unique expression of pagan ways.

Part 2

How to Think Like a Pagan

What do pagans believe? Since most forms of paganism stress spiritual experience over religious doctrine, there's no simple way to answer this question. When it comes to their ideas about spirituality, nearly all pagans stress personal study and development over adherence to dogma.

Nevertheless, some common themes can be identified within most forms of nature spirituality. Many pagans see the universe we live in as having a spiritual nature as well as a material nature. Tradition and folklore play important roles in the pagan world as well, and many witches, druids, and shamans embrace the Goddesses and Gods of world mythology as central spiritual figures. Pagans also celebrate the cyclical and rhythmic nature of the universe, from the endless rhythm of breathing to the rotation of the earth.

An introductory book such as this cannot exhaust the many varieties of pagan beliefs and perspectives, but the chapters in this part of the book will give you enough of an overview to comprehend the basic patterns of pagan thought.

Chapter 7

This World, That World, and the Otherworld

In This Chapter

- ◆ Learning about the otherworld
- ◆ Thinking about the spiritual realm
- ◆ Accessing your inner universe
- ◆ Meeting the residents of the otherworld
- ◆ Understanding the importance of the otherworld

Part of the joy in exploring the pagan path is learning new ways to think about the world in which we live. In this chapter, you'll take a look under the hood of the universe and see how the spiritual and material worlds interact and relate to one another.

A Tale of Two (or More) Worlds: Pagan Cosmology

Take a piece of paper and draw a circle on it. How many sides does the circle have?

Two, of course: an inside and an outside.

To understand the pagan way of comprehending the universe, let's start with this simple principle. A circle reminds us that there are (at least) two sides to everything. Two sides to every object, two sides to every story, two sides to every truth.

The God and the Goddess, whom you will get to know better in Chapter 8, "Getting to Know the Goddess," and Chapter 9, "All About the God," represent the two sides of deity. Likewise, there are two "sides" to every human being: a body and a soul. Even the entire universe itself can be seen to have two sides: an "inside" (the spiritual realms) and an "outside" (the manifest, or physical realm). Think about your own inner consciousness: You have an entire "universe" of thoughts, emotions, experiences, dreams, and imagination inside of you. But of course, there's also the physical, manifest universe that is outside of you. You are a part of this outer universe. But here's the kicker: You are also connected to a vast inner universe as well, and the far-reaching riches of your mind and consciousness, of your dreams and daydreams, are just as connected to the spiritual domain of the universe as your body is connected to the physical domain.

The Psychic Linkup

Indeed, one of the twentieth century's most famous psychologists, Carl Jung, speculated that all human beings have a connection to a unified subconscious reality, which he called the collective unconscious. In this collective *groupmind* can be found all the ancient memories of humankind, all the thoughts, feelings, emotions, and wisdom of the entire sweep of the human race. It's almost as if each human being is a unique computer, but at the subconscious, unconscious level, all of our systems are connected to a universal network that makes the World Wide Web look like small potatoes!

EarthWords

Groupmind, a basic principle of magical philosophy, is achieved when human consciousness extends beyond the limitations of the body, allowing different minds, or souls, to interact to form a unity greater than the sum of its parts. In the pagan world, many groves or covens find that doing rituals together creates a groupmind in which the members have powerful psychic links to one another.

If this sounds pretty far out to you, hang in there with it. Think of some of the more amazing and unexplained mysteries in our world. Mysteries of ESP, like mental telepathy or psychokinesis. How powerful abilities to communicate exist between identical twins or other people with strong genetic or cultural links. How famous prophets or psychics like Nostradamus or Edgar Cayce have been able to predict the future or provide accurate medical information about people they've never met.

These amazing psychic phenomena, which cannot be explained by the current level of scientific knowledge, may point to humankind having profound abilities regarding knowledge, communication, and insight that are not limited by the body. In other words, the human mind appears to have abilities far beyond what "meets the eye." One way to understand these abilities is through Jung's concept of the collective unconscious, which corresponds beautifully with the pagan concept of the otherworld.

> ### Drumbeats
>
> Most pagans believe that everyone has some degree of psychic ability; however, just as everyone may have athletic skill but only a few make it to the Olympics, so, too, on the psychic or spiritual level are there a relatively small number of true "stars." Two of the world's most famous psychics are Nostradamus (1503–1566) and Edgar Cayce (1877–1945). Nostradamus, a French physician and clairvoyant, made hundreds of predictions for the future, extending all the way into the thirty-eighth century! Cayce, who established a psychic research center in Virginia Beach, Virginia, was known as the "sleeping prophet" because he would go into a trance in which he would lose consciousness but would provide startling, accurate medical and psychic readings for clients, even ones located hundreds of miles away.

Understanding the Otherworld

So, if there are two worlds, this world and the otherworld, what can we say about the spiritual realm? What makes the otherworld tick?

To begin with, like everything else in paganism, there are different ways of thinking about the spiritual realm. To get you started learning about the otherworld, I'll present three different ways of thinking about it. The first way is the simplest, seeing the cosmos strictly in terms of the physical universe and the spiritual universe. The second way of understanding the cosmos sees reality as a three-tiered system, with an "upper" world, a "middle" world (that corresponds to the physical universe), and a "lower" world. This is one of the most common maps for the cosmos: It's even found its way into Christianity. Finally, to really complicate matters, I'll show you a traditional occult way of understanding the universe, in which there are no less than eight (!) planes or realms of experience.

As always, I'm presenting these different viewpoints not to confuse you but to provide you with a sense of the variety of ideas in the pagan worldview. You are ultimately responsible for deciding which "map," or *paradigm*, of reality works best for you, based on your own experience and what your intuition tells you feels the most "right."

 EarthWords

Paradigm literally means "pattern" or "example." It refers to a model of something.

The Two-Tiered Paradigm

The most basic way to approach the spiritual reality of the cosmos relies on that circle you drew at the beginning of the chapter. Inside and outside. Physical and spiritual. Manifest world and the world of pure idea. In this way of seeing things, anything that comes from the spiritual or mystical dimension of reality belongs in the "otherworld."

I like this two-tiered approach to understanding how the universe works, but there is a danger to avoid. It's easy to fall in the trap of dualism, in which the "spiritual" world is seen as somehow better, "higher," or more pure than the physical world. The problem with dualism is that it can lead to erroneous ideas, such as thinking that sex is somehow inferior to spirituality or that people who devote their lives to meditation are somehow better than people who just focus on making lots of money.

The antidote to this dualistic way of seeing things is the concept of the Tao, and the yin-yang symbol discussed in Chapter 6, "Other Pieces of the Pagan Puzzle." Remember how it held both black and white in a unified circle? And in the black section was a white dot (and vice versa)? This reminds us that divisions such as "matter" and "spirit" are never meant to imply that one is somehow better than the other. The spirit world may be where we go after we die, where we encounter the Goddess, or where we have access to deep soul wisdom, but none of these things makes it "better" than the material world. Like the yin and the yang, spirit and matter coexist in a unified whole that we call the cosmos.

Oracle _____

Most pagans recognize that any concepts about the ultimate nature of reality can only be models or theories about what is really real. What makes a paradigm useful is how practical it is: If your model of the universe helps you live a happy, mature, and ethical life, most pagans would agree it's a pretty good model.

Taboo! _____

Be careful to avoid dualistic thinking. If you are drawn to spirituality, that doesn't make material pursuits—such as earning money or enjoying sensual pleasure—somehow less worthy. Indeed, most pagans believe that true spirituality consists not only of such things as meditation and ritual, but also learning to have a healthy and appropriate relationship to money, sex, and tasty food!

The Three-Tiered Paradigm

As simple as it may be to see the world as consisting of only physical and material realms, in many traditional cultures, the otherworld is regarded as having two (or more) realms within it. In mythic traditions as well as in modern pagan ritual, concepts such as the "underworld" (not to be confused with the Mafia!) or the "Land of Faery" often point to the idea that a spiritual realm exists below us. By "below," this traditionally meant inside the earth herself, but some modern pagans understand this concept as simply meaning a world of profound depth that may exist inside the mind as easily as inside the earth.

In some cultures, the relationship between the otherworld and the physical universe can be thought of almost as layers, like lasagna:

- The top layer, or celestial realm, is above the physical world and is where the Gods and Goddesses live.

- The middle layer is the manifest, physical universe where we mortals conduct our lives.

- Finally, the underworld is that place of depth and darkness where nature spirits dwell.

If you grew up in the Christian religion, this may sound familiar—almost too familiar. This model of the universe was adopted into Christianity, where the celestial realm is called "heaven" and the underworld is "hell." But unlike pagan and shamanic cultures that see both upper and lower realms as spiritually important, in Christianity, the upper realm is pure good and the lower realm pure evil. Hmmm … sounds like dualism!

> **Drumbeats**
>
> Hell gets its name from a Norse Goddess named Hel, who was the queen of the underworld. Like most pagan cultures, the Norse did not regard the underworld as a place of punishment or suffering. Most pagans consider the concept of "hell" as a place of eternal torment to be absurd.

In contrast to the dualism that sees the celestial otherworld as good and the underworld as bad, pagan tradition simply sees them as different, just like South America is different (but no better or worse than) North America.

Yggdrasil and the Cosmos of Shamanism

In many traditional cultures, a mythic tree is seen as the link joining the various levels of the cosmos together. For example, in the Norse tradition, Yggdrasil, or the Great World Tree, unites the celestial and underworld realms together with the material world. The roots of the great tree reach down into the depths of the underworld, the trunk emerges into the manifest universe, and the branches and leaves reach up, up to the home of the Gods. What's wonderful about the World Tree is that it reminds us that all three levels of reality are interconnected. So the spirits of the earth (nature spirits and faeries) are related to humans, and we in turn are related to the Gods and Goddesses. We are all one family!

The Unbelievably Complicated Paradigm

Okay, now it's time to complicate matters even further. Here is a map of the cosmos that divides reality into eight distinct layers or planes. (Just to complicate matters further, I'll start at the bottom and move up.)

- The *physical plane* is the world we live in, with solids, liquids, gases, and energy.
- The *etheric plane* represents the energies closest to the material world, energies that link physical reality to the spiritual planes "above" it.
- The *lower astral plane* is the realm of instincts, passions, and powerful desires.
- The *upper astral plane* represents "higher" or more pure forms of feeling.
- The *lower mental plane* corresponds to concrete forms of thought.
- The *upper mental plane* is the realm governing abstract or "pure" thought.
- The *lower spiritual plane* is the realm where pure spirit is manifest as various Gods or Goddesses.
- The *upper spiritual plane* is the ultimate reality, where pure spirit resides beyond all possibility of human comprehension.

These various planes represent both stages of consciousness within each human being and realms within the overall world of spirit. In this way of seeing the cosmos, faeries or nature spirits may be citizens of the astral plane, while a true God or Goddess hails from the spiritual plane. And of course, all things proceed from the ultimate source, the upper spiritual plane, which is really beyond all human language and concept.

Some pagans love these kinds of maps for the cosmos, seeing in them helpful ways to understand the variety of spiritual experiences to be encountered in ritual and magic. Meanwhile, other pagans find these kinds of systems to be overly complex and needlessly complicated. Guess what? You get to decide which way of seeing the universe makes the most sense for you.

> **Oracle**
>
> Although there is no one right way to think about the otherworld, it's helpful to know about some of these different ways of understanding the spiritual realm. When you read different myths from around the world or writings from various spiritual teachers, you will run into different ways of thinking about the mystical dimension of the cosmos. On a more practical note, if you choose to study a particular tradition or with a particular teacher or group, you'll probably want to work within your tradition's accepted way of seeing things—remembering, of course, that the ultimate nature of reality is far greater than any human concept could ever capture. Therefore, no one paradigm is perfect.

Doorways to the Otherworld

Whether you prefer to see the otherworld as a unified spiritual realm, a universe with upper and lower dimensions, or an intricate system of layers and realms (or some combination thereof), the practical question is, "How do we visit or contact the otherworld?"

Pagan spirituality is not just a smorgasbord of ideas and abstract principles. For pagans, the existence of the otherworld means we can journey there, gain wisdom and healing power from there, and ultimately make our lives happier, fuller, and more meaningful as a result of our otherworldly voyages.

So, let's begin. First of all, the single most important portal to the otherworld is your own self. Your body, mind, and soul combine to form an intricate system of consciousness. It is through consciousness that you not only experience and interact with the material world but also move "between the worlds" to encounter spirits, guides, faeries, and the Gods. Therefore, the best tools for reaching the otherworld are the tools you create within yourself, including dreams, your imagination, and your psychic or intuitive experiences. Even the other tools discussed here (such as ritual, visualization, and divination) are helpful only because they help you to connect with the power and majesty of your own mind.

Dreams

The dream state is one of the most powerful doorways into the subconscious mind and into the mystical universe to which it is connected. Dreams are fully formed, multidimensional universes and can be gloriously beautiful and resonant with feelings of deep peace, joy, or love. Of course, in a world of both light and shadow, our nightmare dreams can also reveal to us our fears, rage, and other unsettling experiences. For many people, psychic information or contacts with spirits come most easily through dreams.

What I especially love about dreams is how *real* they are. Even when things happen in my dreams that defy the "normal" laws of physics, in the dream state itself, all things have a sense of actual existence about them. To me, dreams are proof positive that the mind is the most important tool when it comes to relating to "reality." After all, modern physics points out that all things that exist, no matter how "solid" or "material," are at their heart merely patterns of dancing energy. Well, so is the mind and so is the dream state. The apparent reality of a dream points to the actual reality of the otherworld.

The Imagination

The saying that "it's just a dream" points out how biased our culture is against the power and meaning of the dream world. Similarly, dismissing something by saying that "it's just your imagination" or "you're just daydreaming" is equally dismissive of the power of the mind. For a child who is trying to feel safe from the monsters that appear in his nightmares or imagination, such dismissive statements may temporarily be useful. But as a society, we've starved ourselves from the powerful wisdom and guidance that can come from the rich landscape of dreams, daydreams, and imagination.

One way to think of imagination (or "daydreams") is simply as the dreaming faculty of the conscious mind. It's a tricky matter, for the inner world must compete with the demands of the outer world. But by practicing such skills as meditation and visualization, you can learn to enter your imagination deeply and thereby attain contact with the spirits and symbols of the otherworld. For more on meditation and visualization, see Chapter 17, "Meditation: Welcome to Magical Boot Camp!"

Intuition and Psychic Experience

Some gifted people are able to receive guidance from the spiritual realm through dreams, imagination, or some other form of inner knowing. These flashes of spiritual insight form the basis of intuition and many kinds of psychic phenomena. There are numerous ways to access wisdom through the mind ("psyche"), too many to cover here. But here are a few of the better-known forms of psychic experience:

- **Clairvoyance ("clear vision")** The ability to see on a psychic level without using your physical eyes.
- **Clairaudience ("clear hearing")** The ability to hear wisdom, psychic truth, or the voice of guidance on an inner, nonphysical level.
- **Clairsentience ("clear sensation")** The ability to access psychic information and guidance by feeling it within the body.
- **Clairempathy ("clear emotion")** The ability to pick up feelings and attitudes on a psychic level or to read the emotional energy encoded within an object or a place.

There's even clairgustance ("clear tasting") and clairscent ("clear smelling"), which enable a person to obtain information or guidance through the psychic equivalent of his or her nose or taste buds!

A psychic is not a special kind of person; we are all special kinds of psychics. Every human being has a tremendous capacity to obtain information, wisdom, guidance, or insight from the spiritual world. It takes practice because we live in a cynical, suspicious culture that dismisses spiritual experience as only so much hokum. Sure, there have been some psychics over the years who have been charlatans. But a few bad eggs do not make the overwhelming reality of spiritual experience invalid. If you take the time to meditate, to learn divination skills, and most of all, to listen to the deep stirrings in your own heart and mind, you can access your own unique psychic skill and gain a deeper connection to the otherworld.

Ritual, Divination, and Magic

So if dreams, imagination, and psychic skill are the most basic ways to access the otherworld, how can we hone our abilities to remember our dreams, use our imagination more vividly, and truly listen to our intuitive side?

The three tools nearly all pagans use are divination, ritual, and magic. I've already touched on each of these concepts in previous chapters, and I'll look at them in closer detail in Parts 3 and 4. For now, let's just say that pagans perform intricate rituals, learn complicated systems of divination, and cast spells with specific goals in mind, not just to have fun. (Actually, most pagans love their spiritual path and would argue that fun is a perfectly valid reason for performing rituals or working magic. But for most pagans, there's far more than just simply enjoyment involved.) To a pagan, the rituals and ceremonies of spirituality not only are a pleasure to perform, they also help a person open up more fully to the beauties and wonders of the universe beyond the five senses. That, ultimately, is the most important reason for doing the "work" of paganism.

Knock, Knock: Who's There?

Think about the many dreams you've had in your life over the years. (Every human being has about five dreams a night, if not more, so you've had thousands of dreams by now!) Think of all the people who appear in your dreams. Family members, friends, associates from work or school, total strangers, loved ones who have died, even famous people. It's amazing to see who can pop up in the theater of the subconscious. Now, psychologists will point out that dream figures tend to be symbolic of aspects of your own mind. So if Jerry Garcia shows up in your dream, he may not be the "real" Garcia coming from the other side; he could just be a symbol of the hippie part of yourself (even if, in the waking world, you are a conservative accountant—even accountants have an inner hippie just dying to get out).

Thoughtful pagans will agree that the people in our dreams are often simply products of our own minds. The same holds true for people we encounter in our imagination. But paganism has a broader view of the mind's connection to the otherworld than does orthodox psychology. Pagans recognize that sometimes the people we encounter in our inner journeys—whether through dreams, visualization, or imagination—actually represent spirits who are contacting us.

But just who are these spirits? And where do they come from? To answer this question, once again we look to two sources: (1) your experience, and (2) the experience of others as recorded in myth, folklore, and the writings of pagans and other spiritual seekers who have gone before us. What we find is that quite a number of different kinds of spirits and entities populate the vast realms of the spiritual universe.

Homes of the Gods, the Ancestors, and the Faeries

To begin with, the otherworld is the home of the Gods (and the Goddesses), the ancestors, and the faeries. These are three particular types of spirit beings, all of whom you will get to know better in the next three chapters. Incidentally, the Gods and Goddesses in the otherworld include all the figures from all the great cultures and spiritual traditions of humankind.

Beyond these three broad distinctions of spirit beings, there are other ways to recognize the kinds of entities you will encounter when you journey into the mystical realms. Here are a few of the beings you are likely to come across:

- ◆ **Spirit Guides**   Entities who come to us as helpers, guides, or mentors.
- ◆ **Allies**   Really just another name for spirit guides, especially those who are members of our "team" that work with us throughout life.

- ◆ **Angels**   Messengers from the Goddess who bring her specific guidance to us.
- ◆ **Ancestors**   Members of our family (biological family or spiritual family) who have gone before us.
- ◆ **Nature spirits**   Faeries, devas, and other spirits with a close relationship with the natural world often reach out for contact with humans.
- ◆ **Ghosts**   Spirits who appear in the form of people who have died; often confused and not even realizing they're dead.
- ◆ **Power Animals/Plants**   These entities come in the form of animals, trees, or sometimes even appearing as mythical beasts like dragons or unicorns.

> **Oracle**
>
> Contacting your spirit guides is one of the most important and basic of tasks as you seek to become more connected with the otherworld. There are many different ways to establish contact with your guides; if you'd like to read more on this subject, one basic and very helpful book is *How to Meet and Work With Spirit Guides* by Ted Andrews (Llewellyn Publications, 1992).

Each of these categories of spirits will be examined more closely in Chapter 10, "A Field Guide to the Spirit World."

Other Spirits (Including the Ones to Avoid)

Working with the spirit realm can mean encountering an endless variety of entities. Here's one thing to keep in mind: Some spirits are unfriendly, hostile, or even scary. These spirits, especially when you're first starting out, are best left alone. Keep your

energies focused on your guides and allies and on
any other spirits you may encounter whose energy
feels safe and light. If you truly want to learn how,
like a shaman, to do battle with negative spirits,
you'll want to find an experienced witch or a shaman
who will teach you. Psychic warfare is an advanced
skill that requires training from a qualified mentor.

What Difference Does It Make?

So there's this limitless wonderland of spiritual experiences that we can call the collective unconscious-
ness, the realm of faeries, or the otherworld. We can
travel there in our dreams and visualizations, and
we'll meet all sorts of interesting beings, from mere aspects of our personality to powerful
guides, allies, and messengers.

Taboo!

Don't put too much
thought, energy, or attention into
dark or negative spirits. They
love to gather around people
who are scared of or obsessed
with them. Sure they exist, just
like common criminals exist in the
material world. But when you
ignore them, leave them alone,
or, better yet, laugh at them, they
will cause no trouble.

But what's the point? Is this just some sort of game we play with our imagination, sort of a
spiritual version of trading Pokémon cards?

Some people criticize the spirituality of paganism, as well as other forms of mysticism, for
being a distraction from the real world. But the whole point behind the spiritual realm is
that it is just one part of the universe: The otherworld and the "real" world fit together as
snugly as do the yin and the yang.

If you find that contacting spirits, recording your dreams, or performing rituals and spells
becomes more important to you than the real-world parts of your life, you may be out of
balance, and you'll need to slow down your spiritual practice. But for most people, spiritual work is actually a way to help them live more productive, meaningful, and ethical
lives in the outer world.

How does this spirit world help? By providing guidance and inspiring creativity.

Turning to the Otherworld for Guidance

You've seen that many of the spirits you'll encounter in the inner universe are guides,
helpers, messengers, and allies. It's important to remember that the wisdom from these
entities is meant to help you in the physical world as well as in the spiritual world. Is your
spiritual practice helping you to be a more loving and trusting person? Is it healing you
and your relationships? Is it inspiring you to do things that make your life better and that
improve the lives of others? The more you can say "yes" to these questions, the more you
are relating to the spirit world in a proper, healthy way.

If you're not sure whether a spirit guide is truly helping you, evaluate its advice according to the preceding questions. Trust your intuition; you'll know when a guide's wisdom is truly beneficial.

Creativity: Envisioning a Better World and Working to Make This One Better

Another benefit of working with the spirit world is that it can bring creativity and vision into your life. After all, the world of dreams and visualizations derives from your own inner and innate creativity. Your creativity helps give the spirit world form. But wait: If you can create beauty and peace in the inner world, doesn't that mean you can help make the outer world a better place, too? Exactly. So when you work with spirit guides, you'll often discover that they'll help you create a better world—both inside and out.

All Acts of Love and Pleasure

So the otherworld, and pagan spirituality in general, can be a source of insight and inspiration, but I don't want to paint too heavy a picture. As long as you don't become overly obsessed with negative spirits or so caught up in the spirit world that it adversely affects the rest of your life, it's perfectly acceptable to journey into the otherworld simply because it's fun. After all, relationships with spirits can be just as powerful and meaningful as relationships with physical beings. Remember what the Goddess says, "All acts of love and pleasure are my rituals." So have fun. In the pagan way of seeing things, fun itself is a spiritual virtue!

The Least You Need to Know

- Most forms of paganism acknowledge that the cosmos has both a material and spiritual dimension; the spiritual realm can be thought of as the otherworld.
- Different pagan traditions have different paradigms, or models, for understanding the spiritual realm (or realms).
- The most powerful ways to connect with the otherworld all come from the mind, including dreams, visualization, imagination, and psychic experience.
- Many different kinds of spirits and entities reside in the nonphysical dimensions.
- Working with spirit guides can be a source of insight and inspiration to help you live a happier and healthier life.

Chapter 8

Getting to Know the Goddess

In This Chapter

- The feminine principle
- Learning about the maiden, the mother, and the crone
- Goddesses from around the world
- Discovering the hidden face of the divine mother
- Recognizing the Goddess in nature

In Chapter 1, "Welcome to the Pagan Path," you learned one of the most basic principles of paganism: devotion to the Goddess in some shape or form. Now it's time to get to know her better. As you'll discover, however, there are many faces to this powerful form of the divine. Because pagans enjoy learning about and performing rituals for Goddesses from all over the world, you have the opportunity to find just the right Goddess (or Goddesses) for you.

There's Always Been a Yin

Before we get too involved in the many different faces of the Goddess, let's refresh our memory regarding the principles of yin and yang. As you saw in Chapter 6, "Other Pieces of the Pagan Puzzle," these Chinese terms, popular in spiritual traditions such as Taoism, refer to the two most powerful and primal forms of energy at work in the universe.

CAUTION

Taboo!

To say yin is feminine and also receptive, dark, or hidden does not mean that women ought to be passive or meek. Remember that these are philosophical ways of understanding the forces and energies in the universe. Women, like men, are healthiest when their personalities incorporate both yin and yang (both receptive and assertive) qualities.

Yang, which is covered in greater depth in Chapter 9, "All About the God," is active, forceful, light, and typically associated with masculinity.

Yin, on the other hand, represents the energies of receptivity, darkness, containment, and form and is traditionally associated with principles of femininity.

So to pagans, the pure essence of Spirit can fundamentally be broken down into yang (or the God) and yin (or the Goddess). Neither one is greater or more important than the other (although some Wiccan groups do place greater emphasis on the Goddess than on the God). Still, for many pagans, the Goddess is "first among equals," if for no other reason than the fact that most religions ignore the Goddess concept altogether, which means one of the ways in which paganism stands out from the crowd is its love and reverence for the principle of yin.

Form

Remember how the Yin-Yang symbol contains both white (yang) and black (yin) areas, but the entire thing is encased in a black circle? This is entirely appropriate because yin represents the form that contains and holds all things. Yin can be thought of as a giant bowl, or open arms, or (most appropriately) as a womb, which is the environment in which new life takes form. If yang represents energy, the yin is the environment in which the energy exists.

Receptivity

Think of yin as a loving mother who opens her arms to receive the embrace of her children. Since yang is considered to be an active principle, some spiritual philosophers label yin as passive. But I don't think that's entirely fair to yin, especially since passive carries the connotation of being weak or vulnerable. Just because yin isn't active doesn't make her wimpy! Indeed, it is out of her towering strength that yin can remain open, accepting, and allowing.

Darkness

Yin's blackness represents qualities of night, darkness, and hiddenness. Just as the womb is hidden from view, so too do the powerful qualities of yin operate mostly behind the scenes. Yin understands that darkness is not a time of defeat or fear, but rather a powerful time of transformation, renewal, and hidden growth.

The History of Mom

The powerful qualities of the yin principle relate to the Goddess, but there are many ways to think about the Goddess (or the Goddesses). As the principle of yin, she may be one unified feminine essence, but in the pages of world myth, she has many faces, personalities, and attributes.

The Goddess in Ancient Times

Experts are divided over whether ancient humanity worshipped a single, great, mother Goddess. Some scholars, like Marija Gimbutas (author of *The Language of the Goddess*), maintain that at the dawn of civilization, a wonderful society based on peace, cooperation, and Goddess worship thrived. Others believe that this notion is really just a romantic fantasy. Whether there was "one" Goddess or merely many different female deities honored in different places is a question equally up for debate. One thing is for sure: The evidence for some sort of pervasive Goddess devotion in ancient times is compelling. Goddess figurines from as far back as 35,000 B.C.E. have been unearthed in Europe, and the Acheulian Goddess figurine, found near Jerusalem, is perhaps 150,000 years old! Many of these ancient statues suggest that the Goddess was revered as a fertility figure: She represented the power to create and nurture life, so her statues had exaggerated breasts and swollen bellies.

Mythology shows us that, at least by the time cultures developed the ability to write, many different God-desses were venerated. These include mother figures (like Hera, the great queen of the Greek *pantheon*, or Isis, the mother Goddess of the Egyptians); Goddesses of love, sex, and beauty (such as the Greek Aphrodite or her Roman equivalent, Venus); Goddesses of wisdom (Athena) and even of war (also Athena, or the Celtic Goddess known as the Morrigan). The many faces of the Goddess reveal just how richly ancient cultures viewed femininity. Goddesses were not limited to confining roles such as wife, mother, teacher, or nurse. The Goddesses of the great pagan religions exhibited a wide variety of skills, talents, and abilities.

> **EarthWords**
>
> **Pantheon** literally means "all the Gods." Originally, the term referred to a temple in which all the deities of a society were worshiped; later it simply came to mean the sum total of all Gods and Goddesses of a given culture. Thus, we can speak of the Greek pantheon, the Roman pantheon, the Egyptian pantheon, and so forth.

The Goddess Reborn

When monotheism became the preferred form of religion in places like Egypt and Europe, Goddess worship pretty much fell out of favor. If there could only be one God—and that single deity was pretty much seen as a guy—that left no room for the Goddesses. Interestingly, common people often preserved some form of Goddess spirituality, even when the official religion forbade it. Thus, in Christianity, much reverence and adoration is paid to Jesus' mother, Mary, elevating her almost to the status of a Goddess (although such language was never used—it would be too true to be comfortable). So even during the many centuries when Europe was officially Christian, Goddess worship never totally died out.

Drumbeats

Closely related to the theory of one great Goddess whom the ancients worshipped is a theory that, until about 5,000 years ago, people in Europe and the Middle East lived in a peaceful paradise governed by Goddess worship, which was ruined when warriors who worshiped a Sky Father God invaded from the east. This theory is highly controversial, even among feminists. Some say that a lost matrifocal civilization can be an inspiration to fight for equality between men and women today; others say that an untrue, romanticized picture of the past cannot further the cause of feminism or paganism. In either event, what makes the most sense is to focus on making the *future* better for women, men, and nature alike.

After the great Renaissance when the leading thinkers became interested in classical (pre-Christian) culture, the ancients Goddesses (and Gods) became acceptable subjects for artists, poets, and musicians to depict in their creations. From there, it was really only a matter of time before people began to recognize that Gods and Goddesses are more than just relics of an ancient time, they actually represent powerful ways to understand the mysteries of the Spirit world.

But if we can't be sure whether there was just one great Goddess in ancient times, we do know this: In modern times, not only has interest in all the many Goddesses of mythology grown, there is an increasing movement to see "the Goddess" in a universal way, as representing at least one half of the ultimate Spirit. Just as religions like Judaism, Christianity, and Islam replaced the worship of many Gods and Goddesses with a single (male) God, so in our time has the revival of Goddess worship, on an important level, meant the celebration of a single female Goddess who is as great as the single male God. Hmmm … sounds a lot like the Yin-Yang symbol, doesn't it?

The "Phases" of the Goddess

To begin to understand the majesty of the divine feminine, take a look at the moon. Because the moon's orbit does not synchronize with the speed of the earth's rotation, over the course of a 28- to 29-day period, the moon's appearance changes in the night sky. At the beginning of the cycle, the "new" moon is barely a sliver that sets in the western sky not long after the setting of the sun. Midway through the cycle the moon is "full," rising as the sun sets and then setting as the sun rises. Eventually, the waning moon becomes a sliver again, although now it rises shortly before the sun.

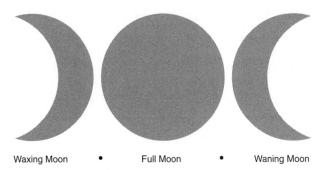

Left: The waxing moon.
Center: The full moon.
Right: The waning moon.

Waxing Moon　•　Full Moon　•　Waning Moon

Notice that the "horns" of the waxing moon point to the left, while the horns of the waning moon point to the right. The waxing moon represents the beginning of a cycle, while the waning moon represents the ending of the cycle. The full moon, meanwhile, represents the cycle at its peak, or midpoint.

This natural progression of the phases of the moon corresponds with three "phases" of the Goddess, which correspond to the life journey of women.

The Maiden

In her youngest aspect, the Goddess comes to us as a maiden: innocent, beautiful, and filled with joy. She is the lovely young girl who catches the boys' eyes. She is confident and self-possessed, living her life for the sheer joy of it. She corresponds to the fresh and new life of springtime. She represents new beginnings and hope for the future. She is both an innocent child before her menstrual cycle begins and also an attractive young woman who is nearing her time of fertility and motherhood. But the maiden comes before the mother, so she always stands for youth and newness. For many pagan women, the most important quality of the maiden is independence. In this sense, a woman of any age can embody the spirit of the maiden, when she chooses to live a life of self-directed freedom.

Oracle

When a girl enters puberty and when a woman enters menopause can be times for celebration and rites of passage. Puberty signifies moving from the maiden phase to (at least the potential for) the mother phase; menopause, likewise, signifies entry into the crone phase. You can honor these important transitions very simply (with meditation and prayers to the Goddess) or through elaborate rituals and a rip-roaring party.

EarthWords

As we enjoy longer lifespans in modern society, some pagans have suggested seeing the stages of a woman's life as embodying four phases. Between the mother and the crone comes the queen, the time when a woman reaches the zenith of her power and authority.

The Mother

Just a young woman matures, begins her monthly cycle, and takes on the adult responsibilities of motherhood (or some other creative endeavor), so, too, does the Goddess in her fullness become a mother. Of course, in mythological terms, this motherhood is often literal: Many Goddesses are depicted as bearing babies and nurturing children. At the same time, it's important not to be too literal about the Goddess' motherhood; a woman can be a "mother" in many ways, as long as she is using her creative power to "give birth to" and "nurture" a project, a work of art, or any other enterprise. The Goddess as mother represents a woman at the height of her creative and generative abilities. She is the one who can make things happen.

The Crone

As the summer turns to autumn and harvest time, so, too, does a woman eventually reach menopause and enter into a time of greatest maturity and wisdom. The Goddess as crone represents this final stage of life, a stage that is often misunderstood and underappreciated by our youth-worshipping culture. The crone represents some dark qualities that many of us might want to forget, from aging to declining health to death. But she also is the destiny of all women, so she represents a deep power. This is the power of wisdom, intuition, and experience. Through the crone, we learn the beauty of acceptance, not only the acceptance of our own mortality but also of the ongoing cycles of nature and life. Her wisdom can light the way for those who are younger than her.

Drumbeats

One of the most famous Greek myths captures the essence of maiden, mother, and crone in the three Goddesses who figure in the myth. This is the story of the maiden Persephone, a young Goddess who was abducted by Hades and carried off to the underworld to be his bride. When Demeter, Persephone's mother and the Goddess of agriculture, realized that her daughter was missing, her anger and grief caused the earth to turn barren. Eventually, another Goddess, the crone Hecate, helped Demeter find her daughter in the underworld. Because Persephone had eaten the food of the underworld, she couldn't leave there entirely, but a deal was struck with Hades in which she spent half the year with her mother and half the year with Hades. Thus, half the year is a time of fertility and abundance (summer), while the winter, when Persephone descends to the underworld, is a time of barrenness.

The Hidden Face of the Goddess

Like any other aspect of the Goddess, the crone is not a permanent state; she eventually yields to the greatest of mysteries: death. In this final release, the crone moves into the "hidden face" of the Goddess, the time of transformation and rebirth in which the aged crone is reformed into the new maiden once again. If the crone represents the autumn, the hidden face is the time of winter, when the Goddess is silent, the earth is dark, and renewal and transformation slowly take place.

We can see the different faces of the Goddess in the movement of the seasons as well as the seasons of any woman's life. Of course, these different Goddess forms are immortalized in the great mythologies of the world. When we become familiar with the maiden, mother, and crone, we become connected to the deepest and most powerful rhythms of Mother Nature herself.

The maiden, mother, and crone (as well as the queen and the hidden face) are powerful symbols for understanding the Goddess. But they do not necessarily represent all the many ways in which human beings can approach and relate to the Spirit in her feminine form. Ultimately, the Goddess is far greater than any images or words could ever convey.

Light and Dark: Two Aspects of the Goddess

We've looked at how the Goddess and the God complement each other, just as yin and yang complement one another. It would be a mistake, however, to assume that all Goddess energy is "passive" and all God energy is "active." Indeed, within the Goddess herself we can find tremendous diversity, as expressed through the many different Goddesses of world mythology. Some Goddesses are sexy, erotic, loving, or kind. Others are maternal, nurturing, and creative. Still others are aged and wise. Some Goddesses are warriors, powerful leaders, and fierce fighters. Finally, some Goddesses are fearsome destroyers and forces of chaos.

Among devotees of the Goddess, many Goddess figures are known as "dark Goddesses." These are the ones who represent forces of death, destruction, war, and chaos. Some examples include the Indian Goddess Kali Ma, a warrior Goddess with a knack for killing demons; Circe, a Greek Goddess who made a sport out of turning men into swine and other beasts; and the Morrigan, an Irish deity who governed war and battle as well as sex and death.

> **CAUTION**
>
> **Taboo!**
>
> The term "dark Goddess" does not imply a Goddess who is bad or evil, nor should this term be seen in a racist or ethnically biased way. A dark Goddess was simply one who governed the powerful forces of night, the subconscious, or who ruled over death and the underworld. In paganism, darkness is just as spiritually important and valuable as is light.

These dark Goddesses look and sound scary, but there's an important lesson in them. Almost all of the dark Goddesses, in addition to representing forces of destruction and death, also carry more life-affirming powers: powers of sex and regeneration, of transformation and rebirth, of renewal in some significant way. In other words, the dark Goddesses teach us that every ending leads to a new beginning. They remind us that we all have powers of destruction inside ourselves—powers that we should use for good. In other words, powers to destroy what needs to go and thereby create room for something new and positive to take its place.

A Few Goddesses from Around the World

To really appreciate the Goddess in her many faces and attributes—from the maiden, mother, and crone to the many Goddesses of love and darkness—the best thing to do is to begin to learn about the many figures out of world myth. So here are a few mini introductions to some of the best-known Goddesses from around the world.

◆ **Aphrodite** (Greek/Eastern Mediterranean)   Goddess of love and sexuality. Although married to the God Hephaestus, she refused to be tied down to one man and took numerous lovers, including Ares (the God of war) and Adonis (a God of youthful beauty). Originally a powerful creator Goddess, she only became a "sexpot" after Greek culture became patriarchal.

> **Oracle**
>
> These brief introductions are just a start on your journey to getting to know the Goddesses of the world. From here, take the time to read all the mythology from cultures that appeal to you. Check out *The New Book of Goddesses and Heroines* by Patricia Monaghan (Llewellyn Publications, 1997) or *Goddesses in World Mythology: A Biographical Dictionary* by Martha Ann & Dorothy Myers Imel (Oxford University Press, 1993) to explore world mythology further.

◆ **Artemis** (Greek)   If Aphrodite couldn't get enough of male attention, Artemis couldn't be bothered with it. A virginal Goddess of the moon and nature, she governed both wild animals and the woods in which they lived. Among other skills, she served as a midwife.

◆ **Athena** (Greek)   A powerful figure, Athena was Goddess of war but also of wisdom and the arts. She was considered to be a powerful source of protection. Patroness of Athens, she probably was an ancient Goddess from a culture other than Greece, possibly Crete or Egypt.

◆ **Brighid** (Celtic)   One of the few deities found throughout the Celtic lands, she was Brighid in Ireland, Brigantia in Britain, and Brigindo or Brigan in continental Europe. She was a Goddess of poetry, inspiration, fire, and healing. She was Christianized as St. Bridget.

◆ **Cerridwen** (Welsh)   A dark Goddess originally associated with the moon and grain. Cerridwen's cauldron was famous as a vessel that governed rebirth, inspiration, and wisdom. She gave birth to the wise bard Taliesin.

- **Freya** (Norse)   Leader of the Valkyries, Freya ruled over both war and love. When warriors died valiantly in battle, Freya and the other Valkyries would escort their spirits to *Valhalla*. She was a beautiful Goddess who dressed in shamanic attire. Like Aphrodite, she wasn't one to be held back by marriage vows.

- **Hathor** (Egyptian)   Both mother of the sun and Goddess of the underworld, Hathor was depicted as a cow who gave birth to the universe. A Goddess of joy, love, and music, she governed the body and the pleasures of physical existence.

- **Isis** (Egyptian)   Not only one of the greatest Egyptian Goddesses but also one of the greatest Goddesses of all cultures, Isis loved her brother Osiris and revived him after he was killed by their brother Set. She was considered to be Queen of Heaven and Star of the Sea. Much of the imagery surrounding Isis was adopted by Chris-tians who venerated the Virgin Mary.

> **EarthWords**
>
> **Valhalla**, in Norse myth, is the paradise where brave soldiers and the Gods dwelled together in eternal feasting and merry-making.

- **Kali Ma** (Hindu)   Her name means "black mother," and indeed, she's the most terrifying dark Goddess of them all. She first came into being to destroy a demon who threatened the Gods of India; to this day she is worshiped as a figure of not only horrific destruction but also powerful protection and creativity.

- **Kuan Yin** (Chinese)   This mythic figure was a Buddhist woman who achieved enlightenment but renounced it because she wanted to help alleviate the suffering of others. Highly popular, Kuan Yin is still revered as a Goddess of compassion, mercy, and love.

- **Rhea** (Cretan/Greek)   Probably the original Mother Goddess of Crete, Rhea later was adopted into Greek myth as the wife of Cronos (Father Time) and the mother of many of the Olympian Goddesses. Symbolically, she may be thought of as "Grandmother Earth."

- **Rhiannon** (Welsh)   Her name means "great queen," and she mirrors a Goddess from Gaul (modern France) named Epona. A queen of the underworld, she was a Goddess of horses, sorrowful mothers, and sovereignty. She had three birds whose otherworldly song could fill the listener with magical joy.

- **Xochiquetzal** (Aztec)   She was Goddess of flowers and patroness of the arts, marriage, love, and sexuality. She was known as the mother of the world who repopulated the earth after a great flood destroyed all but her and her partner.

The Secret Goddess

So is the Goddess just some ancient mythical figure who runs around in Roman togas and really is not that relevant to modern life? No way. Even today, when most people think of spirituality as involving a male God only, the Goddess has in fact played an important role in our culture, even though she has tended to keep her presence very low key.

Let's look at a few of these "secret" Goddesses and the roles they play in today's world.

The Virgin Mary

After Europe made the transition from paganism to Christianity in the early centuries of the common era, devotion to the Goddess did not just wither up and blow away. Instead, people transferred their devotion from the old Goddesses to saints (like St. Bridget, the most popular of Irish women saints, who took on many of the attributes of the old Goddess Brighid) and especially to Mary, the mother of Jesus. After all, since Christianity teaches that Jesus was one with God, that makes Mary the mother of God. And the difference between "mother of God" and "Goddess" really is not that great.

Mind you, most faithful Christians, both in the past and today, would stop short of actually calling Mary a Goddess. But in the devotion that people have shown to Mary, in seeing her as someone to whom prayers can be offered and in giving her titles like "Queen of Heaven," she has, in function if not in name, been a powerful Goddess in the Christian world.

Mother Earth and Mother Nature

We've already talked about how the Goddess can be equated with the folklore personalities of Mother Earth and Mother Nature. Indeed, in a society in which worship of one father God is the norm, honoring the earth and nature as mother is a safe and quiet way for Goddess devotion to persist. Like the Virgin Mary, Mother Nature never gets the full credit she deserves. But even in a silly TV commercial that proclaimed, "You can't fool Mother Nature," there's a subconscious acknowledgement in our culture of just how important this female figure is.

Liberty

In countries like America and France, another important hidden Goddess has been Lady Liberty. She graces the logo of Columbia movies, she watches over New York Harbor, and until about 1948, she was on U.S. coins (she still appears on French coins). Is Lady Liberty just an abstract female personification of a political principle? Well, maybe. But think of all the brave soldiers who have been willing to fight and die to defend her. For an abstraction, she has played a pretty powerful role in people's lives.

Marilyn Monroe and Princess Diana

In the world of entertainment, there are celebrities, stars, and icons—and then there are figures like Marilyn Monroe and Princess Diana, who were beautiful, charismatic, sexy, and who died tragically before their time. Marilyn Monroe has been called a modern Aphrodite, and at her funeral Diana was compared to her namesake, the Roman Goddess. The devotion people show to these larger-than-life figures may not make them true Goddesses, but it does say something about the human need to show love and devotion to a powerful symbol of the feminine.

The Goddess in Nature

Finally, let's look at some specific ways in which nature can be seen as a Goddess. I've talked generally about the way nature plays the role of a mother Goddess, but there are specific elements of the natural world that have long been regarded as embodying aspects of divine femininity. Here are a few of those powerful elements.

The Moon

From time immemorial, women have seen how the rhythm of their menstrual cycle patterns the rhythm of the waxing and waning moon. In some Native American cultures, when women would have their periods (or "moon time"), they would retreat into a "moon lodge" where no men were allowed and the women could be together. Many women experience a deeper access to their psychic and intuitive abilities during their "moon time." Although not all traditional cultures regarded the moon as feminine, most did, and Goddesses like Selena or Diana have a powerful lunar association.

> **Oracle**
>
> Many Wiccans and other pagans express their love to the Goddess through devotion to the moon. If you don't know the phases of the moon, try getting a calendar that specifically lists moon phases. One of the best ones is called "The Lunar Calendar," and it can be purchased through any feminist or metaphysical bookstore.

The Soil

Traditional cultures saw a link between the fertile soil of the earth and a woman's womb. Just as a man plants his "seed" (semen) into the woman to trigger her reproductive power, so, too, by planting seeds into the rich humus can the fecundity of the earth give rise to new crops. Goddesses like the Greek Demeter or the Irish Danu have powerful associations with the soil. When we think of Mother Earth, it is the soil that is truly her "body."

The Night

Identifying the night with the Goddess is really an extension of the moon's association with the Goddess. The day belongs to Gods associated with the sky and the sun, but the night belongs to Mom. Some Goddesses, like the Egyptian Nuit, are specifically linked to the night. The darkness of nighttime is full of yin energy, a time of rest and receptivity to dreams and psychic guidance.

The Ocean

Like the soil, the oceans of the earth have a powerful womb-like role to play in the ongoing drama of terrestrial life. Out of the oceans the first life emerged, and the oceans continue to play a vital role in the planetary biosystem. The tides, of course, are linked to the moon, strengthening the sense of feminine rhythm. Goddesses like Aphrodite have a powerful link to the ocean.

And Everything Else!

Of course, while the moon and the soil and the night have traditional associations with various Goddesses, it's important to note also that other Goddesses were associated with the sun, with daylight, with rivers and mountains, and just about any other aspect of the natural world. Just about any aspect of nature will have one or more Goddesses from world mythology associated with it. Truly, Mother Nature comes to us in many disguises.

The Least You Need to Know

- The modern concept of "the Goddess" has its roots in the ancient practice of worshipping many different Goddesses.
- The Goddess, as maiden, mother, and crone, represents the fullness of the feminine lifespan.
- The mythological Goddesses from around the world represent a wide variety of qualities, personality traits, and abilities.
- Even in cultures that do not officially worship Goddesses, other figures, from the Virgin Mary to movie stars, have had divine or semidivine status attributed to them.
- One simple way to acknowledge the Goddess's presence in your life is by celebrating the feminine dimension of the natural world.

Chapter 9

All About the God

In This Chapter

- Yang (Yin's other half)
- The horned God and the Green Man
- Many Gods from many cultures
- How the God and the Goddess relate
- The natural side of the God

Although devotion to the Goddess is what truly makes paganism unique, it's a mistake to assume that pagans only worship a female deity. True, some pagans are so Goddess-oriented that the concept of a male God means nothing to them, but the majority of nature mystics, witches, and druids believe very strongly in the duality of male and female within that mystery called "the divine." Put into English: Pagan spirituality seeks balance between honoring a motherly Goddess and a fatherly God. After all, it's nature's way to have two genders, male and female. And paganism takes its cue from nature.

Yang (Yin's Dance Partner)

The preceding chapter looked at the fundamental universal polarity of yin and yang as expressed in Chinese philosophy. Yin, the feminine aspect of this polarity, represents darkness, receptivity, and form. Many (but not all) of the Goddesses from traditions the world over embody these yin qualities.

But yin, by itself, would be incomplete. Yang, the other half of the polarity, represents the masculine, active, penetrative qualities of all things. Let's take a closer look at some of these qualities, which can help us un-derstand the pagan notion of God.

> **Oracle**
>
> For many pagans, the sun symbolizes the God, and the moon symbolizes the Goddess. This directly relates to yin and yang. The moon rules over night (the darkness of yin), while the sun rules over day (the brightness of yang).

Force

If yin represents form (that in which all things are con-tained), yang represents force (the divine energy that sets all things in motion). Yin is a bowl, while yang is the rushing water poured into the bowl. Yang energy is assertive, dynamic, and on the move.

Activity

Yang energy does not sit around, waiting passively for events to occur. On the contrary, yang takes the meta-phorical bull by the horns and makes things happen. Yang is the spark of ignition that lights a fire, the initial impulse that arouses you to take action.

Light

In the Chinese yin-yang symbol, the dark parts of the symbol represent yin, and the white parts represent yang. Seen in terms of the universe, the vast darkness of infinite space is yin, while the illuminating light from stars and other energy sources embodies yang energy. Yang illuminates and enlightens. While the subconscious mind and the moon belong to the mysterious energies of yin, the conscious, rational mind and the brilliant light of the sun are symbolically linked to yang.

Putting It All Together

If the universe were all yin and no yang, it would be a dark, mysterious, and enchanting place, where nothing would seem to happen. Likewise, if the universe were all yang and no yin, it would be a blinding, frenetic ball of bursting energy that would soon burn itself out in a blaze of hyperactive glory. The restless movement of yang needs the deep con-templation of yin for renewal and transformation, while the dark stillness of yin needs the dynamic power of yang to stimulate growth and change.

In the pages to come, I'll look at many different images of Gods from around the world. Like the Goddesses discussed in Chapter 8, "Getting to Know the Goddess," these mas-culine forms of divinity come in many shapes and sizes. Just as the force of yang dance with the form of yin, so, too, does the energies of the God complement and balance the Goddess.

As a reminder, the feminine yin and the masculine yang are only symbols of the fundamental polarities in the universe as we know it. These symbols, however, are not meant to imply that women are by nature passive and men are by nature aggressive. Nor, for that matter, do these symbols imply that the Goddess is only receptive and the God only active. Yin and yang dance together in all things: This means every human being, male or female, has both yin and yang qualities, and for that matter, every God and Goddess also contains within himself or herself this fundamental polarity.

How the Pagan Idea of God Differs from the Monotheist God

For many people, God is a concept that comes straight out of the three major religions from the Middle East: Judaism, Christianity, and Islam. Not only are these the three largest religious traditions in the United States today, their concept of God truly affects everyone, regardless of creed or spiritual path. When you pick up a dollar bill that says "In God We Trust" or say the Pledge of Allegiance, which speaks of "One Nation, Under God," keep in mind that, for most people, this refers to the God of monotheism. And although both pagans and monotheists believe that the true source of life is ultimately beyond all words, images, or concepts, the fact remains that our culture's most common images and concepts of "God" have a very specific flavor to them—a flavor derived from monotheism.

Drumbeats

Monotheism, the concept that there is only one God, may seem at odds with paganism, which emphasizes both God and Goddess and in many forms accepts all the various Gods and Goddesses of world mythology. But to pagans, this is mostly a difference of language or philosophy. Many pagans believe that there is ultimately one source for divinity in the universe; to a pagan, that single source can be seen in many ways, as many different Gods. To Christians, Jews, or Muslims, that source can only be seen in one way, as the God of their approved teachings. So although monotheists and pagans have different ways of understanding Spirit, many pagans would see these differences as mostly a matter of interpretation.

Before we go any further in looking at how pagans understand the masculine God, let's clear up some misunderstandings that can come out of the monotheistic notions of divinity.

◆ **The ultimate bully**   Monotheistic religions teach that God is all knowing, all powerful, and all present. (The fancy words for these are omniscient, omnipotent, and omnipresent, respectively.) It's also a common belief among monotheists, however, especially among some Christians and Muslims, that God is going to punish people he doesn't like. Pagans have a problem with this. If God is all powerful and all knowing, why would God create people he knew would be "sinful" and then make them spend eternity in hell? It makes God look like a bully, and pagans aren't interested in worshiping a bully.

◆ **No jealousy here**   Another common concept of God is that he's jealous. "You shall have no other Gods before me," states the first of the Ten Commandments, "for I am a jealous God." What gives here? Is God insecure? Pagans believe that the divine is large enough and loving enough to understand that true devotion, whether offered to Christ, Buddha, Krishna, or Gaia, ultimately serves the purpose of love, light, and healing—and, therefore, need never be rejected as "blasphemy" just because it doesn't fit in with one religion's way of doing things.

◆ **Temper, temper**   One of the ways in which God is depicted, not only in religious circles but in popular culture, is as a wrathful figure. This is tied in with the hell bit. God sends sinners to hell because, well, they irritate him so much. Pagans do believe that we have to take responsibility for our actions (that's what the law of karma is all about) but few would accept the idea that punishment should be eternal, just because the heavenly daddy's in a foul mood. That makes God look like the emotional equivalent of a two year old. Pagans believe the God is much, much wiser than that.

◆ **A God who matters**   One of the crowning characteristics of the mainstream, monotheistic concept of God is his total lack of physical nature. God is pure spirit, without any relationship to the physical world (except that he created it). For most pagans, this is a dualistic concept that places God and spirit above the earth and physical matter—and therefore is a subtle way of saying that the material world isn't as good as the spiritual realms. In contrast to this, most pagan concepts of the God imply that both spirituality and materiality "matter" (sorry about the pun) to the yang principle. The God may be a spiritual being, but he comes to us in many physical ways: as the Green Man, the Horned One, the Lord of the Forest and the Animals (images we'll get to later in this chapter). Pagans believe that both matter and spirit are sacred to the God (and the Goddess).

> **CAUTION**
>
> **Taboo!** _____
>
> The God of monotheism is a complex spiritual figure. Don't assume that what you've read or been taught about this God-form is complete. In many ways, the monotheist God represents both the best and worst qualities of _human_ behavior. Actually, the same can be said about pagan Gods and Goddesses—although pagans tend to see different Gods as embodying different qualities.

In fairness to monotheism, many (perhaps most) Christians, Jews, and Muslims see God as kind and loving, not as wrathful or jealous. Still, those images are present in the customs and traditions, sacred scriptures, and popular imagery associated with these major religions. When pagans talk about the masculine God, it's important to remember that the jealous, almighty, angry bully is not a useful way to understand pagan ideas of the divine.

My, What Strong Horns You Have!

Some pagans (especially Dianic witches) worship only a Goddess, with no God in their spiritual observance. For most pagans, however, who draw their primary inspiration from nature, the idea of a Goddess without a God is as absurd as the idea of a God without a Goddess. So for the yin of the great Goddess, there needs to be a yang figure, a great God.

If the most ancient images of the Goddess include symbols of fertility and motherhood (images that live on in our modern-day notions of Mother Earth or Mother Nature), then for the God, pagans likewise find inspiration in ancient images. One of the most ancient of all images is that of the horned figure who is the lord of hunting, wildlife, and the forest. If the Goddess blessed the people through abundant crops, the God's blessings came through success in hunting. The male face of the divine was the Goddess' lover, her son, and also her partner in the natural world.

Oracle

Many pagans keep a set of deer antlers as a symbol of the God. On a pagan altar, antlers can be a lovely and simple way to honor the masculine dimension of Spirit.

God of Many Faces

The primal deity whom the ancients called on to bless their hunting may have been an overarching God figure, just like the earth mother may be a primal Goddess figure. But once again, we have no way of knowing this for sure. We do know that Gods, like Goddesses, appeared in many forms in the written mythic tradition. Like their feminine counterparts, Gods ruled over the sky (Zeus), the sun (Apollo), war (Mars or Ares), love (Eros or Cupid), and the world of the dead (Hades or Pluto). A figure like Apollo represented civilization, rational thinking, and moral restraint, but other deities (like Dionysus, the God of wine, or Pan, the God of the wilderness) represented the forces of chaos, passion, unfettered sexuality, and indulgence. So Gods, like Goddesses, covered the entire spectrum of life.

The Attack on the Pagan God

If the coming of monotheism basically rendered Goddesses invisible, it had a similar effect on the many Gods who served as the lovers of the Goddesses. There was crucial difference, however. The horned God of passion and wilderness (such as the Greek Pan or the Celtic Cernunnos) was still useful to the new religions, so they kept him on the payroll. They just demoted him from his God status, turning him into a demon instead.

The concept of the devil, or Satan, is not found anywhere in native European paganism. It is a concept from the Middle East that had a minor role in the Hebrew scriptures (the Old Testament) but took on a major role in the relatively young religion of Christianity.

Oracle _____

Some people have difficulty relating to the horned God simply because of the long-standing cultural idea that horns symbolize evil. Even when pagans intellectually understand that the horned one represents positive life force, emotionally it can be hard to shake off old programming. Try focusing on the Green Man as your primary symbol for the God. He represents a joyful image of divinity that anyone could love!

EarthWords _____

A **foliate head** is a depiction of a human face, usually male, covered with foliage, almost as if the leaves were actually part of the face or growing out of it. Most Green Man images are strikingly beautiful in their depiction of wise consciousness merged with the life force of the forest.

In the Christian way of seeing things, the universe is a giant battleground where the good God and the bad devil are perpetually duking it out. The point behind being religious is to make sure you're on the right side. Paganism, however, is much more like Taoism than Christianity. The universe is not a battleground; it's more like a marriage chamber where Yin (the Goddess) and Yang (the God) come together. But according to the Christian way of seeing things, God had an opponent, and when Christianity came to Europe, who better to be depicted as God's enemy than the wild, passionate God of the old religion?

This smear job against the horned God may have helped consolidate the power of Christianity in ancient times, but today's pagan understands the difference between the Christian concept of Satan and the pagan ways of understanding deity. Increasingly in modern times, God figures like Pan and Cernunnos have been valued as powerful representations of the passionate, untamed energy of the Goddess's consort.

The Green Man: The God Today

When the first public Wiccans came forward to teach others about their spiritual path, they almost always spoke of the God in terms of his role as the horned deity. In recent years, however, another powerful image of pagan masculinity has become popular: the Green Man, or *foliate head* images of the God. Many examples of the Green Man can be found in the architecture of churches and other old buildings in Western Europe. Is he a specific God or simply a general figure of the masculine energy of the forest? Whatever his ancient origins may be, today the Green Man is a powerful symbol for pagan devotion to the masculine aspect of deity.

Some Gods from Around the World

Here's a brief introduction to 13 important Gods from world mythology. These brief introductions don't even begin to cover the many stories, attributes, and characteristics associated with each God. You can learn more about your favorite Gods by reading the great myths in which they appear or—to get you started—by exploring a reference work like Janet and Stewart Farrar's *The Witches' God: Lord of the Dance.*

- **Apollo** (Greek/Roman)   Son of the God Zeus and brother of the Goddess Artemis, Apollo was the classical God of the sun. He pulled the sun across the sky in his mighty chariot. Whereas Dionysus represented the deep power of passion, Apollo stands for the orderly structure of a disciplined, rational mind.

- **Cernunnos** (Celtic)   His name literally meant "the horned one," and Cernunnos appeared in Celtic art as a shaman-like figure, often meditating with animals like snakes or stags attending him. He represented the primal masculine energies of the forest and the natural world. In English folklore, he became a character known as Herne the Hunter.

- **Dionysus** (Thracian/Greek)   He was a vegetation God who became associated with fertility, wine, and ecstatic ritual. Women who were dedicated to Dionysus engaged in frenzied rituals that, early on, even included human sacrifice. His equivalent in Roman mythology was Bacchus. Compared to the rational order of Apollo, Dionysus stood for the chaotic powers of the body and passions.

- **Ganesh** (Hindu)   A benevolent God known as the remover of obstacles, Ganesh (or Ganesha) appeared as an elephant or as a man with an elephant's head. He was a great lover of literature and the arts and sometimes was portrayed riding on a mouse. He was a God of good fortune.

- **Hephaestus** (Greek)   The God of smithcraft, he became Vulcan in Roman mythology. He was lame but highly skilled and talented. Among other things, he fashioned Zeus's thunderbolts. Hephaestus represented the spirit of creativity and pride in one's craft.

- **Hermes** (Greek)   Hermes was an intelligent deity who didn't always see the need to play by the rules. He was the God of magic and learning but also the patron of thieves. In Roman myth, he became identified with Mercury. As Hermes Trismegistos ("thrice-great Hermes"), he was the father of alchemy and occultism.

- **Loki** (Nordic)   He was a clever God who originally was just a practical joker, but his jokes took on an increasingly chaotic, destructive edge until eventually Loki's envy of another God set into motion a chain of events that led to the downfall of the old Norse Gods. Loki's brilliant mind but unpredictable status as a trickster made him a dangerous God to mess around with. He represented the destructive power of jealousy.

- **Lugh** (Irish)   A Celtic warrior God who was said to be a master of all skills, Lugh represented the spirit of talented youth. According to Irish myth, he was the grandson of Balor, a leader of the evil Fomorians whom the Irish Gods and Goddesses were fighting. During a climactic battle, Lugh killed his own grandfather, making him a savior figure.

- **Manannan** (Irish/Manx)   The Isle of Man in Britain was named after this powerful God, son of the sea God Lir. Like Poseidon, he traveled over the waves in a magic chariot drawn by otherworldly horses. Celtic myth held that after a human died, Manannan escorted his or her spirit to an Island of Apple Trees, where an everlasting feast was served.

- **Odin** (Nordic)   Chief of the Scandinavian Gods, Odin ruled over magic, poetry, and war. A God of warriors, he was said to have set the sun and moon into motion. He and his brothers Vili and Ve were credited with creating the Norse cosmos, held together by the great world tree Yggdrasil.

- **Osiris** (Egyptian)   A God of the underworld who also governed vegetation and fertility, Osiris played a major role in Egyptian myth. Killed by his brother Set, he was brought back to life by the actions of his resourceful wife Isis. Hmmm … a God who dies and then is brought back to life. Can you think of another religion that uses this theme?

- **Pan** (Greek)   A powerful nature deity and (along with Cernunnos) one of the two most loved images of a horned God, he represented zesty, lusty sexuality and procreation. Maybe he's the originator of the word "horny"? But nothing immoral, here—to Pan, exuberant sexuality is innocent and good.

- **Zeus** (Greek)   The father of the Gods in Greek myth, Zeus was a great example of how the pagan Gods became corrupt in the latter days of ancient paganism. Originally a God of thunder, Zeus eventually became known primarily as a philanderer, thereby earning his "father" status in a rather literal way.

The God in Relation to the Goddess

To fully understand yang, we need to consider how it (or he) functions in relation to yin. Once again, if you're used to seeing God as a monotheistic unity that represents the sum total of divinity, this will take some new thinking. In the neopagan view of Spirit, the God always shares the responsibility and power of divinity with his feminine counterpart, whether she is his mother, his lover, or plays yet another role. If anything, most pagans would say the Goddess precedes the God, so it is she who shares her divinity with him!

The Son

While many pagans insist the God and the Goddess are equal, in some ways she gets top billing. After all, she represents the earth and, as such, is the mother of all things—even the masculine dimension of her own divinity. The Goddess giving birth to the God is a theme that appears again and again in ancient mythology and even can be felt in the powerful veneration offered to the Virgin Mary among some branches of Christianity. Isis gave birth to Horus … Aphrodite gave birth to Eros … Cerridwen gave birth to Taliesin … Gaia gave birth to Cronos (Saturn).

In many cultures, the Goddess, who is one with the earth, represents the principle of *sovereignty.* Just as her son derives his Godhood from the mother, so too does an earthly king derive his sovereignty from the land he governs. In some pagan cultures (such as the ancient Celts), when a king was crowned, he was expected to "mate" with the earth Goddess herself (sometimes symbolically, sometimes embodied by a priestess of the mother). This actually leads us to the second important way in which the God relates to the Goddess.

> **EarthWords**
>
> **Sovereignty** means "supreme authority" and refers to the right of a king or other leader to govern. In democracy, sovereignty comes from the will of the people; in Christian monarchy, sovereignty is believed to come from God. Pagans, however, regarded sovereignty as derived from the land herself—that is to say, from the Goddess.

The Lover God

Many wonderful examples of the sexy lover God can be found in world mythology. Eros (or Cupid), the son of Aphrodite, was a gorgeous being who fell in love with Psyche in one of the most beautiful of Greek myths. Adonis was one of Aphrodite's lovers, as were Ares, Hermes, and Hephaestus (okay, so Aphrodite got around). In Hindu myth, Shiva was the consort of Kali; in Celtic myth, the God called the Dagda got down with the Goddess known as the Morrigan. Again and again, Gods and Goddesses do what comes naturally.

The God as a lover of the Goddess teaches us several important things. On one level, he reminds us to "make love, not war." Sure, there is a time and place for fighting for what's right, but even a crusty war God like Ares couldn't resist the loving embrace of the Goddess. Pagans may believe that there's a place for fighting, but love comes first.

On another level, the lover God reminds us that the best way to deal with evil is not by killing it but by healing it. Among the many Gods and Goddesses of world mythology, there are personalities of every moral persuasion, from saintly to treacherous. Instead of seeing "good" and "evil" as two pure forces that remain ever at odds, pagans take the more naturalist perspective of recognizing that both qualities can be found in just about every living being. We all have the power to create and the power to destroy; we all can choose goodness and healing or opt for selfishness and hurtful behavior. When the Goddess and God are lovers, their "marriage" isn't perfect. But it's a symbol to remind us that love and healing energy works best in dealing with the problems, conflicts, and tragedies of the world.

Other Important Roles for the God

Although it's important to understand the God and the Goddess in relation to each other, pagans also find that the God has many valuable qualities in his own right. Here are three themes often associated with God energies: the warrior, the craftsman, and the king.

Oracle

When reading the mythology of your favorite pagan culture, notice which Gods and Goddesses are lovers (or at least friends). When you do pagan rituals or even just offer prayers, it helps to work with a God and a Goddess who like—or love—each other. This makes for a more harmonious and effective spiritual experience for you and for them.

The Warrior

We just finished looking at the God as lover. No matter how much truth there may be in choosing to "make love, not war," the world we live in sometimes requires us to take a stand. We have to defend our land, our loved ones, and our freedom. For this reason, warrior Gods can be meaningful to pagans, especially those who serve in the armed forces.

Even if you're not a military pagan, a proud fighter like the Roman God of war Mars or the Irish warrior God Ogma can symbolize the best of yang energy: setting and enforcing important boundaries and providing protection to your principles, your family, and your community. A person can be a warrior whenever he (or she) stands up for what's right in any situation. The warrior Gods inspire us to do just that.

The Artist and Craftsman

From Hephaestus and Hermes among the Greek deities to Lugh and Goibhniu (the God of smithcraft and brewing) among the Celts, many Gods have distinctive artistic, intellectual, or technological skills. These crafty Gods are artists, musicians, poets, blacksmiths, magicians, brewers, shipbuilders, or masters of countless other skills. Sometimes they use their skills specifically in service of others (like Hephaestus, the blacksmith who forged Zeus's thunderbolts) and sometimes for selfish purposes (the intelligent Hermes had a reputation for thievery). If you have a skill, or more importantly are trying to develop one, chances are there's a God somewhere in the pantheons of the world who embodies the mastery of your craft. Learning to honor that God can be a spiritual source of inspiration for your own work in that particular skill.

The Regal God

Many Gods are known as kings, princes, or rulers. The God of Abraham, who became the only acceptable God in the monotheist religions, has much royal imagery surrounding him, but this is true of many other Gods from around the world, including Zeus, Hades,

Odin, Osiris, and Krishna. Some kings and other royal figures in literature are derived from ancient mythic figures, such as Shakespeare's King Lear, who was derived from a Celtic God of the sea, Lir.

In some Wiccan traditions, the God takes on two kingly forms that symbolize the transitions of the seasons. Known as the Oak King and the Holly King, they symbolize how different aspects of nature are prominent at different times of the year. Like the mighty oak's transformation from stillness in winter to budding in spring and fertility in summer, the Oak King comes into power at the winter solstice, gaining steadily in might until the summer solstice. At that time, he is eclipsed by the power of the Holly King, who like the holly remains vibrant and robust during the period of decline when other trees, like the oak, lose their leaves. So the Oak King symbolizes the growth and development of spring and summer, and the Holly King represents survival in the declining periods of fall and winter. Although some Wiccan traditions maintain that they fight at every solstice for supremacy, it can be just as meaningful to see them as brothers who share power in an eternal cycle of birth, death, and rebirth.

> **Taboo!**
>
> Not all the Gods (or for that matter, the Goddesses) of ancient mythology were moral or honorable. Here are just a few examples: Hermes looked out for thieves, Kali demanded human sacrifice, and Zeus was a rapist. Remember, the Gods of mythology have weaknesses just like human beings, but that doesn't make their behavior excusable.

The Sacrifice

Yet another kingly God from Wiccan tradition is the Corn King, who grows during the hot summer months only to give himself up for the good of others when harvest comes. The death of the Corn King is a powerful image of sacrifice—of one who lays down his life for the welfare of those he loves. Many vegetation Gods play this sacrificial role, one well-known example being Dumuzi, the Sumerian consort of the Goddess Inanna. In most mythic stories, the sacrificial God dies and is reborn at the beginning of the next season. Of course, this theme of the dying-and-reviving God found its most enduring form in the mythic story of the death and resurrection of the Christian God, Jesus of Nazareth.

The sacrificial God is a combination of the lover God and the warrior God. He loves others enough to die for them, and his warrior spirit gives him the bravery and courage to do so. In these mythic tales of death and rebirth, we can find inspiration

> **Oracle**
>
> Even though the sacrificial Gods of mythology always made the ultimate sacrifice (in other words, they gave up their lives), for most of us, the sacrifices we make to help others are usually much smaller. Still, even a small sacrifice can be meaningful when seen in the light of the love of the Goddess and God.

to live our own lives with courage, bravery, and the strength to make sacrifices (when necessary) for the good of our community.

> ### Drumbeats
>
> Here's a reminder not to hold the gender stereotypes between the Gods and Goddesses too rigidly. This chapter has looked at the God as a warrior, a king, and a sacrifice. But remember that Kali, the Hindu Goddess, is as fierce a warrior as they come; Rhiannon, the Welsh Goddess, is considered a great queen (that's what her name literally means); and Selu, the Cherokee Corn Goddess, is a sacrificial figure who died so that her people could live. The moral of the story is that, together, the God and Goddess hold all the key themes of life!

The God in Nature

Finally, let's take a brief look at how the God, like the Goddess, fits into the natural world. Both in terms of ancient mythic figures and the modern concept of Yang energy at play in the universe, we can see the face of the father in the cosmos.

The Sun and the Sky

For many pagans, the earth is the mother, and therefore the sky is the father. We human beings, then, live our lives in the embrace between mom and dad. The sky provides nurturing rain and sunshine to stir the mother's fertility so that new crops may grow each year. Some of the better-known Gods of the sun or sky include Ra, Apollo, and even Yahweh (Jehovah).

Storms and Fire

Zeus and Thor are Gods of thunder, and Aeolus is the Greek God of storms and winds. In storms, we see the force aspect of Yang energy unleashed in nature. The fire aspect of Gods appears not only among the blacksmith Gods like Vulcan but also among Gods devoted purely to fire, like the Hindu deity Agni (from whom words like "ignite" are derived).

The Forest and the Stag

Pan and Cernunnos, among others, naturally reside in the forest and the stag. Away from the hum and whirr of modern life, in the sylvan glades of the unspoiled forest, the horned Gods of many cultures still reign. These are the Gods who provide bounty to the hunter and peace to the weary soul who just wants to get away from it all.

The Least You Need to Know

- Closely related to pagan views of God is the Chinese concept of Yang, or masculine, assertive, powerful, penetrating energy.

- The monotheistic concept of God as wrathful, jealous, and all controlling simply does not apply to most pagan concepts of the God.

- Two of the most popular and enduring images of the God include the horned God of the wilderness and wild animals, and the Green Man, who symbolizes the abundance of foliage and vegetation.

- The many different Gods throughout world mythology can help us understand the diverse ways of appreciating divinity in paganism.

- Some of the most enduring images of the God include the lover, the son of the Goddess, the warrior, the king, the sacrifice, and forces of nature like the sun, the sky, and the forest.

Chapter 10

A Field Guide to the Spirit World

In This Chapter

- ◆ Who lives in the otherworld?
- ◆ Spirits, real and imagined
- ◆ Guides, allies, and other entities
- ◆ Faeries and devas and dragons (Oh, my!)
- ◆ Making sense of the spirit world

Chapter 7, "This World, That World, and the Otherworld," explored some of the ideas that many pagans hold regarding the otherworld—the spiritual realm that's distinct from, but closely related to, the manifest, physical universe. Chapter 8, "Getting to Know the Goddess," and Chapter 9, "All About the God," then took a closer look at the God and the Goddess, who manifest as many different Gods and Goddesses from throughout world mythology. Now it's time to take a closer look at all the other spiritual beings who populate the mysterious realms of the otherworld—and with whom you might come into contact during your pagan meditations and rituals.

The Many Varieties of Spirits

To pagans, the spiritual realm has many qualities that are similar to our mundane existence. It's not like the otherworld is some sort of wispy, nebulous place where just a few Gods and Goddesses hang out. On the contrary, the inner world is teeming with life, filled with beings great and small, powerful and humble, ordinary and fantastic. Because it is limited not by the laws of ordinary physics but only by the far reaches of our imagination, the spiritual realm has everything in it that can be found in ordinary reality, along with an infinite array of magical beings, marvelous creatures, and spiritual beings from the most powerful of God forms down to the most delicate of faeries.

> **Oracle**
>
> Remember that pagan spirituality celebrates what is natural. Since dreams and the imagination are natural parts of human consciousness, to pagans they are perfectly valid ways to connect with spiritual truth. Many pagans endorse the words of Albert Einstein: "Imagination is more important than knowledge."

Through imagination and dreams, ritual and meditation, folklore and faery tales, pagans find meaningful connection to the many spiritual beings who can be found throughout the otherworld. Some of these beings are celestial messengers; others are nature spirits closely allied with the earth. Still others have powerful connections to our own bodies, representing the souls of our ancestors who have gone before us. Pagans believe that the inhabitants of the spirit world can come to us in an almost unlimited variety of forms.

Of course, because there are different traditions and types of paganism, many different ideas and theories about spirit beings can be found among pagans. The information presented in this chapter provides an overview of many varieties of spirits that some, most, or maybe even all, pagans might work with. But different pagan groups emphasize different kinds of spiritual beings. For example, druids may work very closely with faeries and ancestors, while shamans might prefer to focus on power animals and spirit guides. As always, the rule in pagan spirituality is to trust your own experience and intuition and then to work with the teachers or community to which you feel called. Because the spiritual world is fueled by imagination and dreams, there is no one right way to understand it or experience it. If your adventures in the other world are helping you lead a happier, more balanced life and be kind and loving toward others, your spirituality is as valid as it gets.

Are Spirits Real?

Do faeries, spirit guides, power animals, and all the other denizens of the otherworld really exist? Depending on your beliefs regarding the nature of the universe, there are two ways to answer this question. Traditionally, spirits and the otherworld in which they lived were seen as a sort of parallel universe, existing alongside our own. In contrast, many modern people prefer to see the spiritual realm as existing wholly and only within human consciousness—that is to say, within the realm of dreams and imagination.

Drumbeats

Ever notice how similar the words "magic" and "imagine" are? Although there's no evidence that they're related etymologically, it seems as if they should be. Use of the imagination is a central part of magical work. Incidentally, the word "imagine" is related to the Latin word for "imitate," as if the mind imitates reality in forming mental images. The word "magic," however, derives from the Greek word for "ability or power"—the same root that the word "machine" comes from.

Which of these is more "real" or "true" is probably an unanswerable question, especially since the spiritual world is so subjectively influenced by human thoughts, feelings, and beliefs. For that matter, since paganism is nature spirituality, this question is irrelevant because the vast inner sphere of the human mind/imagination/dream realm is just as much a part of nature, and therefore worthy of spiritual devotion, as the physical world "out there."

One thing is for sure: Whether spirits exist only within the theater of the human mind or have an existence separate from us, they can entertain, delight, teach, guide, and even heal us. In that sense, they most certainly are real.

A Closer Look at Spirit Guides

Chapter 3, "Please Don't Squeeze the Shaman!" briefly touched on the concept of spirit guides as an important feature in shamanism. Now it's time to look at this concept more closely, as many of the spirits we will encounter in our journeys to the magical realm will function as our guides, advisors, and teachers.

Spirit guides are the most helpful and friendly of the beings in the otherworldly realms. They provide support and guidance, drawing on their wisdom and knowledge (not to mention their vantage point—as spirits they have a wider field of vision than mere mortals!). Since spirits come to each of us in unique ways that match our own individual expectations and imagination, there's no one correct description for what spirit guides or spirit allies look like. For that matter, there's no one standard way in which guides behave. Some guides are loyal spirits who work with us throughout our entire life, almost like a "support team" that watches over us throughout this incarnation. But other guides may come and go, helping us out with a specific problem or issue and then leaving when they're no longer needed. Some people have only one all-purpose spirit guide, while others may have literally dozens of helper spirits who provide support along the way.

Contacting Your Guide(s)

Spirit guides can speak to us in many different ways. They come to us in dreams or daydreams and during ritual, meditation, or deep-trance experiences. Sometimes we can even see them, hear them, or feel their presence in the midst of everyday life.

Oracle

Spend time getting to know your spirit guides or allies. Whenever you meditate or do rituals, take the time to still your mind and reach out to your guides. The more attention you give them, the more helpful and beneficial they will be to you.

Taboo!

Spiritual guides can help you connect with your own inner wisdom—but don't become superstitious about the role they play in your life. Their advice, like that of any other friend, must be in accordance with your own intuition for it to be truly useful. You remain responsible for your decisions. Remember that spirit guides make mistakes like everybody else!

Getting in touch with your spirit guides does not require profound training in meditation or a mastery of arcane metaphysical principles. It can be as simple as taking time to meditate and to allow your imagination to run free, trusting that in the deep mysterious place where your imagination touches the world of spirit, you can encounter, and relate to, spirits who are your allies and your guides.

Communication with spiritual entities happens more quickly and naturally when spirits have a sense that you are open and willing to relate. Thus, approach your guides with the same degree of care and attention that you would give to a job interview or a first date. Set aside a special time when you won't be interrupted and remove any possible disturbances like the television or telephone. Light a candle and/or incense to create an atmosphere of spiritual reverence. Take several deep breaths and close your eyes. Say, either out loud or in your mind, something along these lines, "I now choose to communicate with my spirit guides and allies. Please reveal yourself to me and bring to me any word you wish to share." Allow yourself to remain quiet with your eyes closed, breathing deeply and naturally. Notice any images or sounds that come to you. If in your mind's eye you hear a voice or see a person, make note of that experience. You may want to ask the person or voice questions or tell the spirit a bit about yourself. Just follow your intuition to communicate in a way that feels natural.

When it feels like you've interacted with your guide(s) long enough, say good-bye and mention when you'll next be attempting to contact them. Make notes of your experiences in your journal.

If the first time or two you don't have any sense of spirits contacting you, don't give up. You may be trying too hard or not be paying attention to the voices or images that naturally come to you. Just relax and pay attention. You will be amazed at the richness of your inner experience once you start noticing!

Black and White ... or a Variety of Colors?

Not all spirits in the spirit world are necessarily our guides or our allies. For that matter, not all of them are friendly or worth having as friends. Among shamans and other practitioners of traditional spirituality, it was commonly understood that spirits could be friendly, hostile, or neutral. Just because you encounter a spirit in your dreams or meditation does not automatically mean that spirit is your friend.

If you grew up in a monotheistic religion, you may be accustomed to thinking of the spiritual world as including only two categories of spirits: angels and demons. Angels are the servants and messengers of God, while demons are spirits who have rejected goodness and serve evil. To make matters worse, demons are not only hostile but treacherous, so they might masquerade as good spirits, meaning you always have to be on your guard! This black-and-white approach to the spirit world might have made for a dramatic mythological story, but it doesn't really stack up well with the way things really are in nature. Remember that paganism looks to nature as its ultimate spiritual authority. We know that the world we live in doesn't have just "good" and "bad" people; it has an endless variety of personalities—some good, some bad, many incorporating both good and bad qualities in the same individual. Pagans, like shamans of old, assume that the spirit world has a similar variety of entities with an almost endless array of personality types.

Practicing Safe Spirituality

While I don't think pagans need to be utterly suspicious and paranoid of the spirits they encounter, it does make sense to treat the citizens of the otherworld with the same common sense and caution you would apply to physical beings who come into your life. In other words, it makes sense to keep some precautions in mind while meditating, doing ritual, reflecting on your dreams, or doing any other spiritual work that may involve contact with spirits. Here are some common-sense precautions to take when contacting the spirit world:

- Don't automatically believe everything you hear. Just because a spirit says something doesn't make it so.

- Pay attention to your emotions when in contact with a spirit. Does its presence feel light and joyful or heavy and depressing?

- How does the spirit treat you? With basic dignity and respect? Or is the spirit nasty, sneering, or sarcastic? A friendly but powerful spirit may treat you like a student, but even so, the basic sense of the spirit's behavior is positive.

- Does the spirit ask you to do things that make you feel uncomfortable or that seem to go against your deeper intuition? If so, this is a major warning sign to steer this entity a wide berth.

CAUTION

Taboo!

Pagans reject the idea that some spirits are "demons" who want to tempt their soul away from God. Because the Goddess is in all things, it's impossible to be separated from her. Pagans see unfriendly spirits as more of a nuisance than anything else, but even as nuisances, they should be avoided.

♦ If a spirit is truly a guide, you'll learn this over time as the spirit earns your trust and respect the way any close friend would. Not only that, the spirit will provide you with real, helpful advice as to how to live your own life fully and well.

I don't want to scare you into thinking the spirit world is full of nasties and psychos, but like any other aspect of life, an appropriate amount of caution goes a long way. Take the time to get to know the spirits in your life fully, and you'll learn which ones truly deserve your attention, your trust, and your friendship.

Some of the Spirits You Could Meet

Here's a quick look at some of the more common types of spiritual beings that might appear during your otherworldly journeys.

♦ **Ancestors** Some of the inhabitants of the Otherworld are ancestral spirits, including relatives you might recognize (like grandmothers or grandfathers) and early ancestors from many generations back. These are the spirits who gave you your DNA. They can offer you advice or could just as easily ask a favor of you.

♦ **Angels and Archangels** As mentioned earlier, an angel is literally a "messenger" from God (or, in pagan parlance, the Goddess). When angels appear in your life, they bring important news from the ultimate source of reality. They are celestial, radiant beings and are usually (but not always) winged. The most important of the angels are called archangels. Not all pagans choose to work with angels, since the angelic tradition arises out of monotheistic religion, and all named angels (such as Michael and Gabriel) are male. Angels, like faeries, are sometimes portrayed as cute, wispy androgynous figures in modern culture, but in reality angels are powerful and awe-inspiring figures.

♦ **Devas, faeries, and dakini** Throughout the world, spirits with a powerful connection to nature and the land have been seen and related to since time immemorial. In the Celtic regions of the British Isles, such nature spirits are known as faeries; in Sanskrit, they are called devas; and in Tibet, they are known as the dakini. See more about nature spirits later in this chapter.

♦ **Elementals** Many spirits, both great and small, have powerful connections to the elements of air, water, fire, and earth. Indeed, entire categories of spirit beings are associated with each element. For more information on this important category of entities, see Chapter 11, "Elementary, My Dear Pagan!"

◆ **Extraterrestrials**   Do aliens visit us? Do they come to us in our dreams and visions? Some people certainly have had experiences that lead them to believe this. Others believe that "extraterrestrials" are, like angels, simply another category of spiritual beings that may not have a direct connection to the earth. I'll leave it up to you and your drinking buddies to argue over whether extraterrestrials (and any other category of entities) are "real" or "imaginary" (or both). For now, let's just say that on your otherworldly journeys, it is possible to meet up with beings who claim no earthly origin.

> **Oracle**
>
> Friendly spirits do not want to upset or alarm us, so they will appear to us in a form that feels safe and comfortable. For many people, even pagans, the angel is a powerful symbol of goodness and hope, so don't be surprised if you meet spirits with wings!

◆ **Ghosts**   Ghosts are different from ancestors in two important ways. For one thing, they may not have any ancestral connection to you whatsoever. But even if they do, a ghost represents a spirit who is somehow "stuck" between this world and the otherworld. In fact, some psychics believe that ghosts are not even real spirits at all but are more like an ethereal imprint or "recording" of a spirit's powerful thoughts or energy.

◆ **Power animals (and plants)**   From normal creatures you may see in everyday life (dogs, cats, blackbirds) to powerful beasts from the wild (tigers, wolves, stags) and even to mythical creatures like unicorns and dragons (which I'll take a closer look at later in this chapter), animals play a prominent role in the spiritual world. Some may talk, some may communicate telepathically, and many may just ignore you altogether! All, however, can have rich magical or symbolic information to impart to those who are willing to learn. For that matter, sometimes you'll even encounter a plant spirit, such as a tree that appears to communicate with you telepathically.

Spirits of Land, Sea, and Sky

If otherworldly entities were to be organized into two large groupings, the most common-sense way to categorize them would be as celestial beings and nature spirits. Celestial beings include any spirit whose origin is heavenly rather than earthly, including angels and extraterrestrials. The other category, nature spirits, includes a worldwide variety of beings associated with the natural world. From the faeries of Celtic lore to the *devas* of Hindu tradition to the *naiads* and *dryads* of Greek myth, cultures from around the world have acknowledged the existence of nature spirits and have contacted them and worked with them in various ways. Here's some insight into the spirits who have a special kinship to nature and into how we can cultivate a meaningful relationship with them today.

EarthWords

The Sanskrit word **deva** literally means "shining one," suggesting that the citizens of the spiritual world are luminous, radiant beings. According to Greek tradition, a **dryad** is a spirit associated with a specific tree or forest, while a **naiad** is a nymph connected to a particular body of water.

Oracle

An old principle of the magical art of alchemy states: "As above, so below." In other words, there are natural correspondences between the physical and spiritual worlds. The faeries and other nature spirits are entities whose existence is based on those natural correspondences. This is why nature spirits can sometimes be seen in the physical world. Their existence, like our souls, bridges the two worlds.

The Relationship Between the Land and the Otherworld

What makes a nature spirit a nature spirit? Primarily, it involves some sort of direct and physical connection with one or more elements within the earth. Many nature spirits have a specific connection to a place such as a river, lake, hill, or mountain. Others may be connected with specific plants or animals or even with an entire species.

Traditional lore suggests that the otherworld is, in many ways, a parallel world to our own. In other words, when you enter the otherworld, you may find geographical locations that resemble or match physical characteristics of the actual world. Spirits who are associated with Pike's Peak in the otherworld have a similar connection to the real Pike's Peak in the manifest universe.

Does this mean you have to be physically present in a certain location to communicate with the natural spirits of that place? No, because in the otherworld you can connect with any place in the universe instantly. But of course, if you want to contact the spirits of a place, it makes sense to go physically to that place. Just as its easier to talk to another human being in person than over the phone, it can be easier to connect with faeries when you make the effort to meet them on their home turf.

Faeries: More Than Just Tinkerbell ...

In the popular imagination, faeries are often depicted as tiny, delicate little winged critters no bigger than a butterfly or a dragonfly. These little beings live in gardens or other pastoral settings, frolicking gaily among the plants, birds, and bees. They sit on toadstools, glow like fireflies in the moonlight, and dance in rings on forest floors.

Such little faery sprites may make for charming pictures on greeting cards and certainly have contributed to children's literature in the form of Tinkerbell, the famous faery from *Peter Pan*'s Neverland. And to the extent that such itty-bitty sprites exist in our imagination, well, I suppose they can be lovely guides to the inner realms. But as a pagan, don't limit your concept of faeries to this rather sentimental picture. The authentic faeries of

Celtic myth, legend, and folklore come in all shapes and sizes. Yes, they are "little people," but little could just as easily mean 4 feet tall as 4 inches. For that matter, some faeries are not little at all but are the same size as—or larger than—human beings! There's no reason to insist that all faeries have wings, live in gardens, or look like cute little girls. On the contrary, faeries can be male as well as female, can live underground or even underwater, and—most important of all—have a variety of personality types. In other words, not all faeries are necessarily "nice." Just like any group of individuals, some faeries are friendly and kind, and others can be frightening or standoffish. Some are best just left alone.

Drumbeats
The Irish word for faery is *sidhe* (pronounced "shee"), which means "hill-dweller." In pre-historic Ireland, many graves for important members of the tribe were actually built like small hills, called barrows. When later generations forgot that these little hills were gravesites, a feeling of mystery and awe surrounded them. Among the Celts, the idea took root that these mound-graves were actually doorways to the otherworld where the spirits lived. The sidhe could be Gods or Goddesses, nature spirits, or ancestors. (Since the little hills were actually graves, associating them with ancestors was not far off the mark!)

The idea of faeries as nature spirits may come from the original Celtic understanding of the many Gods and Goddesses as having connections to the natural world. In Irish myth, for example, there were Goddesses associated with specific rivers, wells, hills, and other natural features. Even when these Gods were "demoted" to faeries, the nature association remained strong. So today, most people think of faeries as mere spirits and not deities, but they are spirits with strong ties to the world of nature.

Although faeries come out of the Celtic tradition, it's important to remember that nature spirits have been encountered in many cultures from around the world. Hinduism, Greek and Roman paganism, and shamanism from Tibet and other parts of the world all have powerful traditions of nature-based spirits who connect with human beings. No matter what you call an entity, if it is connected with the earth in some way, it is a nature spirit.

Ancestors: Those Who Came Before Us

Ancestors deserve special mention as spirits whom you may encounter because many cultures have included traditions of revering or even worshiping ancestors as part of the their spiritual practice. Many pagans today carry on this tradition, offering prayers and even small tokens of sacrifice to ancestral spirits as part of their ritual work. The ancestors you honor can be physical ancestors (those who gave you your DNA), spiritual ancestors (those who gave you your beliefs or values), or both.

Blood Ancestors: They're in Your Genes

If you go back 10 generations, every human being living today had a thousand ancestors. (Obviously, most of us share many common ancestors!) When they died, their bodies returned to the earth to nourish the soil and, eventually, those who came after. Their spirits, meanwhile, can likewise serve as guides and guardians to those of us who have come later. Presumably, ancestral spirits are very interested in us; after all, we carry their DNA. If you connect with an ancestral spirit, remember that he or she is a family member. Of course, like all family members, every ancestor is different. Some may be wise and powerful; others may just want to stir up trouble. Dysfunctional families exist in the otherworld, too! So when you encounter an ancestor in your spiritual work, be thankful and respectful—and always listen to your intuition to know the best way to relate.

Ancestors of the Soul: The Ultimate Inspiration

Some ancestors may not have a physical relationship to us (in other words, as a great-great-great-great-grandma) but may be spiritual ancestors—they may have been pioneers in the beliefs and values we hold dear today. These ancestors can come to us as shamans, priests or priestesses, sages, or crones with wisdom to impart. They deserve the same respect and honor that we would give to our flesh-and-blood ancestors.

> **Oracle**
>
> In the Roman Catholic church, saints are venerated. This is an example of how spiritual ancestors can play an important role in the spiritual lives of people living today.

Unicorns, Dragons, and Other Mythical Creatures

Although the most common beings we encounter in the spirit world will have some obvious connection to the physical universe—whether in the form of human-like spirits or recognizable power animals—the endless possibilities inherent in the otherworld mean that this is a realm where fantastic beasts and semihuman beings can and do appear. The next time you enter into a deep meditative state, you could find yourself face to face with a fire-breathing dragon, a lovely unicorn, a sexy and playful mermaid, or some other entirely *imaginal* being.

> **EarthWords**
>
> If something is **imaginal**, it comes out of the realm of imaginary or mental images.

Here are just a few examples of mythical beings whose origins lie shrouded in the mists of ancient legend but whose spirit just might welcome you on your next sojourn in the otherworld:

- **Centaurs** have the body of a horse but the torso and head of a human. They are said to possess intelligence far superior to humans.

- **Dragons,** one of the more fearsome beasts of legend, are basically giant fire-breathing flying lizards. They may be worth fighting (or better yet, negotiating with) because often they guard valuable treasure.

- **Fauns** are humanlike beings with goat horns, legs, and cloven hooves. Playful and sexy, they help us connect with our primal, animal nature.

- **Griffins** possess the head and wings of an eagle and the body of a lion. As such, they represent royalty and sovereignty because the eagle is the king of birds and the lion is the king of beasts.

- **Mermaids** (and mermen) are part human, part fish. Beautiful and dreamlike, they can also be treacherous sirens, luring a sailor to his death with their hypnotic singing.

- **The Phoenix,** unique among magical beasts, is a single, immortal bird. Every 500 years, the phoenix immolates itself in a funeral pyre, from which it rises again, young and renewed.

- **Unicorns,** as popular as dragons, represent chastity and virtue. Horses with a single luminous horn, they trust only the pure of heart.

Putting It All Together

Gods and Goddesses … ancestors and faeries … dragons and unicorns. By now you may be wondering, "Is paganism just an excuse to live in la-la land?" Fair enough. It needs to be said that many people adopt a pagan spirituality *without* paying a lot of attention to mythology or getting to know the inhabitants of the imaginal realms. As always, paganism respects diversity and personal choice. If exploring the landscape of the otherworld doesn't appeal to you, that's fine. You might still enjoy paganism as a simple way to revere nature.

CAUTION

Taboo!

Scientifically minded pagans may not feel drawn toward working with spirits or faeries as part of their spiritual practice. Don't assume, however, that pagans who do engage in spirit contact are "superstitious" or ignorant. Remember that brilliant people (such as the eminent psychologist Carl Jung) have believed in, revered, and learned from spirits—and so can you if you keep an open mind!

Yet many pagans do love the rich treasures of the mythic world. Why? On one level, it's entertaining, but few pagans would say they embrace the Gods and spirits just to be entertained. For most pagans, the many faces of the mythic realm of Gods, ancestors, and spirits represent a way to honor the spiritual dimension of nature in all her diversity. Whether Gods and spirits are just symbols from within our own minds or are genuine beings with lives of their own, pagans find them worthy of veneration and devotion—just as Mother Earth herself is worthy of such love. Furthermore, as in the case of spirit guides or many of the Goddesses and Gods, pagans find the inhabitants of the otherworld to be powerful teachers and mentors. They can teach us about the dynamics of our own souls and can give us a glimpse of immortal truth that has been passed down through myth and folklore since time immemorial.

The Fuzzy Logic of the Otherworld

If you feel drawn toward the many deities, spirits, and beings who inhabit the otherworld, you'll want to explore your own dreams and visualizations but also become familiar with the rich treasures of world mythology, folklore, and legend. (See Appendix A, "Recommended Reading," for books to get you started on this quest.) One thing you'll notice is how fuzzy and indistinct the spirit world really is. The same beings may be portrayed as mighty Gods in one story and as mere nature spirits in another. Great heroes and ancestors can sometimes cross the line and be treated as Gods. Sometimes the line separating Goddesses and Gods from ancestors, heroes, and nature spirits can be very thin and blurry.

Don't worry about such imprecision, even if you are by nature a stickler for details. Remember that the otherworld is a realm of poetry and myth, not science and technology. One of the lessons it can teach us is to be comfortable with ambiguity and mystery. You can spend a lifetime exploring the depths of the inner universe and still not have it all figured out. So don't try. Simply enjoy the experience and learn what you can. And remember: The honor and respect you show to deities, ancestors, or nature spirits is ultimately reverence for the earth and the great Goddess she symbolizes.

How to Navigate Through the Spirit Realms

Here's one final word of advice: There are so many wonderful mythological and folkloric traditions in the world that you can easily become overwhelmed by how much there is to learn and discover. From the Egyptians to the Celts, from the Norse to the Greeks, from the Native Americans to the Yoruba, from Australian Aborigines to the Tibetans … every great culture has a vast tradition of myth and legend in which Gods, Goddesses, and other powerful spirits may be encountered.

Don't try to master it all. Your best bet is to pick one or two cultures that especially resonate with you and become a specialist in that or those traditions. It's helpful to stick with a culture from which you are physically descended, although that's not entirely necessary. Perhaps you'll find one culture that is your family culture and another to which you feel personally drawn. These two cultures can be your magical specialties.

Of course, there's always your own intuition, which is ultimately the best guide of all. Remember that, as a pagan, your job is not to follow my instructions but to be true to your own inner wisdom. It can be a trustworthy guide to the wonders of faeryland.

The Least You Need to Know

- Just as most pagans accept many faces of Gods and Goddesses, most accept the idea that many spirits exist in the universe.
- While the "home" of spirits is the mythic inner or Otherworld, spirits (especially nature spirits) can sometimes be encountered in the physical world.
- Pagans find that working with spirits is meaningful and educational and tend not to worry about whether these entities are "real" or "imaginary."
- Aside from Gods and Goddesses, spirits can appear as ancestors, nature spirits, animals, or mythic beings, among many other forms.
- Spirits have many different personality types, and few are totally "good" or "evil." Like human beings, they can have complex identities with both positive and negative traits.

Chapter 11

Elementary, My Dear Pagan!

In This Chapter

- ◆ The four basic spiritual building blocks
- ◆ Elemental yang: air and fire
- ◆ Elemental yin: water and earth
- ◆ A fifth element?
- ◆ The pentagram: tying the elements together

The preceding three chapters took a closer look at the Goddess, the God, and the many other varieties of spirits you might encounter while exploring the pagan path. Paganism, however, is more than just some sort of "head trip" about the spiritual realm. First and foremost, paganism is a way of relating to nature. Since spirituality is part of nature, it's important to give the deities and the other spirits their due. But now it's time to reconnect with the earthy dimension of the pagan way.

The Goddess and the God represent the two most fundamental energies at work in our lives and in the universe. These are the energies of yin and yang, force and form, light and dark, activity and receptivity. Now we'll begin to consider some of the distinctions within these primal energies. Instead of the *two* most basic energies, this chapter considers *four* basic energies that are known as the elements.

What are the elements? In modern science, the elements include more than 90 different essential atoms that make up the basic building blocks of the physical universe: from the lightest and most basic atoms like hydrogen, helium, oxygen, and so forth, all the way to the heaviest, most complex, and frequently unstable elements like uranium and plutonium.

For the purposes of pagan spirituality, things are kept on a simpler level, with only four basic elements: fire, air, water, and earth. These are the elements that were identified in ancient Greek philosophy and that have influenced various esoteric schools of thought from magic to astrology to Tarot. Some pagans also regard spirit as a fifth element. (I'll take a closer look at that concept later in this chapter.) In this chapter, we'll consider each element not only as an abstract philosophical and metaphysical concept but also as a tool for relating more closely to the earth as our living Mother Gaia.

Basic Principles of the Elements

For understanding the four elements, it's helpful to keep the principles of yin and yang in mind. Earth and water are yin elements, while air and fire are yang elements. Thus, earth and water have qualities such as receptivity, darkness, and form, while air and fire have qualities such as light, activity, and force. This means that air and fire are considered masculine elements, and water and earth are considered feminine elements.

Various magical and metaphysical traditions assign a variety of symbols, or correspondences, to each of the four elements. This information is helpful to understanding how ritual works or to doing magical work (if you are so inclined). Because so many different traditions fall under the pagan umbrella, it's impossible to present just one set of correspondences and say, "This is the way pagans do it." All that can be said is, "This is the way some pagans understand the elements." For the sake of simplicity, I'll be using correspondences based on one of the most popular Tarot decks, the Rider-Waite-Smith deck, which in turn was adapted from the teachings of a famous magical order called the Golden Dawn.

> **Drumbeats**
>
> The Rider-Waite-Smith Tarot deck remains the most popular and best-selling deck, even though it is almost a hundred years old. It was designed by Pamela Colman Smith under the direction of the famed occultist A. E. Waite and was published by the Rider Company in London. It is famous for its simple drawings and vivid use of esoteric and magical imagery to illustrate the themes of the cards.

In the Rider-Waite-Smith deck, as well as in many other traditional Tarot decks, there are four suits: wands, swords, cups, and pentacles (also known as coins). The suit of wands corresponds with fire, the suit of swords with air, cups with water, and pentacles with earth.

- ◆ **Air (swords)** corresponds to the direction east, the season of spring, and childhood. Its color is yellow.
- ◆ **Fire (wands)** corresponds to the direction south, the season of summer, and youth. Its color is red.
- ◆ **Water (cups)** corresponds to the direction west, the season of autumn, and maturity. Its color is blue.
- ◆ **Earth (pentacles or coins)** corresponds to the direction north, the season of winter, and old age. Its color is green.

Oracle

Many pagans believe that wands should represent air and swords should represent fire because fire would destroy a wand but not a sword. This book follows the Rider-Waite-Smith symbolism, but this is one example of how some pagans have different ways of understanding the elements and their correspondences.

Got that? Now, here's a different way of looking at the elements, just to confuse you (just kidding!):

- ◆ **Air** corresponds to the atmosphere of our planet or to the lungs of the Goddess. As such, its color is sky blue.
- ◆ **Water** corresponds to the oceans of our planet or to the bloodstream of the Goddess. As such, its color is aqua.
- ◆ **Earth** corresponds to the soil and rocky crust of the planet or to the flesh and bones of the Goddess. As such, its color is brown.
- ◆ **Fire** corresponds to the molten core of the planet or to the mind and emotions of the Goddess. As such, its color is orange.

See? There are many different ways of understanding the elements and how they relate to each other, to the earth, and to the Goddess. The important thing is to find a system that resonates with your intuition. Of course, if you are working within a specific pagan tradition, you'll want to learn the elemental correspondences appropriate for that tradition.

Think of the elements as the basic building blocks of the universe, as seen from a pagan spiritual point of view. Each of these building blocks has energies that relate to different aspects of life, different personality types, or different objectives

Taboo!

Not all pagans even use the four-element (or five-element) system. Most druids, for example, don't think in terms of air/fire/water/earth but in a more nature-based division of land, sea, and sky, with fire simply as a sacred center around which rituals are held. So don't assume that all pagans see things the way you do—or, for that matter, the way they're depicted in this book.

that a person might have. Working with the energies of the elements becomes a way for you to invoke or call the specific energies you desire at this point in your life.

Elemental Symbols

Magical and pagan people sometimes use four symbols, one for each element, in their spiritual work. These symbols, which have their origins in alchemy, can be inscribed on ritual tools or set up in a ritual space to signify which element is honored in which direction.

Alchemical symbols of the elements.

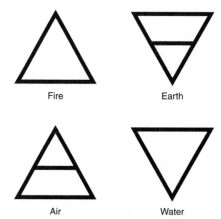

Fire

Earth

Air

Water

Symbols of the four elements include an upward pointing triangle for Fire, an upward pointing triangle with a horizontal line for Air, a downward pointing triangle for Water, and a downward pointing triangle with a horizontal line for Earth.

The yang elements both have upward pointing triangles, while the yin elements both have downward pointing triangles. This is symbolic of the genders: An upward pointing triangle is symbolic of the phallus (and therefore masculine energy), while a downward pointing triangle is symbolic of a womb (and, therefore, feminine energy).

Now let's take a closer look at each element and at some of the ways to think about that element in relation to the whole of life. We'll begin with the yang elements of fire and air.

Come On, Baby, Light My Fire

Some pagan traditions teach that creation began with fire. When you relate to the scientific notion of the big bang, it makes sense. Fire represents the primal spark of divine energy that set all things into motion. As a yang element, fire represents the force that came into being within the context of the pre-existing form, the primal darkness that is the ultimate womb of the Goddess. As sperm enters the womb to co-create new life, so did the masculine spark enter the feminine darkness to co-create the universe.

Just as fire began with the big bang at the center of the universe, so too does fire reside to this day at the center of the earth in her molten core. Fire also resides at the center of the solar system in the great fiery sphere we call the sun. Fire, as pure energy, is the element closest to spirit and farthest removed from the solidity of earthy matter. Because of its association with light, it is related to the human sense of sight.

Oracle

Candles are, naturally, the best tools for working with the element fire. It's fun to make your own candles; wax, wicks, and candle-making kits can be found at craft stores to help you get started. Dye your candle red (or whatever color represents fire in your tradition). Unscented candles are best.

Fire has long held a powerful place in humanity's imagination. When we think of the earliest humans discovering fire, we see that as a key step toward civilization and toward setting us apart from the rest of the animal kingdom. From ancient times, people sat around the fire to eat, stay warm, share time together, and even do spiritual work. Gazing into a roaring fire can be a powerful way to engage psychic skills to see into the otherworld.

Astrologically, the signs of Aries, Leo, and Sagittarius correspond with fire. Like Aries, the energy of fire is aggressive, self-confident, and warlike when necessary. Like Leo, fire energy is highly loyal, proud, and flamboyant and perhaps even a bit of a showoff. Like Sagittarius, the element fire can be philosophical and quite the explorer.

Power and Energy

In terms of magic and ritual, the two keywords for fire are power and energy. You'll want to invoke the energies of fire when you're seeking greater dynamic activity in your life. Whether you just want more energy to get an important project done or you need assistance in dealing with a conflict fairly and courageously, the energies of fire can be your most important ally.

Fire governs the passion and energy of life. Think of when we say that someone is "hot tempered" or has a "fiery disposition." In business, Fire governs entrepreneurship—the gumption to start and succeed at one's own business rather than just going to work for somebody else.

Meet Commander Salamander

According to magical lore, the spirits of the element fire are known as salamanders. These are not the same as the amphibian salamanders we find in the wild; they are magical creatures that make their home in fire. Of course, being magical creatures, they can take any of a number of forms, appearing not only as lizards but as dragons or merely as the abstract spirit of fire. Some pagans actually invoke, or visualize, the salamander kingdom when invoking the energies of fire into their rituals.

The king of the fire spirits is named Djinn, and the archangel associated with fire is Michael.

A Fire Meditation

Here's an exercise you can do to help connect with the energies of fire. You'll need a quiet place where you can spend 10 to 15 minutes or more of uninterrupted time. Ideally, you will be outdoors with a bonfire or indoors near a fireplace with a roaring blaze. If all else fails, light a candle. Sit in a comfortable position facing south with the candle or other flame in front of you.

Close your eyes (before doing so, make sure the fire is safely contained!) and take several deep breaths, allowing your body to relax. Now visualize the color red as if your entire field of vision were red. Then, in the center of the red, visualize an upward pointing triangle. Imagine that the center of this triangle is a doorway leading to the realm of Fire. When you're ready, imagine yourself stepping through the triangular door, into the realm of the salamander. In front of you a flame burns bright and hot, and in the flame, you can sense a presence—the salamander, the spirit of fire. Notice how the salamander appears to you; it may come as a lizard-like creature or in some other form, or it may simply appear as a flame. As you visualize the salamander, ask it any question you may have about the power of fire and the lessons this element may have for you. Take as long as you need to connect with the wisdom of fire. When ready, say farewell to the element and visualize yourself returning through the triangle to your ordinary self, sitting in meditation.

When you're ready, open your eyes. You may want to make notes in your journal about your experience during this meditation. Be sure to note whether the spirit of fire said anything, asked you any questions, or provided answers to your questions.

Airheads, Unite!

It's ironic that we call people who are ditzy or forgetful "airheads" because, in magical terms, air is the element that governs intellectual ability. In other words, to be a magical airhead is to be quite clever!

Fire may be the most primal of the elements, but air comes next. As a gas, it is the most ethereal of the material elements and, therefore, is the closest to the spiritual realm. After the initial fire created the universe, matter coalesced first into gaseous forms before condensing into liquids and solids. So this element is associated with beginnings, with springtime, and with childhood.

Oracle

What power animals are most associated with the element air? Why, birds, of course—from eagles and hawks to ravens and starlings. If a bird appears in your life, it could be an omen of something new or a lesson to be learned.

We live and move in the element air, and of course, we breathe this element throughout the span of our lives. Air is related to the sense of hearing because sound waves travel through the atmosphere. It is associated with mental skill, communication, logic, analysis, and discernment. It also is associated with law and order and, by extension, with defense and self-defense.

Astrologically, the signs of Gemini, Libra, and Aquarius correspond with air. Like Gemini, the element air governs talented communication and sharp mental skills. Like Libra, the energy of air has a keen sense of justice and order and will fight for what's right. Like Aquarius, this energy can be idealistic and have a strong sense of community ties.

Playfulness and Communication

Two keywords that can be associated with air are playfulness and communication. As a child frolics on a warm spring day or as the wind blows playfully over the landscape, so does air signify a kind of light, carefree movement. It has a heavier side, though, in its earnest focus on mental acuity and communication, from the most casual of small talk to the most weighty of legal documents. This is the element most associated with writers and journalists, lawyers and teachers, and the military.

Invoke the energies of the element air when you are trying to learn something new or to communicate an important matter, whether by speaking or writing. In general, air is the element to count on to support new endeavors. Finally, if you're facing a conflict, call on the spirit of air to help you keep a clear mind and a keen understanding of strategy and issues.

Improve Your Sylph-Esteem

The spirits associated with air are known as sylphs, and they can take the form of lovely and delicate winged creatures. They are light and playful like the wind but can assume different appearances if they so choose. For some pagans, visualizing sylphs is an important part of working with the element air.

The king of the spirits of air is named Paralda, and the archangel Raphael is associated with this element.

An Air Meditation

This brief meditation can help you connect with the energies of air. You can return to the same place where you did your fire meditation, or you can find some other location where you can spend 10 to 15 minutes or more of uninterrupted time. Ideally, you will be outdoors under the clear blue sky or, if indoors, near a window where you can see the vastness of the atmosphere. You can be creative: A fan blowing on you can be symbolic of the breeze outdoors. Whether indoors or out, light incense, which is a traditional symbol for the element air. Sit in a comfortable position facing east with the incense in front of you.

Light the incense and then close your eyes, taking several deep breaths and allowing your body to relax. Visualize the color yellow as if it filled your entire field of vision. Now, in the center of the yellow, visualize an upward pointing triangle with a horizontal line in its center. Imagine that this triangle is a doorway leading into the realm of Air. When you're ready, imagine yourself stepping through the door, into the home of the sylphs and the winds. Once within the door, feel the wind blowing across your face, invigorating your skin as it brushes over you. In the heart of the wind, you sense a presence—the sylph, the spirit of air. In your mind's eye, see how the sylph appears to you; it may come as a small, winged being or in some other form, or it may simply appear as a "presence" within the wind. Take time to ask it any question you may have about the power of air and the lessons this element may have for you. Allow yourself as long as necessary to connect with the wisdom of the sylph. When ready, say farewell to the element and visualize yourself returning through the triangle to your ordinary self, sitting in meditation.

Open your eyes when you feel ready to do so. Take a few moments to record your feelings and any experiences you may have had in your journal.

Water, Water, Everywhere

Out of the deep blue vastness of the sky, water condenses and falls as rain. This is the element most closely related to us human beings because our bodies contain more water than anything else. It is out of the oceans, the magnificent bloodstream of Mother Earth, that all organic life emerged.

Like air, water has a playful quality, manifesting as rain, puddles, streams, rivers, lakes, and oceans. Water flows but can also take on the solid form of ice or the gaseous form of steam. Water represents flexibility and change. Magically, water is related to the emotions and the intuition. From love to joy to anger to fear, all feelings (which we experience in our mostly water bodies) are related to this element. In a way, intuition is simply the deepest, most powerful feeling of all, a feeling that transmits knowledge and wisdom through the awareness of the body.

Water is associated with the autumn and with maturity. It is the element of letting go and going with the flow, and of washing away or flowing around obstacles. It does not seek to master so much as to relate. It relates to the senses of taste and smell.

Astrologically, the signs of Cancer, Scorpio, and Pisces correspond with water. Like Cancer, water energy is deeply emotional and nurturing, as loving as a mother but also somewhat self-protective. Like Scorpio, this element has strong psychic connections to the subconscious and to the most basic physical needs of life. Like Pisces, water is the most deeply romantic and even mystical of the elements.

> **Oracle**
>
> To bring the energies of water into your life, try keeping an aquarium filled with beautiful exotic fish. Place it in the western part of your house (or on the western side of its room). Collecting seashells can be another way to connect with this element.

Fluidity and Buoyancy

When working with the element of water, you'll be riding a wave of energies like fluidity, buoyancy, and heartfelt emotion. This is the element to call on when concerned with matters involving feelings and relationships, whether mending a broken heart or seeking greater intimacy with a loved one. This is also the key element to invoke when you are seeking to develop your psychic or intuitive skills or to learn a divination technique such as the Tarot.

If there's an area of life that feels rigid and inflexible, call on water to teach you how to go with the flow. Work wise, if you are a counselor, a spiritual healer or minister, or a child-care provider, you'll want to manifest lots of watery energy in your life.

Don't Be Mean to the Undine

The spirits who inhabit the watery realms of this element are known as undines. Traditionally, undines have been seen as humanlike figures whose natural habitat is underwater, almost like merfolk. Of course, since they are spirit beings, they can assume many different forms. To invoke the energies of water into your own ritual or spiritual work, it can be helpful to envision the undines.

The king of the water spirits is named Necksa, and the archangel associated with this element is Gabriel.

A Water Meditation

The best time to do this water meditation is at sunset. Try to find a time and location when you won't be disturbed; ideally, you will be near a natural body of water like a lake or a stream, but if necessary, simply sit with a bowl of water in front of you.

Begin by assuming a comfortable seated position facing west.

Before closing your eyes, gaze silently into the water. Take a few deep breaths, perhaps reflecting on how the human body is more water than anything else. Finally, allow your eyes to close and your body to relax. If the water is close enough, you can even immerse your hands in it while doing this exercise. Use your imagination to see the color blue filling your entire inner awareness, as if you were standing and moving in a sea of blue. In the midst of this sea, notice a downward pointing triangle. This is the doorway that opens into the realm of water. When you feel inspired to do so, visualize yourself opening this triangular doorway and moving into the watery depths of the elemental realm. Visualize yourself floating in, or perhaps just above, an endless lake or ocean. Feel the cool liquid against your skin, the movement of the currents as the water flows around you.

Now, looking into the water, visualize the spirit of the element, the undine. As you become aware of its presence, look to see what form the undine has taken. Perhaps it appears like a mermaid or merman or perhaps like some unearthly aquatic being. Regardless of its appearance, send a telepathic greeting to it and listen to your inner voice to see if any message or word of wisdom comes to you from the undine. Listen for any teachings it may have to offer you and ask any questions regarding Water that you may have. Do not rush in your quest to connect with the wisdom of the undine. Eventually, though, it will be time to say good-bye. Imagine yourself returning through the triangle to your ordinary self, sitting in meditation.

Open your eyes and take time to recount your inner journey within the pages of your journal.

Earth (and the Land)

Finally, we come to the most solid and stable of all the elements, the element earth. Don't confuse earth the element with Earth the planet. Remember, the planet consists of all four elements plus spirit, while the element earth is a specific energy found as part of the overall planetary system.

As an element, earth represents matter in its most hard, concrete, stable form. Whether this is the moist nurturing matter of the soil or the firm, solid, foundational mass of rocks and minerals, earth carries the energy of all that is fixed, structured, and set in place. This is the energy of ultimate manifestation. The journey that began with the pure energy of fire, coalescing first into gases and then into liquid form, has now reached its most dense form as a solid.

Earth represents completion and endings. It is associated with winter and old age. It is practical, results driven, and dependable. As the most grossly physical of the elements, earth is associated with the sense of touch.

Oracle

Do you love quartz crystal? If so, you may have a strong connection to the element earth. Place a beautiful quartz crystal in the northern quadrant of your ritual space to honor this element.

Astrologically, the signs of Taurus, Virgo, and Capricorn correspond with Earth. Like Taurus, earth energy is practical and sensuous, reveling in the material comforts and pleasures of life. Like Virgo, this element has a humble commitment to service and to paying keen attention to detail. Like Capricorn, it can be a hard worker, a shrewd businessman, and a champion of discipline.

Practicality and Stability

Do you have money concerns or practical concerns regarding physical health, house repairs, or merely bringing a project to its completion? Then earth is the element for you. Bankers, miners, and construction workers represent the kind of people who live especially earthy lives, although since everyone has a body and uses money in daily life, everyone works with this most hardnosed of elements. Invoke the energies of Earth whenever you want to cultivate more stability and security in your life.

Have You Ever Known a Gnome?

Earth spirits are called gnomes. They are small, stocky beings who dwell in subterranean passages and who have a particular affinity for precious gems and minerals. Remember that these are magical spirits, so they can appear in many different forms. When working with the energies of the element earth, many pagans find it useful to envision the community of gnomes.

The king of the earth spirits is named Ghob, and the archangel of the element earth is Uriel.

An Earth Meditation

This brief meditation can help you connect with the energies of Earth. Since Earth is a yin element, this is a good meditation to do in darkness or at least in subdued lighting. Return to your favorite place for meditating, either indoors or out; wherever you choose to do this exercise, find a large rock or crystal that you can hold or place in front of you to set your hands on. Sit in a comfortable position facing north.

Close your eyes and take several deep breaths, allowing your body to relax while you hold (or touch) the stone. Allow your mind's eye to see a rich forest green filling your entire field of inner vision. In the center of the green, visualize a downward pointing triangle with a horizontal line in its center. This triangle is the doorway that opens into the realm of earth. When ready, imagine yourself stepping through the door into the deep, subterranean home of the gnomes. As you move into the elemental realm, it may feel as if you've stepped into a cave—cold, dark, and silent. Imagine that the rock or crystal you are holding gives forth a ghostly light that enables your eyes to adjust to the darkness. As your eyes adjust, you become aware of a presence—the gnome, the spirit of the earth. Visualize the gnome and pay attention to its form; it may appear as a stocky little person or perhaps in some other form. For that matter, it may come to you simply as a "presence" within the earth. Listen for any words it may have to share with you and ask any questions you may have about the element of earth and its power. Take as long as you want to connect with the wisdom of the gnome. When the time comes, say good-bye and imagine yourself returning through the triangle to your ordinary self, sitting in meditation.

Open your eyes when it feels right to do so. Give yourself the time you need to record your impressions in your journal.

Spirit, the Fifth Element

The four elements represent the four states of matter and energy: solids, liquids, gasses, and pure energy. As such, they cover the entire sweep of physical reality. But there's still the fifth element: Spirit. This is the life force, the God and Goddess and all other beings, whether with or without a physical body.

Spirit is the quintessence (literally, the "fifth essence") that holds the other elements together. This is where the word "quintessential" comes from. To symbolize the relationship between spirit and the elements, many pagans rely on one of the most recognizable symbols of magic: the pentagram.

EarthWords

A **pentagram** is a five-pointed star. A pentagram inscribed by a circle is called a pentacle.

The Pentagram: Uniting the Five Elements

The *pentagram* is probably the symbol most associated with paganism. It is a magical symbol that is much loved by ceremonial magicians and also by witches, and by extension, it has become part of general neopagan symbolism even though some forms of paganism (like druidism and shamanism) don't really use the pentagram in their rituals.

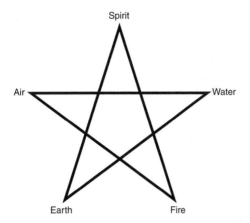

The pentagram with elemental correspondences.

The five points of the pentagram stand for the four elements in relation to the fifth element of spirit. The top point of the pentagram stands for spirit as the most important of these energies. From spirit, the elements manifest in this order: fire, air, water, and finally earth, the most dense and "manifest" of all the elements. If you trace the path of the line that forms the pentagram, beginning at the top with Spirit and moving down toward the bottom right, you'll find that the line follows this progression: spirit—fire—air—water—earth. See the illustration of the pentagram with its elemental correspondences.

The Magic of the Elements: Weaving the Energies Together

Now that you've learned about the four elements and the qualities associated with each one, let's consider how they work together. Of course, future chapters will look at ritual in more detail, and you'll be consciously interacting with each elemental energy, but for now, let's take a beginning look at how they fit together.

> ### Drumbeats
>
> If you're a Harry Potter fan, you can see the different energies of the four elements by comparing the four houses at Hogwarts. Griffindor (the house where Harry and his friends live) is known for its courage, thereby corresponding with the element water. Slytherin (the home of Harry's nemesis, Draco) is known for ambition, thereby corresponding with the element fire. Hufflepuff, known for its loyalty, corresponds with the element earth, and Ravenclaw, known for its intellectual prowess, corresponds with the element air.

Each element complements the other three. Each one represents a different direction, a different color, a different personality type, and a different time of day, season, and phase of life.

Ideally, as a well-balanced person, you would have the energies of all four elements in your life. Air would provide you with mental skill and clear communication, fire would give you self-confidence and passion, water would deepen your emotional sensitivity and intuitive skill, and earth would involve being healthy, physically fit, and financially stable.

Paganism is a path of growth and healing. Look at the four elements. Which of them represent areas of your life where you need to grow or heal? Answering this question can help you determine which element you may want to feature more prominently in your life. If you need to sharpen your intellectual skills, you may want to meditate on the color yellow and burn incense as part of your rituals. If you want more ambition and courage, meditate on red and burn candles to bring fire into your spiritual life. If you yearn for deeper psychic skill or sensitivity, meditate on blue and spend time with water (either indoors or out). If you seek greater health, stamina, or even just a bigger bank account, crystals and the color green may be the areas for your focus.

> **Oracle**
>
> There's much more to learn about the elements and how they can play an important part in your spiritual practice. One helpful book is Margie McArthur's *Wisdom of the Elements: The Sacred Wheel of Earth, Air, Fire and Water.*

The Least You Need to Know

- Many pagans find the lore surrounding the four classical elements of air, fire, water, and earth to be helpful in their quest for a more spiritual relationship with the Goddess.

- The fifth element, spirit, can be seen as the power that holds the other elements together.

- The pentacle, or five-pointed star, symbolizes the connection between spirit, fire, air, water, and earth.

Chapter 12

Going in Circles

In This Chapter

- The rhythm of the pagan cycle
- Is there recycling after death?
- Pagan perspectives on paradise
- Why reincarnation makes sense to pagans
- Paganism and life's big questions

To most pagans, one of the most important ways to understand life, nature, the universe, and spirituality is through the simplest of geometric shapes: the circle. A circle can be a powerful tool for understanding the mysteries of life and death, the nature of time and space, the rhythms of the earth, and the meaning and purpose of ritual.

So, in this chapter, we'll be going in circles. When most people say they're going in circles, it has a negative connotation, as if they're not making any progress. Pagans see circles differently. To a pagan, a circle can be as small as the pupil of your eyes or as large as the universe itself. Going in circles is not negative; rather, it's a description of the way things really work. This chapter will especially consider how life itself is a circle—even when we die, we just continue to move along the great cycle of life.

Nature: The Ultimate Teacher

Before we go any further, let's remind ourselves that, for most pagans, nature is the ultimate teacher. In other words, when we talk about circles or cycles of life or anything similar, let's be thinking in terms of what we can see in the world around us. If something makes sense from a natural perspective, it probably can help us to understand spirituality better as well.

Small Cycles, Big Cycles, Eternal Cycles

The cycles of nature begin with the beating of your heart. The heart is a primal drum, pounding the eternal rhythm of life itself. Dancing alongside the drum of your heart is the silent, slower pulse of the respiratory system. The lungs are the bellows of life, taking in and recycling the nurturing power of oxygen. Our bodies are precision instruments based on the logic and mechanics of rhythm.

> **Oracle**
>
> The rhythm of the breath contains within itself the fundamental energies of yin and yang. Breathing in is a yin process of receptivity and nurture, while breathing out is a fundamental act of trust, a yang process of giving back to the universe.

> **Drumbeats**
>
> Aside from the circle, another symbol popular among pagans is the spiral. Like a circle, it is rhythmic and nonhierarchical, but it also symbolizes movement and transformation. Many Wiccans and other pagans love to dance in a spiral during rituals, a practice that gave its name to one of the most popular introductory books on the craft, Starhawk's *The Spiral Dance*.

The next rhythm we see involves the endless round of day and night. Like a steady drumbeat, sunlight strikes the atmosphere, filling the sky with a luminous iridescence. Then the sun sets and the rich darkness of the universe settles over our horizon for another night.

Then there's the cycle of the moon. Each month (29.5 days to be more precise), the moon goes through a cycle of phases based on how the moon appears from the earth in relation to the sun. A waxing moon appears as a crescent that each night gets slightly fatter and fatter until the moon is full. Then the moon wanes, losing a little bit of its light each night until it is once again a crescent. Finally, the moon disappears from the night sky altogether and is called a new moon. The new moon begins to wax again, and the monthly cycle repeats itself.

Finally, there is the annual cycle of the four seasons. Spring, summer, winter, and fall—each season represents a different time of the year based on where the earth is in its yearly orbit around the sun. Through winter and spring, days gradually get longer and nights shorter until the summer solstice arrives, after which, through summer and fall, the days get shorter and the nights longer. Finally, winter solstice arrives, and the cycle repeats itself.

Because of all these rhythms and cycles, most pagans think it makes more sense to talk about life, time, and other important elements of existence in terms of cycles. For pagans, life is not a linear process of getting from point A (birth) to point B (death); rather, it's a cyclical process that occurs within all the great rhythms of nature.

Nature: The Ultimate Recycler

All this talk about cycles and rhythms is great, but what happens when the cycle comes to a halt? In other words, what happens after we die?

> **Drumbeats**
>
> The phases of the moon and the seasons of the year parallel one another. The new moon corresponds to winter solstice, and the full moon corresponds to summer solstice. The waxing moon corresponds to days getting longer, while the waning moon corresponds to days getting shorter.

When most people grapple with this question, they get so involved with the fate of the soul (Do we go to heaven? Do we reincarnate? Do we just lose consciousness forever?) that they ignore what is obvious from the point of view of nature and the body. No one can see or measure the soul, so no one can speak with final authority about its fate after death. But we can see the body, and from its fate, perhaps we can guess about the fate of the soul.

The body, simply put, gets recycled. Every part of the body—from the air in the lungs to the moisture in the blood stream and cell structure to the calcium in the bones—gets recycled in the natural processes of the earth. Of course, in modern times, our culture, which is insanely afraid of death, has taken to pumping the body full of disgusting chemicals that hinder the natural process of decay. Ironic, isn't it? We treat our bodily remains after death the same way we're treating the entire earth ecosystem. In other words, we're filling it with chemicals and pollutants that aren't

> **Drumbeats**
>
> In some parts of England, "green" cemeteries have been established with ecological principles in mind. Bodies are buried in biodegradable coffins, and instead of a headstone, a tree is planted to mark the person's final resting place. Let's hope this idea catches on!

environmentally friendly, but we do it anyway because we think it makes us feel better. But an embalmed body does nothing for anybody except interrupt nature's normal processes.

If a body doesn't get embalmed and locked up in a concrete vault, what naturally happens is … recycling. From organisms that accelerate the process of decay to the gradual breakdown of the body's fluids and minerals back into the soil and water and atmosphere of the earth, death is a radical giving-back to the earth. It's almost as if the soul says to Mother Earth, "Here, take all this water and minerals back. I don't need them any more."

The recycling, of course, means that the material remains of a dead body become nutrients for other life forms, whether it's the bacteria that cause the decay or the plants that are nourished by the soil in which the body is buried. From there, these life forms in turn nourish other life forms and so on and so forth. All of nature operates in a grand cycle of birth, life, death, and decay, and organisms that die then nourish other life forms. And on and on it goes. Recycling: It's nature's way.

So What About the Soul?

I hope the preceding section didn't give you the creeps too much. Meanwhile, you may be wondering, "Okay, so it's nature's way to recycle a body after it dies. But still, what about the soul? What happens to consciousness when there's no body left in which it can reside?"

As I said before, we can't see or measure the soul (yet), so there's no absolutely certain answer to this question. But given that nature tends to be reasonably consistent in how she does things, most pagans assume that if the body is recycled, so is the soul.

And that's what we call reincarnation.

Beyond the idea that it parallels the way nature recycles the body, pagans generally accept reincarnation because of how universal belief in reincarnation is. Many Westerners think reincarnation is some sort of exotic Eastern concept that only Hindus and Buddhists believe in. Well, they're about half right. Not only is reincarnation widely accepted in the East, there is a long history of belief in reincarnation in the West as well. Julius Caesar remarked that Celtic warriors were so fierce because they didn't fear death—and they didn't fear death because they believed so strongly in reincarnation. Great philosophers like Plato and Pythagoras believed in reincarnation, and even in the Jewish mystical school known as Kabbalah there has been some acceptance of soul recycling. Even some Christians, including the great third-century theologian Origen, accepted reincarnation.

> ### Drumbeats
>
> People who oppose belief in reincarnation say that we have one lifetime to choose whether we are good or bad and then God will judge us accordingly. Most pagans consider this to be evidence that some people believe in a harsh, abusive God. If God really wanted people to be good, wouldn't he give them every possible opportunity to learn from their mistakes and choose the right path? Of course, he would. That's why pagans generally accept reincarnation: It suggests that Spirit (the God and the Goddess) gives us all the time and lessons we need to grow into our full magnificence—even if it takes an eternity of lifetimes!

Recycling after death, whether of the body or the soul, is just one more example of the fundamental cyclical nature of the universe in which we live. See why the circle is such a powerful image for pagans? As pagans see it, it's the symbol that explains, better than anything else, how the universe really works.

The Summerland: The Ultimate Pagan Vacation Spot

So where do we go after we die? Many cultures have different ways of describing what comes after mortality. From the *Tibetan Book of the Dead* to Celtic images of a land of eternal youth, culture after culture has proclaimed the promise of a world to come.

In other words, this process of soul recycling isn't just a matter of going to sleep in an old body and then waking up at some later date as a baby. What a shock that would be! Instead, culture after culture has proclaimed the existence of what the Welsh called "the Summerland"—a paradise of rest and renewal where souls go to charge their batteries, so to speak, in between incarnations.

A Brief Tour of the Afterlife

So what is the Summerland like? Once again, it's hard to say, because everybody who has come back from it comes as a baby who has forgotten the experience. But pagans believe we have encoded in our souls memories of the otherworldly paradise, memories that crop up in culture after culture as mythological depictions of heaven or paradise. So let's look at what some different cultures around the world have had to say about this ultimate destiny.

Tir na n'Og

Tir na n'Og is Irish for "the land of the young." According to Irish myth, this paradise exists over the waters to the west (or underground—remember that exact locations for otherworld sites are hard to come by) as a land where disease and suffering are unknown, where shimmering waves crash on beautiful shores and lovely, heroic women and men enjoy the blessings of eternal youth. To get to this heavenly island, those who die are escorted by the God Manannan to the Island of the Apples, where a feast is served. Eating the apples from this island confers eternal life.

The Elysian Fields

Greek myth doesn't have the happiest concept of the afterlife, with Hades ruling a dark underworld populated by ghostly spirits. But do not despair: Mortals who live worthy lives

Oracle

The movie *What Dreams May Come* explores ideas about the afterlife similar to what many pagans believe. According to the story, everyone is responsible for creating his or her own heaven (or hell); individuals can stay in paradise as long as they wish and then reincarnate when ready. Hell is not a place of eternal punishment from which there is no escape, but a karmic manifestation of the consequences of making unloving choices.

find a home in the Elysian Fields, a place of shimmering sunlight and sensual pleasure. Like the Celtic Island of the Apples, Elysium is a place of feasting, parties, and joy.

Valhalla

If you're a peacenik pagan, Valhalla may not exactly appeal to you, but to the sturdy, stocky, tough-as-nails warriors of Norse myth and legend, this paradise for Gods and great warriors was as fine an afterlife as one could imagine. Not only did the brave and valiant heroes of northern lands feast and make merry in this glorious setting, they would regularly don their armor and hack at each other just for fun! Hey, if combat is your thing, why not go to an afterlife setting where someone's always up for a good knockdown drag-out fight?

The Happy Hunting Grounds

This concept of the otherworldly paradise comes from Native American societies that were particularly oriented toward hunting. If the inhabitants of Valhalla loved to fight in their Summerlands, the inhabitants of the happy hunting ground enjoy a bounteous land where there's always plenty of game and fish. The theme of the happy hunting ground is abundance, and even if work is required, it's a joyful work—*happy* hunting.

You Reap What You Sow

A common theme among different cultures is that a happy home awaits us after death—that is, if we're worthy. Although pagans don't believe in any sort of divine judgment, that doesn't mean paganism is some sort of spiritual free ride where anything goes without consequence. The concept of worthiness as a requirement for enjoying paradise is linked to the notion of karma, another important aspect of the cyclical nature of reality. As you saw in Chapter 6, "Other Pieces of the Pagan Puzzle," karma involves the concept of the wheel of destiny. Put in simpler terms, karma means, "You reap what you sow."

When pagans of old spoke of the afterlife as being dark and shadowy (like Hades's underworld) or as being sunny and joyous (like the Elysian Fields), this is not a matter of some God arbitrarily deciding who gets rewarded and who gets punished. On the contrary, the idea of karma states that we create our own reality, both here and in the afterlife. In other words, if you want a happy afterlife—not to mention a pleasant "job assignment" with your next incarnation—you are 100-percent responsible for making it happen. You do this by living according to principles of justice, fairness, honor, and most of all love and nonharm.

The Ultimate Justice Program

In our imperfect world, justice is handled poorly (if at all). Many people get away with murder (literally), while others wind up in prison just because they happened to be at the wrong place at the wrong time. Especially in the United States, our "justice" system (which is really a punishment system) unfairly targets minorities and the poor. Even when a person really deserves to be imprisoned for doing something wrong, what does he or she get? Time in a facility where prisoners either are abused or are schooled by their peers in how to be an even better criminal.

Karma suffers from none of these faults. You can keep your dirty deeds secret from everybody, but the forces of karma know what's up. It's important to remember, however, that *karma is not a system of punishment*. It is a system of justice. In other words, karma sets up future circumstances that redress our wrongs and reward our good deeds. Here's one way to look at it: Think of the universe as an ultra-fine-tuned precision instrument. Whenever someone does something wrong, it throws the instrument out of balance. Karma is the force that brings all things back into balance. Of course, this means that some form of compensation needs to occur. If you do something wrong, you get to clean up the mess. You don't get punished, but you aren't let off the hook, either.

Instant Karma: The Ultimate Incentive

You might think, what good is karma? If I do bad things but don't face the consequences of my actions for another lifetime or two, won't I just keep doing more harm, at least this go round? And if I do good, what's the point if I won't enjoy any benefits for lifetimes to come?

Taboo!

Don't assume that paganism is "easier" than other religions just because pagans don't believe in an eternal hell. Religions that believe in hell say that if a person obeys his or her God, he will be spared from punishment. Paganism, on the other hand, maintains that you remain responsible for your karma no matter what God you worship! But karma is based on fairness and justice, never punishment.

EarthWords

Instant karma is more than just an old song by John Lennon. It's actually a term referring to karmic energy that gets worked out in the same lifetime as the deed(s) that created the karma. In other words, every time you deal with the consequences of your actions before you die, you've experienced the force of instant karma.

Ah, no one said karma only influences the distant future. One important element of karma is often overlooked: the force of *instant karma*. This is karma that shapes your current life, not some future incarnation. In other words, you face the consequences of your actions, whether good or bad, in the same lifetime as the actions themselves.

Obviously, instant karma is a powerful incentive to clean up your act (or keep doing the good stuff) now. When an alcoholic loses his job or marriage, that's instant karma at work. When a philanthropist gets a reward from the government for her good deeds, that's a bit of instant karma as well. Karma is always at work in our lives. Remember that karma is the force of destiny by which our actions shape our future. Future, however, could mean the next few minutes or 500 lifetimes from now.

The Psychology of Reincarnation

It's important to emphasize that reincarnation and karma involve justice, not punishment. For many people, the model of the afterlife presented to them as children involved an angry God who punishes sinners for the slightest of misdeeds. This way of seeing things can feel terrifying to a child and can even unsettle an adult. Pagans believe that such talk of hellfire and damnation is a form of religious abuse in which those who make their living as religious clergy have basically scared people into being obedient (and financially generous) churchgoers.

> **Drumbeats**
>
> Paganism is optimistic. Rather than focusing on some divine judge who tells us if we're good or not, pagans emphasize each person's unique ability to create the circumstances of his or her own life. No matter how bad things are, your attitude and choices can make them better. Your good choices will benefit you not only now but in future lifetimes as well.

Punishment is a linear process. You do something wrong; you get punished. It all happens in a line. This is why mainstream notions of heaven and hell are so scary: If you go to hell, you're stuck there forever. Reincarnation, by contrast, is cyclical. What goes around comes around. Instead of getting punished for our misdeeds, we do what is necessary to put things back into balance. No eternal punishment. Of course, there's no eternal reward either, but there is the promise of growth and evolution over the course of many lifetimes.

Psychologically speaking, reincarnation removes the "fear of God" as a factor of life. In its place are the energies of trust and love: trusting that our deeds, whether good or bad, shape our future and therefore trusting that we are always capable of making good choices that will lead to a better tomorrow. Love, meanwhile, is at the heart of all good choices, which in turn lead to the bliss of a happy sojourn in the afterlife before reincarnating in a positive new cycle.

The Cosmic Amusement Park

Since pagans don't believe in everlasting punishment, they don't see the world as some sort of mighty testing ground where the sheep and the goats get divided up for all eternity. Instead, pagans believe that the world exists, among other reasons, for the sheer pleasure of existence. From sex to chocolate to a cold shower on a hot day, life is filled with countless pleasures, large and small. Since pagans believe "harm none and do what you will," part of the joy in living is getting to sample the many pleasures of existence.

Think of the universe as a cosmic amusement park. Yes, that's a silly image, but it's not all that inaccurate when considering the pagan view of things. We get to have fun, and it's okay. We don't have to cower before some angry-parent-God who only is concerned about whether or not we're good enough. We get to relax into life and exult in its many joys.

> **Oracle**
>
> Next time you say that something is silly, here's something to keep in mind. The word "silly" comes from the ancient word *selie*, which means spiritually blessed or happy. Perhaps silliness is a spiritual virtue. After all, the Charge of the Goddess calls us to have mirth as well as reverence within us. Pagans believe in having fun!

The Cosmic Classroom

Among the many pleasures of life is the pleasure of learning. It is a joy to master a new skill, to develop new insight, to learn better ways to relate to others or to understand oneself. So more than just a cosmic funhouse, the universe can be seen as a cosmic university (pun intended) where life itself is the course of study. Everyone we meet becomes a teacher or a resource person. We learn, we study, and we grow as part of the grand cycles of life.

This ties in with the "harm none" aspect of the Wiccan Rede you learned about in Chapter 4, "Wicked Good!" In our quest for the pleasures of life, inevitably we make mistakes, and somebody (sometimes our own self) gets hurt in the process, which takes away from life's pleasure. So we are all involved in the intricate process of learning how to maximize love, pleasure, and joy while minimizing pain, suffering, and harm. That alone is a challenge that could keep all of us going for many lifetimes! Then add to that the philosophical lessons to learn: What is the meaning of life? What is the nature of love? How can I know the Goddess and the God more closely? You can see that the cosmic classroom will keep us occupied for eternity.

The Big Questions

This chapter began by considering how pagans see the world and nature in terms of cycles, but it has expanded to become a rather philosophical chapter that has looked at some of the "big questions." Here are a few of the biggest of the big:

◆ What is the meaning of life?

◆ What happens after we die?

◆ Why is there suffering in the world?

◆ Can we truly know love (or God and the Goddess)?

EarthWords

Orthodox means "correct teaching." It refers to the officially accepted beliefs of a religion. A heretic is, literally, "one who chooses," which implies someone who has chosen a path that deviates from the orthodox straight and narrow.

Such questions are the natural purview of religion and spirituality. Pagans, however, don't need to have one ultimate truth. After all, the universe we live in is so vast and diverse and teeming with different life forms and cultures that most pagans assume the "truth" can be described in many different ways, with many different ideas and concepts used to answer the big questions. So for pagans, it really is okay if people have different ways of understanding or answering these questions. It doesn't mean that one person is "right" and the other "wrong" or that one person is *orthodox* and the other a *heretic*. Since pagans don't believe in a punishing God or an eternal hell, there is no reason to worry if people have differing views on life. Instead of trying to prove what's right and what's not right, we can approach the big questions like scientists, doing research and study to try and come up with answers that make the most sense, most of the time.

Lessons and Love

Having said all this, let me share my personal opinion on what, in pagan terms, the meaning of life might be. To do this, I'll quote my favorite poet, William Blake (who is said to have been a druid priest), from his *Songs of Innocence:*

> *And we are put on earth a little space*
> *That we may learn to bear the beams of love.*

I believe that life is about learning and love. I also think Blake put a fabulous pun in this poem because the "beams" could be heavy like a wooden beam or light as a sunbeam. In other words, sometimes the lessons of life are truly hard, but other times they're easy as can be. We've signed up for the ride, and we'll get both kinds of lessons. But always, the goal is love. This can mean the love of our own selves, the love of others (whether family, friends, strangers, or sexual/romantic partners), and the love of nature and of the Gods. There are many ways to love, many objects of love. We are here for a time to learn to bear love's beams.

Life for the Sheer Joy of It

For me, seeing life as a grand lesson in love is much more joyful than seeing it as some sort of test to determine how high the temperature will be for me once I've died. Love, after all, is related to joy. So when we focus on love in life, I believe we also open ourselves up to deeper and more lasting joy.

To bring this all full circle (this *is* a chapter about nature's cycles, you know), let's remember what the most popular symbol of love is in our culture: the heart. From Cupid's arrow that pierces a young lover's heart to a box of candies shaped like one, the heart as a symbol is synonymous with love. The heart, as we saw at the beginning of this chapter, is the pump that keeps our lifeblood flowing in an ongoing cycle. With the beating of the heart, we have the most fundamental rhythm of all. As babies in our mother's wombs, we listened to her beating heart and the pulse of her blood as it swirled around us. So even love is, ultimately, related to cycles and rhythms. Anyone who has ever been in love understands this: Lovers quarrel and make up, go through dry spells and times of intense passion, and experience ups and downs in their journey together. Love, too, is built on cycles and rhythms.

After all, it's only natural.

The Least You Need to Know

- Since nature is cyclical, pagans believe spirituality works in cycles as well.
- The cycles of life can be felt in a heartbeat or in the lungs' breath, and they also show up in the rhythms of day and night, the phases of the moon, and the seasons of the year.
- Because the body is recycled after death, most pagans believe the soul is recycled, too, in the process of reincarnation.
- Because pagans believe in reincarnation and karma, life is seen not as a test but as a joyful experience with pleasures and lessons to learn.

Part 3

Ritual

Ritual plays an essential role in spirituality throughout the world. From the Catholic Mass to the Hindu Puja to the Jewish Passover Seder, ceremonial observance is a central feature of the human quest for meaning.

Pagans are no exception. True to their reverence for nature, most pagans perform rituals to observe and honor the changing of the seasons or the phases of the moon. Pagan rituals can serve a variety of functions, from simply honoring the Goddess and the God, to seeking blessings or healing for those on whose behalf the ritual is performed, to acknowledging important life transitions like birth, marriage, or death. The diversity in pagan ritual mirrors the diversity in paganism itself.

In Part 3, you'll learn about rituals performed in accordance with the solar cycle (involving eight ceremonies over the course of a year) and the lunar cycle (the new and full moons). You'll find out about tools commonly used in rituals and the role of ceremony in marking the major passages of life.

Chapter 13

The Wheel of the Year

In This Chapter

- ◆ How to tell a Sabbat from an Esbat
- ◆ The solstices and the equinoxes
- ◆ The four great Celtic fire festivals
- ◆ The spiritual significance of the moon phases
- ◆ The meaning of the 13 lunar cycles

The preceding chapter briefly touched on how pagans honor the rhythms of nature, including the phases of the moon and the seasons of the year. This chapter takes a closer look at how these two fundamental cycles contribute to the pagan approach to ritual and spiritual observance.

The way time is measured has to do with the relationships between the sun, the moon, and Earth. The day, our most basic unit of time, represents the cycle of Earth spinning on its axis. The concept of the month is related to the phases of the moon, the approximately 29.5-day cycle of new, waxing, full, and waning moons. A year is simply the time it takes Earth to make one full revolution all the way around the sun (traveling a distance of approximately 584 million miles!). This period of time involves the four seasons of spring, summer, winter, and fall.

The two primary forms of ritual for pagans correspond to the cycles of the moon and the sun.

Sabbats and Esbats: Understanding the Two Kinds of Pagan Ritual

The two kinds of pagan rituals are known among Wiccans and many other pagans as Sabbats and Esbats. Sabbats are related to the sun and occur at eight specified times throughout the year. Four of the Sabbats are based on ancient Celtic festivals, and the other four are based on the solstices and equinoxes, which mark the first days of the four seasons. As such, the Sabbats are basically fixed days from year to year, varying at the most only by a day or two.

Esbats, by contrast, are based on the cycles of the moon. Most Wiccans—but some other pagans as well—have a special reverence for the full moon, the new moon, or both. Esbats mark these key days in the lunar cycle. Because the 29.5-day lunar month does not correspond exactly with the 30- to 31-day calendar months, the dates of full and new moons vary considerably from year to year. Thus, there are no fixed days for Esbat celebrations. You'll need a good calendar that shows the phases of the moon (or you could get in the habit of watching the night sky) to know when the next Esbat celebration will be.

> **Oracle**
>
> Although astronomically the seasons begin with the solstices and equinoxes, to pagans, the solstices and equinoxes actually represent the midpoint of each season. So, in pagan terms, winter begins on October 31, and the solstice represents the middle of winter. The same is true for the other seasons: Spring begins on February 2, summer on May 1, and autumn on August 1.

The Yin and Yang of Ritual

The Sabbats and moons (as the Esbats are often called) represent both a masculine and feminine cycle of rituals. The sun, traditionally associated with yang energy by Wiccans and many other pagan groups, represents the masculine cycle. The moon, traditionally associated with yin energy, represents the feminine cycle.

Of course, these yin and yang designations do not apply to every single variety of paganism. Some traditions see the sun as feminine and the moon as masculine. For the purposes of this book, however, I'll stick with the commonly accepted Wiccan understanding.

> **Oracle**
>
> "Esbats" is something of a tongue-twister word. Try saying it three times fast! For this reason, many pagans simply refer to the rituals of full and new moon as "moons." This might not be as fancy or romantic a term, but it's certainly practical.

The dates of the Sabbats and moons all serve to support the nature emphasis of paganism. Solstices, equinoxes, and new and full moons obviously have a connection with events in the natural world. Even the other four Sabbats, however, the ones from Celtic tradition, all have their origin in specific events that occurred in nature.

Let's take a look at the eight Sabbats and how they fit together to form what pagans call the "Wheel of the Year." The following picture of the Wheel of the Year will help you understand this concept. By depicting the year as a circle (much like the path of Earth as it orbits the sun), the eight Sabbats function like spokes on a wheel.

Taboo!

Don't make the mistake of thinking you *must* do ritual to be a good pagan. There is no such thing as required attendance at pagan rites. Some pagan groups may ask members to attend rituals regularly, but that's a group decision, not a religious requirement. Do only the spiritual observances that you find to be meaningful and rewarding. This will keep your spirituality fresh and alive.

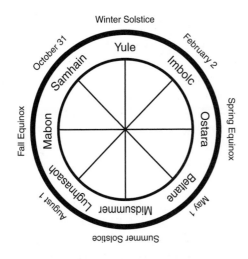

The circle represents Earth's orbit around the sun. Note that the dates given for the Sabbats correspond to the Northern Hemisphere. Pagans in the Southern Hemisphere will need to transpose the dates. (For example, Samhain in the Southern Hemisphere falls on April 30, Yule falls on June 21, and so forth.)

The Cycle of the Sun: The Dark Half

In many traditional cultures, from the ancient Jews to the Celts, a day was thought to begin at sundown. Night and day together formed a single "day." In the pagan ritual year, this same principle applies: The dark or wintry half of the year precedes the light or summery half. To the ancient Celts, there weren't four seasons but merely two: winter (November through April) and summer (May through October). The year began with the onset of winter in November, and thus the first Sabbat was Samhain (pronounced SOW-in), which literally means "summer's end." Most pagans today continue to regard Samhain as the first Sabbat on the Wheel of the Year.

Samhain, or Harvest's End—October 31

Traditionally, Samhain marked the end of harvest. In ancient times, when all the crops had been gathered from the fields, farmers needed to determine whether any of their livestock were too weak to survive the winter. The weaker animals were then slaughtered to provide meat for the winter. Thus, Samhain was a somber time when summer and harvest both came to an end and death seemed especially near. Over time, Samhain came to be associated with those who have died and was regarded as a time when the veil separating this world from the otherworld was especially thin, enabling living mortals to converse more easily with departed loved ones.

Many ceremonies and festivals came to be associated with this most sacred of pagan nights but always with a theme of ending and new beginnings and/or contact with the dead. After the arrival of Christianity in pagan Europe, this holiday became Christianized as All Saints' Day, in which the dead of the Christian family were venerated. The night before All Saints' Day came to be known as Halloween and continued to be associated in the popular mind with the mysteries of ancient pagan ways.

Yule, or Winter Solstice—Approximately December 21

The onset of winter is marked by the days growing increasingly shorter until finally the shortest day and longest night of the year occur around December 21, the winter solstice. In ancient times, this would have been seen as a bleak time because the sun seemed so far away. Yet it also marks a turning point, for immediately after the solstice the days begin lengthening. So the Sabbat of Yule came to represent the rebirth of the sun. It also marked the time when the Oak King triumphs over the Holly King (see Chapter 9, "All About the God").

This rebirth of the sun means that Yule, despite the darkness of the season, is a time for merriment and rejoicing. It has become a traditional time for exchanging gifts. Some pagans perform rituals at this solstice to "help" the sun return. Others note with a wry sense of humor that Yule has become overshadowed by the Christian holiday of Christmas, which in its own way is a celebration of the birth of the "sun." Indeed, much of the folklore and popular imagery associated with this Christian holiday has its roots in pagan spirituality. From kissing beneath the mistletoe to setting up a Christmas tree to burning a Yule log and decking the halls with boughs of holly, many of the customs connected with this holiday have roots in our ancient pagan past.

> **Drumbeats**
>
> Although carols (songs for the season) are associated primarily with the Christian festival of Christmas, some of them have clearly pagan origins. "Deck the Halls" and "The Holly and the Ivy" are two with strong pagan imagery, even though they eventually were Christianized.

Chapter 9 talked about the Oak King and the Holly King as two different faces of the pagan God. The Oak King rules over the waxing half of the year (when days are lengthening and nights getting shorter) and the Holly King rules the waning half (when days get shorter and nights get longer). Yule represents the time when the Oak King triumphs over the Holly King; with the turning of the solstice, the days begin to get longer. Even though the coldest part of the winter lies ahead, Yule represents the rebirth of the sun and the promise of the eventual return of warmth and light.

Imbolc, or Candlemas—February 2

The ancient Celtic festival of Imbolc (pronounced *IM-molc*) is associated with Brighid, a Goddess deeply loved throughout the Celtic lands. She was a Goddess of poetry, magic, inspiration, and healing. Farm animals and milk were especially sacred to her. Brighid was such a popular Goddess that she survived as a "saint" when Ireland converted to Christianity and was regarded as the "foster mother" of Christ (and since a foster mother feeds a baby with her own milk, this image preserved one of Brighid's most sacred attributes). Historically, Imbolc was celebrated when the pregnant ewes began lactating. The milk of the animals symbolized the coming of spring, so this was truly a time of rejoicing. Winter was receding, the days were noticeably getting longer, and warmth and new fertility lay ahead.

Many folk customs surround this holiday. In Gaelic Scotland, Imbolc was traditionally a woman's holiday, celebrated indoors around the hearth fire. (Fire was an important element of Celtic spirituality.) The women would make corn dolls to symbolize Brighid, the fertile mother, and lay them in specially prepared "Brighid's beds." They would also make wands with a pinecone at the end to symbolize the God whom Brighid takes as her lover. This was especially important for women who were hoping for a new baby.

Imbolc survived in the Christian church as Candlemas, a feast day dedicated to the Virgin Mary (who is as close as the Christian church ever got to honoring the Goddess). Many pagans like to refer to this Sabbat as Candlemas, if for no other reason than it's a pretty name! Of course, the candles associated with this holiday serve as reminders of the ancient use of fire in pagan worship. Because it marks the beginning of spring, Candlemas is considered a day of beginnings. For this reason, it is a popular time in many pagan traditions for initiations.

Drumbeats
In popular culture, Imbolc survives as Groundhog Day. The connection between Imbolc and the beginning of spring lives on in this folksy holiday in which a groundhog forecasts how soon spring will arrive by whether or not it sees its shadow.

Ostara, or Spring Equinox—Approximately March 21

Ostara (pronounced *OH-star-uh*) took its name from the Germanic Goddess of spring, the dawn, and new beginnings. Traditionally, her sacred objects included the egg and the rabbit. Her name can also be spelled Eostre. It doesn't take a rocket scientist to figure out how Ostara has survived in Christianity. The Christian festival that celebrates Jesus's resurrection from the dead is known as Easter, a holiday that takes its name from a pagan Goddess. Easter customs include coloring eggs and telling children the story of a bunny that will bring them sweets. It's interesting to note how ancient pagan traditions survived into modern culture, even after Christianity became the mainstream religion. Of course, today's pagans often reclaim these ancient customs, only within the context of nature spirituality.

For pagans, the vernal (spring) equinox continues Imbolc's themes of new beginnings and new birth. Obviously, it is related to the agricultural cycle of sowing and planting seeds. It is also a time of balance because day and night are equal in length on this date. This equinox symbolizes not only the beginning of the new growing season but also the culmination of the dark half the year. In ritual terms, this is a good time for celebrating balance and equilibrium while resolving to nurture all the "seeds" that have been planted in the preceding dark half of the year. Even modern urban pagans who don't plant crops still have projects and plans in their lives; this Sabbat is a time for celebrating such endeavors and asking for spiritual blessings upon them.

The Cycle of the Sun: The Light Half

After the spring equinox comes the light half of the year.

From the perspective of agriculture, all the hard work of tilling and planting now begins in earnest, as farmers begin the work that will bear fruit in the fall harvest season. Even for pagans who live in cities and don't directly work with the land, this is still the time of year in which projects are nurtured to fruition. From the fertility rites of Beltane through to the triumph of the Holly King at the summer solstice and on to the Sabbats that celebrate the harvest, this is the time of completion and celebration.

Beltane, or May Day—May 1

Beltane (pronounced *BEL-tane*), named after the sun God Belenos, marked the beginning of the summer season, when Celtic farmers took their livestock out to pasture. In ancient Ireland, this festival began with the lighting of two great bonfires. The livestock would be driven between the fires as a ritual of cleansing and fertility.

As the third of the great Celtic fire festivals, Beltane occurs halfway around the year from Samhain, and just as Samhain represents the end of summer, this festival represents the beginning. Even for modern pagans who see the year as divided into four seasons, this is a joyful time of celebrating the arrival of the hottest of the seasons.

Beltane is the happiest and friskiest of the Sabbats. In ancient times, the focus of this Sabbat was fertility, and people would take this literally, often spending the night out in the fields, making love to energetically rouse the fertility of the land. Among modern urban pagans, the theme of fertility can still be meaningful, not only in a literal sense for those who want to have babies but in a symbolic sense for people who are working toward manifesting something new in their lives.

Beltane survived in Christian times as May Day, a secularized festival of the coming of spring. Perhaps the most familiar May Day ceremony involves the Maypole dance, in which young couples dance around a beautiful pole, weaving ribbons together to decorate it. The fertility origins of this festival survive in the phallic symbolism of the pole (the God) penetrating the soil of the earth (the Goddess).

Oracle

A modern Beltane custom derives from the ancient practice of driving livestock between the fires. Light your own Beltane bonfire (safely), take your sweetheart's hand in yours, and run together and jump over the fire. While jumping, think of whatever it is you wish to manifest in your life. But be careful—don't think about fertility and babies unless you really want one!

Midsummer, or Summer Solstice—Approximately June 21

Halfway around the Wheel of the Year from Yule is Midsummer, or the summer solstice. Because in pagan reckoning summer actually begins with Beltane, it makes sense to think of the solstice as summer's midpoint.

We don't have much information about how the ancients celebrated Midsummer. But considering that Stonehenge was oriented toward the sunrise on the summer solstice, it's apparent that the ancients considered this a pivotal day.

Modern pagans celebrate Midsummer as a time when the Goddess is swollen with her "pregnancy" as the crops grow onward through the hot and languid days toward maturity. The Oak King, who governs the waxing of the year, is now

Drumbeats

William Shakespeare's *A Midsummer Night's Dream* is filled with magic, fairies, and sprites, thereby keeping alive the ancient pagan belief that it was easier than usual to communicate with the otherworld on the Sabbats.

defeated by the Holly King, who oversees the waning year. The sun that was reborn at Yule is now reaching its zenith, but with the solstice, the days begin to get shorter. This is a time of celebrating the imminent harvest but also recognizing the cyclical nature of life in that the dark time of the year will surely come again.

Lughnasadh, or the Beginning of Harvest—August 1

Lughnasadh (pronounced *LOO-nuh-suh*) literally means "Lugh's festival" and is named after one of the great Irish Gods. This festival may be thought of as the Celtic Olympics because, in ancient Ireland, it lasted an entire month and involved sporting competitions to celebrate the beginning of harvest. Even after the coming of Christianity, this festival survived as Lammas (to celebrate the baking of the first loaves of bread from the new grain), and in the British Isles it survived into modern times as Harvest Home.

In some traditions, sacrifice is the theme of this festival because the harvest is a sacrifice the God makes to feed the children of the Goddess. As the Corn King, the God now lays down his life so that the grain may be "killed" (harvested) that others may live. This somber element of Lughnasadh reminds us that our lives depend on the bounty of nature.

When celebrating Lughnasadh, light a bonfire or some other form of fire to honor the life-giving spirit of the earth. If at all possible, bake a loaf of bread. Give thanks for the fruits you are harvesting in your own life, whether literally or symbolically.

Mabon, or Fall Equinox—Approximately September 21

The harvest continues, and the days grow shorter. Finally, the festival of Mabon (named after a Welsh God) arrives, the opposite of the spring equinox. Like Ostara, this is a time when day and night are of equal length, but the light will soon surrender to the growing dark. This is a festival that celebrates getting the job done. What is unfinished in your life? What needs to be "harvested" before it's too late? These are the areas to focus on at this festival.

After Mabon, the days continue to grow shorter until finally harvest is done and it is time to celebrate another Samhain. And so, the great Wheel of the Year keeps turning.

The Cycles of the Moon

The sun, symbolically speaking, represents the yang energies in time: the energies of force, of power, of activity and assertion. These are the energies that are "out there" in the world, making a visible impact in the manifest world. Remember, however, that yang dances with yin. In terms of the cycles of time, this means that the sun dances with the moon. So, for pagans, the lunar cycles represent the darker, more mysterious, receptive, encompassing, and deeply intuitive yin qualities. These are the energies of magic; of rest, renewal, and transformation; of healing and wisdom, quiet and contemplation; and of the great Goddess in her aspects of maiden, mother, and crone.

Of all the various types of pagans, Wiccans are the most likely to honor the moon. Indeed, Wicca tends to place the moon above the sun, just as it sees the Goddess as "first among equals" in relation to the God. You don't have to be Wiccan, however, to appreciate and benefit from the rhythms of the moon. The profound symbolism of the nocturnal light that waxes and wanes over the course of a month can be inspiring to pagans of any stripe.

Taboo!

Just because the moon reflects light from the sun doesn't mean that, spiritually speaking, the sun is more important. To pagans, moonlight has its own magical energy.

Here's a look at some of the symbolism of the moon. You'll notice that, in some ways, it parallels the solar cycle. Remember, however, that in the solar cycle, concepts such as "planting," "nurturing," "harvesting," and "resting" are understood in more external ways (how these energies manifest in the world), whereas in the lunar cycle, these same energies are cultivated in the inner world, deep within the interior landscape of our own conscious and subconscious minds.

New Moon

Each lunar cycle begins at a time when the sun and the moon occupy more or less the same position in the sky. But because the moon revolves around the earth at a different rate than the earth spins, over the course of about 29.5 days, the moon seems to move around the earth in relation to the sun. Thus, at the beginning of the lunar cycle, the moon is basically invisible because it is in the sky at the same time as the sun, and the brilliance of the sun hides it from view. Two weeks later, however, the moon rises as the sun sets and therefore appears fully illuminated in the night sky because it reflects light from the sun back to the earth. Another two weeks go by, and the cycle renews itself.

At the moment the lunar cycle begins, the moon is said to be "new." Basically invisible to the human eye, the new moon is a time for rest and renewal.

First Quarter/Waxing Moon

The first two weeks of the lunar cycle are the *waxing* period. At first, the moon appears only as a sliver in the evening sky, setting not long after the sun. Every night the moon appears a bit larger (fatter) and sets later in the evening. One week into the cycle, the moon appears to be about half full. This is the first quarter. From the first quarter, the moon enters its *gibbous* phase until it becomes full.

EarthWords

Waxing means "getting bigger," whereas **waning** means "getting smaller." A waxing moon appears, night after night, to be growing larger; a waning moon appears to be getting smaller over time.

EarthWords _____

Gibbous means "rounded and bulging" and refers to the shape of the moon when it is more than half full but not yet entirely full.

The time of the waxing moon is a time of increase. Magically speaking, it is a time to focus on projects or endeavors you want to grow. Whether it is growing a business, cultivating deeper love for your spouse, or fattening your bank account, if there's something you want more of in your life, the waxing phase of the moon is the time to focus on these goals. Depending on your personal preferences, you might pray, meditate, perform ritual, or work magic to support the increases you seek.

Full Moon

Approximately two weeks into the cycle, the moon appears full in the night sky, rising more or less just as the sun sets and setting in the morning just before the sun rises. Lots of folklore surrounds the full moon; this is when werewolves are said to walk the earth,

Oracle _____

Not only are the phases of the moon a cycle, when the moon is full, it forms a circle in the sky (hence the tendency of most pagan groups to do rituals in a circular space). Once again, the pagan fondness for circles and cycles is based on what may be found in nature.

when babies are more likely to be born, and when accidents more likely to happen. A "lunatic" is someone who is driven crazy by the powerful energies of the full moon.

To pagans, the full moon is not something to be frightened of; it simply represents the peak of energy and, therefore, should be treated with appropriate respect and reverence. Most traditions of witchcraft teach that the full moon is the single best time to perform rituals or magic. Think of the full moon as an energy pipeline between you and the Goddess; as you stand outside basking in that pale light, you are in a special place for seeking healing, transformation, and prosperity.

Like the new moon, the full moon is a turning point. The energies of increase have reached their fullest potential, but now it is time to clear the decks. As soon as the moon reaches her fullest point, she enters the waning phase.

Last Quarter/Waning Moon

Now the moon is getting smaller and smaller with each passing night. The *waning* moon rises later in the night, and toward the end of the cycle, it will rise in the eastern night sky just before the sun appears. This is a time of letting go and releasing, to correspond with the moon's energy of decrease. What in your life do you need to discard or clear away? Is your house cluttered and in need of a good cleaning out? Are you trying to lose weight, reduce debt, or finally end an unhealthy relationship? For any of these goals, seek the energy of the waning moon to support your prayer, meditation, ritual, or magical work.

Finally, the moon disappears in the night sky. Many witches consider this dark phase, before the first sliver of the next new moon, to be the ideal time for profound inner transformation—for releasing of the old, to prepare for the new. With the dark moon, the cycle is complete, but of course every ending is also a beginning.

Significance of the 13 Moons

Each year there are approximately 13 lunar cycles, in other words 13 opportunities to celebrate the full and new moons. In various pagan traditions, different systems exist to explain the spiritual significance of each moon. Here is one way to understand the meaning of the moon. If you work within a specific pagan tradition, the lore surrounding the 13 moons you'll learn could be somewhat different than this.

- **January, the Wolf Moon**   Wolves may howl, but this deep winter moon is a time of contemplation and inner reflection. It is a good time to be planning what you will sow in the coming spring.

- **February, the Storm Moon**   Like Imbolc, this is a time for lighting candles, not bonfires. Honor winter's last few weeks of fury and begin planning new projects (like spring cleaning).

- **March, the Innocent Moon**   The first stirrings of spring are now upon us. Pay special honor to the spirits of nature during this moon, perhaps celebrating it in your garden or yard.

- **April, the Seed Moon**   The name says it all; this is a moon for planting, sowing, or simply setting new projects into motion. Dance for joy at the coming warmth and celebrate beginnings.

- **May, the Hare Moon**   Frisky as the rabbits for which it is named, this is the moon for celebrating sensuality, love, and the power of life. Celebrate your body on this magical night!

- **June, the Dyad Moon**   This is another moon that is especially sacred to fairies and nature spirits. Honor the growth that occurs in the fields, like the swelling of a pregnant woman's belly.

- **July, the** Mead **Moon**   As the crops continue to grow, take time for a mini celebration beneath this moon. Relax, tell stories and jokes, and have fun. Drink a toast to the lady of the night.

- **August, the Corn Moon**   Harvest begins with the first grains of August. This is a time for baking bread, settling old disputes, and preparing for the hard but joyful work of harvesting.

- **September, the Harvest Moon**   This is a time for thanksgiving. The harvest is in full swing, so this moon is a time for acknowledging our abundance and sharing with those in need.

- **October, the Blood Moon** Like the blood shed at Samhain, this is a moon for letting go of what is unnecessary and planning for the cold months to come.

- **November, the Snow Moon** Brrr! As the snows of winter descend upon the land, turn your attention inward. Do divination, exercise your intuitive and psychic skills, and make final preparations for the cold season.

- **December, the Oak Moon** The oak symbolizes strength, so this is a moon for trust during the darkest days of the year. Light a bright fire, tell happy stories, and sing songs of joy.

- **The Blue Moon** This is the "wild card" of moons. It occurs in a calendar month with two full moons; which month varies from year to year. Use it to be spontaneous, do something you've never had the gumption to try, or do whatever else your zaniest imaginings inspire you to do!

Remember that this is just one tradition's way of understanding the significance of the moons. Like most other elements of paganism, different traditions or cultures may have their own way of finding significance in the different lunar cycles. If you want, you can even develop your own system.

Chapter 15, "A Basic Ritual," and Chapter 18, "Magic, or Flexing Your Spiritual Muscles," will go over ritual and magic, two of the most important elements to pagan spirituality. You'll find that the new moons, full moons, and Sabbats are the best times for celebrating a ritual or performing a magical working. But even if you are a solitary pagan and don't want to go to the trouble of setting up an entire ritual or spell, try to keep the Sabbats and moons in mind. With them, you mark the passage of time and the cycle of the seasons. These sacred days can help you be more attuned to the rhythms of nature, which after all is one of the primary goals of the pagan path.

The Least You Need to Know

- Most pagans celebrate days determined by the sun (Sabbats) and by the moon (Esbats).

- The Sabbat cycle consists of eight holidays, including the solstices, equinoxes, and four ancient Celtic festivals.

- Each of the Sabbats has a different meaning with regard to what's going on in nature at that point in the year.

- The lunar cycle involves honoring the phases of the moon, including the mystical new moon and the magical full moon.

- There are approximately 13 lunar cycles each year, and pagans (especially Wiccans) try to honor each one.

Chapter 14

Tools for Ritual

In This Chapter

◆ The basic purpose of tools in pagan ritual

◆ The tools commonly linked to the four elements

◆ Getting in touch with your altar ego

◆ How to prepare tools for ritual use

Different pagan traditions use a variety of tools in their rituals. A ritual tool can be defined as any object, supply, or implement used to make the ritual effective and pleasing, both for its participants and (hopefully) for the Gods as well. Some tools are virtually universal: Candles, incense, water, and fire can be found in rituals not only throughout paganism but in various other religious traditions the world over. Other tools may be specific to one particular pagan lineage.

This chapter provides an introduction to various ritual tools. These tools can make your ritual come alive. Remember, however, that the most important element of a ritual is the spiritual contact between you and the realm of the otherworld. Such contact may be fostered by the use of fancy tools, but the tools ultimately aren't necessary. You can be all by yourself, sitting in front of a tree in the city, and still have a powerful ritual experience. Furthermore, if you get so caught up in using "the right tools" in "just the right way," it can actually sabotage the inner, spiritual aspect of your ritual work. You might be so busy worrying about the tools that you forget about connecting with the Gods! So enjoy learning about the tools, but remember to keep them in perspective.

What Are Tools, and How Are They Used?

For a ritual tool to be effective, it must be the right tool for the intention of the ritual. In pagan ritual, the intention involves revering, honoring, and hopefully communing with the Gods and Goddesses and spirits of nature and the otherworld. Pagans perform rituals to express their love of nature, to find healing and transformation, and simply to celebrate being alive. A ritual tool is anything that can make this process easier or more effective.

Oracle

In the popular imagination, witches, druids, and shamans all use lots of paraphernalia to work their magic. Ritual tools are the items you will use as you develop your spiritual life as a pagan. Just remember, the magic is in you, not the object!

Obviously, since there are so many different ways to express spiritual yearning and the intent to communicate with the divine, there's almost no limit to what can function as a ritual tool. This chapter will focus on some common tools found throughout the pagan world. As you learn more about these ritual items, you'll develop a better understanding of how ritual works and how you can incorporate it into your life to become more closely connected to the Goddess and the other spirits of nature.

Elemental Tools

Let's begin by drawing from the Wiccan tradition the tools associated with each of the elements. Chapter 11, "Elementary, My Dear Pagan!" looked at the power of the elements: air, fire, water, and earth. In ritual, these elemental energies can be symbolized, channeled, and contained by four powerful tools. If you're familiar with a traditional deck of Tarot cards (like the Rider-Waite-Smith deck), these tools will make sense to you—they correspond with the four suits of the Tarot.

EarthWords

An **athame** (pronounced *AH-the-may*) is a black-handled dagger—a double-edged knife—used strictly for ritual or magical purposes. In most pagan traditions, the athame should never be used to cut anything other than magical energy.

The Sword and the Athame

Representing the element air is the sword or its smaller equivalent, the *athame*. They represent not only the element air but also all the magical attributes related to this element, such as learning, discernment, intelligence, communication, and conflict. Most groups have one sword that represents the group as a whole, but each individual participant who has been properly trained and initiated can carry an athame. Wiccans and many other pagans use the ritual blade to focus and direct *psychic energy*, which is used to set up a ritual space. Similarly, the athame is used to dismantle the energy after the ritual is over.

Swords and athames may seem sinister, but there are strict protocols governing their use. They are never to be used to cut material things, only for the spiritual or magical use of cutting energy. Cutting meat or flesh is especially forbidden. In fact, some traditions insist that if an athame comes into contact with blood, it is no longer fit for use as a magical tool.

EarthWords _____

In many pagan traditions, **psychic energy** plays an important role in ritual and magic. This is energy created and directed by the mind as the "fuel" which propels the ritual and gives power to magic. Some traditions create a circle of energy as the boundary of their ritual space.

Oracle _____

Wiccans perform ritual in a sacred circle, an energetically-created boundary "between the worlds." Although this magical circle can be created without any tools, most witches prefer to use an athame to focus and direct the energy used to create the circle's boundary. Other pagans may use different tools to set up their ritual space (as in the sample ritual in Chapter 15, "A Basic Ritual," which uses the tools of the elements to create the circle).

The Wand

Representing the element fire is the wand. Like the sword, this tool can be large or small. It is used in directing the energy of a ritual, but it also is symbolic of the particular characteristics of the element fire, including passion, vigor, enterprising spirit, and sexual energy.

Notice that the sword and wand, as the tools related to the Yang elements of fire and air, are both essentially phallic in nature.

The Chalice

Next are the feminine elements and their tools. The chalice (cup) is associated with the element water and is used to symbolize all that water characterizes, including intuition, fluidity, emotional

Oracle _____

Elemental tools, like any other ritual tool, can be ornate and valuable or simple and inexpensive. Chalices, for example, can be intricately made silver goblets or handmade clay vessels. What you (or your group) use as ritual tools can in large measure be determined as a matter of taste.

power, and love. In some pagan traditions, an altar will have two chalices on it. One is filled with water and represents the element proper, while the other is used as part of the ritual and contains wine, mead, or some other drink that the ritual participants will share.

This priest and priestess are holding the sword, wand, chalice, and pentacle, typical tools to symbolize the four elements.

(© 2001 Fox Gradin)

The Pentacle

The final elemental tool, as found in the Rider-Waite-Smith Tarot and as used by many pagans, is the pentacle, which is a symbol of the element earth. For ritual purposes, the pentacle is often a circular dish, plate, or *paten* with a circle and pentagram engraved or painted on it. This tool represents the energies of its element, including stability, practicality, abundance, structure, and humility.

EarthWords

A **paten** is a metal plate used to hold food in a ritual setting. Catholic and some other Christian churches use patens to hold the communion wafers in their rituals.

Like the chalice, the pentacle represents the yin qualities of receiving, holding, embracing, and accepting. Some pagans may use their altar pentacle as a dish on which to place food to be used in the ritual, although most will have a separate dish for this purpose.

Other Common Wiccan and Pagan Tools

The implements based on the ancient symbolism of the Tarot are just a few of the many possible tools for ritual use. Here are a few more common ritual tools, especially found in Wiccan traditions (but these are also often used by pagans from other traditions).

Incense and Candles

Items commonly used to represent the energies of air and fire include incense and candles. Incense, with its pleasing aroma transmitted through the air, naturally represents that element, while candles just as obviously have a fire connection. Pagans often use a red candle to symbolize fire because red is the color most often associated with that element. Of course, if your tradition associates a different color with that element, you'll want a candle that matches your specific symbolism.

Because incense has a powerful aroma, it's best to use unscented candles. There's no point in having the scent from both incense and a candle competing with one another.

Because many different kinds of incense exist, there's lots of room for creativity and experimentation in your ritual work. You can use a special scent to represent air (frankincense and myrrh have traditionally been associated with this element) or different scents for different Sabbats and Esbats. You can even learn to blend your own unique scent. This can be very powerful; every time you light that special blend of incense, your subconscious mind will be reminded that it's time to do ritual.

Salt and Water

What better symbol for the element of water than … water? As previously mentioned, you can fill a chalice with water to set on your altar. A beautiful shell, bowl, or dish can also hold the water you use to symbolize this element. As for the water itself, try to avoid regular old tap water—if possible, use rainwater or water from a local spring or lake. If that's not available, at least use bottled spring water. Try to use water that is as close to natural as possible. If you collect rainwater or spring water yourself, go ahead and filter it to purify it. You may also want to boil it to remove any impurities. Although altar water is not meant for drinking, you may use it for anointing, so it's good to make sure it's safe.

Salt functions as a beautiful and sacred symbol for the earth element. Once again, find a beautiful dish or bowl in which to keep the "salt of the earth" and use sea salt or non-iodized salt if possible.

Sometimes pagans combine salt and water on their altar to form a cleansing solution that represents the combined energies of water and earth. Likewise, because it takes a flame to light it, incense can be seen as combining the energies of Air and Fire. It can be a lovely process in a pagan ritual to walk around the circumference of the circle first with incense and then sprinkling salt water, to bless and cleanse the circle area with the four elements.

At the end of this chapter, you'll learn a brief mini ritual for *consecrating* your tools. From your altar to the smallest dish of incense, make it a habit to consecrate anything you use in a ritual, no matter how informal the ritual may be. By only using consecrated tools, you add an energy of respect and honor to your spiritual practice. Also, you'll want to keep all your consecrated tools together, either on your altar or in a safe storage place. You'll learn about the important role of the pagan altar shortly.

Oil

Oil is another tool often used in rituals. Like incense, oil comes in countless different fragrances. Oil symbolizes the "fifth element" of Spirit (see Chapter 11). It is especially useful at the beginning of a ritual when you anoint yourself (or the leaders of a ritual anoint the participants) to symbolize cleansing and purification.

As with incense, you or your pagan group may want to blend your own unique fragrance, which can help you subconsciously tune in to the energies of ritual when you use it.

Tools from Other Traditions

All of the tools just discussed originate in ceremonial magic and are commonly used in Wicca, the largest, and most established of the modern pagan religions. But because paganism draws as heavily from shamanism, druidism, and other traditions as it does from Wicca, you may want to incorporate some of these other useful items into your spiritual practice.

The Drum

Thanks to shamanism, drums have become as associated with paganism as the organ is with Christianity. At many pagan gatherings, powerful symphonies of percussion create a throbbing, pulsating soundscape to which pagans will dance and trance the hours away.

Even if you are a solitary pagan creating a single beat on a frame drum, this instrument can greatly contribute to your otherworld journeying and *entrainment* in the rhythms of the Goddess. Probably the best drum to start with is a Native American frame drum, made of a hoop of wood over which skin is tautly pulled to form the drumhead. Using a beater, hit the frame drum in a simple, monotonous beat and then allow your mind to flow with the pulse. It works magic!

From frame drums, you can get really creative. The Irish bodhran and the African djembe are two drums popular among pagans. For a more Middle Eastern rhythm, get a dumbek.

Many pagans get their hands on one or more drums and happily begin pounding away, with no training and only their intuition to guide them. This can be plenty of fun, and rhythm is so powerful that even an untrained drummer can help evoke a trance state. That said, if you feel drawn to drumming, consider taking drum lessons. Not only will you become a better drummer, you'll learn to appreciate the power and versatility of this primal instrument.

EarthWords

Entrainment is the process of changing the body's heartbeat or brain waves to match an external rhythm. Shamanic drumming can entrain brain waves to achieve an altered state of consciousness.

Drumbeats

A frame drum virtuoso named Layne Redmond has done valuable research into the ancient links between drumming, Goddess spirituality, and the priesthood of women. Her book, *When the Drummers Were Women*, should be required reading for all pagans (both men and women!). Check out her CDs, too. Her music is filled with entrancing, danceable beats and rhythms from around the world.

A Druid's Tools

All types of pagan spirituality thrive better outdoors than in, but this is especially true of druidism. This modern revival of Celtic spirituality looks to trees and nature as its "cathedral." Because the ancient druids worshiped in groves called nemetons, most modern druids prefer to take their spirituality out under the blue sky as well. Not surprisingly, the three most important tools for the druid path are all found outdoors.

Druids view three powerful symbols as being central to their spirituality: the fire, the well, and the tree. In many sites in pagan Europe, wells were venerated as holy. Next to these holy wells often were trees on which, to this day, supplicants tie brightly colored pieces of cloth to represent their prayers. As you know from shamanism, the tree symbolizes both the human spine and the axis of the universe and therefore symbolizes the connection between this world and the realms of the otherworld. The well, likewise, suggests a passageway to the underground or underworld abode of the fairies, and in ancient times, offerings of silver or other precious metals often would be thrown into wells.

> **CAUTION**
>
> **Taboo!** _____
>
> Ancient pagans made sacrifices to the Gods by depositing silver or other valuables in wells or rivers. Modern pagans should never do this, even when attempting to worship like the ancestors. Our water supply is so threatened by pollution that you can't afford to risk contamination by throwing any kind of foreign objects into the water. If you want to make offerings, use a bowl to symbolically represent your well.

Miscellaneous—and Optional—Ritual Tools

Here are a few more items you may enjoy using when performing your earth-honoring rituals.

- ◆ **Robe** Pagans like to dress magically for their rituals, and you can, too! Online pagan merchants sell magical robes, or if you're handy with sewing, you can make your own.

- ◆ **Cingulum** The cord you use to tie your robe around your waist is a magical tool in its own right. Wiccans often use a different-colored cingulum for each level of advancement within the craft. For other pagans, the cingulum color can be a matter of personal choice.

- ◆ **Jewelry** From silver pentacles to beautifully cast images of the Goddess or God, jewelry can adorn you not only in your everyday life but in ritual as well. Like anything else you use ritually, however, take the time to consecrate it. (Consecration is discussed later in this chapter.)

- ◆ **Food** Spiritual traditions from around the world incorporate food into their rituals, and paganism is no exception. Something to eat (cake, cookies, or bread) and something to drink (wine, ale, or mead) are both customary parts of ritual. These do not need to be specially consecrated, but it makes sense to bless them as part of the ritual (much like saying grace before a meal).

- ◆ **Book of Shadows** Most traditions of Wicca require you to keep a magical reference book known as a Book of Shadows. Even for most other pagans, having a book of rituals, meditations, and prayers as well as a record of your spiritual journey makes good sense. Once again, consecrate it to highlight the spiritual purpose it plays in your life.

Your Personal Altar

Now let's look at one of the most important pagan tools. Your *altar* will be the center point of your pagan spiritual practice. It will serve as the place where you display (or store) your ritual tools and where you meditate, pray, work magic, and do your rituals, whether by yourself or with others. In other words, the altar is the focus point for your spirituality. As much I believe that all tools are ultimately optional, if you had to have just one pagan tool, I'd recommend that you have an altar.

EarthWords

An **altar** is a place where you honor or make sacrifice to the Gods. The word comes from a Latin root meaning "to burn" or "consume," referring to the ancient practice of making burnt offerings.

Like any other ritual tool, altars can be simple or elaborate, small or large, inexpensive or valuable. There's no one right way to create your sacred place. The following sections take a closer look at the practical uses of an altar and provide some tips for creating your own.

Why Have an Altar?

If you don't come from a religious background that uses altars, this concept of "a place to make offerings" may seem foreign and a little bit scary. Relax. Remember that neopagans never kill animals (or humans!) as part of their spirituality. Blood sacrifice is strictly a thing of the past. But just because they don't kill animals doesn't mean they don't make sacrifices. They just do it in a much more spiritual manner.

Having an altar makes good pagan sense. Even if you aren't used to altars, the following reasons will help you see how valuable they are to pagans.

A Place to Pray and Meditate

Human beings are creatures of habit, and many people find that developing a discipline of daily or regular prayer and meditation is a difficult habit to develop. It's easier to form this positive habit if you have a regular time and place for your spiritual observance. The time part is mostly a matter of scheduling. If you eat breakfast every morning at 7:30, you might want to schedule your spiritual observance a half hour earlier—after all, it's hard to meditate on a full stomach. Having a regular place to be spiritual is just as important (maybe even more so) than a regular time. Your altar will serve as that all-important place to face the Goddess and the spirit world.

A Place for Magic, Ritual, and Sacrifice

Of course, you can just as easily make a *shrine*. But shrines are different from altars in that they are not places where sacrifices are offered. Shrines are places where we keep spiritually significant objects, and can be used as a focus point for prayer, meditation, or lighting devotional candles. An altar, however, is a place specifically created for the more serious magical work where you'll "conduct business" with the spiritual world. Many pagans have a central altar for their ritual work, and numerous shrines throughout their house to create a sense of spiritual ambience.

So if pagans don't kill goats or chickens, what kind of sacrifices do they make? It varies. Some pagans like to make token physical sacrifices such as putting small amounts of fruit, herbs, flowers, or oil on the altar as a symbolic way of making gifts to the Gods. After the ritual, these token sacrifices are scattered in nature for the faeries to enjoy. More and more, however, most pagans see sacrifice as involving gifts of time, energy, money, and skills to the service of Mother Nature and the Gods. This can mean donating to, or working for, environmental advocacy groups. It can mean making recycling a sacred duty. It can mean vowing to give a certain number of hours each week to study, meditation, and helping others. There are endless ways in which you can offer gifts to the Gods. But however you do it, start at your altar. It's the anchor from which your connection with the Goddess (including the gifts you offer her) originates.

> **EarthWords**
>
> A **shrine** is a place where you keep sacred or holy objects. Pagan shrines might include a collection of fossils, water from a sacred well, or a collection of God and Goddess statues.

A Sacred Center for Your Home

Finally (and this is really just a culmination of the other reasons), having an altar gives your home or apartment a sacred center. Remember that paganism is not a religion based on a book; it is a spirituality based in nature. Nature exists in the universe of dimensional space. So when you find a special place to create that anchor described in the preceding section, you have essentially rooted your spirituality in the universe. Having just one spot in your home for sacred observance can help make the entire place feel just a bit more radiant with divine presence.

Elements of a Typical Pagan Altar

For your altar, you will need the following:

- ◆ The actual altar itself
- ◆ Objects to adorn the altar
- ◆ Storage space for magical and ritual tools

Ideally, your altar and your storage space should be in the same location. You might set up your altar on top of a chest of drawers and keep your candles, incense, and other supplies inside. This way, the entire piece of furniture becomes sacred. If you decide to use a coffee table as your altar, the shelves and drawers beneath it can be your storage space.

Remember that the altar itself is a ritual tool and ought to be duly consecrated and treated with reverence just like any other tool.

Drumbeats

Because a pagan altar honors nature, it can be a work of art devoted to the natural world, displaying an attractive collection of natural objects (such as stones, shells, or leaves) that have spiritual meaning to the owner and that will seem beautiful even to the nonpagan. One Wiccan priestess I know has an altar in her living room filled with works of art. Pagans know what it is, but others simply think it's a beautiful accent in her home!

Sometimes pagans will use an item for both ritual and mundane tasks. For example, the aforementioned chest of drawers might be used both as your altar and to store ritual tools, but the other drawers can still be used to contain regular clothing. You can consecrate just certain parts of it for spiritual use or consecrate the entire item—just remember that you're keeping your clothes in a ritual container, so don't be surprised if they feel a bit more magical than the rest of your wardrobe!

Generally, pagans love to set up a permanent altar where they can practice their spirituality at any time. If space is limited or if you live with unsympathetic housemates, however, you may want to set up your altar only when in use. This is okay, too. In between ritual use, still treat the altar with respect. After all, it is a central symbol of your spiritual life.

Adorning the Altar

What do you put on your altar? It depends on your personal preferences and the teachings of your tradition. To set up a general, all-purpose, pagan altar, I recommend including at least the following items:

- **Symbols for the elements** These might be incense for air, a red candle for fire, a chalice with water for water, and a bowl of salt for earth. You can also use more nature-oriented symbols such as a feather for air, a piece of lava for fire, a seashell for water, and a crystal for earth.

- **Your athame, wand, pentacle, and drinking chalice** Placing your elemental tools on your altar makes practical sense, because you'll be using these tools during rituals. Many pagans place the pentacle in the center of the altar, with the chalice to the left of it and the wand and athame to the right.

- ◆ **Symbols or statues of Gods and Goddesses**   If you love mythological art, you can find beautiful statues of Gods and Goddesses from cultures around the world. You can also represent Spirit in more abstract ways such as a symbol of the sun and the moon to represent the polarities of yang and yin.

- ◆ **Tools for ritual**   These include candles, incense, oil, an offering bowl to receive sacrifices, and a paten to hold any food you will eat in ritual.

- ◆ **Other decorations**   A beautiful altar cloth can create a sense of reverence on your altar. Treasures from nature—from crystals to seashells to beautiful leaves—can add a touch of beauty. A living plant can be a nice touch (and symbolic of the World Tree). Two candles, one for the Goddess and one for the God, are also customary.

An eclectic pagan altar. Notice a statue represents the Goddess, and a figurine of a stag represents the God.

(© 2001 Fox Gradin)

Consecrating Your Altar and Tools

Some pagan traditions have elaborate ceremonies for consecrating tools, but this can also be a simple process. The important point to remember is that consecration sets the tools apart for magical and ritual use only. Once you have consecrated a tool, use it only for spiritual purposes.

Here's a simple procedure for consecrating your tools. Do this the first time you use your altar. Then, each time you acquire new tools, you'll be ready to consecrate them as well.

Set up your altar, according to either your tradition or your personal preference. Light the candle(s) and incense on your altar. Take a few moments to breathe deeply, centering yourself in the presence of Mother Nature and her beloved consort.

When ready, hold up (or place your hands on) the object being consecrated. Say, "By the power of the four elements, I consecrate this tool to the Lady and the Lord" (or something similar in your own words).

Now consecrate the tool with the four elements, as follows:

1. Pass incense over or around the tool to consecrate with air.
2. Pass a lit candle over or around the tool to consecrate with fire.
3. Sprinkle the tool with water to consecrate with water.
4. Sprinkle the tool with salt to consecrate with earth.

When done, hold (or place your hands on) the tool for a moment in silence, thanking the God and Goddess for their blessing on your tool.

If you have more than one tool to consecrate, repeat the ritual as needed.

When finished, say a prayer of thanksgiving in your own words and then extinguish the candles on the altar. You can extinguish the incense or let it burn out, as you prefer.

Oracle _____

When consecrating your tools, envision rainbow-colored or golden-white light suffusing through each object, cleansing it inside and out.

Obviously, the first time you do this, everything you use will be unconsecrated. That's okay. Consecrate the objects you use (yes, even the candles and the salt and water) the first time through, and then in future rituals, you will have consecrated items ready for use.

Practical Issues

Here are a few concerns to keep in mind when setting up your ritual place.

Where to Have an Altar

The best place for your altar is the best place for your spiritual work. Ideally, it will be in a private, quiet part of your home. Even if you like to do rituals outdoors, still set up an indoor altar—it creates a sense of sacred presence in your home. Remember that a human home is just as much a part of nature as is an anthill or a beehive.

If your altar is portable, you may want to take it outside for outdoor rituals. Otherwise, find a large rock or outdoor table that you can use as your outdoor altar, consecrate it accordingly, and take your altar supplies outdoors when needed.

More Than One?

I know of pagans who have houses full of altars. That's not really my way. I think it's good to have one altar and then shrines in other parts of the house. In other words, I like having one central place for ritual and magic but other mini locations for prayer and meditation.

There's one exception to this: Families may choose to have a main family altar, with each member of the family also having his or her own personal altar.

Altar Etiquette

Most pagans believe that everything is holy in its own way, so treating an altar with special reverence may seem odd. Such respect is simply a way of expressing devotion and honor to the Goddess and the God.

Here are a few simple principles to keep in mind with regard to your altar or other ritual tools:

CAUTION

Taboo!

Respect, yes. Superstition, no! As a pagan, you'll want to treat your altar and ritual tools with due reverence, but don't overdo it to the point where you freak out if your baby drools on your altar cloth. Remember that the Goddess is levelheaded and has a sense of humor. So be reverent and keep it in perspective.

◆ **Keep it clean**   Even if you're a messy housekeeper, at least keep your altar dusted, neat, and orderly. Maybe it will inspire you to keep the rest of the house looking better!

◆ **No clutter**   Don't fill the altar with so much stuff that you can't find things. Think of your altar as a mirror of your soul. Keep it serene and spacious, almost like the mind of a meditating Buddhist.

◆ **No cigarette butts or drink cans**   Okay, so this is just a reiteration of cleanliness, but it deserves its own mention. Part of respecting a consecrated altar lies in not putting unconsecrated items on it (unless they are about to be consecrated in a ritual).

The Only Truly Necessary Tool: Your Self!

Tools are cool, but like any other material object in our lives, they serve a purpose: to make ritual work easier or more beautiful. It's important to remember that ritual is possible even with no tools whatsoever. That's right. No altar, no athame, no candles, no incense. Just you, your imagination, and nature. True spirituality happens in your heart, not in the pages of a book or the flicker of a candle. If you keep this in mind, you will have a balanced perspective toward your ritual "stuff." Of course, it's fun and can be beautiful and meaningful to light candles on an altar or to bless a chalice of mead before sharing it with your spiritual sisters and brothers. But never forget that an inner sense of reverence and relationship with nature is the true and ultimate goal of pagan ritual and spirituality. If your ritual tools support you in that goal, they are worthy objects. When they stand in the way, it's better to do without them. That's why they're *optional*.

Oracle

You can learn to make many ritual tools, from robes to candles to incense. Pagans who enjoy making things find that making their own ritual tools is not only fun but spiritually powerful, as more of their own energy is contained in items they themselves make.

The Least You Need to Know

- ◆ Pagans use candles, incense, oil, chalices, water, salt, robes, and many other items to help make rituals meaningful and beautiful.

- ◆ The most important place for performing spiritual acts is the altar, which, like any other ritual tool, can be very simple or extremely ornate.

- ◆ Before using a tool in ritual, pagans usually consecrate it (make it sacred by blessing it with the energies of the four elements).

- ◆ Ultimately, the most important—and only necessary—tool is your own self.

Chapter 15

A Basic Ritual

In This Chapter

♦ Why rituals are important to pagans

♦ Preparing your preritual checklist

♦ A simple pagan ritual, step-by-step

If there's one essential way in which pagans practice their spirituality, it is through ritual. Rituals can be simple or elaborate, performed alone or with others. They can be focused on simple devotion to the Goddess and the old Gods, or they can be intricate ceremonies designed for working magic. As a pagan, you get to decide what kind of ritual works best for you.

In this chapter, you'll learn a basic outline for performing a ritual based on the spirituality of Goddess and nature. As you become more comfortable doing the ritual and more knowledgeable about the symbolism of paganism, you can adapt this ritual to your own needs. Of course, if you work with an established pagan group, you'll learn the ritual protocols of that tradition. But whether your chosen path is Wicca, druidism, or some other form of paganism, the basic elements of ritual will be the same.

A Step-by-Step Guide to Your First Ritual

This chapter assumes that you have never done your own ritual before. It will lead you step by step through the why, how, and wherefore of pagan spiritual practice. This is a safe and simple program for honoring nature and the divine as Goddess and God.

First of All: Why Bother?

You may be asking, "Why would I want to do such a thing? What's the point behind ritual?" Well, as you saw in Chapter 1, "Welcome to the Pagan Path," rituals (or religious rites) are universal human experiences, and indeed, everyone's life is filled with rituals that aren't even religious or spiritual in nature. We have courtship rituals, rituals to help us get up in the morning or get through the day at work, and complex rituals around holidays like Thanksgiving or the Fourth of July. Human beings are creatures of habit, and a ritual is a habitual way of expressing spiritual beliefs and principles.

Oracle

The ritual in this chapter is only one example of a pagan ceremony. If you want more ideas for rituals, check out books like Glennie Kindred's *Sacred Celebrations: A Sourcebook* or Ed Fitch's *Magical Rites from the Crystal Well*, both of which have many sample rituals.

Many pagans find it fun and fulfilling to do their own spiritual ceremonies. Others aren't so inclined. Remember that there are no dogmas in the pagan world, so don't do ritual just because you think you're supposed to. If ritual isn't your thing, that's okay. You might also find that you love participating in rituals but just don't want to lead them yourself. In that case, finding a coven or other pagan group may be a helpful way for you to express your spirituality.

If, like many pagans, you really are interested in performing a ritual, here's how to do it.

A Preritual Checklist

You'll want to begin your ritual by setting up a checklist. This will help you stay mindful of the purpose of the ritual, the items you'll need to perform the ritual, and step-by-step instructions for the process of the ritual itself. Let's look at each of these in turn:

   ◆ **The purpose of the ritual**   Why are you doing the ritual? One reason could be to celebrate a Sabbat, a new moon, or a full moon. But is there another reason? Are you going to make a specific request of the Goddess or perhaps offer her your thanks for a miracle that has occurred in your life? Knowing the ritual's purpose can help make it more meaningful. A ritual for Samhain (the festival that shows respect to our departed ancestors) and a ritual for Beltane (which celebrates life, sexuality, and fertility) will naturally have different symbolism and different purposes.

◆ **Items you'll need for the ritual**   This depends on what you'll be doing. Items can include any of a number of ritual tools, musical instruments, special costumes (if you're going to enact a mythic story, for example), or magical herbs and oils (for spell work). Our simple ritual will need the following items:

> An altar with candles for God and Goddess
>
> Incense, a red candle, water, and salt to symbolize the four elements
>
> Oil (for anointing)
>
> Four candles, one for each direction (north, east, west, south)
>
> Bread, cookies, or cake (enough for each participant)
>
> Wine, mead, or nonalcoholic juice
>
> A drum or other musical instrument (optional)
>
> A candle snuffer (optional)

◆ **Step-by-step instructions for doing the ritual itself**   That's what the rest of this chapter is.

If you're doing your ritual alone, you'll perform all the functions of the ritual. If you're working with others, try to share the parts of the ritual. In many pagan groups, the leaders of the group function as priests or priestesses who lead the rituals. For the purposes of this ritual, however, which is designed for individual or small, unstructured group use, no one person is the leader. Different people can be assigned to each of these roles:

◆ Anointing the participants

◆ Lighting the candles and incense on the altar

◆ Creating the circle

◆ Honoring Air

◆ Honoring Fire

◆ Honoring Water

◆ Honoring Earth

◆ Honoring the Goddess

◆ Honoring the God

◆ Leading the main work of the ritual

◆ Blessing the ritual meal

◆ Distributing the ritual meal

◆ Leading a song or chant (optional)

 Oracle

Although many pagan groups have officially designated priests and priestesses who lead rituals, it can be very bonding for a group of pagans to share leadership responsibilities. With more people contributing their energy to the ritual, it can more quickly feel like a true group effort.

You can include up to 13 people in this ritual, and everyone has a part to play. Of course, if you have fewer than 13 participants, just double up on the tasks. If you're doing the ritual by yourself, you get to do it all!

Generally, whoever performs a function at the beginning of the circle will perform the corresponding function at the end. This means that the person who honors air at the beginning will thank air at the end and so forth.

Getting Ready: The Ritual Bath

Before beginning a ritual, you will want to take a special bath. This ritual bath serves a purpose similar to consecrating a tool: It not only makes you physically clean, it symbolically cleans your spirit as well. This way, you can go into your ritual feeling refreshed and properly prepared to encounter the Goddess and God.

To prepare a ritual bath, run your bathwater as normal. Before you get in to the bath, however, consecrate it with air (incense), fire (candle), and earth (salt) and drop a few drops of consecrated oil into it to represent Spirit. The bathwater itself signifies the element water. While actually bathing, try to maintain a meditative state, reflecting on the purpose of the coming ritual.

After your bath, you're ready for the ritual. Put on your robe or some other special garment (or even remain skyclad if you prefer). Don't wear any watches, cell phones, pagers, or anything else that will connect you with the mundane world. Jewelry is okay, but I recommend you limit it to consecrated, spiritually meaningful jewelry. Now it is time to prepare the circle.

Round and Round We Go

Chapter 12, "Going in Circles," looked at how central cycles and rhythms are to paganism. When you do a pagan ritual, you'll honor the centrality of the circle to paganism by working within a circular space. Indeed, most pagans consider the circle to be so essential to their rituals that they use the word "circle" as a synonym for ritual.

If you are working indoors, place your altar in the center of a space large enough for you and your companions to comfortably stand in a circle around it. At each direction (east, south, west, and north), place a candle. If your ritual is outdoors, you can put the altar in the center or, if you prefer, put a bonfire in the center and place the altar to the north or northeast of the fire (a location favored in many Wiccan traditions). Still, mark out a space large enough for your circle and place the candles in each *quarter.*

EarthWords

Pagans talk of the **quarters** as the directions in which the elemental powers are honored.

This ritual honors air in the east, fire in the south, water in the west, and earth in the north.

Anointing the Participants

After everyone has taken his or her ritual bath and is ready, gather around the altar. Begin with a few moments of silence so that everyone can become *centered*. If you like, have the participants hold hands and chant the sacred Hindu syllable OM (pronounced *ohm*) to attune everyone's energy. Or, use the sacred syllable MA to invoke the feminine energy of the Goddess.

EarthWords _____

Spiritually speaking, we become **centered** when we relax our minds and bodies so that we feel comfortable and safe in our environment. We are relaxed but alert, and our minds are in a meditative, peaceful state.

After giving everyone a chance to get centered, go over any last-minute instructions before the ritual begins. Then, to start the ritual, take the consecrated oil (or have the appointed person do this) and begin in the east, moving *deosil* (clockwise) around the circle. Go to each person and, with a tiny amount of oil, draw a circle on his or her forehead. Say, "You are the earth, and you embody her cycles. Blessed be." Give the participant a hug and then move on to the next person. The last person to receive the anointing should take the oil and anoint the person who did the anointing so that everyone receives the blessing.

EarthWords _____

Deosil means "sunwise" and refers to moving clockwise around a circle. The opposite direction, counterclockwise, is called **widdershins**.

Lighting the Altar

Now everyone turns to face the altar. The appointed person steps to the altar and, in a slow and reverent manner, lights first the candle representing the element Fire, then the incense representing the element Earth, then the candle symbolizing the Goddess, and finally the candle symbolizing the God. In some pagan traditions, this process is known as lighting the altar and is very complex, with complicated ritual movements. That's not necessary for this simple ritual, but you'll want to do this process in silence, with reverence for the elements and spirits that the altar represents. This can be a beautiful and moving part of any ritual and, if done in a spirit of reverence, will set the tone for all that follows.

Creating Sacred Space (Casting the Circle)

Now that the altar is lit, it's time to cast the circle. Take the incense from the altar to the point where the east candle is situated (or have the person appointed to cast the circle do it). From there, walk deosil around the circle, saying, "With the element of air I cast this circle." Walk all the way back to the east and then return the incense to the altar. Repeat the process with the candle, now saying, "With the element of fire I cast this circle." Repeat again with the water and then with the salt. With the water and salt, sprinkle small amounts of the element on the circumference of the circle while doing the casting.

> ### Drumbeats
>
> In traditional Wicca and ceremonial magic, casting a circle is a powerful process designed to create an energetic barrier for advanced magical work. The circle described here, while meaningful on a spiritual level, will not attain that same level of energy.

As the elements are taken around the circle, it's helpful for all the participants to envision a bluish-gold energy hanging like a curtain around the circumference. Once the circle has been cast, don't move through this energy field unless absolutely necessary.

A World Between the Worlds

When the circle has been cast, say, "The circle is cast. We now stand in a world between the worlds." This means that the ritual space has been set apart for magical and ritual purposes. Spiritually speaking, the space now functions as a meeting place between the mundane world and the otherworld. It is now a place where it is easier to establish communication with the Gods and other spirits.

Take a moment to savor the subtle shifts in energy that you might feel. Welcome to the world of magic!

Invoking the Spirits (Calling the Quarters and the Deities)

The next six parts of the ritual call in powerful spirits to watch, support, and connect with the ritual participants. This is a time for reverence and respect. Think of it as asking to have a meeting with the president of the United States or a major spiritual figure like the Dalai Lama. Of course, the Gods are more accessible than those figures, but they deserve at least the same amount of respect.

201 A Basic Ritual

The Ancient and Mighty Ones

To honor the spirit of air, take the God candle from the altar (or have the person appointed to honor the spirit of air do it) and move to the east. Holding the God candle in your right hand, hold it above your head and say, "Spirits of the east, element of air! We invite you to come and join us in our sacred rites."

Feel free to improvise with these words. You can write a poem or a brief song. Speak to the characteristics of the element air. (Or it's fine to use the simple greeting given here.)

Pause after speaking, and then light the candle at this quarter. Then return the God candle to the altar.

Drumbeats

Some pagans love to have beautifully choreographed rituals with flowery prose, lilting poetry, and eloquent prayers. But these need to be either memorized (which can be nerve wracking) or read from a script (which can seem artificial). Other pagans believe that scripting a ritual destroys its spirit and do everything spontaneously, speaking from the heart (which can also be nerve wracking, too longwinded, or clumsy and awkward). Clearly, there are positives and negatives to both using a script and not using one. The moral of the story: Do what feels right for you, whether it involves memorization, reading from a script, or just being spontaneous.

Next, take the God candle from the altar (or have the person appointed to honor the spirit of fire do it) and move to the west. In a similar manner as before say, "Spirits of the south, element of fire! We invite you to come and join us in our sacred rites."

Return the God candle to the altar. The person who will honor water should then pick up the Goddess candle (remember that the first two elements are yang, while the last two are yin) and perform the same actions in the west, saying, "Spirits of the west, element of water! We invite you to come and join us in our sacred rites."

And then finally, the Goddess candle is used in the north, with these or similar words: "Spirits of the north, element of earth! We invite you to come and join us in our sacred rites."

In each case, feel free to embellish these words with a poem or song of your own, speaking to the unique qualities of the element being honored.

The Lord and the Lady

Now it is time to honor the fifth element, Spirit, in its dual form as Goddess and God. If one person (say, you working alone) does this, he or she should face the altar. If two people call the Goddess and God, they can stand in front of the altar, facing one another. Traditionally, a priest calls in the Goddess, and a priestess calls in the God (or vice versa), but in this ritual, either a man or a woman can call in either deity. To symbolize the polarity of Goddess and God, the person(s) calling them in will use special arm-and-hand positions to signify each. These positions, based in ancient Egyptian symbolism, are called the Isis position (for the Goddess) and the Osiris position (for the God). See the following figure for a demonstration of these positions.

The Isis position includes hands extended in an open and receiving gesture. The Osiris position includes arms crossed over the chest in a position of confident strength.

(© 2001 Fox Gradin)

Since darkness precedes light and form precedes force, call in the Goddess first. The appointed person should open his or her hands in the Isis position and say, "Mother Goddess, we honor you and ask your presence in our sacred rites. Bless us with your protection and guidance."

If desired, this simple prayer can be replaced with a poem or song, celebrating the attributes of the divine feminine such as her nurturing or her deep earthy wisdom. You can also call on the name of a specific Goddess such as Aphrodite (for matters pertaining to love), Athena (for matters pertaining to wisdom), or Hecate (for divination).

When the Goddess has been called, allow several moments of silence to feel her presence.

Then it is time to call the God. The person appointed to call in the divine masculine should hold his or her arms in the Osiris position and say, "Pagan God, we honor you and ask your presence in our sacred rites. Bless us with your protection and guidance."

> **Drumbeats**
>
> Many Wiccans practice a ritual act called "drawing down the moon (or the sun)" in which the energies of the Goddess and the God are ritually invoked in the priestess and priest. Other pagan traditions maintain that human beings carry the energies of the divine in them at all times and thus they don't need to be "drawn down."

You can use "Father" instead of "Pagan," although some people find the concept of "Father God" to be too reminiscent of the angry father-God they were exposed to in their childhood religion. Use whatever feels most comfortable to you.

Once again, feel free to substitute a poem or song that celebrates the energies of the God, perhaps calling him forth as protector of the wilderness and patron of the hunt. Depending on the objectives of your ritual, you may wish to invoke a particular God such as Hermes (for magical pursuits), Apollo (for rational wisdom), or Hephaestus (for skillful work).

Be sure to allow several moments of silence to feel the presence of the masculine face of Spirit.

The Work of the Ritual

At this point, the ritual has attained "cruising altitude." You've purified the participants and the ritual space, set up an energetic circle, and invited the participation of the elements and Spirit. Now it's time to do whatever the primary goal of the ritual might be, which is called the "work" of the ritual.

Perhaps you'll be consecrating tools using a ceremony similar to the one presented in Chapter 14, "Tools for Ritual." Or you might be working a magical spell along the lines of the basic spells presented in Chapter 18, "Magic, or Flexing Your Spiritual Muscles." You may be enacting a skit or miniature play to celebrate the themes of the Sabbat or moon you are observing, or you may be raising energy for healing work (see Chapter 19, "Divination and Omens: Listening for the Divine Whisper").

If you have no purpose at all other than simply wanting to do a ritual, this is an appropriate time to sit in silent meditation, do some shamanic drumming, or even sing a song of love for Mother Nature. Whatever you wish the ritual to celebrate, this is the time for it.

Meditation, Mystery, and Magic

The three key words for the work of the ritual all begin with the letter "M." Meditation allows you to connect more powerfully with your divine essence (more on this in Chapter 17, "Meditation: Welcome to Magical Boot Camp!"). Magic includes any spiritual work you do to effect positive changes in your life (more on this in Chapter 18). The mysteries include the deep spiritual truths of nature and the pagan way, including mythic stories of the Gods or teachings related to the Wheel of the Year. The mysteries can be celebrated in a ritual through poetry, song, drama, or story.

Sacrifice and Omen

Another possibility for the work of the ritual includes the concepts of sacrifice and omen. As you learned in Chapter 14, a sacrifice is an offering to Spirit. It can be a token offering of flowers or herbs, an artistic offering like a song or poem, or even a vow to make a positive changes in your life or to work harder to protect nature. Whatever it is, see your sacrifice as a gift you're giving to the Goddess. In response, this is a great time for taking an omen—looking for a sign of what word(s) the Goddess and God may have for you. This can be done through divination or simply listening for whispers from the Spirit in your own heart. Some people are even gifted at seeing the guidance of Spirit in the flame of a candle or bonfire. If your psychic skills run in that direction, this is the time in ritual to seek the words of the divine.

The Ritual Meal

After the work of the ritual, it is time to begin grounding yourself. This is the process of letting go of the heightened state of consciousness that often accompanies ritual work and returning to the normal awareness of everyday life.

> ### Oracle
> Many pagans experience profound shifts in consciousness when doing ritual. Others may only experience slight changes in awareness or no change at all. However you experience ritual is fine for you. If it doesn't cause you to "see the Goddess," keep an open mind. It takes practice. Sometimes when you least expect it, a ritual can have a profound impact on your way of relating to consciousness and the world.

The first (and a very effective) way to do this is through eating and drinking. This is a great time to share a small amount of food in a ceremonial way. Wiccans refer to this as "cakes and ale" or "cakes and wine," but it can be any sort of food. Try to pick something wholesome: Fresh apples are better than candy bars (unless your ritual is honoring a Goddess who is particularly fond of chocolate!). Fresh-baked bread, homemade cookies, and fresh fruit are all excellent choices. As for the beverage, although wine, mead, and ale are all traditional choices, nonalcoholic choices may be preferred, especially if anyone in your circle needs to avoid alcohol for medical or spiritual reasons.

Taboo!

Paganism is a path of personal liberty, so among other things, there is no rule against alcohol. But remember the charge to harm none. Alcoholics, minors, and those who will be driving are all at risk of causing harm to themselves or others when they drink. So the freedom of paganism is also balanced by common-sense responsibility.

Some good choices for ceremonial drink include fruit juice, milk, and sparkling water.

When it's time to share the food and drink, the person appointed moves to the altar and holds up first the cakes and then the chalice, saying these words of blessing:

> O Lady, bless this meal we are about to share in honor of you.
>
> Great Mother, bless this chalice we are about to share in honor of you.

The food and drink are then passed deosil around the circle. This can be a time for sharing, for singing a chant, or for listening to a lovely song if someone has one to share. If your ritual has been very solemn and reverent up to now, here's a time to loosen up and maybe make a bad pun or two. Remember that reverence doesn't mean being too serious to have fun!

Putting Things Back Where They Belong

Now the ritual is almost over. The remainder of the ceremony involves dismantling the energies of the ritual, saying thanks and goodbye to the spirits who have attended the ritual, and making sure the altar and ritual areas are clean and everything is back in its place.

Grounding and Centering

Sharing food and beverage began this process of reentry into ordinary consciousness, but now is a good time to do something to officially mark this transition. The process of grounding and centering implies getting in touch with your body (grounding) while keeping your thoughts, breathing, and heartbeat at an even keel (centering). To do this is a simple matter involving one or more of the following:

- Standing up and stretching
- Holding hands in a circle or, better yet, a group hug
- Briskly patting your whole body with your hands, from head to toe
- Taking several deep, relaxing breaths while focusing your attention on your body

If anyone feels dizzy, lightheaded, or especially light and airy, this is a time to make sure they reconnect with their bodies. After all, no one wants to drive a car while still stuck in a spiritual high!

Thanking the Deities and Opening the Circle

From here on out, the ritual basically operates in reverse of how it began. Begin by saying farewell and thank you to the Goddess and the God, with the appointed person(s) facing the altar (or each other). Use these or similar words, with the person thanking the God standing in the Osiris position and the person thanking the Goddess standing in the Isis position: "Pagan God, thank you for your presence in our sacred rites, and for your ongoing presence in our lives. We bid you hail and farewell."

Others present may respond in unison, "Hail and farewell."

Then the person thanking the Goddess says, "Mother Goddess, thank you for your presence in our sacred rites, and for your ongoing presence in our lives. We bid you hail and farewell."

Others present may respond in unison, "Hail and farewell."

Taboo!

When extinguishing a candle, never blow it out or lick your fingers before snuffing it. Either use a candle snuffer or dry fingers. (If you do it quickly, it doesn't hurt.) Using air (blowing) or water (licked fingers) amounts to using one element to vanquish another element. Spiritually speaking, it's impolite!

Now, beginning in the north and moving widdershins around the circle (north, west, south, and east), the quarters are thanked and dismissed with these or similar words. At each quarter, the appointed person may stand, speak the words, and then extinguish the candle.

Spirits of the north, element of earth! Thank you for joining us in our sacred rites. As you depart to your fair and lovely realm, we bid you hail and farewell.

Spirits of the west, element of water! Thank you for joining us in our sacred rites. As you depart to your fair and lovely realm, we bid you hail and farewell.

Spirits of the south, element of fire! Thank you for joining us in our sacred rites. As you depart to your fair and lovely realm, we bid you hail and farewell.

Spirits of the east, element of air! Thank you for joining us in our sacred rites. As you depart to your fair and lovely realm, we bid you hail and farewell.

Others present may respond with "Hail and farewell" after each candle is extinguished.

Finally, the person appointed extinguishes the candles on the altar: first the God candle, then the Goddess candle, and finally the fire candle. You can allow the incense to burn out on its own unless the altar is to be dismantled right away (such as in an outdoor ritual for which the altar tools will be taken back indoors).

Once the altar candles have been extinguished, turn to the others present and join hands to form a circle. The person who tended the altar now says, "The rite has ended. We have returned to ordinary space and time. Our circle is open, but never broken. Merry meet, merry part, and merry meet again."

To which the others reply, "Merry meet, merry part, and merry meet again!"

Your ritual has now ended.

Reentering Ordinary Space and Time

The ceremonial part of the ritual may be over, but there are still a few final steps.

♦ **Clean up** Make sure tools are put away in their proper places and move the altar to its normal home, if necessary.

♦ **Stay grounded** Many participants in ritual need extra grounding, especially after a powerful ceremony. It's helpful to eat a full meal after a ritual or at least share some hors d'oeuvres. Many pagan groups finish off their rituals with a potluck feast.

♦ **Review the ritual** What did you like about it? What didn't you like? What worked and what didn't? Remember that you can change and adapt pagan rituals to suit your needs. Take the time to review your experience so that you can plan better for next time.

Oracle

If you are keeping a diary or Book of Shadows, make notes in it about your ritual. Keep not only a copy of the ritual script but also your comments on how the ritual felt, whether it seemed to succeed in its objective, and what you plan to do differently next time.

The Many Faces of Ritual

You may be getting tired of hearing this, but it bears lots of repeating: Paganism is a many-faceted thing, so there are countless ways to do ritual. If you participate in a particular tradition, its elders will teach you their way of doing things (usually with lots of rhetoric about why it's the "right" or "best" way). That's perfectly fine as long as the rituals feel right to you. Of course, many pagan groups love to experiment and try different rituals for different occasions. Some groups may emphasize sacrifice and omens more, others may have specific mini rituals for lighting the altar or invoking the Gods, and so on. Plus, there are many writings that can be incorporated into ritual, such as the Charge of the Goddess (see Chapter 4, "Wicked Good!"). If ritual becomes a major part of your spiritual life, you'll want to get some of the many pagan books available that include sample rituals, chants, invocations, and other resources to make your ceremonies the best they can be!

The Least You Need to Know

- For most pagans, performing rituals is a primary way to honor the Goddess and the God.
- Rituals can be done privately or with a group.
- For the best results, plan your ritual ahead of time and make sure you have the proper tools, a clear understanding of the ritual's purpose, and roles for each participant.
- Central to a pagan ritual is casting the circle, or creating the psychic space in which the ceremony takes place.
- After the ritual, it is important to ground and center (return to ordinary, relaxed but alert consciousness).
- You can adapt your rituals to fit your specific spiritual needs.

Chapter 16

Rites of Passage

In This Chapter

- Rituals of transition
- The two types of life passages
- How pagans honor births, weddings, and deaths
- Taking a magical name
- The spiritual side of life transitions

Over the course of a lifetime, a person goes through many stages, and changes. This is recognized in the Goddess as she moves from her maiden aspect, young and sensuous, to the maturity of her nurturing and life-giving mother aspect, to her final stage of wisdom and dark power as the aged crone. Each of us likewise goes through phases, from birth and infancy to childhood and adolescence, from young adulthood to maturity and middle age, eventually becoming elders.

A One-Way Trip to a New You!

Pagans believe that the stages of life are different points on the great cycle of life, death, and rebirth. As such, the transitions from one stage of life to another ought to be honored and celebrated. A rite of passage is a specific ritual designed to mark an important transition point of life. This chapter looks at some of the common turning points in most people's lives and at how pagans celebrate and commemorate these important passages.

Drumbeats

The title of the movie *Four Weddings and a Funeral* makes a subtle comment on the role of religion today. For many people, religion serves only two purposes: It's for marrying and burying. This shows how powerful rites of passage are, even among people who have abandoned the religion of their parents. Paganism not only strives to fill the need for rituals in people's lives, its basis in nature makes it a user-friendly spiritual path for all of life, not just the transition times.

The Philosophy of Rites of Passage

Why is this necessary? What's the point of marking a transition in life?

In every part of life, from infancy and childhood all the way to old age, we have different functions and roles to play, especially in terms of how we relate to others. While a parent needs to be responsible, loyal, and dedicated, a child's job is to respond to the parent's guidance so that he or she can grow safely and healthily. An elderly person does not have to be in charge but can be a valuable source of wisdom, guidance, and reassurance to younger adults who have lots of responsibilities—just like the elder once did. With the passage of time, the way in which we function in our families and our society inevitably changes.

Drumbeats

Writers like Robert Bly have argued that the reason society has become so violent is because of a lack of effective rites of passage to teach boys how to become mature adult men. Likewise, our society has not provided meaningful rituals to celebrate girls as they transition into womanhood. Many pagans believe both genders would make a smoother transition into adulthood if meaningful rituals accompanied their journey.

This makes perfect sense, but for many people, making the transition from child to adult, from single person to married person, or from parent to grandparent is not always easy. We are creatures of habit and are used to doing things a certain way. When the circumstances of our lives change and we have a new role to play, it may take some getting used to.

Rites of passage are tremendously valuable for helping us adjust to life's changes. They encapsulate the wisdom and traditions of our forebears into a spiritual program that helps make transitions easier, more meaningful, and more real. Rituals speak not only to our conscious, rational mind but also to the deeper parts of our minds—our subconscious—as well as the "right side of the brain" that understands symbols better than words or logical concepts. When we enact a ceremonial rite of passage, we engage all parts of the mind to work together to take on our new role of life. This, in turn, makes the transition (and the forming of new habits) easier.

Our Cultural Rites of Passage

To understand the concept of rites of passage better, let's look at some of the ways in which we celebrate life transitions in our society at large.

- ◆ **Birth**   As a society, we celebrate expectant mothers by throwing baby showers, and when the baby arrives, the proud father might just hand out cigars (unless he doesn't approve of smoking). Naming the newborn, setting up a nursery in the home, and applying for a Social Security number are all part of the process of bringing a new life into the world.

- ◆ **Driver's license**   Getting your first driver's license (usually around age 16) is a pretty big deal to most teens. Not only does this "rite" involve taking driver's education classes, learning to feel confident behind the wheel, passing the exam, and taking the first solo drive, it then extends to buying (or, for those lucky few, being given) your first car, along with all the accompanying responsibilities.

- ◆ **Graduation**   Successfully completing your schooling, whether high school or college, culminates in ceremonial "commencement exercises" (complete with robes—how pagan can you get?), lots of parties and gift giving, and most important of all, the excitement of planning for the future, whether it involves more schooling or entering the work force.

- ◆ **Marriage**   Many people who never participate in any kind of religious ceremony suddenly become devout when the subject of weddings come up. But weddings, like Christmas, are a curious blend of religious and social customs. Even people who get married in a strictly secular, justice-of-the-peace ceremony still undergo a ritual process of getting engaged, applying for a marriage license (which in some states requires blood tests), getting family and friends involved in the celebration, and finally dashing off to a honeymoon.

Oracle

Many people have no religious affiliation but then try to find a church to get married in. Many Christian churches, however, either require people to join the church before they can get married there or charge large sums of money to host the wedding. Pagans, thankfully, have another alternative. See the section on handfastings later in this chapter to discover why pagans don't need a church to get married.

◆ **Retirement**   After years of hard work, eventually the day comes when you leave the daily grind behind. This calls for more than just turning in your two weeks' notice, however. Not only are there practical financial, medical, and time-management concerns, often fellow employees sponsor a party complete with rituals such as "roasting" the retiree or giving him or her a lovely gift.

While we may not be accustomed to thinking of these normal life transitions as "rites of passage," the fact is that, as a society, we've created ritualistic ways to honor these normal transitions. A wedding without a honeymoon or a retirement without a party just doesn't "feel right." That odd feeling is a sense of unease because our cultural rituals have not been honored. Even the most staunchly nonreligious person is, on many levels, a creature of habit and custom. Rituals and rites are the public way we manage our customs and routines. Even without spiritual intent, rituals can be profoundly meaningful as signposts along life's way.

The Mark of an Effective Rite of Passage

So what makes a rite of passage tick? Essentially, there are two key elements to a successful passage.

You Change

First of all, the person having the transition undergoes some sort of change. It doesn't have to be an overpowering mystical or emotional experience, but it should communicate, either in words or in symbols, the reality of the transition in such a way that the person "gets it."

Your Community Changes

The second key to a successful rite of passage is just as important: The community changes just as much as the individual does. In other words, when two people get married, it affects not only the couple but all their friends, family, and neighbors. For one thing, the newlyweds are no longer romantically available to others (unless they're swingers!). Furthermore, assuming that the marriage is between two reasonably mature and healthy people, the community will want to support the bond. Even a happy marriage has tough times, but when the two have supportive friends and relatives to count on, they can navigate the storms and have a long, happy marriage. Meanwhile, the community benefits from this stability as well, as do any children, who thrive much better in a happy, stable home environment than in a broken or dysfunctional situation.

Since life transitions affect other people in addition to ourselves, an effective transition ritual includes other people and communicates to them the reality of the passage.

Remember that these changes do not necessarily refer to sort of emotional high or mountaintop experience. You don't have to see the Goddess at your wedding for the marriage to be valid. There do need to be specific words, symbols, or actions, however, that communicate to all involved parties that the transition has occurred. This is why the minister's phrase "I now pronounce you husband and wife" is so important in a wedding. Through words, the change is made real.

Taboo! _____

A rite of passage (or any other ritual) doesn't have to be some sort of traumatic or heavenly experience to be successful. Simple rituals that seem to have no emotional impact on us can be very powerful; the real effect of ritual happens subconsciously, below the level of our feelings.

The Two Kinds of Transitions

For pagans—and indeed for anyone who has a spiritual path to follow—there are two basic kinds of rites of passage. This chapter considers both kinds of transitions and how pagans undergo them.

Life Transitions: Pretty Much for Everybody

The first kind of passage involves life transitions. These are universal experiences that pretty much everyone experiences: being born, coming of age, falling in love and choosing a mate, making the transition into old age, and finally, death. Nearly all spiritual traditions have ceremonial ways to mark these significant turning points in the journey of life. Pagan spirituality is no different and has some beautiful and unique rituals to mark these passages.

Spiritual Transitions: Only for Those Who Answer the Call

In addition to the universal, biologically driven turning points of life, people who embrace a particular spiritual path will have rites of passage unique to their tradition. The spiritual rites of mainstream religions are familiar to most people, from baptism and confirmation in Christian religions to bar mitzvahs and bat mitzvahs in the Jewish community. Paganism, like other religions, also has specific ceremonies for embracing spirituality or becoming a teacher, priest or priestess, or elder of the path.

Life Transitions

This section takes a closer look at various ways in which pagans celebrate the universal passages of life. From birth to death, there's a pagan way to honor each major transition in your life.

Wiccanings

A newborn baby is a cause for celebration and joy. Pagans don't believe in original sin, so there's no need to baptize a baby to "cleanse" his or her soul. Instead of the rituals of purification or washing performed in other religions, pagans use rituals to introduce and welcome the baby to the community and the spirits. "Baby, meet the elements and the Gods." "Elements and the Gods, meet this precious newborn baby." The theme of a *Wiccaning* is one of happiness, joy, and welcoming to the precious new being who has come to live with us.

Obviously, the name Wiccaning comes from the word Wicca. For pagans who aren't Wiccan, this ceremony could just as easily be called the "rite of blessing a newborn."

EarthWords

A **Wiccaning** is a special kind of ceremony in which a baby is ceremonially "introduced" to the elements and the God and Goddess.

Wiccanings can take place at a new or full moon or at a Sabbat; in other words, any time pagans normally gather for ritual is appropriate. Begin your ritual in your normal custom and then, when it is time for the work of the ritual, you or the child's parents can bring the baby to the altar. A priest or priestess or some other appointed person should bless the baby, anointing her or him with oil, incense, and salt water. Then the baby and the parents or sponsors move around the circle, starting in the east and moving to each of the quarters. At each quarter, say a short blessing for the baby based on the qualities of that element, like this:

May the element of air bless you with a keen and discerning mind and skills of clear communication.

May the element of fire bless you with passion, vision, and energy to pursue your dreams.

May the element of water bless you with intuition, insight, and a kind and loving heart.

May the element of earth bless you with strength, good health, and a life filled with abundance.

You also could use some similar blessing in your own words.

Finally, bring the baby back to the altar. Similar blessings may be offered from the God and the Goddess.

The Wiccaning does not turn the baby into a pagan. It is simply a blessing offered with no strings attached. Like anyone else, the baby will have to decide for her- or himself what spiritual path, if any, to follow.

Coming of Age

The next significant life transition is puberty, or coming of age. This is a time of celebrating the child's transition into adolescence, which in itself is a long-term transition into adulthood. For girls, this is a special time when menstruation begins. For both girls and boys, their bodies change, and their feelings about themselves and about sexuality will change as well. It's a glorious and sometimes scary time. A rite of passage can be both a celebration and a reassurance.

A coming-of-age rite can be held during a regular Sabbat or moon ritual, or it can be done privately or by invitation only. There are many variations on how such a ritual can be meaningful, both for the new adolescent as well as for his or her family or friends.

♦ As with a Wiccaning, it's a good idea for a coming-of-age ritual to include blessings from the elements and the God and Goddess.

♦ At least part of the ceremony should involve only the gender of the new adolescent. Girls honoring their menarche may want to go on a women's only camping weekend. Boys celebrating their transition into adulthood might enjoy a ritual experience created for them by their fathers and other male elders.

♦ There should be one powerful way to mark the transition. Have everyone younger than the new adolescent stand on one side of the circle and all the adults stand on the other side. The new adolescent might begin with the children and then, to the sound of drumbeat or cheering, walk alone from the kids to the grownups, symbolically crossing the threshold of adolescence.

♦ Like any good rite of passage, make sure the festivities include a party and gifts!

Handfastings

Eventually, the day comes when a young adult (or, for that matter, an older adult!) falls in love and seeks some form of union with his or her beloved. For pagans, the ritual of *handfasting* serves as a joyous and lovely marriage rite. Some pagans have a legal handfasting, complete with a

EarthWords

Handfasting is the pagan term for marriage. It comes from the custom of tying the bride and groom's hands together as part of the ritual.

marriage license and a pagan priest who is recognized by the state as a minister able to perform weddings, but many pagans (especially gay and lesbian pagans, who sadly do not have the same legal rights as heterosexuals regarding marriage) opt for a spiritual hand-fasting in which their love and union are recognized on a spiritual level even without any corresponding legal status.

Like the other rites of passage, a handfasting should include blessing and anointing the bride and groom as well as blessings from each of the elements and the Goddess and God. Like any other wedding, the bride and the groom make vows to one another (which, ide-ally, they will write themselves). The couple may exchange rings or other tokens of their commitment. Finally, what makes a handfasting unique is, well, the handfasting. The priest, priestess, or other appointed leader takes a cingulum or other cord and ties it around the joined hands of the bride and groom. This is an old custom from Europe, and it is the origin of the idea that marriage involves "tying the knot!" Finally, as the newly married couple leaves the circle, they jump over a broom as a final act of blessing on their newly shared lives.

Oracle

If you choose to be handfasted in a pagan marriage ceremony, be sure you understand the legal issues surrounding the ceremony. If you want a legal wed-ding, you need a pagan priest or priestess who is licensed to perform weddings, and you'll need a marriage license in accordance with the laws of the state. As a pagan, you can opt for a spiritual handfasting that does not have legal status, but remember that such an arrangement does not give you or your spouse the legal rights of a marriage.

Croning/Saging

After marriage, many of the life transitions that pagans experience involve their children: their Wiccanings and comings of age. Eventually, though, the kids grow up and move out, and a new season comes to the life of maturing adults. Women reach menopause, and men experience a similar transition into their role as the elders of their families and com-munities. This is the onset of the *crone* or the *sage*.

Becoming a crone or a sage is very special because, unlike the other life transitions, this one tends to be ignored by society. Society is afraid of maturity, old age, and death, so we look the other way as our hair turns gray and our skin becomes wrinkled. The pagan path, however, as the path of celebrating nature, realizes that old age in a human being is (or can be) just as beautiful as colorful leaves in the autumn or a snow-covered field in the depths of winter. The vigor of youth may be fading, but in its place is the wisdom and vision that comes only with age.

Many pagans elect to celebrate their croning or saging around age 50. Like the other rites of passage, it involves anointing and blessings. Like the rite of passage from childhood to adolescence, it can be very powerful to include a physical separation between the younger members of the circle and the elders. One person I know even had the young people at her croning stand on one side of a hill and the elders on the other. Proudly, she marched over the hill, celebrating in true pagan style what most others fear or ridicule.

The theme of this rite of passage is wisdom and perspective. Gifts involving knowledge or teaching are especially appropriate.

EarthWords _____

In paganism, the words **crone** and **sage** refer to women and men, respectively, who are past the age of approximately 50. Thus, a ritual to celebrate and honor this milestone in their lives is known as a croning or saging.

Funerals

Eventually, each of us will make the final transition. Whether death comes at age 11 or 111, there's always a measure of grief or loss associated with it, so this is the one rite of passage in which the needs of the community take precedence over the needs of the individual (who will be partying in the otherworld by the time the funeral takes place). Some traditional Wiccan groups have elaborate rituals for the dead that involve helping the soul pass over to the other side. Others may prefer a very simple and elegant service of saying "Goodbye" (sort of a balance to the "Hello" of a Wiccaning). In either event, this is a ritual for honoring the dead and for offering strength and solace to the bereaved.

Oracle _____

The Pagan Book of Living and Dying by Starhawk and M. Macha Nightmare provides a wealth of resources and rituals related to the process of crossing over. Even if you're not planning a funeral, it's a great book because it contains a section that discusses pagan perspectives on death and dying.

Spiritual Transitions

This section looks at rites of passage specific to the spirituality of paganism. Whereas the rituals of the preceding section involve the normal turning of the wheel of life, these ceremonies specifically focus on the process of walking the pagan path throughout one's life. These rituals are less connected to physical changes in life; instead, they have more to do with celebrating the milestones reached as one matures spiritually.

Dedication

When a person first decides that he or she wishes to formally embrace the spirituality of Goddess and nature, the ritual way to do this involves dedication. Simply put, it's a ceremonial way to dedicate one's self to this path. Dedication can be done alone as a ritual of self-dedication, or it can be part of a group experience in which the priest or priestess or other group leader leads you through your declaration of choosing the pagan way.

Remember the section "A Ritual for Embarking on the Pagan Path" from Chapter 6, "Other Pieces of the Pagan Puzzle"? It contained a simple rite of self-dedication. It was nothing fancy, but often the best rites of passage tend to be simple. Basically, a dedication ritual doesn't change you into some sort of advanced mystic or enlightened master. It's as simple as being willing to stand up and say, "Yes, I am a pagan, and as a beginner, I'm willing to learn the ins and outs of this spiritual tradition." Whether this declaration happens in a simple rite you perform all by yourself or in an elaborate ceremony with a coven, complete with incense, oil, and pentacles inscribed in the air above you, is a matter of personal preference.

Drumbeats

There's no limit to how fancy a pagan ritual can be, and especially among some witches, ceremonies get fancy indeed. One of the fancy elements of ceremonial witchcraft involves inscribing pentacles in the air, often as a sign of blessing and protection. There are even different ways to draw the pentagram based on each of the four elements and based on whether the pentagram is invoking (calling in) energy or banishing (dispersing) energy.

Taking a Magical Name

Many pagans like to take a special magical name by which they will be known to other pagans. Supposedly, this practice began back in the days when witches were persecuted. By only knowing one another by their magical names, a witch could not reveal the identity of other witches if she were ever caught and tortured by the authorities. This is probably more a romanticized notion than a solid historical fact, but regardless of why they do it, most pagans love to adopt a magical name. The process of taking a magical name can be its own meaningful rite of passage.

How do you choose a magical name? The possibilities are almost endless. Many pagans take the name of a God or Goddess who embodies qualities they admire or wish to cultivate in their own lives. Others might take a name from nature, perhaps a power animal or a tree that is spiritually meaningful to them. Names can even come from science fiction or fantasy (one of my teachers is named Galadriel, after the elf-queen in the novels of

J. R. R. Tolkien) or even just from an ancient language. Gerald Gardner, the father of modern Wicca, had the magical name Scire, which comes from the Latin word for "to know."

Here are some popular magical names. When trying to choose one for yourself, don't limit yourself to these choices. In fact, some of these names are a bit overused in the pagan community!

- Names of Gods and heroes: Bran, Gwydion, Hermes, Merlin, Pan, Oberon, Osiris, Taliesin, Theseus

- Names of Goddesses and heroines: Ariadne, Artemis, Brighid, Circe, Freya, Gaia, Hestia, Rhiannon, Minerva

- Names from nature: Ash, Bear, Hawk, Hazel, Holly, Raven, Storm, Thorn, Wolf

> **Taboo!** _____
>
> Don't just choose the first name that comes to you when deciding on your magical name. Take the time to make sure the name you choose is right for you.

Think carefully about your magical name before you decide on one and begin using it. Remember that names have power, and you'll be taking on the energies of the name into your own life.

Avoid Gods and Goddesses known for unpleasant qualities like violence or trickery and also stay away from powerful Gods whose name may be more than you can handle. A man who takes the name Zeus will be regarded by veteran pagans as having delusions of grandeur, while an outgoing young woman who takes the name Aphrodite will probably find she gets lots of attention at parties—but not the kind of attention she wants!

When in doubt, call on your spirit guides or your teachers or friends in the pagan community to help you identify the name you wish to be known by.

Once the name is chosen, you'll want a ritual of name taking to formally declare your name before the elements, the Goddess and God, and (if applicable) the members of your group. You can do this as part of a regular Sabbat or moon ritual. Before the sharing of the cakes and wine, you'll want to stand in front of the altar, tell a little bit about your name and why it's meaningful, and finish with something like this: "So before the elements and the Goddess and God, I now take _____ to be my magical name. May it be!"

That's all there is to it, but as with all passage rites, something will have changed. You'll know that every time somebody addresses you—using your new name.

Initiations

Some (but by no means all) Wiccan and pagan traditions involve a series of ranks that a person works through over the course of his or her magical studies. As you learned in Chapter 4, "Wicked Good!" initiations are the rituals by which a person is admitted into his or her new rank in the craft. Initiation means "beginning," and this rite represents a mystical entry into a new beginning of your spiritual life. In many traditions, initiation is regarded as one of the most powerful and sacred rites you'll ever undergo and, as such, requires considerable preparation beforehand. Since initiation confers certain privileges (in some traditions, an initiation makes you a priest or priestess, and the highest level of initiation gives you the authority to start your own coven or group), most Wiccan elders will only initiate those whom they believe are truly committed to the craft and to their tradition. In other words, this is serious business!

Generally, initiations are secret. Those being initiated take oaths not to reveal the circumstances of their initiation or the teachings they receive once they have been initiated. Some pagans criticize this as elitist, but others see the secrecy as a way to preserve the power and specialness of Wiccan teachings.

In many groups, there are three levels or degrees of initiation. Aspirants must prepare for at least a year and a day before being initiated. Here are the common levels of initiation:

- **First degree: the basics**   In many traditions, a person is not considered a witch until he or she takes the first degree. At this point, the person can lead rituals and assist in the teaching of students.

- **Second degree: middle management**   When a first-degree witch is elevated to the second degree, he or she can take greater responsibility for teaching and managing the group. In some traditions, a second-degree witch can, with proper supervision, start his or her own coven.

- **Third degree: mastery**   When a second-degree witch is elevated to third degree, he or she has the authority to teach and run the entire coven and can start a new group. Basically, at the third degree, the person has completed training and can now turn his or her attention primarily to supporting others on their journey.

As you can see, initiations and degrees make sense primarily within a coven setting. For solitary witches and most other kinds of pagans, initiations and degrees are not necessary. After all, you don't need a merit badge to love and honor the Goddess!

Eldership

Eldership can be thought of as the spiritual dimension to becoming a crone or a sage. Anyone can be a crone or a sage by merely reaching age 50 or so. To become an elder, however, you need to be a long-standing member of the pagan community who has given much over the years to support the community and the spiritual lives of others. Elder status recognizes that you may not be involved in the day-to-day management of a coven or other pagan community, but you are respected as a mentor and resource for those who do have leadership responsibilities.

Like a croning or a saging, a ritual of transition to elder status can be a celebration in which a pagan leader turns over leadership responsibilities and assumes the new role with grace, dignity, and a smile. Like every other rite of passage, it should begin with blessings and end with a party!

The Least You Need to Know

- People of just about every culture have developed ceremonies and customs to spiritually mark the transitions of life.
- There are two kinds of rites of passage: transitions that are universal (like birth, marriage, and death) and transitions that are specifically spiritual in nature (like dedication to a new spiritual path or initiation into the priesthood).
- Wiccans and other pagans have various formal and informal ways of marking rites of passage.
- Although our culture as a whole tends to resist growing older, pagans honor the aging process with appropriate rituals.
- Because of paganism's flexibility, you can mark the transitions in your life with an elaborate ceremony and a huge party or with a simple rite performed all by yourself.

Part 4

Magic

From Gandalf the Grey to Harry Potter to Mickey Mouse as a sorcerer's apprentice, magic has long enthralled both young and old. The use of spiritual power to effect real changes in the world has almost a universal appeal. Although many religions regard magic as a taboo subject, to most pagans it is a legitimate field of spiritual inquiry.

Authentic magic involves far more than pulling rabbits out of hats or turning ex-boyfriends into toads. Indeed, many pagans regard the popular notion of magic-as-wish-fulfillment to be a limited, inaccurate understanding of spiritual power. Genuine magic incorporates meditation as a tool for developing psychic and intuitive skill, divination for accessing inner guidance, and (most important of all) a commitment to healing as the purpose of magical work. For pagans, magic entails cooperation with the Goddess and the God to manifest positive transformation in the world, a process that includes creating changes both ordinary and miraculous.

Part 4 provides an overview of spiritual magic. You won't be able to change anyone into a newt after reading this, but hopefully you will have a better sense of how magic enhances the pagan path.

Chapter 17

Meditation: Welcome to Magical Boot Camp!

In This Chapter

- Don't wait to meditate
- Zen and the art of visualization
- Trance, serenity, and theta waves
- The spirituality of meditation
- How to succeed at your own meditation practice

For many people, the whole point behind becoming a pagan is to master the art of magic. Witches, shamans, druids, and pagans in general have a long-standing reputation for possessing spiritual powers far beyond the reach of ordinary folks. Well, if you're interested in magic, this chapter's the place to begin. That's right, you begin your study of magic by first learning the basics of meditation.

Magic is simply a fancy word for spiritual power. A magical person is some-one who uses spirituality to make positive changes in his or her life. Power, after all, is simply the ability to make changes. Just about anyone who talks about magic could replace the word "magic" with "spiritual power," and the ideas would still make perfect sense. Magical power is perfectly natural and available to anyone who wishes to develop the skills necessary to use it.

Before you can become an accomplished magician, however, filled with spiritual power that can be used for healing and transformation, you must first gain power over the most important magical tool of all: the human mind. Indeed, once you master this tool, all other magical tools are of secondary importance.

Meditation: A Workout for the Mind

Meditation, like paganism, is a broad concept that can mean many different things. To a Buddhist, a Christian, a Wiccan, or a New Age psychic, meditation might mean entirely different things. For pagans, many different styles of meditation mean many different ways to approach the vast miracle of your mind. If you don't care for the radical silence of a Zen monk or the guided visualizations of a ceremonial magician, that's okay. You might find that you prefer the profound shifts in consciousness that result from chanting the sacred Hindu syllable "OM" or the physically induced trance state that comes from the hypnotic beat of a shaman's drum.

In other words, if a certain style of meditation doesn't appeal to you, don't worry! That doesn't mean you have to give up on meditation (or magic). It just means you have to keep looking to find the kind of meditation that fits your style.

Think of meditation as the art of inner listening. It is the ultimate tool for getting to know the riches of your subconscious mind as well as the mysterious ways in which your inner world connects with the vast otherworld where pagans encounter the Gods and Goddesses and other spirits.

Oracle

Reading about meditation is not the same as doing it. Be sure to put the book down and actually spend time sitting in silence!

EarthWords

Zen comes from the Chinese word for meditation, *ch'an*.

Hang Out with Silence Now and Zen

Zen is a word commonly associated with meditation. It refers to a specific tradition within Buddhism, probably the most meditation-filled religion of them all. Zen may be an exotic little word, but all it means is—you guessed it—meditation. Another word from this tradition, *zazen*, means "sitting meditation."

But what kind of meditation is zazen? Well, it tends to be very focused on disciplining the mind. Indeed, in the tradition of Zen Buddhism, monks wrestle with koans, seemingly absurd and irrational questions, that can help free the mind from the cage of ordinary logic and thought, thereby achieving satori, or enlightenment. Zen monks, like most other Buddhists and many other practitioners of meditation around the world, pay close attention to their breathing and their bodily sensation, seeking liberation from the chain of desire that characterizes ordinary human thought and feelings.

Instead of seeing the world as a sorrowful place that they must try to escape through salvation or enlightenment, pagans accept the world as a pretty cool place that just needs some more positive energy, like trust and love, than it currently has. Therefore, pagans don't meditate to achieve some sort of supernatural enlightenment that will liberate them from their desires (unless they happen to want to be liberated, but most pagans think their desires are rather, well, desirable). This is not to say, however, that pagans won't benefit from zazen. For many pagans, zazen represents a way to discipline their minds so that their thoughts and feelings are harmonious and in keeping with their ultimate goals (which usually involve living in harmony and balance with nature). Remember that a disciplined mind is the first step toward developing the power of magic.

Drumbeats

A wonderful tool for cultivating meditative silence is the labyrinth. In many cities, bookstores or even churches will have labyrinths that you can walk through in silence. Don't worry if you're not a member of a church that has a labyrinth—people of all faiths are usually welcome. The simple process of walking a labyrinth may not seem like a form of meditation, but it is surprising how quiet and peaceful the mind can get as you walk silently along the curving path. There are also little labyrinths that you can trace with your fingers, and even these can help you achieve meditative consciousness.

I Spy with the Mind's Eye

For many people, the problem with zazen and many other types of meditation is that they involve the slow and difficult work of disciplining the mind to avoid extraneous thinking and feeling. Meditation, to put it bluntly, is hard work. Sure, anyone can sit still for five minutes, but for five hours? Or for an hour a day, day in and day out? For most of us living our busy lives, the discipline of silent meditation is just too big of a challenge.

Don't despair. There are other ways to develop the skills of meditation and the benefits of a disciplined mind. They may not be as powerful as zazen, but they're enjoyable and easier to get into. These skills involve visualization.

Two generations ago, the concept of visualization would have been considered quite odd, yet today people from all walks of life—from corporate executives to schoolteachers, among others—regularly practice visualization. Basically, it is the skill of using the imaginary powers of the mind to form as realistic an object as possible within the mind's eye. Visualization is a form of mental creativity. It's the film projector inside our skulls, and it can literally show us anything, from real things that exist in the world outside us to fantastic objects that are manifest only on our mental stage.

CAUTION

Taboo!

Don't give up on meditation just because a popular form, like zazen or transcendental meditation, doesn't appeal to you. If you aren't the Zen type, just keep looking; there's bound to be a style of meditation that suits your personality.

What's more, pagans, following in the tradition of shamans, magicians, and occultists from many cultures throughout history, accept that what we visualize just might be far more real than we're typically taught to believe. In other words, the images in our mind may have powerful connections to the collective unconscious (where our ancestral memories are stored) or even to the otherworld (the realm of spirit beings and the God and Goddess) that is larger than the farthest reaches of our soul.

But let's bring this back down to earth for a minute. What does visualization have to do with meditation?

Simply put, if zazen is like training your mind to sit still, then visualization is like training your mind by giving it a vigorous workout. Everyone has an imagination, but for most of us (thanks to television and the Internet and other images that bombard us every day), the image-making skill in our noodle is woefully underdeveloped. Visualization is the exercise program that can bring your image-maker into full spiritual fitness. If you can't figure out why sitting for an hour and just paying attention to your breathing patterns makes sense from a spiritual point of view, maybe you need to be visualizing. If you flex those imagination muscles, your ritual work, your trance work, and your efforts to contact and work with your spirit guides will all become immeasurably deeper, more vivid, and more real.

A Visualization Exercise

Here are two brief exercises to get you started on the journey to meditation through visualization:

♦ Find an apple. Any old apple will do. You'll also need a kitchen timer. (Get the battery-powered kind that makes no noise until time's up.) Sit in a quiet place where you will be free from distractions. Set the timer for a minute or maybe 90 seconds. Use that time to gaze at the apple, concentrating as best as you can on all its details, color, markings, and so on. When the timer goes off, reset it and close your eyes. Now, in your mind's eye, re-create the apple. Don't just draw a little red blob like a kid with a crayon. Concentrate on making your visualized apple as detailed and vivid as possible. See the markings, see how light shines on the apple, and see any soft spots or bruises. When the timer goes off, open your eyes and look at the "real" apple. Make notes in your journal regarding how close your visualized apple came to the manifest apple.

For extra credit, work with the other senses besides sight. While you are visualizing your apple, imagine how it smells. Imagine how it would taste if you took a bite and how it would feel inside your mouth. Again, strive for as vivid and realistic detail as possible.

◆ This next exercise begins the same way as the apple exercise, only now you're using your hand. Hold your hand in front of you and concentrate on it. See the details, the creases in your skin, the veins on the back of your hand, and the lines on you palm. Then, after resetting the timer, visualize your hand, striving for as much vivid detail as possible. With this detail, however, you'll also "feel" your visualized hand, for it is as much a part of your spiritual body as your flesh-and-blood hand is part of your physical body.

Do this several times until you have a sense of being able to clearly visualize your hand. Now set the timer for a longer period (say, three minutes) and, during this time, concentrate on making your visualized hand move. Clench your visualized hand to make a visualized fist. Wave the visualized hand. Point with your visualized finger. With each movement, strive to feel your inner "muscles" move in synchronization with what you are seeing in your imagination. Again, when the timer goes off, open your eyes and write about your experience.

The point of these exercises is not to become adept at giving yourself the imaginary finger, but to develop vivid visualizing skills so that when you go on inner or otherworldly journeys, such as during a shamanic trance, you will be rewarded with a detailed and powerful experience. The greater the detail, the more meaningful, educational, and potentially transformative the experience will be.

> **CAUTION**
>
> **Taboo!**
>
> Resist the temptation to get mad at yourself if you don't do it "perfectly" the first time (or the hundredth time). Meditation is an art, and like all forms of art, it is beautiful and valuable even when not entirely perfect.

May I Have the Next Trance?

Instead of the overwhelming silence of the Zen monastery, perhaps you are more drawn to the throbbing pulse of the shaman's drum. If that's so, perhaps your preferred style of meditation involves *trance*.

There are many different varieties of trance, as evidenced by the many different ways in which shamans access the spirit world. Some can go into a waking trance, in which they retain some degree of normal consciousness but can access the spirits while in the altered state. For others, trance involves a complete loss of normal consciousness, and the person in a trance may appear to observers to be unconscious or sleeping. Some people go into a trance and cannot remember anything about it when they come out again, but for many, trance is a memorable, if dreamy, experience.

> **EarthWords**
>
> A **trance** can take many forms, but it is always an altered state of consciousness in which some form of powerful spiritual contact or transformation may occur.

The great variety of trance states suggests that you can find the path that is unique and proper for you, even if it is different from what other spiritual seekers do.

In Chapter 3, "Please Don't Squeeze the Shaman!" we talked about the role that trance plays in shamanism, and in Chapter 7, "This World, That World, and the Otherworld," you learned about contacting your spirit guides and making journeys into the otherworld. Guess what? You were learning the fundamentals of trance. In many ways, trance is the bridge between meditation and magic. It involves using the skills of relaxation and concentration that are the foundation of meditation to reach out to spirit allies and their otherworldly home.

Why Bother with Meditation?

Think of meditation as a psychic workout.

Whether you like to physically work out or not, you understand that it's good for you. Regular exercise lowers blood pressure and cholesterol levels, improves digestion and regularity, and keeps the body feeling good in general. A person who exercises regularly is not only healthier but happier due to the natural good feelings of a physically fit body.

The same holds true for meditation. It's interesting to note that for people who suffer from life-threatening illnesses such as heart disease or cancer, many physicians consider meditation to be as important as exercise for promoting health. Although meditation has a benefit on our physical bodies, its most enduring and powerful gift is the way it strengthens the psychic dimensions of life. My first meditation teacher used to say, "Meditation is the only thing I know that benefits us in every aspect of our lives: physically, mentally, emotionally, and spiritually."

All Levels

Meditation induces calmness and serenity, which in turn fosters clarity of thought. It also helps manage stress, which can contribute to emotional health and well-being. Most of all, however, meditation opens us up to the vast riches of the spiritual world.

Whether your natural meditation style is more akin to the deep serenity of a Buddhist monk or the inner dynamics of creative visualization, you'll want to get into a regular habit of exercising your meditation muscles. This will enable you to be more adept at trance work and more powerful when it comes to putting magic to work in your life as well.

The Bottom Line

Even if you are a naturally skeptical person who thinks that something has to be measurable to be real, there's evidence to support the importance of regular meditation. The physical changes to the body that meditation can bring about (such as reduced blood pressure and pulse rate) can be measured, and those changes can add years to a person's life. So, if for no other reason, it makes sense to meditate.

The other benefits can't be measured, but they can be experienced. Meditate every day for six months, and you'll impress yourself with how much your life has changed for the better. Thanks to the serenity, clarity, and sense of spiritual union that it brings, meditation may be thought of as the most basic of all happiness spells. When it comes to magic, meditation is truly the bottom line.

Brainwaves: The Physics of Meditation

Here's something you probably didn't learn in high school. The human brain has at least four different speeds. (Who knows, maybe there are more than four brain speeds, assuming there are subtle variations to brain states that can't yet be scientifically measured.) We know about these different speeds through measurable *brainwaves*, and we experience these different speeds as different states of consciousness or awareness. Most people have figured out that there's a difference between being awake and being asleep. But there's also the difference between deep sleep and dreaming, between alertness and daydreaming, and most mysterious of all, that twilight phase in between sleep and wakefulness in which we sometimes get feelings or thoughts that are indescribably powerful.

So, what are these four brain speeds, and what does meditation have to do with them? First let's look at brainwaves and how they relate to different states of consciousness. Depending on the number of cycles per second, brainwaves fall into four states: beta, alpha, theta, and delta. (No, these are not fraternities or sororities; they're simply Greek letters.)

> **EarthWords**
>
> **Brainwaves** are the activity of the mind, and they can be measured as energy patterns on an instrument like an EEG. The EEG depicts brain activity as a line on a graph, revealing the energy of the brain to exhibit repetitive patterns (waves).

Beta Waves

When your brain waves are revved up, moving at more than 14 cycles per second, you are in the beta state. This is the high-alert functioning. When you're in the beta state, you are paying attention, deeply engaged in the business directly before you. Whether you are trying to solve a tricky math problem, get that cutie across the room to notice you, win an argument, or simply understand a book you're reading, you are in the beta state of consciousness. This is what most people think of as "normal" awareness, but it really is only one of three states of waking consciousness.

Alpha Waves

Now we'll slow the brain down to between 7 and 13 cycles per second. Stand up, stretch, take a humongous yawn, sit back down, and relax. Don't think about anything in particular. Allow your mind to wander, maybe even daydream a little. Thoughts may get a little fuzzy … or indistinct … or stop altogether. This is the alpha state of consciousness, the state of moderate relaxation and rest. The mind is on call; the beeper is turned on. At a moment's notice it can be fully revved up again, back into the hurly-burly of beta consciousness. Until the mental pager buzzes, however, the alpha-state mind is happy to kick back and float happily along.

Most people who are reasonably good at meditation can easily attain the alpha state when meditating, but even people who never meditate at all slip into the alpha state at various points throughout the day. It's not the best state for driving or operating heavy machinery, but it does wonders for reducing blood pressure and increasing a sense of spiritual well-being.

> ### Drumbeats
>
> Have you ever listened to music that reminded you of a memory and drifted off into a happy space where you thought about that memory, and then, suddenly, you realized the music had ended without you noticing it? You were lost in a daydream, which usually involves the brain relaxing into an alpha state.

Theta Waves

Next in line are the theta waves. The theta state of consciousness occurs when the brain-waves flow at between four to six cycles per second. This is powerful, deep consciousness. It's not sleeping; rather, it's what we often experience as that deliciously magical zone we pass through in between wakefulness and sleep. When your brain is in the theta state, you're not sleeping, but you're definitely not alert either. To be in the theta state means to be deeply relaxed, profoundly centered in a realm of mystical awareness where ordinary feelings and sensations of time and space are altered, if not abandoned altogether. This is the state most conducive to psychic and paranormal experiences, the state in which contact with the otherworld is most likely. Most people don't spend much time in the theta state, but regular practitioners of meditation often are capable of achieving this deep level of psychic attunement.

Delta Waves (Zzzzzzzzzz)

Get down to three or fewer brain cycles per second, and you are sawing logs. This is the state of sleep consciousness. It feels great after a long day of hard work, and it can be a portal to the mystical realm through the rich symbolism of dreams (which are, after all, windows onto the subconscious). Beyond that, however, it's not something meditators try to attain. If you fall asleep during meditation, that's usually your body saying you haven't been getting enough sleep! As important as meditation is, when that's the case, get the sleep you need and try to meditate another time.

We've already talked about how meditation lowers physical cycles like blood pressure and heart rate. Well, brainwaves are yet another physical cycle that can be favorably, and measurably, impacted through the meditation process. But brain waves are more than just squiggly lines on a graph. They are the energy patterns of the mind and soul where they intersect with the body. As meditation slows down the functioning of the brain, it also opens us up spiritually to be more available for the magic and wonder of connecting with the Goddess and the God.

Oracle

Interested in learning more about brainwaves and the physiology of meditation? You might enjoy the music recordings from the Monroe Institute, a center in Virginia that specializes in body-mind research. Their Hemi-Sync series of recordings uses special technology to induce different brainwave states. Visit them online at www.hemi-sync.com.

The Meditation-Magic Connection

Let me guess. You're squirming in your chair by now, thinking, "All this meditation stuff is great, but I don't want to be a Zen master. I want to be a powerful pagan magician. So when do we stop worrying about how fast my brain is idling and get down to the good stuff?"

Meditation may not be as glamorous or as exciting as casting spells or chanting ancient runes to command the powers of magic, but just as a budding musician needs to learn how to play scales before graduating to performing real music, so do the skills of meditation provide the foundation for all magic. Here are two concepts from ancient magical teachings that underscore this point.

Know Yourself

Tradition holds that the central message of the ancient *mystery religions* of Greek and Egypt was a very simple one: "Know yourself." In other words, if you want to find enlightenment, spiritual mastery, or psychic power, it all begins with the humble but essential process of knowing just what makes you tick. This means knowing your thoughts, your feelings, your triggers (what especially upsets you or fills you with strong feelings like jealousy or anger or fear), and the deep forces inside you that motivate you in every part of your life.

Whew! That may sound like hard work, but this process of knowing yourself is more than just a homework assignment from ancient masters. It's a powerful step toward the spiritual mastery that magic promises.

Bet you can guess how we get to know ourselves. That's right—through meditation.

As Above, So Below

Ancient alchemical teachings held that a powerful stone called the Emerald Tablet existed in the ancient world, and on this tablet was inscribed the simple saying, "As above, so below." As with "Know yourself," these simple words convey profound spiritual truths that form the foundation of all magic.

> **EarthWords**
>
> In the ancient pagan world, **mystery religions** taught spiritual truths that could not be put into words. Using images and secret rituals, these religious groups shared their teachings only with specially-prepared initiates. Incidentally, the magical tradition we looked at in Chapter 6, "Other Pieces of the Pagan Puzzle," began with the ancient mystery religions.

So what does "As above, so below" mean? Basically, it means that the universe as a whole (above) exists in miniature within the universe of the human soul (below). This is the basis of the idea that our imagination or visualization can provide spiritually meaningful experiences. When we delve deep into the "dark" regions of our subconscious, we are journeying into our own connection to the underworld. When we ascend to the radiant light that shines within us, we are soaring into the splendor of the celestial realms. We change the universe as a whole when we change the universe within ourselves. This is probably the single most critical element of magic. And once again, meditation is the key.

Opening Up to Spiritual Contact

"Know yourself" and "As above, so below" have powerful implications for the pagan practice of reaching out for spirit contact. Whether you seek communication with Gods and Goddesses, ancestors or fairies, power animals or spirit guides, the practice of meditation remains the single most important tool you will use to establish a lasting and meaningful contact. When you slow down your brain cycles, you are literally creating a space for spiritual contact to occur. When the spirit beings come to you, even within the guise of your imagination, remember this: "As above, so below." The powerful experiences you conjure within your meditative imagination have repercussions that reach throughout the entire universe. When a spirit guide imparts wisdom or guidance to you, enabling you to live your life more powerfully and more in service to nature and healing, not only are you changed and you benefit, but indeed, the entire universe prospers as well. And it all starts with meditation.

Enlightenment and Ecstasy, or Welcome to Godhood!

Finally, meditation is important to pagans because it carries a promise. As nature spirituality, paganism doesn't see God as some sort of remote deity who lives in a heavenly court far removed from our daily lives; it celebrates the God and Goddess who live in the midst of nature, the midst of our lives, the midst of our very selves. For many pagans, human beings are as much a part of the Goddess as a drop of water is a part of the ocean. This is a lovely image that many nature mystics find deeply comforting and empowering.

But is it just a nice thought, or is there real spiritual power in it? In other words, how can you and I access the latent divinity within ourselves, assuming we really are that closely connected with Spirit?

Mystical and meditative traditions all over the world, from Buddhism to Hinduism to even mystical Christianity, maintain that the discipline of meditation can unleash the most powerful forms of enlightenment and God consciousness that are available to humankind. Zen calls it *satori*, Yoga calls it *samadhi*, and western mysticism calls it Divine Union. But in every case, it means the same thing: unlocking the full range of divine ecstasy within the tiny confines of our own souls.

This, then, is the ultimate promise of meditation. As cool as the thought of casting a magic spell to lose a few extra pounds may be, the promise of ecstatic enlightenment and Goddess consciousness helps put all other forms of magic into proper perspective.

> **EarthWords**
>
> **Samadhi** means "union," as in the union of human consciousness with infinite or divine consciousness. **Satori** means "enlightenment."

No-Nonsense Advice for Starting Your Own Meditation Practice

One significant question remains. If meditation is such a good spiritual practice, how do we go about doing it? The bad news is that it can seem like a tedious chore because it is so basic. The good news is that, like any other habit, a regular meditation practice can be learned and adopted so thoroughly that it becomes unthinkable *not* to do it. Here are a few tips for how to incorporate a regular session of inner listening into your spiritual life.

Same Time, Same Place, Same Routine

Part of what makes a habit a habit is its regularity. We brush our teeth without thinking about it because we do it at the same time and place every day: in the bathroom, right after every meal. It's such a normal part of our routine that we forget what it was like back when we were kids and our parents had to watch over us like eagles to make sure we brushed three times a day.

Whether you are 16 or 69, learning meditation requires that you be your own parent. You have to set the rules and enforce them. You have to say "I'm doing this every day, no matter what" until it acquires the force of habit. To support that, you should at least create a situation in which a habit can more easily flourish: Set up a regular place for meditation (in front of your altar is the best spot, but if that's not available, find another quiet, private place) and a regular time. I especially recommend meditating first thing in the morning, when the busy-ness of our day hasn't yet turned our minds into fast-spinning frenetic machines. Also, the phone is less likely to ring early in the morning, and other interruptions less likely to intrude. If you're not a morning person, pick a time that works for you. If you're in the habit of sleeping every day until noon, perhaps your best meditation time is from 12:00 to 12:30 in the afternoon.

> **Oracle**
>
> Remember the kitchen timer you used in your visualization exercises? Keep it handy whenever you meditate. If you only have a limited amount of time, you can set the timer and focus on meditation rather than the clock. This will allow you to relax more fully into the meditation process.

Keeping a Journal

Chapter 2, "All-Natural Ingredients," talked about the value of keeping a journal as part of your pagan spiritual practice. Now let's take a closer look at the spiritual journal because writing about your meditation experiences can be one of the most effective tools for supporting your adventures with inner listening.

Keeping a journal does not have to be a fancy or involved process. Your meditation diary will never be graded, and no one ever has to read it (unless you want them to). Your writing is meant for you alone, so you don't have to worry about how neat your handwriting is or whether your grammar is correct. As long as you understand what you've written, it's okay if it isn't "perfect."

This is important because, after years of schooling, most of us get so tongue-tied when it comes to writing that we never get down to the important matter of making a record of our thoughts and feelings. That's too bad because if we can let go of our inner critic and write down what we experience when we meditate, we can create a valuable tool we can use for years to come to understand ourselves better and to mark our progress in the journey of the interior life. So tell that twerpy inner voice that's always saying "It isn't good enough" to take a vacation. With a meditation journal, the point is simply to make notes on the joys and challenges you face as you go deeper into the vast regions of your imaginary landscape.

Your Secret Weapon: A Meditation Buddy

As important as having a routine and keeping a record can be for fostering your practice of meditation, you may find it's still hard to keep at it. It's human nature that whenever we try to form a positive habit of any type and at any age, it's easier when we have someone to talk to, ideally someone who's doing something similar. This is one of the main reasons why it makes sense to practice pagan spirituality in a group. Within a group, you have access to friends and loved ones who can support you on your quest to honor the Goddess and nature. Sure, it's okay to be a solitary pagan, but there's a lot to be said for having companionship on your spiritual journey.

The same holds true for meditation. When you have a meditation buddy, whether it's a teacher who is training you on meditative skills, or simply a friend with whom you get together to meditate with once a week or so, that person provides powerful support to assist you in developing your "psychic fitness." So if you don't know anyone with an interest in meditation, consider taking a meditation class or even attending a yoga or Zen center once in a while. There's strength in numbers. Rely on others to help you succeed.

> **Oracle**
>
> Want to explore meditation in greater depth? Try *The Complete Idiot's Guide to Meditation*. This book looks at meditation from both a spiritual perspective and a health-benefit perspective, and it gives some great advice for starting your own meditation practice.

The Least You Need to Know

- Meditation is the single most important skill for magic or any other aspect of spiritual development.

- There are many different kinds of meditation. Two of the most common are zazen (a Buddhist practice of sitting still, clearing the mind and focusing awareness on the body) and visualization (using the mind to strengthen the skills of imagination).

- Meditation has many benefits, including physical benefits like reduced stress levels and spiritual benefits like slowing down our brainwave cycles.

- Pagans appreciate meditation because it supports them in making contact with spirits and even in attaining a sense of union with the Goddess and the God.

- Developing a meditation practice is like learning any other good habit; it takes dedication and commitment, but it's worth it.

Chapter 18

Magic, or Flexing Your Spiritual Muscles

In This Chapter

♦ The highs and lows of magical spirituality

♦ Why psychic power is the key to magic

♦ Seven universal magical principles

♦ How to write your own spells

♦ The trust factor

Bet you turned to this chapter first!

Magic is a lot like sex. As a concept, it's glamorous and desirable. Who wouldn't want to be able to wriggle their nose and get their housework done or drink a potion that would turn them invisible? Who wouldn't want to cast a spell to make someone fall desperately in love with you? For that matter, who wouldn't want to conjure up just the right numbers to win the lottery?

Well, sorry to disappoint you, but the kind of magic that wins you the lottery or gets you the sexy lover only happens in Hollywood. Real magic, as you will learn in the pages to come, is not some sort of supernatural shortcut to happiness. On the contrary, real magic is nothing more—or less—than harnessing your own inherent mental and spiritual power to create the life you desire.

That may not be flashy or glamorous, but it *is* powerful. If you learn the principles of magic, you will find something far better than a winning lottery ticket or a luscious lover: You'll find yourself in control of your own healing and happiness.

Here's a fun definition of magic: **m**aking **a**greements with the **G**oddess to **i**nstitute **c**hange in life. In this definition, "Goddess" can be shorthand for both the Goddess and the God.

Oh, and one more thing for those of you who did turn to this chapter first: Go back and read Chapter 17, "Meditation: Welcome to Magical Boot Camp!" before this one. To do magic, you first must learn to meditate.

Okay, let's get started.

Magic: Not Required (But Not Prohibited Either)

First of all, I need to say something important that doesn't often get mentioned in books about paganism: You don't have to be interested in magic to be a good pagan. There's no requirement that you learn how to astral project, cast spells, or become *adept* at astrology to honor the earth and the Goddess. Many, perhaps even most, pagans and would-be pagans are interested in the spiritual power of magic. For those who aren't, however, it needs to be said: That's okay, too.

You can approach paganism from two distinct perspectives: the devotional/mystical perspective and the magical/metaphysical perspective. Although many pagans combine these two perspectives, others clearly prefer one or the other.

> **EarthWords**
>
> An **adept** is a person who has achieved a high degree of mastery and skill in one or more forms of magic.

> **Oracle**
>
> When you commit to learning magic, you take responsibility for your own happiness and well-being. Magical people think it's boring to be a victim, martyr, whiner, or complainer. Instead of dissipating your energy feeling sorry for yourself, as a magical pagan you take responsibility to transform your life in positive and healthy ways.

Devotional or Mystical Paganism ...

The devotional approach to paganism stresses love and reverence for nature and the Goddess and God. This is a spirituality that finds meaning in taking care of the environment, trying to live a good and ethical life, and honoring the Sabbats and the moons because it helps you feel more attuned to nature's way. As a spiritually oriented pagan, you may or may not be interested in magic, divination, and psychic skills, depending on your personal inclinations. But your primary purpose in being a pagan is your desire to love and honor Mother Earth.

... and the More Magical Variety

In contrast, the magical approach to paganism stresses personal development and the attainment of magical power as the heart of pagan practice. In this approach, the God and the Goddess are found within, so the best way to love and honor the divine is by unleashing our own creative power. This approach tends to place much more emphasis on developing psychic ability, learning divination skills, and spell casting.

For many pagans, mysticism is the yin of spirituality, and magic is the yang. Which means it makes sense to blend the two. In other words, pagan spirituality can combine powerful devotion to the sacred mysteries of the Goddess with a pragmatic emphasis on using spiritual power to achieve one's goals. Think of this as relating to the Gods on two levels: through love, and through power.

Whether your approach to nature spirituality is more mystical or magical or a blend of the two, you have a home in the pagan community. Just remember that not all pagans will have the same feelings about magic or psychic development that you do. Some will place a great deal of emphasis on it; others will be so busy fighting for environmental reform that they don't have time to learn how to astral project. The pagan community is big enough and diverse enough for all kinds.

Having said that, if you are like the many pagans who do want to develop your magical muscles, the remainder of this chapter provides a brief introduction to this ancient power.

> **CAUTION**
>
> **Taboo!**
>
> Whether you are more oriented toward magical (power-oriented) or mystical (devotion-oriented) forms of spirituality, avoid thinking that your way is the better way. Nature is filled with beautiful diversity. Why shouldn't pagan spirituality be just as multifaceted? Your way is the way that's right for you. Respect others who do it differently.

The Spiritual Tool for Making Dreams Come True

Chapter 10, "A Field Guide to the Spirit World," considered how the words "magic" and "imagine" are so very similar, even though they are not related in terms of etymology. Magic is a word that means power or ability manifested in a spiritual way, whereas imagination is connected to imitation: the mind's ability to imitate reality by forming mental images. But there is a closer connection here than you might think. How do we manifest the spiritual power of magic? Often—through a process of imitation.

Take *affirmations*, or words of power, for example. One of the most basic principles in magic is that words shape reality, and if something is desired for your life, the first thing to do is affirm it. "I make all the money I need" is a useful affirmation if you're struggling to make ends meet. Maybe when you first begin using the affirmation, it is not actually true. But saying the words of power sets unconscious brainpower into motion, and the powers of your mind will help make the affirmation come true. Perhaps it will involve working hard enough to get a promotion or spending just enough time networking so that a truly lucrative job opportunity falls into your lap "as if by magic." The more you say positive and powerful things about your life, the more you train yourself to believe that you deserve good things and the more conscious you become of opportunities that come your way.

EarthWords

An **affirmation** is a statement used to program your mind to manifest a positive change in your life.

Visualization, a skill explored in depth in Chapter 17, is also related to magic. You've already seen how visualization is helpful for making contact with spirit guides and other beings from the Otherworld, but this mental skill is more than just a spiritual tool—it can be a powerful magical technique as well. Affirmations employ words to generate change in our lives; visualization uses mental images to the same end. One very powerful way to work magic is to combine affirmations and visualizations, using both techniques in service of attaining a specific goal. In the aforementioned example, that would mean not only affirming "I make all the money I need" but visualizing depositing huge checks into your bank account, getting the promotion at work, or shaking hands with a new employer as you start that job of your dreams.

The process of using an affirmation is a process of imitation. Using positive words and visualizations, your mind imitates the thoughts and feelings of success, health, abundance, or whatever it is you wish to attain. Then your mind works powerfully to make the choices and commitments necessary to manifest the goal—with the help of your spirit guides along the way. This combination of imagination, imitation, and power is what magic is all about.

The Many Faces of Magic

Like paganism itself, magic comes in many shapes and sizes. There is natural magic, folk magic, high magic, ceremonial magic, ritual magic, and so on. There are schools of magic such as Enochian Magic, Thelemic Magic, and the Golden Dawn. Each flavor of magic has its own unique set of rules, symbols, rituals, and protocols for the proper performance of its own magical style. It's beyond the scope of this introductory book to provide an in-depth look at any one magical system. Instead, we'll look at two categories of magic and some general principles that apply to pretty much every school of magic.

Two of the most basic categories of magic are the so-called high magic, favored by occultists and learned magicians over the ages, and the more down-to-earth low magic, often preferred by shamans, village wise women, and folk healers. Both have made their contribution to the multicolored fabric of modern paganism.

High (Ceremonial) Magic

Try to envision a magician from long ago, perhaps from the late Middle Ages: a learned man who has spent a lifetime poring over arcane books, developing precise knowledge of astrology, Eastern mysticism, the esoteric properties of crystals and metals, and so forth, who uses his skills to perform intricately timed and enacted rituals that in turn can literally conjure forth spirits of the dead, angels, or even unfriendly spirits of darkness. This is the classic stereotype of the ceremonial magician. From medieval alchemists to Renaissance astrologers to modern adepts of secret fraternities like the Golden Dawn, the ceremonial magician has combined powerful scholarship with an intricate system of symbols and rituals to master the forces of the spiritual world.

Ironically, even during the eras when midwives, healers, and other folk magicians were being persecuted for witchcraft, the ceremonialist could practice his art in relative peace. Why the difference in treatment? It was all about class and social status. Unlike folk magic, which generally was practiced by peasants and women, the high magic of the ceremonialist thrived among the intelligentsia, meaning that even clergy and monks of the Christian church would sometimes become magical adepts.

Much of the symbolism and ritual structure of modern paganism (such linking the elements with directions and colors) comes out of the ceremonial tradition.

> **CAUTION Taboo!**
>
> "Kids, don't try this at home." Ceremonial magic, like traditional witchcraft, involves powerful spiritual exercises that will, among other things, place you face to face with your deepest doubts and fears. If you are interested in learning more about ceremonial magic, find a reputable teacher or group to study with. See Appendix B, "Resources," for ways to connect with a reputable magical group.

Low (Folk) Magic

Now allow another image to form in your mind from long ago. This time, envision an old woman living alone on the outskirts of a medieval village. This being the so-called Dark Ages, there are no doctors or health clinics. As far as the villagers are concerned, their health needs are perfectly well attended to through the powerful knowledge of herbs, oils, and minerals possessed by the old wise woman. A gifted gardener, midwife, and healer, she knows just what to give a person for a sore throat, sore back, or weary mind. Her love for plants spills over to a natural veneration for the cycles of nature, so much so that the town friar seems suspicious of her and calls her a sorceress instead of a wise woman. To most people, however, her knowledge is so profound that she can make warts disappear, help young lovers conceive a child, and cause a fever to break.

The power of the folk magician relies less on ritual skill and more on a deft understanding of nature's gifts, combined with a keen insight into human psychology. Still, given how this approach to natural living also incorporates deep reverence for the earth's rhythms and abundance, it certainly is a spiritual magic, even if it doesn't involve the pursuit of mastery and power over supernatural forces that characterizes the high magician.

> **Oracle**
>
> One way to understand the difference between high and low magic is to consider the different purposes behind their psychic work. For ceremonialists, the purpose behind magic is to attain spiritual power and control over unseen forces. Natural magicians, however, tend to use their craft more in the service of physical healing or to help improve someone's luck when it comes to love or money.

Modern Magic: The Best of Both Worlds

In the pagan community, some people love the ceremonial side of magic and devote their lives to esoteric knowledge and mastery of intricate rituals. Others gravitate toward the simplicity of working with herbs, crystals, and spiritual forms of healing. Many pagans, however, freely draw from both the symbolism of high magic and the earthy practicality of folk magic to create their own style of spiritual power.

Psychic Power: Magic's "Engine"

With all the talk about candles, incense, and oils that's usually associated with magic, it's easy to think that magic involves lots of superstitious mumbo-jumbo. In truth, magic is about the power of the mind. The various tools and props we use are merely objects to help in the real work of magic: focusing the mind.

A Quantum Approach to the Powers of the Mind

Modern physics reveals that the mind has a direct impact on the external world. Experiments in physics have revealed, on the subatomic level, that merely observing the dynamics of matter and energy changes those dynamics. The implications of this are staggering and show how magic ultimately is consistent with the implications of modern science. Magic involves training and using the powers of the mind to literally create or shape our reality in accordance with our hopes, desires, and spiritual goals.

The Science of Manifestation

The world we live in is marked by change. Nothing is still. Even the smallest atom consists of particles spinning around each other, and even a seemingly immovable rock contains within it the dynamics of atomic energy. Not only does the earth spin and rotate around the sun, the sun itself is moving throughout the galaxy, and the galaxy is in motion relative to all the other galaxies in the universe. Motion, change, and energy are the bottom line of the manifest universe.

Similarly, we human beings are constantly changing and moving. As a Greek philosopher once put it, you can't step in the same river twice. Not only is the river perpetually changing, so are you.

Magic, then, is the art of managing change, primarily the changes within you but also external changes because you have a natural impact on your environment. Occult adepts have long maintained that merely imagining an object causes it to manifest in the astral dimension. Magic is the tool we use to manifest not only in the otherworld or our inner world but fully present in the physical world. We begin by creating changes within: changes in consciousness, changes in beliefs, changes in how we think and feel. We seek spiritual help in bringing these inner changes to bear on our outer lives. And then, like a beautiful dance, Spirit leads us in creating powerful (and real) changes in our lives, both inside and out. As if "by magic."

But how does it happen? How does magic work? No one knows for sure. We do know that the mind is the most creative instrument known to exist, and when we envision or affirm a reality, it sets into motion mental, emotional, and spiritual vibrations that support the manifestation of the image. Of course, this doesn't mean that all we have to do is cast a spell or recite words of power and then sit back and wait for the magic to happen. The true spirituality of magic involves both a spiritual (ritual or spell-casting) component and the real-world work to back up the intention of the ritual.

Oracle

Want to learn more about the connection between magic and science? Here are a couple of books to explore: *Stalking the Wild Pendulum: On the Mechanics of Consciousness* by Itzhak Bentov, and *Space-Time and Beyond: Toward an Explanation of the Unexplainable* by Bob Toben and Fred Alan Wolf.

Meet Me Halfway

Once upon a time, a poor man decided to test the power of magic. Every week he'd cast a spell to win the lottery. Six weeks went by, and he won nothing. The seventh week he decided to give it one more try and began to work on the spell. Just as he was about to say the words that would seal the magic, there was a blinding flash of light, and the Goddess appeared before him. "My Lady!" he gasped. "Are you here to grant me my wish?" "I would have granted your wish weeks ago," she replied. "But for you to win the jackpot, I do need you to meet me halfway. Would you go and actually buy a lottery ticket this time?"

Taboo!

The quickest way to make magic fail is to do nothing on the mundane plane to achieve your goals. The Goddess knows if you are just a slacker trying to get her to do all the work. She may be loving, but she's no fool.

This little joke underscores a key principle of magic: Even when you work a spell, it's still necessary do everything in your everyday power to make your dream come true. If nothing else, it shows the spirit world that you're serious about your goals.

So if you want to cast a spell to lose weight, that's wonderful, but you'll still have to modify your eating or exercise habits for the spell to work. A spell to find a new job will be meaningless if you aren't sending out resumés and setting up interviews. Remember the old saying "God helps those who help themselves"? In magic, this is a core principle. The Goddess helps those who help themselves.

Seven Principles of Magic

To understand magic better, here are seven principles that apply to any form of magic:

- **The power of the mind is the beginning of magic.** We've already seen this principle. The ability to use spiritual power to create positive changes in your life comes ultimately out of the mind.

- **Magic is strengthened by the words we use.** Witches call them "words of power," while mainstream society calls them affirmations. No matter what word you use to describe it, whenever you put your desires into a positive statement, you can use that statement to put your mind's power to work to make your dream come true.

- **We amplify our magic through the energy we devote to it.** Affirmations, visualizations, spells, rituals, prayers, and chanting are examples of actions that pagans take to inject their own energy into their magical work. Putting energy into a magical intention is like feeding it—it nourishes it and makes it grow stronger, thereby bringing us closer to our goal.

- **Our feelings, good or bad, impact our magic.** Because magic begins in the mind, it is affected by your mental state, including whatever you may be feeling. Times of emotional extremes—such as extreme anger, fear, or depression—are not the best time to do magic because such powerful feelings can distract the focus and intention of your magical work. More experienced magicians can use extreme emotional energy to creative and powerful ends, but as a beginner, it's generally better to take the time to be grounded and centered before focusing on your magic. Your feelings don't have to be perfectly calm, but as a rule, the more grounded you are, the better.

Oracle _____

What is the difference between magic and prayer? Some pagans would say there is no difference. Others might see prayer as a tool for friendly or intimate communication with the Goddess and see magic as more of a "business plan" where you and the Goddess are partners in achieving a goal.

♦ **Ultimately, magic involves the power to make positive changes.** The universe is constantly changing, and the energy of magic is no more or less than the energy of this constant flow of change. Magic involves focusing our desires and intentions to shape the flow of energy to positive ends.

♦ **What makes magic "magic" is the spiritual component.** Using your mind to inspire you to make changes in your life is good common sense. What makes it "magic" is the spiritual dimension: calling on the God and Goddess and your spirit guides to bless and guide your magical work. Thanks to the spiritual component, it is more than just "positive thinking." It is actually a partnership between you and the spirit realm to make good things happen.

♦ **Real magic creates real results.** It might be a nice gesture to work magic for world peace or a cure for cancer, but such huge goals tend to dissipate the energy of magic, and so we can't really see the results of our efforts. It's better to focus your magic on a specific goal that you have, such as losing those extra pounds you gained over the winter or seeing local air quality improve. Focus your energy, perform a ritual or spell, and then support it with real-world action (such as going on a diet or supporting local carpooling efforts). That's the best prescription for magic.

Magic: Any Way You Spell It

Many people think of magic purely in terms of spells. The veteran pagan understands that magic is far more than just a list of little rituals you perform to increase your sex appeal or pay down your credit cards. However, here are some thoughts on spells and the role they play in magic.

A spell is simply a recipe for success. In the preceding chapter, we looked at how regular meditation over time can contribute to increased feelings of calm, well-being, and clarity of thought. Well, that right there is a basic recipe for success. You could put it this way:

Spell to Induce Serenity, Clarity of Thought, and Well-Being

1. Light an unscented white candle.

2. Sit in a comfortable position with your back straight. Gaze softly at the candle.

3. For 10 to 30 minutes, focus on your breathing. Allow your mind to go blank. If you start thinking, simply return your attention to your breathing. Breathe deeply enough so that your body relaxes.

4. Repeat this ritual at about the same time every day. You may begin to notice immediate results, although the deepest power of the spell often takes six months to manifest.

Okay, this is a bit tongue-in-cheek, but it points to the heart of natural magic. There's nothing woo-woo about casting a spell. It's simply a tool you use to harness the natural power of your own mind to create positive changes in your life. Candles, incense, trinkets, moonlight … all are props designed to support your mind, where the real magic occurs. To the extent that the spell sets your mind on its path to mastery, a spell is truly a recipe for success.

It's the Window-Dressing That Makes Magic Fun

When you perform a spell, you'll often use any of a variety of ingredients such as candles, oils, incense, crystals, or herbs. You'll choose your ingredients based on specific colors or scents related to your goal. Spells often need to be performed at the correct phase of the moon or the correct time of day. They involve particular instructions such as burying an item at the crossroads under a full moon. All of these "ingredients" in the spell carry magical, elemental, or mythical meanings that support your mind in doing the real work of making the magic happen.

> **Oracle**
>
> Want to learn more about spells? Check out *The Complete Idiot's Guide to Wicca and Witchcraft,* which has sample spells, tips on ingredients, as well as instructions for writing your own.

It is possible for your mind to create the magic in your life without any of these extra ingredients. But just as well-chosen spices can make a meal taste truly superb, so, too, do the unique tools and actions in a magical spell combine to provide just the right support to enable your spirit to work its magic. On top of all this, spellcraft can be fun and pleasurable. Because magic is about healing and positive transformation, it only makes sense to work your magic in ways that are enjoyable for you.

As I Do Will, So Mote It Be: The Ethics of Magic

Some people resist the idea of magic. After all, if everyone cast a spell to get rich, where would all the money come from? Isn't there a level on which magic is selfish or immature? Isn't it wrong to use spiritual power in ways that give one person an unfair advantage over others?

These questions are all well worth considering. Most pagans see these kinds of questions as pointing to the ethics of magic. Magical ethics are the rules that keep magic focused in positive, spiritual ways. This section contains some thoughts about magic, spiritual power, and ethics.

First of all, as you've already seen, everything is constantly changing. Magic is the power we use to create positive changes in our lives through the use of mental and spiritual skill and backed up with real-world choices and actions. Every day we all make hundreds, perhaps thousands, of choices. Some are big and some small, but each one makes a difference in how our life moves forward. Magic, as the spiritual power we use to make changes in our lives, is a tool we use to make changes in alignment with our spiritual or higher self.

But can magic be misused? Absolutely—just like any other choice we make in life can potentially be a bad choice. Magic, by itself, is neither good nor evil. It's our intention and goal that determines whether magic is being used properly.

For most pagans, there are two ways to determine if magic is ethical. The first involves the Wiccan Rede: "An' it harm none, do what ye will." The second involves the traditional role of pagans as healers of the earth.

> **CAUTION**
>
> **Taboo!**
>
> Never cast a spell to change someone else's behavior—to get a person to fall in love with you, for example. Not only is this unethical, it will never make you happy. If you cast a love spell on a person who then says she loves you, does she really love you, or is it just the spell? You'll never know for sure. It's better to cast a spell to make yourself more naturally attractive to the right person and then let nature take its course.

Harm None ...

If your magic will harm someone else, it's unethical. Before you do any spell work, ask yourself this: What is the likely outcome of the work? Could someone get hurt (including yourself)? If so, don't do it.

Pagans take this rule of magic very seriously. Even magic that will influence or control somebody against his or her will is considered unethical because it could potentially harm that person. For this reason, pagans don't cast spells aimed at causing somebody to fall in love with somebody else, for example.

Banishing Evil: Magical Self-Defense

Is it always wrong to harm others? What about a murderer, rapist, or child abuser? Aren't there some situations in which self-defense (or the defense of others) justifies the use of harmful magic?

When we commit to magic, we commit to working for positive transformation not only in our lives but in society. Sometimes the transformation most needed involves stopping evil. From terrorism to verbal abuse, our world unfortunately has far too many people willing to engage in behavior that hurts others.

Naturally, pagans ought to do all they can to stop violence, abuse, or any other evil. This includes using not only magic but whatever mundane means may be at our disposal (such as reporting suspicious activity to the proper authorities). In terms of magic, the two concepts to keep in mind are binding and banishing. Binding involves magic aimed at preventing someone from hurting themselves or others. Banishing involves dissipating negative or harmful energies so that they cannot hurt anyone. Neither binding nor banishing is a form of harming. Basically, these are magical workings designed to prevent evil without directly attacking the evildoer. Both binding and banishing are advanced magical arts that cannot be taught in an introductory book like this. If you are interested in learning forms of magical self-defense, find a reputable teacher of the magical arts.

> **CAUTION**
>
> **Taboo!**
>
> Some people associate witchcraft with curses (spells intended to hurt someone). This is an incorrect understanding of pagan spirituality. Binding and banishing are ethical tools for magical self-defense that honor the spirit of the Wiccan Rede. Leave the curses in the low-budget horror movies where they belong.

Although the thought of using magic as a way to get even with someone who has injured or insulted you may be deliciously tempting, think this through carefully. Remember the wise proverb "Living well is the best revenge." If you use magic properly and ethically, you'll live well—a life full of happiness and personal power.

The Healing Pagan

The other way in which pagans keep magic positive and ethical is by orienting their magic toward healing rather than just toward self-gain. In fact, healing is such an important element of magic that it deserves an entire chapter of its own. See Chapter 20, "The Pagan as Healer: From Medicine Men to Reiki Masters," for more on this essential topic.

Bringing Magic and Spirituality Together: The Alchemy of Transformation

To pagans, magic is not some tool used to order spirits to do their bidding. On the contrary, pagan magic involves relating to the Goddess and God in a spirit of cooperation and harmony. Pagan magic is always aimed at the highest good, which means it works on a deeper level than just "getting what you want." Granted, because pagans believe in the way of nature and it is natural to have strong desires, pagans think it is okay to work magic to make your dreams come true. But the spirituality of magic reminds us that sometimes what you or I want may not be in accordance with the highest good. Spiritual magic is magic that always supports what is best all around.

The Spirituality of Trust

Magic can be a powerful tool for expanding your sense of connection with the Goddess and with nature, as well as your feeling of spiritual self-control. Used in conjunction with a regular spiritual practice of making offerings to the Goddess and God, you can truly find spirituality to be directly supporting your life's dreams and goals. However, one final word needs to be mentioned: trust.

No matter how devoted you are to your spiritual life, no matter how often you meditate, perform rituals, or make offerings, no matter how rigorous and exacting your spellcraft is … some things you desire may not come to you, or not as soon as you would like, or not exactly in the manner you would like. This happens to us all.

Paganism doesn't respond to disappointment with some sort of stern notion that "God knows what's best for you, so you'd better just accept it." On the contrary, because pagans believe the work of magic is a friendly partnership between infinite Spirit and our own finite natures, the disappointments of life are not interpreted as implying in any way that we don't deserve good things. Instead, pagans approach their disappointments and setbacks in terms of trust.

Again and again, the very thing that upsets us most can, at least potentially, open our lives to tremendous new blessings. Breaking up with your high school sweetheart may seem devastating, but it could also clear your life to make you available when you meet your soulmate six months later. Missing out on a promotion may seem a bitter blow, but when the company downsizes and that whole department gets the axe, maybe then you'll be glad you were passed over. And on it goes. When we learn to approach even the setbacks and delays in life with a spirit of trusting in the ultimate wisdom of the universe, we allow our energy to flow in positive, creative ways rather than getting hung up on feelings of self-abasement or resentment. Of course, trusting the process of life doesn't mean you just should passively accept disappointments. Magical people know the meaning of "If at first you don't succeed, try and try again!" When we work from a perspective of trust, we have more energy available for subsequent attempts to manifest our dreams.

The bottom line is this: Magic invites you to dare to believe in your dreams and to work (both spiritually and on a mundane, practical level) to make your dreams come true. When setbacks come your way, try to trust the wisdom of the universe, which knows more than your finite mind about when it's best for your dreams to manifest. But don't give up even when disappointments come your way.

The Least You Need to Know

- Magic is an optional part of pagan spirituality, but because most pagans want to change their lives for the better, most are interested in magic.
- Pagans may pursue high magic (very ceremonial and ritualistic) or low magic (much more informal and based on ancient folk wisdom).
- A spell is basically a recipe for putting magical power into motion.
- The most important tool in magic is your mind—it's the engine that makes change happen.
- Pagans approach magic spiritually. Trusting in the Goddess and the God is more important than always getting your own way.

Chapter 19

Divination and Omens: Listening for the Divine Whisper

In This Chapter

- ◆ Divination: How to get "intuit"
- ◆ The forces behind divination
- ◆ Learning about the major tools for divination
- ◆ Omens, or the natural side of divination

Divination is such a popular form of magic that it deserves its own chapter. Like any other kind of magic, it involves using spiritual power to achieve a specific result—in this case, accessing divine wisdom and knowledge. Chapter 4, "Wicked Good!" already looked at divination briefly because it is so central to the practice of most types of witchcraft. Witches are not the only pagans, however, who seek knowledge through the symbols and correspondences of divination. In this chapter, you'll learn more about the many ways in which pagans can seek a deeper sense of divine wisdom for practical use in their lives.

Getting Into Intuition

If magic is a tool for accessing spiritual power, then divination is a magical tool specifically designed to improve your intuition. Everybody gets knowledge from two essential sources: their senses and their intuition. Sensory knowledge is basically anything that comes in through the eyes, ears, nose, mouth, or skin. Anything you learn through reading, conversations with others, the radio, television, and so forth qualifies as sensory knowledge. But then there's the knowledge that comes from no source other than what's inside us: our imagination, our connection with the spirit world. This is the knowledge that gives us hunches and flashes of insight. The more psychically gifted you are, the more likely it is that you'll receive intuitive knowledge in dramatic or detailed ways such as vivid visions or complex thoughts that arise purely from within. This is intuition, and it is our pipeline to the Otherworld, the guidance of power animals, spirit guides, and the Goddess and God themselves.

It's not as simple as it sounds. Unfortunately, we live in a culture that is in the habit of mistrusting or ignoring intuition. We discount our hunches as silly or superstitious, and we reject any ideas or bits of knowledge that cannot be verified by the world outside of us. We don't want to appear foolish or superstitious to others, so when intuition tries to get our attention, we fervently look the other way. Most of us learned to ignore our intuition at a very young age, perhaps even before we learned how to read and write. By the time we become adults, we are so out of touch with intuition that we can't even tell the difference between intuitive guidance and other emotional processes in the body such as feelings of fear, anxiety, or hope.

> **Oracle**
>
> The choice to use divination, like using magic, is a matter of personal preference among pagans. Some pagans don't feel drawn to these tools at all. If that describes you, you're not alone. Others, however, love to explore the mysteries of astrology, Tarot, and other ancient arts for accessing intuitive wisdom. So if you feel a tug to learn more about these divinatory tools, this chapter will help you get started.

The way most people are out of touch with their intuition is symbolic of our society's overall disconnection from nature and Mother Earth. When we use tools like divination to reconnect with our intuition, we are also contributing to the overall reconnection that needs to occur between the human family as a whole and the earth, which sustains us. When we get in closer touch with the earth, we also get in closer touch with the divine—the Goddess who is manifest as the earth on which we live.

Learning to Recognize Your Own Intuition

If you've read the preceding chapters in this book, you know by now that intuition plays an important role in pagan spirituality. This is because paganism has no central authority that sets down the party line. (In paganism, there is no single party line.) Instead of looking to a bible or a pope to tell you what to think and what to believe, paganism challenges you to think for yourself and decide what's right for you to believe. This requires not only that you take responsibility for educating yourself (so you can make informed decisions) but, just as important, that you get in the habit of listening to your own intuition so that you can follow your own internal guidance to the path that is right for you.

For many of us, this is easier said than done. How do we learn to listen to that inner voice, especially if we're so alienated from it?

This is where divination comes in. If you were perfectly attuned to your psychic sources of knowledge and wisdom, you wouldn't need tools like astrology or Tarot or the I Ching to access divine guidance. You'd just naturally know what you needed to know. But because so few of us are that well connected to our intuition, the tools of divination can help us to become reconnected.

Taboo!

Intuition is no more perfect than any other form of knowledge. Just as you can make a mistake when you read or when you listen to someone, your intuition can sometimes be compromised by human error. Don't treat divination as if it were infallible. It isn't.

Psychic Skill, or Intuition on Steroids

The way most pagans see it, everyone is intuitive to some degree. Just as everyone has some sort of athletic skill and the ability to master a talent or a craft, so, too, does everyone have an innate ability to access spiritual guidance totally from within.

That said, intuition is also like athletic skill or any other talent in that different people have different abilities. Some of us are klutzes, while others are Olympians. In terms of intuition, those with world-class ability are said to be psychic. This word simply means "in touch with the powers of the mind," and the power referred to is the power of intuition.

Psychic skill, like any other talent, is somewhat based on the aptitude you're born with. Not everyone can be an Edgar Cayce or a Jane Roberts, but that's like saying not everyone can be a Jackie Joyner-Kersee or a Michael Jordan. No matter how strong (or modest) your natural psychic ability may be, you can improve your skill through spiritual practices such as meditation and making the effort to master one or more divination tools.

Drumbeats

Edgar Cayce (1877–1945) and Jane Roberts (1929–1984) are two of the best-known psychics to have lived in recent years. Both were celebrities during their lifetime, well known for the accuracy and depth of their intuitive abilities.

Divination Tools: Ways to Reconnect with Our Intuitive Power

Because the purpose of divination is to help you develop your own intuition, it's important to remember where the power of divination truly originates. Sometimes people think that astrological charts or Tarot cards or stones with runes carved on them have some sort of mysterious, inherent power that contains the key to the future. Granted, the information we can access through divination can be amazing in its accuracy and relevance to our lives, but we need to remember that the power comes from within us, not from the tool itself.

> **Drumbeats**
>
> The fancy word for predicting the future (or "fortune-telling") is *prognostication*, which means literally "foreknowledge." Some psychics and diviners do claim to have this extraordinary power. Many others, however, prefer to say that their gift only forecasts the future, acknowledging that many differing factors—including the choices you'll make as a result of consulting with divination—will inevitably shape the future in ways that no one can ever predict.

Some people even get scared of divination. After all, because these tools are so powerful, perhaps we need to be careful when we use them, for they might tell us more than we want to know about the future.

This may be a romanticized way of viewing divination, but it is not really in keeping with the wisdom of pagan spirituality. Remember that, to pagans, the power of divine guidance exists not in some external tool but within the magnificence of the human mind and imagination. In other words, *you* are the ultimate divination tool. Any system you use, from astrology to Tarot to runes to whatever, is simply a tool like a hammer or a screwdriver. Like all tools, they make your job easier, but ultimately, you're still the one doing the work.

What is the "work" of divination? Accessing your own powers of intuition and psychic skill to discern guidance and knowledge.

Past, Present, and Future

Some psychics advertise their wares in the newspaper with an ad that says something like, "Madame Susanna reveals your past, present, and future." Doesn't that sound exciting—to go to a psychic and get the lowdown on what's going to happen in your life in the next month, year, or whenever? Because these professional psychics stay in business, we can assume that many people do think this is an exciting offer.

Well, the wonders of the mind are so vast and powerful that it certainly is possible to receive psychic information about the past or future. By the same token, for most everyday purposes, divination is mainly about the present.

That may seem odd on the surface. Why would I want to ask the Tarot cards or the I Ching about something happening today? If I'm going to consult my intuition, doesn't it make more sense to look ahead a little?

Naturally, we always wonder what the future holds. But even if we gain information about the future, it can only benefit us in the present. After all, we don't live in the future—or the past. We only live right now in the present moment. So the best divination will always reveal to us hidden truths about ourselves, right here and now, that can help us to be happier, be more fulfilled, and live more meaningful lives in the present moment.

Okay, so that may not seem as glamorous as revealing all the hidden secrets of the future, but it's spiritually healthier. It also honors our own free will. What if the stars or the cards told you what would happen a year from now, and you didn't like it? What if there was nothing you could do to change it? Most pagans reject the idea that the universe is so predetermined. We believe that the Goddess and God share their power with every living being, which means each of us has an impact on how the future unfolds. In other words, the choices you make *today* (here we are back in the present) influence and shape what your tomorrows will look like. So, once again, the best divination helps us create our own future by accessing our divine guidance for the present.

Whadduzit Mean?

Now let's look at what you'll find in most divination tools. Whether you're working with astrology, Tarot, *I Ching*, numerology, tea leaves, runes, or some other method of accessing intuitive guidance, your divinatory tool will always consist of two key elements: symbols and interpretations. The divination tool gives you the chance to assemble the symbols in a random fashion (as in Tarot or runes), or they can be predetermined (as in astrology, where the symbols correspond to the location of planets in the heavens). The symbols themselves require interpretation to make sense to the person seeking guidance.

The interpretation usually involves two levels. The first level is based on established meanings associated with the symbols. For example, in astrology, the sun symbolizes your ego, your rational mind, and your father, among many other things, and the moon symbolizes your subconscious, your mother, and your feelings, among many other things. To be a true master of divination requires plenty of practice in learning the various correspondences associated with each symbol. Complex methods of divination, like astrology and Tarot, not only involve a complex set of symbols, but the meaning of each symbol is influenced by its placement in a reading. Thus, in Tarot, if you do a spread of 10 cards, the moon card will have a different meaning in each position in the spread. So, as you can see, the possibilities of interpretation are practically endless. Memorizing these correspondences marks only the first layer of doing a reading.

Oracle

It's possible to read Tarot cards or use other divination tools without ever learning the "right" meanings of the symbols. If you are able to listen to your intuition, you probably could use a divination tool effectively even with little or no knowledge of its traditional meanings. However, learning the meanings associated with your favorite tool can help you be even more accurate in your divination.

The second layer involves pure reliance on your inner guidance. In other words, a gifted reader not only will know the "standard" meaning of each symbol but will also be able to listen to his or her own inner voice, which will sometimes lead to an interpretation of a symbol that is entirely different from its standard meaning. This is especially true in Tarot, where the rich symbolism of the cards includes not only pictures but colors, numbers, elemental correspondences, and various magical or esoteric symbols encoded in the cards. To a gifted reader, any one element of the symbol may trigger a sense of what the reading's guidance may be.

Does all this sound overwhelming? It's good to understand just how profound and complex divination can be, but if you're just beginning, you don't have to master all the complexities at first. As a beginner, you can quickly learn to do accurate and useful divinatory readings as long as you take the time to try to learn at least basic meanings for the symbols of your divination method while also remembering to listen to your inner guidance to help you when you interpret a reading.

Cycles and Chance

Most systems of divination involve the element of chance because the symbols (whether runes, Tarot cards, or I Ching sticks) are picked at random. This in itself is the intuitive mind at work. Pagans recognize that the power of the mind is such that subconsciously you can pick just the right cards (or whatever system you're using) to be given the guidance you need right now.

Drumbeats

How can divination work if chance plays such a large part in which cards or runes or whatever you'll be interpreting? Many pagans see it this way: Everything in the universe is part of the Goddess and the God; therefore, everything has some aspect of divinity about it. Even seemingly random events, like picking cards out of a stack, can therefore contain elements of divine wisdom. This is why reading omens in nature (such as the chance occurrence of a certain species of bird flying above you at a particular moment in time) can also be meaningful. On the other hand, remembering the randomness of divination is important to keep from taking it so seriously that you give up your ability to make your own choices.

Two popular systems of divination, numerology and astrology, don't involve this random element of chance. Instead, these systems find meaning in the cycles of the universe. Numbers, the symbols used in numerology, work in a series of fixed cycles. The planets and stars, the symbols used in astrology, appear to revolve in a series of cycles around our position on the earth.

Numerology and astrology are meaningful because we live in a cyclical universe in which certain energies, lessons, and principles come to bear in our lives in a rhythmic manner. So, although random/chance methods of divination put us in touch with our subconscious ability to choose meaningful symbols, tools like astrology and numerology help us become better attuned with the natural rhythms and cycles of life.

Well, that's enough theory for now. Let's look at several of the better known and more commonly used divination systems.

Astrology and Tarot: The Big Two in Divination

Far and away, the two most common and popular tools for accessing divine wisdom and inner guidance are astrology and Tarot. Notice that these represent the two main types of divination: the cyclical and random methods of creating a reading. Some psychics even say that astrology represents the science of divination, while the Tarot represents the art.

In both of these tools, like all the other great methods of divination, you'll find an intricate set of symbols, each of which has many correspondences that can be used in interpreting a reading.

Astrology

When William Shakespeare called Romeo and Juliet "star-crossed lovers," he was making a reference to the ancient tool of astrology. This divination system relies on three distinct sets of symbols—known as planets, houses, and signs—to create a reading (commonly called a "chart" in astrology).

The signs refer to 12 constellations that form a ring in the heavens. These 12 signs, also called the zodiac, represent the path that the sun and planets appear to take through the sky over the course of time.

The planets include all the planets in our solar system, from Mercury (closest to the sun) to Pluto (farthest away). Even though they are not technically planets, the sun and the moon are considered planets for the purposes of astrology. There are 10 planets in every horoscope. Some astrologers also use asteroids (the small planet-like objects that orbit the sun between Mars and Jupiter) to add additional layers of meaning to their charts.

The houses are like 12 spokes on a wheel. Each house, like each sign and each planet, has a different set of meanings. The position of the houses depends on the time of day for which a chart is cast.

Generally speaking, the signs rule aspects of your personality. The houses rule people, places, or things that play a role in your life, and the planets signify the energy or dynamics that impact your life. Not only does the position of the planets in the signs and houses make a difference in interpreting your horoscope, but if planets are close to one other, opposite one another, or at specific angles to one another on the chart, that makes a difference as well.

> **Drumbeats**
>
> Every horoscope chart is unique. Each of the planets moves at different speeds around the zodiac (from the moon's 29-day cycle to Pluto, which takes more than 240 years to complete one circuit). Even an interval as short as five minutes will result in the planets having different positions on a chart.

If you decide to explore astrology as a divination tool, you'll first want a natal horoscope. This will give you a snapshot of the heavens at the moment of your birth. A natal chart is like a blueprint of your personality. From there, you'll want to explore progressions and transits. These are charts based on your natal horoscope that look at how the planets have continued to move in the skies over the time since your birth. By comparing your natal chart to where the planets are presently in the sky, you can learn how your life issues, as encoded in your natal chart, impact the current situation of your life and where your personal strengths are for dealing with current and future problems.

Astrology is such a large and vast discipline that you could literally devote your entire life to it. If you feel drawn to it, look for a professional astrologer in your community who can teach you how to cast and interpret charts.

Tarot

Like astrology, Tarot is an ancient tool that has enjoyed an upsurge of popularity in recent years. The origins of the Tarot cards are lost in the mists of time, although some occultists believe that the symbolism of the cards contains powerful teachings that date back to the golden age of Egyptian paganism. As for solid evidence, the cards can be traced back to medieval Europe and have been used for divination since the middle of the nineteenth century. No matter how old Tarot is or just how much "secret" information is contained in the cards, it is certainly a vivid tool for deep inner insight that anyone can learn how to use. Divination with Tarot cards (or any other deck of cards) is called *cartomancy*.

> **EarthWords**
>
> **Cartomancy** is the practice of using playing cards for divination.

On the most basic level, the Tarot is a fancy deck of cards. Traditional Tarot decks include 78 cards, divided into two sections. The Major Arcana consists of 22 cards, each of which has a name like "The Fool," "The Wheel of Fortune," "The Lovers," and so forth. The remaining 56 cards form the Minor Arcana, which is very similar to an ordinary deck of playing cards. The Minor Arcana includes four suits called Wands, Swords, Cups, and Pentacles (which in older decks are called Coins). Each suit includes an Ace card, numbered cards from 2 to 10, and four court cards: the Page, the Knight, the Queen, and the King.

Oracle

You don't need a fancy Tarot deck to practice cartomancy. An ordinary deck of playing cards works just as nicely. The suits of Spades, Clubs, Diamonds, and Hearts correspond to the Tarot's suits of Swords, Wands, Pentacles, and Cups. Whether you use Tarot or playing cards, you'll use the cards to inspire your intuitive powers, which is where the real magic of divination lies.

The Tarot, with its colorful images, is one of the most popular forms of divination.

(© 2001 Fox Gradin)

As a system of divination, Tarot is much less structured than astrology. Many different systems have developed over the years to help unlock the mysteries of these cards. Among ceremonial magicians and other occultists, the cards (especially the Major Arcana) have very specific meanings, often tied in with ancient Egyptian mythology, the Kabbalah (Jewish mysticism), or the esoteric teachings of a magical order like the Golden Dawn. The Minor Arcana combines elemental symbolism, numerology, and even family psychology (the Kings represent fathers, the Queens mothers, and so forth) to assign meanings to each card. Learning the traditional meanings of the 78 cards can be a daunting task, but it's really no more complicated than learning how to play the 88 keys of a piano. Like a piano, the Tarot can be a powerful tool in the hands of an experienced player. All it takes is practice.

Many people have found that the Tarot can be a powerful tool for divination even if you do not know all the traditional meanings behind each card. Simply picking three or four cards at random; laying them out and looking at the colors, numbers, and pictures on each card; and then allowing your intuition to speak can be an amazing way to access your deep inner wisdom. The Tarot, as a collection of images (rather than words), helps us to access the right side of our brain, the part of the human mind more accustomed to thinking in images rather than words. For many people, this is the part of the mind that is more naturally intuitive.

If you want to read Tarot, it's still a good idea to learn all you can about the traditional lore and meanings associated with the Tarot cards. As you get to know the depth of each of the symbols in the cards, your ability to tap into your intuition will be enriched.

Many different Tarot decks are available today, thanks to the explosion of interest in divination and spirituality in general. Artists have developed Tarot decks based on ancient mythology, Native American spirituality, herbalism, and even baseball. Here are a few Tarot decks that are especially well-suited for pagans.

- ◆ **The Rider-Waite-Smith Tarot**   One of the most famous decks, it is filled with imagery based on the magical teachings of the Golden Dawn.

- ◆ **The Robin Wood Tarot**   Inspired by the Rider-Waite-Smith deck, this beautiful deck by artist Robin Wood replaces the Golden Dawn imagery with purely pagan symbolism.

- ◆ **The Motherpeace Tarot**   This famous round deck (the cards are round) features almost purely feminine imagery. It is perfect for intensive work with the Goddess.

- ◆ **The Witches Tarot**   Designed by Wiccan elder Ellen Cannon Reed, this deck makes effective use of Kabbalistic imagery in the Major Arcana.

- ◆ **Tarot of the Old Path**   This gorgeous deck is filled with imagery from traditional witchcraft.

- ◆ **The Celtic Wisdom Tarot**   Created by Celtic scholar Caitlín Matthews, this deck replaces traditional Tarot imagery with symbolism drawn directly from Celtic myth. It is perfect for druids and other Celtic-oriented pagans.

♦ **The Aleister Crowley Thoth Tarot** Crowley was the "bad boy" of ceremonial magic, but this beautiful and symbolically powerful deck reveals his profound knowledge of the inner mysteries.

Sacred Alphabets: Spelling Out Intuition

The power of the Tarot comes mainly from its effective use of symbolism and imagery to coax our natural powers of intuition into action. Pictures, however, are not the only tool that can be psychically stimulating. The runes and the ogham are two examples of alphabets that can be used for divination, and each letter of the alphabet carries a rich and profound set of symbolic meanings.

The Runes

The word "rune" means "hidden secret" and points to the fact that this sacred Norse alphabet has magical as well as linguistic uses. The oldest set of runes, the Elder Futhark, consists of 24 characters. According to Norse myth, the runes were discovered by the God Odin. After being suspended from Yggdrasil, the great shamanistic world tree, for nine days and nights, Odin received mystical visions in which the secrets of the runes were revealed to him.

Several different versions of the runes exist, all based on ancient alphabets from northern Europe. Today, use of the runes as a tool for divination is based on each rune having its own set of meanings. You can buy a set of runes or create your own, carving the characters into stones or painting them onto small pieces of wood. To use the runes in divination, you simply draw at random one or more runes out of a bag, interpreting each character in light of the question you're asking.

> **Drumbeats**
>
> Technically, it's incorrect to call the runes an alphabet. Alphabets are collections of letters that begin with the letters A and B (or their Greek equivalents, alpha and beta). Because the runes begin with the letters F, U, Th, A, R, and K, it's more proper to refer to the runes as a futhark.

Because of the powerful symbolism associated with each rune, you can use the runes in ways other than just for divination. You may want to carve a specific rune on your magical tools, embroider it on your robe or other ritual clothing, or even get a runic tattoo. Whichever rune you use, you are inviting the energies represented by that character to manifest more fully in your life. Thus, if you are seeking spiritual protection, you may want to carve the rune Elhaz on your tools. If you seek to grow in knowledge, the runic energy you'll want to invoke is that of Kenaz, the rune of knowledge.

The Ogham

Chapter 5, "The Philosophical Pagans: Druids and Other Revivalist Groups," looked at the ogham, the ancient alphabet used by the druids. Although there's no evidence that the ancient druids used this alphabet as a system of divination, modern writers like Robert Graves, Edred Thorsson, and Caitlín Matthews have created divinatory systems using the ogham letters and the magical lore surrounding the trees or plants that each letter represents. Like the runes, each character of the ogham signifies a specific kind of energy, concept, or theme that can impart wisdom to the person seeking a spiritual answer to a question. Thus, the ogham character Beith, for the birch tree, calls the seeker to embark on a new beginning of some sort. Saille, corresponding to the willow tree, represents awareness of and trusting your own inner wisdom.

Like the runes, you can buy a set of ogham to work with, or you can make your own. See Appendix A for recommended resources to learn more about these divination tools.

Other Common Divination Tools

Any one tool of divination could take up an entire book all by itself, so needless to say, the following list of divination tools is only the most basic of introductions. As you pursue your own unique path of nature spirituality, trust your own interests and intuition to discern which divination tool or tools may be right for you. If you feel drawn to a system of divination, take the time to learn more about it. Trust your own inner guidance to direct you to the tool that is best for you for accessing intuitive wisdom.

The *I Ching*

One of the oldest forms of divination comes from China and is based on principles associated with Yin and Yang energies. The *I Ching*, or *Book of Changes*, involves 64 different patterns called hexagrams that are selected by throwing special coins or sticks. Each hexagram has a profound meaning that has been encapsulated in a classic text called *The Book of Changes*. Reading the densely written, enigmatic words associated with each hexagram can provide striking insights into your intuitive guidance.

Tea Leaves

Popular in the Victorian era, the practice of reading tea leaves is not as widespread nowadays (probably because tea usually comes in bags), but as a venerable practice, it might be worth checking out if you're interested. After drinking a cup of tea made with loose tea leaves, turn your cup upside down on your saucer and look at the patterns the tea leaves form. Several books have been published that suggest meanings related to different images that can appear in the tea leaves.

Numerology

Every number, from 1 to 9, has a particular resonance, a particular set of meanings associated with it. "Master numbers," such as 11, 22, 33, and so forth, also carry their own particular meanings. Numerology is the art of determining the numbers that are meaningful to you, through your birth date, numbers associated with the letters in your name, and even your Social Security number and telephone number. Every year has its own numerological value, so if you choose to master the lore of numerology, you can begin to create plans for each year of your life based on its numerological value.

Scrying and the Second Sight

From crystal balls to bowls of water to sheets of glass painted black, psychics and diviners through the ages have used tools to aid them in the art of scrying.

Scrying is the art of seeing psychic images in an empty item such as a crystal or a dark glass plane. It comes from the same root as the word "describe." It is the practice of describing what is seen psychically.

Omens: Listening for the Voice of the Spirits in the Natural World

For many pagans, working with runes, Tarot cards, or *I Ching* coins has a man-made feel about it. Instead of relying on such artificial tools for divination, these pagans, true to their devotion to nature, prefer to rely on signs and omens from the great outdoors to inspire their intuitive prowess. This comes straight out of the world of shamanism, where the movement of animals, the patterns of birds in flight, or the pattern found in rocks lying on the ground all can contribute to your intuitive guidance.

Omen is a Latin word that means "foreboding." For pagans, an omen is anything that suggests something to come. It's not necessarily good or bad; omens can point to positive developments as well as negative ones. Remember that the power of an omen lies in its ability to speak to your intuition. If you see two birds fighting on the morning of your wedding, it doesn't necessarily mean your marriage will be full of strife. What's important, from a divinatory perspective, is how you interpret the omen. If you saw the birds fight, you could interpret it as a warning to control your temper. Or perhaps you would interpret it as a sign that your marriage will be filled with passion and energy, energy that could lead to fighting if not properly channeled. To pagans, an omen is not something "carved in stone;" rather, it is a natural event that helps a person to connect with his or her own inner wisdom.

The Least You Need to Know

◆ Divination involves using your intuition to access the wisdom of the spiritual world.

◆ Many tools exist to help you develop your natural intuitive abilities.

◆ Two of the most popular forms of divination are astrology and the Tarot.

◆ Divination is meant to help you live a happier and more fulfilled life. It's a mistake to take divination so seriously that you cannot make your own decisions.

◆ You can use omens, or signs in nature, as a means of divination, or you can learn to rely on your intuition so thoroughly that you don't need any external tools at all.

Chapter 20

The Pagan as Healer: From Medicine Men to Reiki Masters

In This Chapter

- ◆ Why healing is central to pagan spirituality
- ◆ The varieties of spiritual healing, from herbalism to reiki
- ◆ Why magical healing complements—but doesn't replace—mundane methods of healthcare and environmental work

From meditation to magic to divination, the various spiritual skills of the pagan path all serve to increase your power to relate to life, the Goddess and God, and nature. The more magical you become, the more powerful you are.

But what is the point of developing all this spiritual power?

It has been said, "Power corrupts, and absolute power corrupts absolutely." Most pagans would not entirely agree with this dour assessment of power. To pagans, the power that corrupts is the power that seeks to control other people. However, there is a healthy, appropriate kind of power—the power that comes from within, which is the power to heal. Basically, power can be used for one of two things. It can be used to shove people around so that you can get your own way (the power that corrupts). But there's also the power that seeks to live in harmony with nature and the Goddess and God and that seeks to change things when something is out of balance to make the world more harmonious, more balanced, more in alignment with Spirit. This is the power of healing. For pagans, the point behind developing spiritual power—whether you call it magic, divination, enlightenment, or whatever—is to facilitate the work of healing and love in the world.

"Healing" can mean a lot of things, including physical healing (the promotion of bodily health), mental, emotional, and spiritual healing, as well as healing work done in the name of protecting the environment or fostering peace and social justice in the word. For pagans, every aspect of healing can be part of our magical work.

This chapter takes a closer look at the healing tradition within paganism. You may have been drawn to paganism just because you liked nature, thought the Goddess was cool, or secretly wanted to learn how to cast spells. There's nothing wrong with that. But here's a surprise: If you stick around the world of paganism, you will become more than just a nature mystic or a conjurer. You will become a healer. Not because you're forced to (remember, there's no one in the pagan world telling you what you "should" do) but because you'll just naturally want to. You'll want to heal yourself of all the physical, mental, and spiritual ailments and wounds that you have. The more healed you become, the more you'll naturally reach out to others—including to nature herself—to help them heal.

Witches, Shamans, Magicians: All Are Healers

So what do the three main types of pagans (witches, shamans, and druids) have in common? They are all, at least in some significant way, healers.

Let's take a look at the wonderful healing tradition within these branches of paganism.

Shamans engage in what may be the world's longest-standing healing practice. Indeed, in traditional societies, the shaman basically performs two functions: He or she negotiates with the spirit world to ensure favorable conditions for the people (like a successful hunt or a bountiful harvest) and then also intercedes in the spirit world to help heal the sick. With the practice of soul retrieval, shamans travel into the Otherworld to help a person regain spiritual wholeness.

Witchcraft, as you saw in Chapter 4, "Wicked Good!" is basically the modern expression of European forms of shamanism. The witch as healer is particularly evident in the tradition of the village wise woman, midwife, and herbalist. Before the rise of the institutionalized medical profession in the early modern era, most people resorted to traditional wisdom—including the wisdom of herbs and other natural remedies—for their health and well-being. And who were the custodians of this healing knowledge? The wise women, of course. Remember that the word "witch" comes from the same root as the word "wise."

Druids, as the Celtic priesthood, represented not only shamanic and magical power but a true flowering of scientific and mental knowledge. The druids were the philosophers, scientists, and lawyers of their culture. They also were the doctors. Indeed, in Celtic mythology, several Gods (most notably Dian Cecht) were honored specifically for their medical skills. In some ways, the druids were also psychological counselors because they served the chieftains of the Celtic world, sharing their knowledge and spiritual wisdom to help the chieftains rule effectively.

Drumbeats

The words "heal" and "healing" come from an Old English word related to wholeness. To pagans, healing is more than just getting better when we're sick. Spiritual healing means doing what it takes to make every aspect of life full of happiness, vitality, and wholeness. Such healing may include learning to think positively, getting proper exercise and rest, developing skills for intimacy and interpersonal communication, and making other efforts to improve the quality of life. Therefore, healing is something that can benefit us even when we're physically healthy.

Here is where the true beauty of paganism begins to flower. There are two sides to spirituality. The first side involves personal feelings of spiritual wholeness and satisfaction. Different religious traditions around the world label this in different ways, such as "salvation," "enlightenment," "being born again," "getting right with God," or merely "improving your karmic bank account." Paganism's emphasis on harmony with nature and finding joy through magic and ritual falls within this important aspect of spirituality, but taking care of yourself is only half of the spiritual adventure.

The other half involves recognizing that your health and well-being depend on the health and well-being of others (including the environment in which you live). So, ultimately, spirituality involves service and healing. In Buddhism, there's the concept of the boddhisattva, who is on the verge of enlightenment but chooses to reincarnate to serve others. Christianity has the concept of the saint, who dedicates his or her life to alleviating suffering in the world. Pagans don't think of themselves in such high-faluting ways as saints or bodhisattvas, but that's because pagans believe that everyone can be a healer, not just specially advanced mystics or holy people. If you choose to walk the pagan path, you are choosing the path of healing.

Oracle

Remember the old saying that "an ounce of prevention is worth a pound of cure"? This applies to spiritual healing as well. You can use visualization, herbal supplements, healing touch, and other spiritual tools for wellness at any time. If you get into the habit of taking care of yourself when you're healthy, you'll be less likely to get sick in the future.

The rest of this chapter will look at several ways in which pagans practice healing. Here's an important point, one that we'll revisit toward the end of the chapter: Spiritual healing is meant to complement, not replace, scientific forms of medicine and healing. In other words, if you decide to practice reiki or herbalism, that's great, but don't turn your back on other forms of physical care. A pagan friend of mine recently suffered from chest pains. He asked his girlfriend to give him reiki. She very responsibly told him that he didn't need reiki, he needed a trip to the emergency room. Sure enough, he was suffering from a heart attack, and her common sense most likely saved his life. The moral of the story: Pagan healing is never meant to diagnose illness or prescribe medical treatment. You remain responsible for consulting with your doctor whenever you have health concerns that require care.

This doesn't mean that spiritual healing is useless. On the contrary, most pagans will report that their use of spiritual as well as traditional forms of healing help them to stay healthier and, when they do get sick, to recover more quickly.

How Pagans Heal

Pagans basically have four tools to help them heal themselves, others, and even the planet as a whole. These tools include herbalism, energy work (which includes reiki), magic and spellcraft, and visualization and affirmation. Pagans also understand that the healing process requires action. In the pagan world, each person is responsible for his or her own life and well-being, including his or her own healing. If you are sick, you don't just passively go to the doctor's office and let him or her "fix" you like you are a broken engine. Instead, you partner with the doctor, making the necessary changes in your diet, lifestyle, and even thought patterns to support the healing process.

Let's look at each of these healing tools. This chapter only gives you the most basic of information. If you find that a particular healing modality appeals to you, you'll want to do further studying on your own.

Drumbeats

Here are four of the most common herbs and how they are used:

- **Echinacea** (coneflower) is used to boost the human immune system, especially to fight common ailments like head colds.
- **St. John's Wort** is used to combat depression.
- **Garlic** has a reputation not only for supporting the immune system but also for removing toxins from the bloodstream, making it a supportive herb for cardiac health.
- **Ginseng** is taken to support the body's overall sense of wellness and energy levels (and, in older men, to increase sexual vitality).

Herbs: Plants of Healing

Question: What do echinacea, St. John's Wort, garlic, and ginseng have in common?

Answer: All are botanical products that have gained attention in recent years for having beneficial properties for human health and vitality.

The first doctors were the herbalists: the women and men who learned the properties associated with plants that could help reduce a fever, stop an infection, cleanse the bowels, or elevate a person's mood. For most of human history, herbal remedies were the primary tools used in supporting health and wellness.

In the modern era, humankind has developed pharmaceutical skill: the ability to synthesize powerful drugs to support the healing process. Most people forget that today's wonder drugs often have a foundation in the world of plants. Aspirin originally was manufactured from the bark of willow trees, and penicillin originally was developed from a mold.

Taboo!

> Herbs can heal, but they can also be dangerous. Consult with a reputable herbalist if you are interested in using herbal remedies. If you are interested in herbal healing, you need to study with a qualified herbal master.

Many drugs are truly wonderful miracles of science. Others have side effects that are almost as bad as the condition the drug treats. To many pagans, it simply makes good sense to rely on the curative powers of plants whenever possible as a natural, organic way to support the body's quest for health and well-being.

Reiki and Other Forms of Psychic Healing

Pagans, like the followers of many other spiritual traditions, understand that healing involves more than just taking a pill or having surgery. The human body is more than just a machine that needs a tune-up every few thousand miles. It's a precise energetic system in which the subtle energies of one's spirit interact with the more gross energies of physical manifestation (the body) to create a shell or home in which the spirit resides. As an energy system, the body needs to maintain balance to function properly. When things get out of balance, we experience illness ranging from little problems like sore throats and headaches to major, life-threatening problems such as cancer or heart disease. No matter how large or small the malady, regaining energetic balance is a key to healing. We do this in several ways: through proper diet, adequate rest, appropriate levels of exercise, maintaining mental health through close contact with loved ones, and keeping a hopeful, faithful attitude first and foremost in our consciousness. All of these practices are key to maintaining optimum health.

Psychic healing brings together several of these principles. It is a loving form of interaction between two (or more) human beings, thus nurturing our body's need for intimacy, love, and physical contact with others. It involves the healer's energy interacting with that of the person in need of healing, recognizing that energy patterns tend to harmonize and stabilize. It also involves the healer opening up his or her energy to allow the healing energies of spirit to flow through. This also supports the faith and hope of the person in need of healing.

Psychic forms of healing work on several levels: restoring energetic balance, fostering intimacy and human contact, and nurturing a sense of faith and hope. No wonder so many people find it an effective healing tool.

In this section, we're going to look at one particular form of psychic healing that has become increasingly popular in recent years: reiki, a healing practice that originated in Japan and made its way to America in the mid-twentieth century. Other disciplines of psychic healing employ similar practices. The common element of all psychic healing is loving interaction between healer and client, the flow of energy (including energy from Spirit), and an atmosphere of trusting faith in the healing process.

What Is Reiki?

The word "reiki" literally means "universal life-force energy." It was discovered (or some would say rediscovered) by a Japanese Doctor, Mikao Usui, in the mid-nineteenth century. On a quest to learn how to perform spiritual healing like that practiced by spiritual masters such as Christ or the Buddha, Dr. Usui found instructions in an ancient manuscript in a Buddhist monastery on how to become a spiritual healer. Following the guidance of the ancient text, he spent a 21-day period fasting and meditating on a mountaintop in Japan. The morning of the twenty-first day, Usui underwent a profound mystical experience during which he received a number of powerful symbols and instructions on how to use them in psychic healing work. Thus was he attuned, or initiated, into the practice of reiki.

> **Drumbeats**
>
> Mikao Usui's original quest to find reiki arose out of his desire to learn how Jesus healed with the laying-on of hands. Of course, reiki itself transcends all religious and spiritual boundaries; it is a healing method that anyone with goodwill, right intention, and proper training can master. It is something pagans, Buddhists, Christians, or members of any other faith can practice.

Usui spent the rest of his life practicing this unique form of spiritual healing and trained others to become masters in the art of reiki. One of his students trained Hawayo Takato, a woman who brought reiki to North America in the mid-twentieth century. From her, countless numbers of individuals have received training in how to perform this powerful healing art.

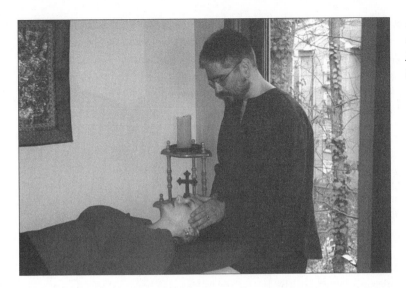

Reiki is a gentle practice of channeling universal life-force energy through the practitioner's hands.

(© 2001 Peter Manzi)

Reiki involves the practitioner envisioning one or more of the sacred reiki symbols as conduits of the healing energy known as the universal life force. Indeed, the practitioner him- or herself is a conduit for this energy. The practitioner places his or her hands on the recipient, either on or near the source of pain, on the chakras, or on a series of positions throughout the body, channeling the reiki energy through the practitioner's hands and into the recipient. Reiki is safe, noninvasive, gentle, and an effective way to integrate spiritual energy into physical healing and well-being.

Get Those Chakras Spinning!

Like reiki, most forms of psychic healing involve interacting with the chakra system. You learned in Chapter 6, "Other Pieces of the Pagan Puzzle," that the chakra system is the energy field intimately associated with the human body. Each of the seven spinning wheels of light governs different parts of the body as well as different aspects of soul consciousness. Depending on how balanced and harmonious the body's energy is, any or all of the chakras may be opened or closed. An opened chakra is one in which energy flows smoothly through it and around it. Think of the chakra as the hubs of major highways and the energy of the human body/soul as traffic on the highway. When there's a traffic jam, the chakra

Oracle

Some healers find that using a pendulum is a handy tool to assess how open a chakra is. Simply take a small pendulum and suspend it over a person's chakra. If the chakra is closed, the pendulum will either hang limply or move in a back and forth motion. When a chakra has opened up, the pendulum swings in a smooth circular motion.

shuts down and energy doesn't flow. When the chakra is open, however, the energy flows smoothly through it. Obviously, stress (which medical science recognizes as a major cause of disease) is like a sudden inflow of excess energy (or traffic, to continue the highway metaphor), leading to jammed-up energy (and closed chakras). One of the main benefits of psychic healing work is that it balances out the body's energy flow and enables the chakras to open and function smoothly.

Healing Touch

Reiki and other forms of psychic healing are known as healing touch. This is because they generally involve gentle touching of hands on the body of the person seeking healing. Some psychic healers may not touch the physical body; instead, they use their hands to interact with the aura, or psychic/spiritual body, that surrounds the physical. Even so, this is still a form of healing touch because contact is occurring, even if only on a spiritual level. Healing touch is gentle and nonthreatening. It works because the energy of the healer (or the energy channeled through the healer) stabilizes and harmonizes the energy of the recipient.

If you are a skeptical sort of person who finds talk of "energy work" and "psychic healing" not to your liking, don't write it off just yet. More and more members of the medical and scientific community have come to recognize that spiritual practices like meditation and prayer play a measurably significant role in the healing process. There is certainly no harm in fostering a spirit of hope or the warmth of physical intimacy between people. The next time you have a headache or backache and someone offers you reiki, give your skepticism a vacation and just try it. I bet you'll be pleasantly surprised at how good and healing it feels.

Ritual as a Healing Process

Pagans recognize that ritual plays an important role in many areas of life. Chapter 16, "Rites of Passage," pointed out how rites of passage (like handfastings/weddings and funerals) help us make sense of the transitions we go through in life. Indeed, there's a powerful level on which a rite of passage actually makes the transition more real.

For pagans, using ritual as a healing tool is a way to make the body's natural healing abilities more real. A person may believe that he or she contains natural power for self-healing and may believe that medical care, dietary and herbal treatments, and spiritual healing practices all can support the body's natural healing ability. Even so, in performing a ritual to facilitate and celebrate the magic of healing, we send messages to our subconscious mind to make the healing more truly a reality in our experience.

In this section, we'll look at how ritual and magical processes can provide that kind of "make it so" support. Whether it's creating a spell to facilitate the healing process, raising energy in a magic circle, or simply engaging in regular use of visualization during meditation, pagans find these rituals of healing to be valuable and transformative exercises.

Magic

Magic is about change and so is healing. Whether you're seeking healing for yourself, a loved one, or the earth, whether you're seeking a cure for a disease, a release of an emotional or mental block, or a new attainment of vitality and wellness, why not support your efforts with a little bit of fairy dust? In a way, all ethical magic is healing magic because positive magic seeks positive transformation, and what is healing but change for the better? One function of magic involves the concept of charging, or imbuing a person or object with energy focused on a particular purpose or desired outcome. Many pagans will charge their medicine, herbs, or other healing items with their own energies in support of the healing process. To charge an item, hold it or place it on your altar. Visualize golden white light radiating from your heart, your third eye, and the crown of your head, infusing the item with magical power for the purpose you seek. It's also helpful to say a brief prayer to the Goddess, asking for her blessing on the item being charged.

Here are several ways to bring magic into your quest for healing:

- **Cast a spell.** One simple and effective healing spell involves two objects: one that symbolizes your illness and another that symbolizes the healing you seek. Perhaps if you suffer from lower-back pain, a box of pain killers symbolizes your affliction, while a photograph of a strong, happy body builder can symbolize your own back becoming healthy and whole. The spell itself involves two steps. First, during the waning moon, cast a circle and charge the item symbolizing the illness. Envision healing energy flowing from Spirit through you into the object, therefore symbolically representing the actual healing. Next, bury or burn the object symbolizing the affliction to represent its demise. Then, after the new moon (during the waxing moon), cast another circle and charge the object representing health as a symbol for the new health that is arriving. Keep this object on your altar (or give it to the person on whose behalf the magic is performed).

> **CAUTION** **Taboo!**
>
> However tempting it may be, don't ever perform magic for someone without his or her consent. If you want to do healing work for a loved one who doesn't understand paganism or doesn't know you're a pagan, offer to "say prayers" for them instead. Pagans believe even prayer can be a source of magical healing.

◆ **Create or use an *amulet, talisman,* or spirit bag.** Amulets and talismans are magical terms for objects you wear or keep to support your magical intention. Use an amulet for protection from illness, infection, or anything else that would inhibit healing. A talisman may be used to attract healing or healthy energy. Shamans use spirit bags to hold amulets, talismans, crystals, herbs, or any other items that may have powerful magical or spiritual meaning. Although some pagan or magical traditions have very precise instructions for how to create powerful amulets and talisans, you can also use a simple natural object (like a crystal or an acorn) and magically charge it to represent your goal for healing (or prevention).

EarthWords

An **amulet** is a natural object which is energetically charged to protect the wearer/owner from negative energies. A **talisman** is also a magical object, but one created by a human being and then imbued with protective or healing energy.

◆ **Take a shamanic journey.** If you practice a more shamanic form of paganism, you may find that going on an inner journey to your spirit contacts in the otherworld can be a healing and educational process. The spirit guides will work to support your healing on a spiritual level, and they often have practical advice to help you with your efforts for healing.

Visualization and Affirmation

Your skills in visualization and affirmation can deeply benefit your quest for magical healing, whether for yourself or for someone else. Take time while meditating, on a regular basis, to visualize yourself or the person involved as healthy and well. Also visualize the healing process itself. If you're working on healing cancer, visualize the body's white blood cells effectively destroying the cancer cells. The visualization doesn't even need to be literal. You can see two "armies" fighting, with the army representing health and healing emerging victorious.

Similarly, words of power support healing because they train the mind to think in healing, nurturing ways. Here's a few sample affirmations. You also can write your own to support your specific healing needs.

I exercise regularly and eat a balanced diet to support my body maintaining my ideal weight.

I think positive and loving thoughts and enjoy a happy, optimistic mood.

Aunt Tracey gets stronger every day, regaining more and more of the skills she lost after her stroke.

The earth's ozone layer repairs itself, and humankind reduces our dangerous emissions.

Granted, some of these affirmations (like the last one) may seem a long way off from events as they currently stand. But the more we train our minds to think in positive, healing ways, the more we'll manifest such healing both in mundane and spiritual ways. For that matter, there is the concept of critical mass—that when enough people align their consciousness with the same goal (such as healing the ozone layer or fostering world peace), that goal will become manifest. So start focusing your mind in healing ways, and you can contribute to positive transformation.

Oracle

Write your affirmations on sticky notes and put them in places where you're likely to see them, such as on your bathroom mirror, near your computer monitor, and above the kitchen sink. Then, each time you see one, you'll have another reminder to put these words of power into action.

A Simple Healing Ceremony

Any of these magical tools can be incorporated into a healing ceremony, which is basically using ritual and magic together to support your healing work. You can cast a circle like the sample one described in Chapter 15, "A Basic Ritual," or you can use the ritual format from the particular tradition you've chosen to follow. Either way, it's a good spiritual practice to include time for special magical or healing work in your rituals. Devote this part of the ritual to healing, including raising energy, charging amulets or talismans, or simply meditating and sharpening your tools for visualization and affirmation. It's also powerful to perform reiki or other healing-touch work in a ritual (provided the person receiving the healing work is comfortable being in a ritual). That's like adding extra "oomph" to the psychic work you're doing.

Paganism and Mainstream Medicine

Pagans believe that every human being is a unique manifestation of the life force of Spirit. In other words, each person has his or her own connection to the Goddess and the God. Healing simply involves using tools (from mainstream medicine to alternative therapies to spiritual practices like those discussed in this chapter) to reconnect with our spiritual essence and thereby bring our bodies back into energetic balance and harmony. In other words, even if you are fighting cancer and have chosen to rely on mainstream forms of healing like chemotherapy and radiation, you can still approach your therapy from a position of faith in your own spiritual essence and optimism that you can generate healing. Indeed, even people in the last stages of cancer have experienced dramatic (and scientifically unexplainable) healing. Keep your faith focused on the healing you desire, and it will serve you well.

The Importance of Being Informed

Health and healing (whether for ourselves, those we love, or the entire ecosystem of planet Earth) requires several important qualities, including knowledge, commitment, and love.

Pagans trust in the goodness of nature and rely not only on magic and mythology but on the wisdom of human knowledge to point the way toward health and wellness. Pagans take responsibility for healing by being informed about what it takes to maintain or gain maximum health. If you or someone you love is facing a health crisis, be sure to learn all you can about the treatment for the disease. Ask the doctor questions and play an active role in treatment and care. The more you know, the more powerful your work for healing will be, both mundane and magical.

The knowledge we gain counts for little unless we also have the commitment to put that knowledge to good use. If you know what dietary changes you need to make to control your medical condition, make a commitment to do it now. If you see a way in which your lifestyle is wasteful and therefore harmful to the earth, take responsibility for simplifying your life in appropriate ways. Once you gain the knowledge necessary to be a true healer, you will also be responsible for living your life in accordance with that knowledge.

Finally—and perhaps most important of all—is love. Pagans are spiritual people, and healing is a way they celebrate life and make the love of the Goddess and God manifest in their lives. Remember that the work you do for healing (both mundane and magical) is a way of expressing divine love. Think of love itself as a vibration that heals whatever it touches. Resolve to live your life in resonance with that vibration as much as possible. This alone can bring powerful healing energy into your life. Plus, it feels good to love. Pagans understand that love needs to be directed in many ways. Learn to love yourself, your family and friends, and the earth that supports you. All of these types of love are ways to bring healing into the world.

Keep It in Balance

Psychic, spiritual, and magical healing practices are very similar to divination in one important respect. It's important to keep your use of magical tools in balance when taking care of your health. In other words, don't become so reliant on spiritual practices like reiki or visualization that you avoid getting regular checkups from your family doctor. Also, if you are battling an illness, remember that spiritual tools complement regular healthcare but never replace it.

Just as divination can become a problem if you give so much power to astrology or Tarot cards that you stop making decisions for yourself, so, too, does spiritual healing cease to be useful if it gets out of balance or you approach it superstitiously or with a reckless disregard for other forms of healthcare. Just because you use guided visualization in an attempt to lose weight doesn't mean you don't have to exercise or avoid fatty foods.

Keep your spiritual efforts at healing in balance with the mundane things you do to stay (or become) healthy. As long as you do that, your spiritual efforts will truly benefit your overall well-being.

The Least You Need to Know

- ◆ Nearly all pagan traditions emphasize healing as an important part of spirituality.
- ◆ Healing is something pagans do for themselves, for others, and even for Earth as a whole.
- ◆ Popular methods of healing employed by pagans include herbalism, healing-touch practices such as reiki, and magical work such as affirmations and ritual.
- ◆ Although pagans regard magical healing methods as essential to health and well-being, these practices are never meant to replace seeing a physician when necessary.

Part 5

Living the Pagan Life

Paganism is more than a hobby or a pastime. Like any other spiritual tradition, it is a way of life. People who embrace the pagan path find that it can shed meaningful light on every aspect of life, from work to relationships to managing a home. To pagans, the spirituality of everyday life means incorporating respect for the environment and an appreciation for magic into the ordinary choices and commitments of daily living.

How do pagans understand the difference between right and wrong? What's the best way to connect with other pagans, whether in a small group setting or a large national gathering? What kind of cultural and entertainment resources are available with a nature spirituality theme? When is it appropriate for pagans to tell others about their spiritual practice? How can the Internet be used to enhance your understanding of and connection to the pagan world?

Chapter **21**

Pagan Ethics: How to Behave Like an Earthkeeper

In This Chapter

◆ Pagan morality: from flower power to personal power
◆ Wiccan teachings on the ethical life
◆ Tried and true tribal values
◆ Pagan perspectives on sex
◆ Taking simple steps to care for the earth

How do pagans tell the difference between right and wrong? What do pagans believe is necessary to live a good and upstanding life? These are questions of ethics. Paganism, like any other religious or spiritual system, has its own approach to ethical and moral issues. This chapter will look at the unique perspective of pagan values—values that are grounded in nature and in the primacy of trust and love.

Flower Power Lives Again!

Back in the counterculture of the 1960s, the term "flower power" applied to the hippies and antiwar activists who believed that our technological, industrialized, pollutant-heavy society had gotten out of control. Instead of more factories, automobiles, and bombs, they felt that cleaner air, organic produce, and conservation of nature was what our world really needed.

Flower power as a slogan may be out of style, but the values it embodied still live on in the pagan community. Many Goddess worshipers work hard to make the world more environmentally balanced and to preserve precious natural resources for future generations. Of course, not all environmental activists are pagans, and for that matter, not all pagans are environmental activists. But the two fit together beautifully, and indeed many practitioners of nature spirituality consider it their religious duty to take good care of Mother Nature. These are the folks whom many pagans call *earthkeepers*. It's a term of honor. If you would like to live an ethical pagan life, perhaps you're an earthkeeper, too.

EarthWords

An **earthkeeper** is a person who has taken spiritual responsibility for living in harmony with the environment and teaching or encouraging others to do the same.

Obviously, living your life in ecological harmony with nature is the fullest expression of a spirituality devoted to Mother Earth, but pagan ethics involve more than just being green. This chapter will take a closer look at the environmental dimension of paganism, but first let's look at issues of power, freedom, love, trust, and even that big bugaboo that so many people get worked up over: sexual ethics. Pagans have a perspective on each of these topics that is, as you'll see, strictly natural.

Power from Within Instead of Power Over

In Chapter 18, "Magic, or Flexing Your Spiritual Muscles," you learned how pagans understand power in terms of magic. Now let's take a closer look at pagan view of power and how it shapes the way pagans understand ethics.

Oracle

Pagans tend to have a very responsible approach to power. Power is good when it helps you reach your own full potential, but it's suspect when it is used to control or oppress others. This, of course, is the same position pagans take with regard to magic: Use it for healing and personal transformation but never to harm another.

Many pagans have a unique perspective on power. Power, of course, is simply the ability to make things happen, to make changes (or to block an unwanted change), to influence others to behave in certain ways, and so forth. From family dynamics to international politics, power is central to the way in which human beings interact. But not all power is created equal. Indeed, the Wiccan author/philosopher Starhawk identified three distinct kinds of power in her groundbreaking book, *Truth or Dare*. They include:

- ◆ **Power over**   This is the power of people who have control over others. Parents have power over their children, and prison wardens have power over the inmates. It's unhealthy power when it turns into a form of social privilege, such as racism or sexism, in which one group of people has power over another group by virtue of privilege.

- ◆ **Power with**   This is the power of equals who work together. People who form a food co-op, countries that work together for a common goal, even a husband and wife in a nonsexist marriage—all have equal power that they share with each other.

- ◆ **Power from within**   This is the innate power that every human being has, the power to make his or her own way through life, his or her own choices, his or her own destiny. Sadly, many of the features of our culture often keep people from expressing their own natural power; they're too busy fitting into the ideals of society to ever express themselves naturally.

Most pagans feel deeply suspicious of "power over" but really approve of "power from within." To pagans, the ideal society would be one in which people have little or no power over others, where each person is free to develop his or her natural power. Most pagans believe in values like freedom, personal responsibility, and personal empowerment.

> **Drumbeats**
>
> Do pagans believe that everyone should be equal? In nature it's normal for some animals to be dominant. Most pagans accept that society will always have rich and poor, hard workers and slackers. Pagans object, however, to social forces like racism and sexism or to laws that benefit a privileged group at the expense of others.

Freedom Rules

Do pagans reject rules? Not really. Most pagans believe that there's a place for law and order. But a rule needs to make practical sense and not be in place just because of tradition. A case in point would be laws (and social views) that are antihomosexual. Most pagans, whether straight or gay, think it's wrong for society to dictate how gay people should behave. This is an example of how "power over" gets misused. A society based on "power from within" allows each person to decide for him- or herself whether he or she prefers gay or straight relationships.

Thus, most pagan traditions have few rules of personal conduct. To pagans, adopting an overall commitment to values like love, trust, not harming others, and personal freedom and empowerment is the best guide for moral and ethical behavior. After all, not all moral rules apply equally to all situations.

Many pagan groups work hard to govern their communities in egalitarian or nonhierarchical ways, such as using *consensus*. For pagans, this is not only a spiritual way of recognizing that the Goddess and the God speak to all people, but also a small way to contribute to healing our society as a whole. The more people become comfortable with different models of shared power and leadership, the more we can build a truly democratic society.

Perfect Love and Perfect Trust

In many forms of Wicca, the phrase "perfect love and perfect trust" is used as a password to gain admittance into rituals. This is a wonderful thing because it encourages the participant to think about these supreme ethical values as a part of attending the circle. Our thoughts shape our lives, so thinking about trust and love is a great way to engage in spirituality.

But what exactly is "perfect" trust and love? How do they go together? How do we manifest these values in our lives?

> **Drumbeats**
>
> Nobody's perfect, right? So why do pagans talk about perfect love and trust? To most people, perfect means "spotless" or "without blemish." Pagans, however, don't use the word in that way. One traditional meaning of perfect is "completed," as in a perfected formula for success—a formula that is tried and true and therefore completely developed. So perfect love and perfect trust can be thought of as completed—that is, mature and adult—love and trust. Such love and trust need not be spotless or without blemish. To pagans, even perfect love and perfect trust will have their share of mistakes.

Perfect Love: The Power of Relationship

Perfect, or mature, love involves relating to others in positive ways. It's not only sexual or romantic love; it also includes goodwill toward others and a commitment to behaving honestly and honorably, thereby being a good partner in relationship. Love always balances your own needs with the needs of your loved ones. Love is as personal as caring for your family and as universal as being a good citizen. Love also means standing up for what's right, even when it may be an unpopular position.

Perfect love means doing our best to behave like adults in relationships. It means not acting inappropriately—like a sulking teenager or a child throwing a temper tantrum. It means being mature, reasonable, and compassionate in dealing with others. It means taking good care of oneself.

 **Oracle** _____

Love and trust are more than just feelings. They are commitments we make to behave in positive ways toward both ourselves and others.

Perfect Trust: The Fruits of Personal Power

If love is in short supply in our present society, trust is even more rare. Unfortunately, we live in a society that does not encourage people to find and express their own power. Trust is the basic faith in human nature that you can feel when you have deep faith in your own power and your own goodwill. Trust is not naive—it doesn't mean leaving our doors unlocked or leaving money lying around. But given that we take responsible measures to protect ourselves, trust is the emotional tool we use to honor both our own power and the power of others, including the power for people to make good and loving choices in their lives.

When I trust you, I expect you to behave in good ways. For pagans, that trust creates an energetic resonance that actually supports them in making good choices. The more people love and trust one another, the more they will naturally and freely make choices in their lives that reflect the love in their hearts. Trust, like love, can never be imposed by the government, by religion, or by any other authority. Love and trust are the ultimate energies that can only find expression through power from within. Without love and trust, our world turns into a nightmare of violence and paranoia. When we love and trust one another, however, society functions, and healing and growth can occur.

Harm None and Do What You Will

If you've been reading this book from the beginning, by now you are well familiar with the Wiccan Rede: "An' it harm none, do what ye will" (or more simply, "Harm none and do what you will"). This simple and universally applicable mandate embodies perfect love and perfect trust in a single statement. Furthermore, it contains three virtues that most pagans would agree are essential to the spiritual life: nonviolence, authentic and appropriate power, and freedom. Let's look at each of these in turn.

Nonviolence

Nonviolence ("harm none") is upheld by spiritual traditions throughout the world as a worthy and necessary foundation to any code of conduct. From the Biblical injunction

"Thou shalt not kill" to the Buddhist commitment to refrain from contributing to suffering, spiritual seekers have joined together in recognizing that being nice to one another is essential to life, and when we can't be nice, let's at least avoid being not nice. In this, the Wiccan Rede is not so much a radical position; rather, it conforms beautifully with the wisdom of the world.

Drumbeats

Pagans have differing opinions on issues like capital punishment, military service, and violence in self-defense. Some pagans are like Buddhists or Quakers, deeply opposed to *any* form of violence, period. Other pagans proudly serve in the military, support capital punishment, and view the Wiccan Rede as an ethical ideal that sometimes must be broken in the interest of self- or national defense.

Act Now!

After "harm none," the next element of the Wiccan Rede is the simple word "do." This is an action word, and it points out the second principle of the rede: authentic power. You've already looked at pagan views on power, and the rede supports the idea that personal empowerment is a good thing. Pagan ethics are the ethics of doing, of action, of creative power. This is not a spirituality that tells people they must be passive, weak-willed, or submissive.

Freedom

The final element in the Wiccan Rede is "what you will." This stands for the principle of freedom. The Wiccan Rede isn't about doing your high priestess's will, or your father's will, or your boss's will. It's about the freedom to live life according to your own designs—your own will. The ethics of paganism are based on trusting people to decide what is best for themselves.

That doesn't mean we should never express our opinions about what is right or wrong; nor does it imply that we shouldn't learn from those who are older and wiser than ourselves. It makes sense for children to learn from their parents and for adults to learn from their mentors and elders. We learn, however, not to be submissive and obedient but to find the wisdom so that our freely chosen actions may truly serve ourselves, the Gods, and the highest good.

Tribal Values

Not all pagans are Wiccan, so not all pagans consider the rede to be their source of ethical wisdom. Still, most pagans consider nonharm, freedom, and appropriate uses of power to be hallmarks of pagan virtue. Among pagans whose tradition is shaped by ancient cultures (such as the druids or the Norse), often there is great devotion to what has come to be known as *tribal values*. These are values that govern conduct within each pagan community (the "tribe"), and also govern how pagans behave in society at large. Even for pagans who live in large cities in today's world, tribal values can be a meaningful compass for living a good life. Some of the most important tribal values are honor, hospitality, loyalty, and respect.

> **EarthWords** _____
>
> **Tribal values** are the virtues that guided the social lives of people who lived in clans, tribes, or other small communities in ancient times (and even up to the present).

Honor

Honor refers to the sense of pride a person takes in his or her own life, family, and tribe. To be an honorable person means to be one whom others hold in high esteem. It's a value based on relationship: Honor is not just something you give to yourself; it's something you receive and enjoy from the other members of your tribe. Honor is interconnected: When you behave honorably, your entire tribe is honored; when other members of your tribe behave honorably, you enjoy a share of that honor as well.

Honorable behavior includes honesty, compassion, bravery, hard work, and a willingness to make personal sacrifices for the good of others or for the tribe as a whole. Furthermore, it is honorable to be kind, considerate, and civil toward both loved ones and strangers. In a real sense, honor is the keystone of a virtuous life. Honor also implies fulfilling one's duty effectively. Thus, an honorable warrior is strong and fearless in battle, and an honorable farmer is dedicated and hardworking in raising and harvesting the crops.

> **Oracle** _____
>
> Some religions teach that pride is a sin. To pagans, true pride (self-esteem) is a natural part of honor.
>
> Honor assumes that healthy self-respect, integrated with the positive opinion of others, makes for a happy and virtuous life. We live honorably when we live in ways that we—and that other members of our tribe—can be proud of.

Hospitality

Closely related to honor is hospitality, or openness and goodwill shown to strangers and travelers. Hospitality brings together virtues such as generosity, charity, and kindness and is a core value of civilized society. Showing hospitality is a way of giving thanks to the Gods for the abundance of life. Sharing our abundance with the needy or with anyone who may need a helping hand is a way of fostering a better world. Honor also dictates that when receiving hospitality, one should be gracious, thankful, and respectful of those who are offering it.

Loyalty

Another core tribal value, loyalty involves supporting and remaining faithful to the tribe and to other members of the tribe, even when the going gets rough. A loyal person can be counted on to do the work that needs to be done, even when it's unpopular or unpleasant.

Loyalty, incidentally, involves being faithful not only to other people but to the Gods and to the virtues. Loyalty to the Wiccan Rede, for example, takes precedence over being loyal to someone whose irresponsible actions may harm others.

Respect

Modern society often emphasizes young people above their elders, students above teachers, workers above managers. Much humor is built on how the young are naturally smarter than their elders (one example is the movie *Ferris Bueller's Day Off*). While this perspective can be entertaining, pagans believe it's also important to remember the traditional tribal values of honoring the elders, the wisdomkeepers, and the leaders of the tribe. Whether male or female, young or old, those in authority deserve respect and support to help them do their best for the good of all.

Respect is not the same as blind obedience. Those who hold positions of authority still need to behave honorably. But assuming they are doing so, respect is the energy that supports the leaders, teachers, and elders in carrying out their duties on behalf of the entire tribe.

Pagan Virtues and the Urban Tribe

Very few pagans nowadays live in a setting that can truly be called tribal, but that doesn't mean they don't have their own "tribes." Their family, their workplace, their neighborhoods, and even their pagan community all function as tribes in their lives, and in a larger sense, the nation and the entire planetary family are tribes as well. To pagans, each of these arenas is a place where values like honorable living, respect and loyalty, and hospitality can and should be practiced. These are the bedrock virtues that make the world a more civilized and happier place to be.

Pagans and Sex

Pagans, like everyone else in society, believe it's wrong to kill, lie, and steal. After all, such actions harm others, and pagans believe it's wrong to harm. When it comes to sexual ethics, however, pagans generally prefer the diversity of nature over the artificial rules that came out of a book somewhere.

Ward and June Let Their Hair Down

According to most mainstream religions, sex is only okay between a married man and woman. Period. For pagans, marriage is a lovely way to express love, intimacy, and commitment, but many pagans acknowledge that there are ethical situations in which sex outside of marriage is okay. Here are a few examples:

- **Gay and lesbian sexuality** Because a legal marriage requires a man and a woman, gays and lesbians have no choice but to express their love outside of marriage. Since pagans accept responsible lesbian, bisexual, or gay sexuality, same-sex relationships are okay, even without a marriage certificate.

- **Situations in which it doesn't make sense to get married** Perhaps the lovers live in different states or are elderly and stand to lose retirement benefits if they wed. Or they could be in college and acknowledge that it's too soon to get married. As long as they make their sexual choices with adult responsibility, to pagans, these extramarital relationships are entirely okay.

- **Responsible recreational sex** To mainstream religions, the concept of recreational sex is utterly taboo. To pagans, it's no big

> **Oracle**
>
> *Leave it to Beaver,* a popular 1950s television show, portrayed a happy suburban family with a dad named Ward and a mom named June. Ward and June symbolized the traditional heterosexual marriage favored by most religions. Although many pagans live in traditional heterosexual marriages, nearly all pagans believe it's okay for mature adults to choose other sexual options.

> **Taboo!**
>
> Even the most liberal pagans follow these strict sexual limits: Rape, sexual assault, and sex with minors are totally forbidden, and any situation involving harassment, exploitation, or manipulation is also out of bounds. Cheating on your spouse is a form of lying, so that's not okay. Unsafe sex, since it is potentially harmful, is also against pagan ethics.

deal. Sex is fun. Honest, responsible, safe sex between consenting adults is permissible. This includes swinging and premarital sex.

Although the media sometimes portrays pagans as sexy libertines who love to have orgies, the truth is far less titillating. The vast majority of pagans live very ordinary lives in which they fall in love with one special someone and form a family unit. Where paganism differs from other spiritual paths, however, is that the traditional "Ward and June" option is not the only acceptable lifestyle in the pagan world.

From Heinlein to Harrad: The Polyamory Option

To look at just how open the pagan community is to sexual alternatives, let's look at the concept of polyamory. This is popular among some pagan groups (like the Church of All Worlds) and generally is accepted or tolerated among most pagans. Basically, polyamory is the belief that it's okay to love more than one person at the same time, as long as the love is expressed ethically and honestly to all persons involved. Such love can be expressed sexually or not. It might involve people who live together in a group marriage, or it might involve people who love several different partners who live in different places.

There are many possibilities to polyamory, but the main emphasis is on sexual and romantic freedom balanced by honesty, integrity, and responsibility. It's not exactly the same thing as swinging. Swinging is the freedom to have sex with others outside marriage, whereas polyamory stresses love more than sex. It's not the same as having an affair either. Polyamory is based on being honest—in other words, everyone knows who's loving whom. It's not an easy lifestyle and requires emotional maturity and effective communication skills.

Drumbeats

Like many elements of paganism, polyamory has its connection to nature. The bonobo, a species of chimpanzee whose genetic makeup is extremely similar to humans, is remarkable for living in peaceful societies where there's lots of monkey business going on—literally. Most bonobos are bisexual and, to put it delicately, *very* active. They enjoy group sex and oral sex as well as sex with a variety of partners—and they are among the most nonviolent of primates. They truly embody the old slogan of "Make love, not war." Polyamorous pagans cite the bonobos as evidence that sexual freedom occurs in nature and therefore is a valid lifestyle option.

The idea of group marriages or open relationships became popular in the 1960s with books like Robert Rimmer's *The Harrad Experiment* or Robert Heinlein's *Stranger in a Strange Land* (which inspired the founding of the Church of All Worlds). For a while, the concept of open or group marriages was a mainstream idea in the "swinging '60s."

Eventually, such lifestyles fell out of favor, partially because they are difficult lifestyles to maintain and partially because public attitudes toward sex became much more conservative with the rise of diseases like herpes and AIDS in the 1980s. Less than a generation after the swinging '60s, conservatives declared the sexual revolution to be over.

Well, it wasn't over; it had just gone underground. Swinging clubs continued to proliferate all across the United States and other parts of the world. Polyamory even today continues to attract a small but dedicated number of idealists (many of whom are pagan) who believe it's okay to love and/or be sexual with more than one person at the same time, as long as it's done with honesty and integrity.

Pagans who practice polyamory often say it's better for the environment to have more than two adults living together in a home. Our economy is based on every two-adult household having its own computer, stereo, kitchen appliances, furniture, and so forth. If more adults lived under the same roof, they could share such belongings, live more simply, and use fewer precious natural resources.

Polyamory isn't for everyone, just like swinging isn't. Only a small percentage of pagans practice polyamory, and many pagans believe polyamory is a big mistake. But even the pagans who are opposed to it wouldn't call it a "sin." In the pagan world, it's okay for people to have conflicting views on what sexual or romantic lifestyle is best for them.

> **CAUTION**
>
> **Taboo!**
>
> Some people think pagan sexuality sounds like a big party. Just because pagans believe in freedom, however, it doesn't mean anything goes. No matter what sexual lifestyle you choose, as a pagan, you need to treat others with honesty, respect, maturity, and kindness. Anything else is wrong, even by pagan standards.

Sex and the Wiccan Rede

For pagans, sex is a personal matter, and different lifestyles and sexual preferences are part of the diverse world we live in. If you're straight, gay, or bisexual, celibate, married, a swinger, or polyamorous, it's okay—as long as you follow the demands of the Wiccan Rede. Remember to "harm none." In other words, be honest, ethical, and responsible and maintain integrity in all your sexual relationships. And then do what you will. Don't judge others and don't let them judge you. As long as you're behaving honorably and without harm, be true to your own heart.

Weaving It All Together

What is the spiritual foundation of pagan ethics? In other words, how do the Goddess and the God fit into pagan concepts of right and wrong?

Oracle

A wonderful book that explores living in balance and harmony with the earth is *The Education of Little Tree* by Forrest Carter. A charming and funny novel based on Carter's childhood, it tells the story of a half-Indian boy learning from his Cherokee grandparents how to live in a proper relationship with nature.

The best answer to this question involves the concept this chapter began with: the concept of the earthkeeper. Pagans who take their devotion to Mother Nature seriously will naturally apply the values of honor, loyalty, respect, hospitality, and other traditional virtues to their relationship with the earth.

Harmony and Balance

When it comes to being an earthkeeper, pagans are inspired by traditional cultures. Many Native American tribes, for example, teach values such as respect for the natural world, the importance of conservation, and the need to preserve the environment for our children's children. One native tradition holds that we should consider the impact of our decisions for up to seven generations. Obviously, a world in which fossil fuels are being consumed, forests cut down, and the ozone layer destroyed is not a world in which the environment is respected and the needs of the seventh generation are taken into account. Pagans try to live their lives according to nature-based, tribal principles instead of just blindly following the consumerist habits of society.

Environmental Charity Begins at Home

It's easy to complain about the ozone layer, acid rain, or the destruction of the rainforests; after all, few of us have the power to do anything about these huge problems. Everybody, however, pagan or nonpagan, can make a difference in preserving the environment, cleaning up the mess we've created, and saving our world for generations to come. Even just making changes in our own home makes a difference.

- If you don't recycle, now's the time to start. You can recycle glass, aluminum, cardboard, office paper, newspaper, batteries, motor oil, plastics, and many other household items. Many communities now have convenient curbside recycling pickup. If yours doesn't, let your city council representatives know that you want it.

- Don't throw away food scraps. Make compost instead. Use the compost to fertilize your garden. (If you don't have a garden, start one. Growing your own food is a great way to connect with nature.)

- Disposable diapers may be convenient, but they're horrible for the environment. Our grandmothers made do with cloth diapers, and we can, too. It's actually *less* expensive to use cloth diapers and pay for a diaper-cleaning service than to use disposables!

- Many common cleaning detergents, pesticides, laundry soaps, and personal-care products are filled with ingredients that are environmentally unfriendly. Give your home a green makeover and start buying products that are biodegradable and nontoxic. Visit your local natural-food store to find such eco-friendly products.

- Whenever possible, eat organic. Not only are organic foods better for the environment, they're also better for our "inner" environment as well. Also, wear clothing made of natural fabrics and organic materials whenever possible.

Oracle

Most of the things you can do to protect the environment at home will also save you money. Even some expensive choices, such as buying organic food, may be cheaper in the long run. (Eating organic, for example, may reduce your risk of cancer.)

- Watch that thermostat. Keep the house a few degrees cooler in the winter and wear an extra sweater (or snuggle up to your honey). In the summer, consider using fans instead of air conditioning.

- Use a clothesline instead of a dryer. The sun will dry your clothes without contributing to your monthly power bill.

- Next time you buy a car, consider an alternative-fuel vehicle or a hybrid. The less gasoline you consume, the lower your monthly transportation costs.

- Do you own a bicycle? It's a great alternative to a car for many short trips such as to the grocery store or post office. Plus, using a bicycle is good exercise—here's a way to take care of the environment and yourself at the same time. Walking or using public transportation is another great alternative to running the car.

Perhaps you can think of other ways to make a positive impact on the environment. Remember that, as a pagan, every time you do something (however little) to benefit Mother Earth, you are putting your spirituality into action. Think of yourself as a champion for Mother Earth. We're in the middle of a war: a war that will determine the quality of the environment for ages to come. Fight like a warrior to protect your Mother Earth.

Toward the Future: A Pagan Vision

For most religions and philosophies, ethics are related to living a good life. What then is the pagan view of "the good life"?

Most pagans would say it involves a world in which people can reach their full potential as individuals while still living in a creative and harmonious community with others. It is a world that values creativity, personal freedom, and family relationships. It is a world that values diversity in terms of race, culture, gender, sexual lifestyle, and spiritual beliefs.

Most important of all, it is a world in which everyone works together to live in harmony with the earth, choosing carefully to preserve and protect our planet both for now and for the future.

It's a vision worth working for. As a pagan, you can take steps today to help make this vision come true.

The Least You Need to Know

- ◆ Pagans consider a healthy understanding of power to be an important part of ethical living.
- ◆ Concepts like perfect love, perfect trust, and the Wiccan Rede contribute to pagan perspectives on right and wrong.
- ◆ Many pagans embrace tribal values such as honor, hospitality, loyalty, and respect.
- ◆ Most pagans lead typical sexual lives and are tolerant toward those who choose alternative lifestyles.
- ◆ Reverence for the Goddess can best be expressed by taking good care of the environment.

Chapter 22

Groups, Groves, and Gatherings

In This Chapter

◆ No pagan is an island (unless she's a solitary)

◆ Circles and groves: the heart of pagan community

◆ All about pagan gatherings

◆ How to find the right group for you

Human beings are social creatures, and pagans are no exception. You can find all sorts of ways to meet and interact with other pagans, including a variety of groups and organizations aimed at serving the pagan community. This chapter will introduce you to the many resources available in the pagan world. Some of them will probably be just right for you.

The Four Ways to Be a Pagan

In pagan spirituality, there is no church to join, no membership cards to fill out, no pledge to make. If you choose to affiliate with other pagans, it is entirely voluntary. Many pagans practice their spirituality all alone or with just their immediate families or closest friends. Others participate in covens, groves, lodges, or groups of varying sizes and structures. The following sections provide a brief rundown of the ways in which you can be a pagan.

EarthWords

Pagan groups have many different names, an indication of how many different kinds of groups there are. A **coven** is a small group of witches (typically no more than 13), while a **grove** is a larger group of witches or a group (of any size) of druids. A group dedicated specifically to ceremonial magic calls itself a **temple** or **lodge**. Other pagan organizations may identify themselves as a **circle**, a **hearth**, a **clan**, a **sisterhood** (or brotherhood), or a *tuath* (Gaelic for "people").

Solitary Practice: Just You and the Gods

The most basic unit of paganism is the individual. If you want to form a spiritual relationship with nature itself and with the spirit of Mother Earth, you have all it takes to be a pagan. In other words, joining a group is not a requirement. For many, this is deeply satisfying and a wonderful way to practice spiritual beliefs. In Wicca, a witch who practices alone is called a solitary, and most other pagans use the same term to describe their solo practitioners.

Small Groups (Covens or Circles): The Crucible of Intimacy

Perhaps the most common form of pagan community is the small group, often called a coven, circle, or grove. These groups typically have anywhere from 3 to 30 members. Among some Wiccan traditions, a coven refers to groups of 13 or fewer, and once the group has 14 or more members it is called a grove. Regardless of what you call it, a small pagan group usually is an informal, casual gathering that meets in people's homes and operates entirely on volunteer energy. In other words, there's no clergy getting paid to run the show. Everyone has to pitch in to keep the group functioning.

Large Groups, Gatherings, Alliances: Power in Numbers

As the pagan community grows, more and more large groups have appeared on the scene. Like the smaller groups, these take a number of forms. Some longstanding pagan groups have grown so large (50 or more members) that they can manage property and offer a variety of services and ministries. Meanwhile, large national organizations provide support to the many smaller groups that are members of the umbrella community. Especially in Wicca, covens that belong to the same tradition often form alliances or communities that provide leadership, training, and other resources to the local groups.

Festivals and Gatherings: Short-Term Pagan Community

One of the most popular ways for pagans to get together involves regional or national pagan festivals and gatherings, most of which occur on an annual basis. These events usually take place over the course of a weekend or a week-long period. They involve hundreds of pagans who gather at a state park or on private land for time spent close to nature and in community with other like-minded folks. Activities at festivals include classes and workshops, rituals, and plenty of free time for fun and fellowship. Some pagan gatherings are invitation-only events designed specifically for the members of one particular tradition or lineage, but many festivals are open to all pagans—whether solitary or group members—of any tradition.

The Pleasures of Solitude

Community plays an important role in spirituality. Some religions, such as Buddhism and Christianity, place great emphasis on belonging to the community as a core part of their tradition. To pagans, community matters mainly because it is natural for human beings to connect with one another, but pagans don't believe in any particular divine mandate for people to form an organization.

Like everything else in paganism, nature is our teacher. Since it is natural for humans to live in a community, most pagans like to have the company of others. Meanwhile, it is just as natural for humans to value time alone, and some have always preferred solitude. Therefore, many pagans find it more natural to express their spirituality in a solitary way. They may live active and full lives with a family and career, but when it comes to connecting with Mother Nature, being alone is their preferred way to go.

Being a Lone Ranger

Solitude is a gift. We live in a world that is increasingly overcrowded, and for many of us (especially city dwellers), the constant presence of other people seems to crowd peacefulness right out of our lives. For the solitary pagan, taking time out on a regular basis to sit alone in front of an altar or in a wooded grove, savoring the quiet and emptiness of a personal, intimate, one-on-one interaction with the Goddess, is a rare and precious pleasure.

Oracle

The responsibility of solitary paganism involves strict self-discipline. As a solitary, you must make and keep your own agreements about how you'll live the pagan life. If you enjoy being alone and can adhere to your own discipline, you'll probably find the rewards of solo practice to be deeply fulfilling.

With this gift of solitary practice comes responsibility. If you want to grow in your spirituality, it's up to you. If you want to overcome a bad habit or learn a new skill, no one is going to hold your feet to the fire. As a solitary, no one will be disappointed if you start blowing off rituals or magical work. No one, that is, but yourself when you wake up one morning and realize you've done nothing spiritual in more than six months.

Spiritual Lessons of Solo Practice

What are the benefits of being a solitary pagan? For those pagans who have walked the solitary path for a long period of time, here are some of the most valuable and important lessons to be learned:

◆ **Self-reliance** As a solitary, no one does anything for you. You are responsible for what you learn, the rituals you do, the magic you achieve. If you don't do it, it doesn't get done. But you don't have to worry about someone letting you down either.

◆ **Personal responsibility** Are you spiritually unhappy or restless? As a solitary, there's no one to blame but yourself. The solo pagan is 100-percent responsible for his or her spiritual growth, happiness, and mastery. There's only one person to please (and only one person to do the pleasing).

◆ **The pleasures of silence and solitude** In many of the world's great mystical traditions, divine union is only possible when a person dedicates his or her life to profound silence and solitude. Think of the proverbial wise man who lives all alone on the mountaintop. That's the ideal of silence and solitude common to world mysticism; as a solitary pagan, you can cultivate these mystical qualities in your own spiritual life. There will be no one to interrupt your meditation (but also no one to listen when you want to talk about your spirituality).

> ⚠ CAUTION
>
> **Taboo!**
>
> Don't decide you're a pagan solitary just because you didn't like the institutional religious group you grew up with. Pagan groups tend to be much more tolerant, flexible, and upbeat than many mainstream churches. If you're new to paganism, give group membership a chance.

Solitary Pros and Cons

With solitary spirituality, you always can chart your own course. You answer to no one but yourself (and the Gods). If you feel that your spirituality is a private matter or feel self-conscious doing ritual, the solitary path may be perfect for you. And if you don't have any access to other pagans for whatever reason, solitary practice means you can still honor the Goddess and God in ways that are meaningful for you.

The downside of solitary paganism, not surprisingly, is its loneliness. Human beings tend to be social creatures, and when we love something (like the Goddess and nature), we naturally want to share that with others. Even many people who are dedicated solitaries will still occasionally want to reach out to others, through groups as well as various pagan gatherings held at the local, regional, and national level.

Small Group Spirituality: A Backyard Full of Pagans

Solitary paganism can be very nurturing, but for many people, nothing can replace the sheer pleasure of sharing rituals and beliefs with a small group of like-minded folks. This is why, for many pagans, the circle, coven, or small grove remains the best kind of community.

Unlike religions that are based in churches (where members are expected to make hefty financial pledges and participate in all sorts of volunteer work), paganism's orientation toward the small group means that spirituality happens in more intimate settings such as the living rooms or backyards of group members. Because there's no church building to maintain or preacher to pay, the financial burden of such a group is minimal. There usually is a time commitment if you want to be involved in a pagan group, but most pagans find it's a joyful commitment. After all, when doing coven work, you're hanging out with your closest and best friends.

Small groups not only do ritual together, they also form close bonds that for many pagans feel like a family.

(© 2001 Fox Gradin)

Most small pagan groups consist of 3 to 20 members. Traditional Wiccan covens are not supposed to grow beyond 13 members, although some groups will allow their size to go beyond that limitation. Still, for many people, the smaller the better. I participated for two years in a group with only six members, and I still consider that group to be one of the best experiences I've had in a pagan community.

The Structure of the Small Group

There are probably as many different group structures as there are pagan groups. Depending on the tradition you follow, the personalities of the group members, and other factors (such as how old the group is and the group's primary mission or objective), your group may take any of a countless number of forms.

Here are a few of the more common types of pagan organization:

- ◆ **Working groups** What most people think of when they think of a coven of witches, these groups get together to do magic and ritual. Often working groups consist of veteran pagans and may not be open to newcomers.

- ◆ **Teaching groups** Here's where newcomers can connect with the pagan world. These communities focus on teaching pagan ways to beginners, often leading the students through a series of degrees to reach the level where they can successfully start their own group.

- ◆ **Study groups** Not everyone with an interest in paganism wants to do magic or ritual, and that's okay. Study groups may gather to discuss a book the members have read or to debate topics of interest to the community. Such groups are often very flexible and open to newcomers.

- ◆ **Fellowship or social groups** Pagans love a good party, and some groups convene for no other reason than the pure joy of getting together. These groups may sponsor camping weekends, drum circles, or a night out to a concert or movie.

Some groups are very informal, just getting together for a cup of coffee and conversation once a month with no set leader or agenda. Once in a while, someone will offer to lead a ritual or teach a class. The emphasis is on little or no structure, and each member of the group is responsible for his or her own spiritual happiness and development. This kind of group can feel safe for people who are uncomfortable in structured situations, but unfortunately, such loose-knit groups often don't last long.

At the other end of the spectrum are tightly organized groups, usually under the direction of an efficient and confident high priestess. These groups have set schedules, a clear chain of command, and specific protocols for joining the group, earning initiations, and leading rituals. It's almost like a tiny little military outfit, and everyone knows his or her rank and responsibilities. Groups like this tend to be more stable and long lasting, but sometimes they only work for people who like high amounts of structure in their lives.

Naturally, most pagan groups fall somewhere in between these two extremes. As a general rule, the smaller the group, the more it can afford to be loosely organized and flexible. By the same token, the larger the group, the more it has to offer in the way of quality instruction, meaningful rituals, and ongoing stability.

Spiritual Lessons of Small Group Practice

Most pagans find that participating in a coven or circle has a powerful impact on their spiritual life. While group membership is often fun and rewarding, there are also lessons to be learned. Many of these lessons are not specific to paganism: Any small group in which you become involved will teach you these things. Indeed, the most important lessons that a small pagan group will teach you are general lessons about life.

In a small group, generally there are few secrets. Everyone knows which member is the hardest worker and which one is the slacker, which member is the intellectual and which member has the most loving heart, which member is the most insecure and which member has a tendency to lie. In short, everyone figures out sooner or later each person's strengths and weaknesses. When you join a small pagan group, your ego will pretty soon bump up against the concerns and needs of others in the group. If you have difficulty managing conflict, compromising, or admitting when you're wrong, you'll find participating in a small group to be full of growth opportunities.

The conflicts in small pagan groups rarely have to do with the proper way to perform a ritual or the best magic to use in a given situation. Instead, people bicker over dividing the workload in a fair manner and making sure everyone gets treated fairly (especially by the group leaders). Small groups often will take on the personality of a family, with the priest and priestess playing the roles of "mom" and "dad" and everyone else functioning as the kids. Like any other family, it will have its measure of dysfunctional behavior.

> **CAUTION**
>
> **Taboo!**
>
> Pagan groups often function like families. If you join a group and then leave, it can feel as wrenching as a divorce. Don't switch groups every time your ego gets bruised. Try to work through any conflicts or differences that arise.

It is a pagan's responsibility to remain committed to the values of perfect love and trust as he or she seeks to grow and to help others grow. The small group can be a wonderful setting in which people mature as human beings. Unfortunately, if the dysfunction takes over, small pagan groups can turn into war zones where there's constant bickering and fighting and people getting emotionally hurt.

When joining a new pagan group, always keep your psychic feelers out to make sure the group is basically happy and healthy, with only a normal amount of conflict and dysfunction. Also, remember no group is perfect, and part of the normal journey of any pagan community is learning to work through conflicts and difficulties. When you join a pagan group, you will have an impact on that group's dynamics. Make sure your contribution to the group helps, rather than hinders, the group's functioning.

Larger Groups and National Organizations

Larger pagan groups are like small groups, only more so. The emergence of pagan communities with 50 or more members has occurred mainly within the last few years, and it is a sign of how rapidly the pagan community is growing.

Larger groups have strength in numbers and often use that strength to make a real difference in the world. Such groups may buy land to make a nature preserve or to build an authentic stone circle where powerful rituals can take place. Others may sponsor a ministry such as feeding homeless persons or participating in local environmental programs. Still others may publish a pagan magazine or newsletter.

Larger groups have the same the limitations as any large institution. You may be asked to make a pledge or to commit to a certain number of volunteer hours each week. It may be harder to get to know the group leaders. Although it can be exciting to participate in a large group project, you probably won't have the intimacy that comes with a group small enough to fit in your living room.

The Best of Both Worlds: Alliances and National Organizations

Instead of growing into ever-larger organizations, many pagan circles have instead opted to form alliances with other small groups. Such umbrella organizations provide resources to serve the small group, such as national or international gatherings, credentials for clergy, and networking. Three of the best-known pagan alliances are the Covenant of the Goddess (or COG, a federation of covens and Wiccan solitaries), the Pagan Federation (similar to COG but more international and pan-pagan in scope), and Ár nDraíocht Féin (a confederation of druid groves).

> **Oracle**
>
> Large pagan groups often have websites with networking information that can help you locate member covens or circles in your area. The Church of All Worlds (www.caw.org) and Ár nDraíocht Féin (www.adf.org) run two such websites.

The Pagan Gathering (and Festivals)

Both solitary pagans and members of pagan groups enjoy gathering with others for occasional weekends or weeks in a natural setting. These large-scale gatherings, also known as festivals, have become a significant aspect of the pagan community. For many solitaries, gatherings are their only link to the larger pagan world. For that matter, many covens and groves go to festivals for much the same purpose—to connect with other pagans, many of whom may not even practice the same tradition but share a general commitment to nature and the Goddess.

Although some festivals are sponsored by a specific lineage or tradition of pagans and are open only to members of that lineage, many others welcome pagans of any tradition (as well as anyone who is sincere and respectful of pagan ways).

Anatomy of a Gathering/Festival

Most pagan gatherings take place in rural settings. Generally, pagans love to get as close to nature as possible and will gravitate toward settings that are as far off the beaten track as they can find. Many pagan individuals and groups own large tracts of land that have been converted into primitive campsites. Other gatherings take place at private campgrounds or state parks that have been leased for use by the community. Occasionally, pagan gatherings will even take place at urban hotels or conference centers.

What happens at a pagan gathering? Usually it's a blend of ritual, education, and socializing. Since most pagans love to do ritual, large ceremonial circles are generally a highlight at any gathering. Larger gatherings may have a circle every night or may even have multiple circles occurring simultaneously, each one featuring the ceremonies of a different tradition. Many gatherings will have classes on how to write and lead rituals or on learning the many chants pagans use in ceremonies.

The educational component includes workshops on a variety of topics, from magic to myth to herbalism to Paganism 101. Since gatherings tend to foster a relaxed atmosphere, these classes are often taught in a casual, conversational discussion format. It's a great setting in which to meet pagans from other traditions (or other parts of the country) and learn their views on certain subjects.

> **Drumbeats**
>
> When local laws permit, gatherings may include some areas that are clothing optional, since some pagans prefer to do ritual skyclad and others simply enjoy the naturalness of nudity. Of course, no authentic pagan event will ever require participants to forgo clothing. That's why it's called clothing *optional*. Also, most gatherings permit nudity only in limited areas.

Finally, pagan gatherings have a strong social focus. A gathering is a place where you can let your hair down and simply be yourself among other pagans. Many pagans feel the need to keep their spirituality secret in their normal, "mundane" lives. Thus, going to a gathering in the woods with other pagans can truly be a liberating experience where, for at least a weekend or a week, you can just be you without worrying about offending or confusing those who don't understand your spirituality.

The Pros and Cons of Pagan Gatherings

As a rule, pagan gatherings are not a community you join; rather, they're an opportunity that occurs only from time to time to connect with a large group of other pagans. As such, you can remain a solitary pagan or be involved in a small group, and when the gathering occurs, you can immerse yourself in the larger community just for that short period of time.

The chief advantage of a pagan gathering is that it's fun! You can learn a lot about paganism, ritual, and people in general by hanging out at gatherings. You'll likely make plenty of new friends, and if it's a gathering where different pagan groups and traditions are present, you can shop around to find the group or coven that feels just right for you. Pagans originally sponsored gatherings as a networking enterprise, so take advantage of the unique opportunity to connect with others who share your interests and spiritual beliefs.

The biggest disadvantage of a pagan gathering is its impermanence. Sometimes it can feel disorienting to return to the mundane world after a week in the woods with 600 other druids, shamans, and witches. It's easy to feel a sense of community while attending a gathering, but you have to make an effort to keep the community going once you return to your daily life.

Finding Groups and Gatherings

Okay, so you've decided you'd like to take the plunge and connect with a group of pagans or even attend a pagan gathering. How do you find the group that's right for you? Unfortunately, pagans rarely, if ever, advertise in the yellow pages, but there are some effective ways to meet people of a like mind.

◆ **Talk to your friends.** Do you have friends who know you're interested in paganism? If you're comfortable discussing this with them, you can ask if they know of a pagan group they can recommend. Many groups find new members strictly by word of mouth, so this may be your only avenue for reaching them. Of course, if your friends don't know of a group, they won't be much help, but there's no harm in asking.

- **Check at your local new-age or meta-physical bookstore.** Some semipublic pagan groups will leave flyers at bookstores that sell Wiccan and pagan books, or they will host a monthly open house or occasionally teach a class through the store. One advantage of meeting groups in this kind of public arena is that it gives you and the group a chance to get to know one another in a comfortable environment.

- **Check online.** Several websites, such as the Witches' Voice (www.witchvox.com) specialize in pagan networking. These sites can be excellent resources and often list so many different options that you'll have a hard time figuring out which one(s) to contact. The downside is that a group could sound great online but not really be right for you once you meet face to face. If you decide to contact pagans online, use the same common sense you would use when connecting with anyone over the Internet. Don't give out your personal information and be sure to arrange to meet in a safe, public location.

 Oracle

Many people feel drawn to starting their own pagan group. If you and several friends are interested, you can find books to help you get started, such as *Wicca Covens: How to Start and Organize Your Own* by Judy Harrow. The downside is that if no one in your group has experience with a pagan community, you'll be reinventing the wheel. So if possible, find an existing group of experienced pagans who can share their wisdom with you.

Drumbeats

Are you interested in finding a pagan community but also want the structure and resources that only a church can provide? Then you might feel especially comfortable with the Covenant of Unitarian Universalist Pagans (CUUPs). This is an organization devoted to the theology and ritual of nature and Goddess spirituality under the auspices of Unitarian Universalism. The UU church is a liberal church that advocates freedom to follow your conscience in what you believe, tolerance of diversity, and respect for science and world religions—qualities that most pagans heartily endorse. CUUPs is a national organization with chapters meeting at local UU churches. Visit the group's website at www.cuups.org for more information.

The resources for finding pagan gatherings are pretty much the same as for finding groups. Some gatherings are private, invitation-only affairs; you'll need to become involved with an existing group that participates in a private gathering before you'll get invited to it. Others, however, are more open. Again, use your common sense in looking for gatherings to attend. Talk to the gathering's organizers before registering and make sure you feel comfortable with the energy of the people involved.

Is a Group or Gathering Right For You?

When looking to connect with other pagans, the most important point to remember is to take good care of yourself. Fortunately, most of the pagans you'll meet are gentle, kind, caring people. But with all the different traditions and styles of paganism out there, remember that many groups or individuals may simply not be to your liking. That's okay! Your job as a pagan will be to find the group that's right for you and not try to fit in with a group where the energy isn't a good match.

Oracle

A pagan gathering with 500 participants at a remote campground can be a powerful, spiritually moving experience. But it can also be overwhelming to someone new to nature spirituality. Ease your way into the pagan community: look for a small group in your area to participate in, before going to large regional or national gatherings.

When you meet a group, ask yourself these questions: Do you feel comfortable with the members? Do they seem to be kind, respectful, mature people? Are the leaders humble and down to earth? Is it okay for members to disagree with the leaders? Do people seem to be having fun? Can you accept the ideas put forth in the group's classes? Do you enjoy the group's rituals? Is it clear that spirituality is important to these people? The more "yes" answers you have, the more comfortable you'll likely feel with this group. Remember that it's okay to decide a group isn't for you and seek another one. When you do find a group that truly feels right, make a commitment to stick around. That's how you'll learn.

What to Expect from a Pagan Group

When you do find the group that's right for you, here's what you can look forward to experiencing as a group member:

- **Training** The group will teach you its particular pagan traditions. Many groups have special secrets that only their dedicated members learn.

- **Rituals** Pagan groups gather at the full moons, new moons, Sabbats, and sometimes other occasions to perform circles or other rituals. Before you officially join the group, you may only be allowed to attend part of the ritual or only certain rituals (others are members only). Be patient. Once you're initiated into the group, you'll be able to participate more fully.

- **Opportunities to serve** Every group requires a certain amount of effort just to function, from preparing supplies for ritual to organizing events. As a group member, you'll be expected to roll up your sleeves and participate in the work. Many pagan groups also do service projects for society at large, such as cleaning litter by the side of a highway or volunteering at a soup kitchen. You'll want to participate in these efforts as well.

- ◆ **Fun**   Spirituality isn't all work and no play (at least not in paganism). Pagans are some of the most gregarious, happy, and joyful people you'll ever meet. Pagan parties are usually boisterous events. Enjoy your coven or group; you'll soon be thinking of its members as your extended family.

- ◆ **Leadership opportunities**   All groups need people who are willing to assume positions of responsibility: to teach the newcomers, to handle administrative work, and to lead rituals. When you're just beginning, you won't need to worry about these jobs, but if you stay with a group long enough, you'll have the chance to steer the boat from time to time. This not only is a way to serve others, it's a special way to serve the God and Goddess as well.

Group membership is not for all pagans. For that matter, some people may enjoy being solitary and then later on participating in a group (or vice versa). As always, trust your intuition when it comes to connecting with other practitioners of nature spirituality. Whether you take the plunge and connect with a circle or a grove, or you choose to practice your spirituality in a solitary manner, it's good to know so many other pagans are out there, honoring the Goddess and the old Gods.

The Least You Need to Know

- ◆ Pagans can practice their spirituality by themselves as solitaries, in small circles, in larger groups, and even at major regional or national gatherings.

- ◆ Each different style of pagan group has its own lessons to impart, and sometimes working in a pagan community teaches us as much about life in general as about paganism.

- ◆ Gatherings are a great place to meet pagans of different traditions, to learn and participate in pagan rituals, and most of all, to enjoy a relaxing few days in the woods.

- ◆ When finding a pagan group, always use common sense and trust your intuition. Don't join a group that makes you feel uncomfortable or that espouses values contrary to your own.

Chapter 23

Harry Potter and Beyond: Paganism in Popular Culture

In This Chapter

- ◆ Books with pagan and pagan-friendly themes
- ◆ Enchanting television shows
- ◆ Pagans on the silver screen
- ◆ Witchy elements in popular and classical music
- ◆ The pagan music scene

The themes of magic, myth, and the spirit of nature play a major role in the arts, including literature, film, and music. For that matter, many creative works explore the mysterious worlds of witchcraft, druidism, and other forms of paganism. Most people who embrace pagan spirituality find that it's great fun to read books, watch films, and listen to music with pagan or nature-spirituality themes. This chapter will introduce you to a variety of artistic and cultural works that explore the pagan world.

Books for Pagans

Well, you're reading a book right now, and by doing so you are engaging in one of the favorite activities of pagans. Pagans tend to be intelligent, well-educated folks with a curious nature, so reading is a natural endeavor for many of them.

Here's a list of some books that many pagans enjoy. Some of these books (like *The Mists of Avalon*) have very specific pagan themes. Others, like *The Lord of the Rings*, aren't necessarily pagan in focus but have magical, mythical, or other elements that pagans love. Happy reading!

♦ *The Lord of the Rings* by **J. R. R. Tolkien**   The great-granddaddy of fantasy novels, Tolkien's epic tale of war and magic draws on northern mythology to create a wondrous world of elves, dwarves, and hobbits, or halfling humans. Tolkien was a devout Catholic, so there's plenty of good-versus-evil dualism in his story. Still, for sheer mythic grandeur, this three-volume classic should be read by every pagan.

♦ *The Mists of Avalon* by **Marion Zimmer Bradley**   Another classic, this retelling of the legends of King Arthur focuses on Morgan Le Fay, Arthur's half sister who is regarded as an evil sorceress in most versions of the myth but here is revisioned as a priestess of the Goddess. There's a sense of tragedy and loss in this tale of the old order of paganism yielding before the onset of the new religion (Christianity), but even in the end, there's a sense that the Goddess lives ever on.

♦ The *Harry Potter* books by **J. K. Rowling**   The hottest British export since The Beatles is a series of children's books about an orphan boy who discovers he's a wizard. Although the world of witchcraft and wizardry as portrayed in the Harry Potter series doesn't exactly match up with real-world Wicca, these stories nevertheless employ magic as a symbol for personal power and an ethical message that love is better than force. These entertaining books are required reading for the next generation of witches, so even if you're a grownup, check 'em out.

♦ *David and the Phoenix* by **Edward Ormondroyd**   This is another kids' book with a strong pagan message. David is a young boy who discovers the great phoenix of mythic legend living in the mountains behind his home. He and the phoenix become friends and embark on a series of otherworldly journeys before finally David must protect his friend from the threat of a decidedly unmagical scientist.

> **Drumbeats**
>
> The *Harry Potter* books have been criticized by religious fundamentalists because they allegedly promote occultism and witchcraft. This is ironic because the author does not consider herself a pagan or a witch, and the portrayal of wizardry in the books bears little resemblance to real paganism. Most pagans, however, enjoy the books for what they are: good clean fun.

◆ *Lammas Night* by **Katherine Kurtz**   A powerful glimpse into the world of traditional British witchcraft, this book is set in the nerve-wracking days of 1940 when England scrambled to protect itself from a likely Nazi invasion. While everyone was doing his or her part to aid the war effort, the witches and other magical folks took matters into their psychic hands and performed a powerful ritual to ward off the enemy. This novel, based on an actual magical effort by the witches of England, weaves together a modern suspense story with the mythic lore surrounding the pagan concept of sacrifice to create a compelling, if slightly spooky, story.

◆ *Druids* by **Morgan Llewellyn**   We know very little about the rituals, beliefs, and day-to-day lives of the ancient druids, but they certainly have captured the imagination of pagans as well as lovers of mystery and myth in general. This book, by a popular Irish author, speculates on what life may have been like for a druid living in Celtic Gaul on the eve of the Roman conquest. It's a sad story, but Llewellyn provides a believable portrait of the mystical spirituality underpinning a proud people in the twilight of their freedom.

◆ *The Teachings of Don Juan* by **Carlos Castaneda**   This book is based on anthropological research Castaneda conducted with a Yaqui shaman in Mexico. It's controversial in that it has been portrayed as a true story, but critics charge that it is fictionalized. Pagans can recognize that even if this is more fiction than fact, it is a powerful and spiritually viable portrayal of shamanism as it still exists on the fringes of "civilized" society.

◆ *Moonheart* by **Charles De Lint**   Many science-fiction and fantasy writers explore pagan or nature-mystical themes in their writing, but Canadian author Charles De Lint has been especially well received by the pagan community, thanks to his lyrical and vivid portrayals of the pagan world intersecting with the mysterious and magical Otherworld. *Moonheart* tells the story of some ordinary folks in modern Ottawa who find a link to the magical past of ancient Wales, the land of Merlin the magician and Taliesin the bard.

◆ *Thomas the Rhymer* by **Ellen Kushner**   Here's a contemporary novel based on retelling a fairy tale from an old Scottish ballad. Thomas is a minstrel who is spirited away by the Queen of Elfland (a.k.a. the Fairy Queen) to live in the otherworldly paradise before finally returning to the mundane world, but now with a magical inability to speak anything other than the truth.

Oracle _____

If you really love to read and want to get to know nature mysticism and Goddess spirituality inside and out, check out *The Well-Read Witch: Essential Books for your Magickal Library* by Carl McColman. It's a directory of more than 400 books on topics of interest to witches and other pagans.

TV Shows for Pagans

One of the most telling signs that paganism is growing as a spiritual movement is that it has become increasingly visible on television. TV is truly a marker of our society's mainstream, and a generation ago, paganism only made it onto the tube in funny ways (such as the classic show *Bewitched*). Nowadays, the humor is still there, but other shows—from *Charmed* to *Buffy the Vampire Slayer*—explore pagan, Wiccan, and magical themes in respectful and thought-provoking ways. The next time you feel like being a couch potato, perhaps you'll enjoy some of these shows:

◆ *Bewitched* This grandmother of magical television involved an ordinary man married to a very special witch. Elizabeth Montgomery, in her classic role, portrayed Samantha, who could do her housework just be wriggling her nose (now *that's* magic!). Part suburban satire and part family comedy, this show portrayed witchcraft only as magical ability, not as an ethical spirituality. (Some of Samantha's relatives were not very nice.)

◆ *Buffy the Vampire Slayer* What began as a goofy story of a high-school girl with the ability to kick supernatural butt developed into a multilayered glimpse into the perennial struggle of good versus evil. Most important for pagans is Willow, Buffy's best friend who embraces the spiritual dimensions of Wicca.

◆ *Charmed* This is the story of three sisters who practice witchcraft and use their magical abilities to fight all sorts of evils. As with most other pagan-oriented television shows, the good-versus-evil theme is a bit over the top, and the sisters are stereotypically Hollywood gorgeous. Still, for mind candy that's reasonably fair in its portrayal of magical spirituality, this is worth a watch.

◆ *Sabrina the Teenage Witch* Okay, so teenagers have problems even when they're witches! Like *Bewitched*, this show (based on the children's comic book) is more silly than anything else. But the overall message—that it's okay to practice an alternative spirituality—is one most pagans can support.

◆ *Xena* and *Hercules* Not all pagan-friendly shows on TV involve witchcraft. These two fantasy adventures explore the world of ancient mythology, not only through the eyes of the Greek hero Hercules but also occasionally featuring various other Gods and Goddesses, most of whom are petulant, self-centered, and given to wreaking havoc. That may seem goofy, but it's important to remember that, in the world of ancient mythology, many of the divine and semidivine figures *were* given to behave in ways that weren't always commendable. These shows may be valuable only as entertainment, but at least they entertain us by creating a world where Gods and Goddesses (however imperfect) exist.

Movies for Pagans

Thankfully, paganism has fared better on the silver screen than on the TV screen. As with television, movies have gone from mostly stereotypical depictions of pagan and nature spirituality to very profound and sometimes deeply pagan-friendly examinations of our spirituality. Of the movies listed here, not all of them are necessarily "pagan" (such as *What Dreams May Come*), but they have elements in the story that pagans can relate to.

◆ *The Craft*   Four alienated high-school girls learn the ways of witchcraft and have fun doing mean things to the people who get on their nerves—until it all backfires on them. Some witches don't like this movie because it suggests that there's a strong link between witchcraft and evil, but others see it as a warning of what happens when you ignore the Wiccan Rede.

◆ *Practical Magic*   This delightful film tells the story of two sisters born into a family of hereditary witches and their adventures (and misadventures) growing up and falling in love. It has a strong message about how witches face discrimination in our society. A happy ending and two delightfully kooky witch aunts make this an enjoyable flick.

◆ *Bell, Book and Candle*   Set in the 1950s, this love story features a nonmagical man (James Stewart) who becomes romantically involved with a very bewitching woman (Kim Novak). Silly stereotypes abound in this film, but it's fun if you don't take it too seriously. Plus it features a wonderful jazz nightclub called the Zodiac, where all the witches and warlocks hang out. The Zodiac is located underground—a metaphor for the "underground" status of pagan spirituality in the not-too-distant past.

◆ *The Wicker Man*   This horror movie from 1973 builds its story around the stereotype of paganism as a primitive religion of human sacrifice. That's too bad because if you can ignore the horror elements, everything else about this film actually portrays modern paganism in a fairly positive and sympathetic manner. The story involves a very Christian Scottish policeman who travels to a remote island to investigate the disappearance of a missing child. He finds a thriving pagan community there and uncovers a plot with a powerful surprise ending. If you don't like horror movies, skip the last 10 minutes (and in any event, remember that all real pagans today renounce any kind of blood sacrifice).

◆ *Harvey*   Here's a movie from classic Hollywood that playfully and artfully showcases a pagan theme. In this case, it's the concept of the pooka, the power animal of Celtic shamanism. *Harvey* tells the story of an amiable drunk named Elwood P. Dowd (masterfully portrayed by James Stewart) who has an "imaginary" friend—a five-foot-tall rabbit named Harvey. It's a one-joke movie with the humor being driven by the many ways in which all the "normal" people react to Elwood's apparent delusion. By the end of the movie, it appears that maybe Elwood and his pooka are the sanest characters around.

Drumbeats

Movies like *Bell, Book and Candle, The Craft,* and *The Wicker Man* are mixed blessings—they are marred by unfortunate stereotyping of pagans, but they also have some entertaining or interesting perspectives that make the inaccuracies almost forgivable. Yet many other movies, such as *Rosemary's Baby, The Witches of Eastwick,* or the 1940s classic *I Married a Witch,* are totally unfair in their depiction of witches as evildoers. Films dealing with supernatural themes are meant to entertain people, not enlighten them, so many unfortunate stereotypes continue to appear even in new films. Hopefully, as increasing numbers of people embrace paganism as their chosen spiritual path, Hollywood will respond with more movies that accurately convey the beauty and honor of nature spirituality.

◆ *Final Fantasy: The Spirits Within*   This stunning animated epic, based on the popular video game, has a strong message of environmental awareness and honoring the spirits of the land. What happens when the spirits of the "land" from a meteor strikes the earth? A strong spiritual theme in the story argues against the blind use of force to subdue the wild energies of nature.

◆ *Cast a Deadly Spell*   What if magic defined the world of Hollywood? This movie explores a parallel Los Angeles where a private detective gets involved in a plot by a scheming magician to awake Cthulu, the dark forces of underworld chaos. It's a tongue-in-cheek story with fun special effects.

◆ *The Sorceress*   A beautiful film with a strong pagan message, *The Sorceress* tells the story of a medieval village where a Catholic friar comes to root out heretics. He takes aim at the village wise woman, an herbalist/midwife who is too busy communing with nature to go to church. What's especially interesting about this story is its depiction of the village priest, who tolerates the paganism of the herbalist. The story ends with a hopeful and positive message of goodwill between competing belief systems.

◆ *Anchoress*   A visually gorgeous film, this is the story of a medieval peasant girl who, after having visions of the Virgin Mother, becomes an anchoress—a holy woman enclosed in a small cell attached to a church. It quickly becomes apparent, however, that the divine figure who appears in her visions is not exactly the Virgin Mary that the priest approves of. This is a stark, mysterious story that explores the tension between Christianity and paganism in an earlier era.

◆ *What Dreams May Come*   This is not a pagan film in itself, but it features themes warmly embraced by many pagans, such as the otherworld to which we go after we die, the possibility of at least partial communication between the dead and the living, and the promise of reincarnation with those you love. Robin Williams delivers a nuanced performance as a dead man who cannot shake his love for his surviving wife. Thanks to computer graphics, this film is a visual spectacle.

◆ *Mary Poppins*   Walt Disney's 1964 masterpiece makes an upbeat statement about magic, adventure, and living life playfully. The magical nanny, Mary Poppins, promptly turns a proper English home upside down with her unorthodox ways of caring for her young charges. From a floating tea party to a merry-go-round ride in the otherworld, this kid's movie captures the magic of magic.

Popular Music for Pagans

Music plays a pivotal role in any spiritual path. From the organ preludes associated with Christianity to the harmonic chanting of Tibetan monks, from time immemorial, music has helped shape humanity's inner experience. Pagans, too, have their own musical culture. (Later in this chapter, you'll learn about recordings by artists who specifically create music for the Goddess/nature spirituality community.) This section, however, looks at a variety of recordings by popular musicians whose music touches on one or more pagan or pagan-friendly themes. Then comes a list of pagan-themed classical music and finally a list of music by pagans themselves. Think of these lists as the soundtrack for your spiritual journey.

◆ **Jethro Tull,** *Songs from the Wood*   This progressive rock album, originally released in 1976, features a number of songs that celebrate the love of nature, British style. Songs like "Ring Out Solstice Bells" and "Jack-in-the-Green" are filled with earthy imagery from English folklore.

◆ **Peter Gabriel,** *Security*   This moody and ritualistic album features songs brimming with pagan, shamanic, and magical imagery. Standout tracks include "San Jacinto," an elegy for the culture of southwestern Native Americans, and "Lay Your Hands on Me," a ceremonial number evoking the spirit of initiation into sacred mysteries.

◆ **Kate Bush,** *Hounds of Love*   This lovely and melodic album features a 20-minute suite of songs (back in the days of vinyl records, it took up the entire side of the album) that explores a powerful dream sequence, filled with imagery of witchcraft and Irish magic, that climaxes with a song of love for the earth, just before the dream ends and the singer awakes into a morning filled with love.

Drumbeats

The Grateful Dead was a popular band among many pagans, not only because many of the group's songs had nature-positive lyrics but also because their concerts usually featured long periods of shamanic-inspired drumming, to which the fans would enthusiastically clap or dance along. A Dead concert was, to those who understood, full of pagan ritualistic elements.

♦ **Incredible String Band,** *The Hangman's Beautiful Daughter* An old hippie classic from 1968, this recording has songs that honor the elements ("The Water Song" and the unpronounceable "Koeeoaddi There") and the moon ("Waltz of the New Moon"). It also features an epic tune called "A Very Cellular Song," parts of which have been adopted as chants by the pagan community. Robin Williamson, one of the founders of the Incredible String Band, has recorded a number of folksy solo recordings that evoke the spirit of the ancient bards.

♦ **Mickey Hart,** *Planet Drum* Former Grateful Dead drummer Mickey Hart has released a number of albums that celebrate the diversity and beauty of world percussion. This album is a powerful statement of how drums and percussion instruments from around the globe can be used together to create an integrated and harmonious musical statement of world unity through rhythm.

♦ **Fairport Convention,** *Liege and Lief* Fairport is a British folk-rock band that made a reputation from playing old traditional songs in a modern, electric style. Their most famous album is the 1969 recording *Liege and Lief*, which consisted mostly of traditional ballads along with a couple of original compositions. Both the traditional and new material has pagan themes, especially "Tam Lin," a song about a fairy abduction in Scotland, and "Come All Ye," about using music to rouse the spirit of the earth.

♦ **Gilli Smyth,** *Mother* This obscure recording is from the female vocalist of the avant-garde band Gong of the 1970s. It features songs about the Goddess, feminist spirituality, and reincarnation. A highlight is a retelling of the ancient Welsh myth about the birth of Taliesin, the magical bard.

♦ **Loreena McKennitt,** *The Visit* This deeply magical recording from a Canadian harpist/vocalist features a lovely version of "Greensleeves" and an 11-minute setting of Tennyson's Arthurian poem, "The Lady of Shalott." "Bonny Portmore" has a strong environmental theme, and "All Soul's Night" is a paganesque celebration of the Samhain rituals. McKennitt even looks witchy in the cover photo.

♦ **Libana,** *A Circle is Cast* This is a collection of chants and songs from an all-women chorus. This eclectic anthology includes selections from a variety of cultures but also plenty of feminist and nature-oriented material. Even the song titles reveal how pagan-friendly this recording is. In addition to the title song, there's "In May, That Lusty Season," "Full Moonlight Dance," "The Earth, the Air, the Fire, the Water," and "The Earth is Our Mother."

◆ **Faith and the Muse,** *Annwn, Beneath the Waves*   This is a powerful and brooding darkwave song cycle based on the mythology of the ancient Welsh. This is not your mother's hippified pagan music; rather, it's a gothic masterpiece filled with the energies of Gods and Goddesses like Cernunnos and Arianrhod.

◆ **Dagda,** *Celtic Trance*   This is an excursion into Irish myth by way of Enigma-esque ambient/dance music. Uillean bagpipes join with synthesizers and chanting to create a hypnotic otherworldly soundscape.

◆ **Sarah Brightman,** *La Luna*   This classical-crossover singer best known for her appearance in *Phantom of the Opera* delivers a collection of songs based on the moon. It's not especially pagan, but since witches and other pagans love the moon and revere her as a symbol of the Goddess, this is a natural addition to any pagan music library.

Classical Music for Pagans

Over the years, many classical musicians have drawn on the rich traditions of ancient mythology to inspire their compositions. Even if these musicians are (or were) not themselves pagan, their music, imbued with the spirits of Goddesses and Gods, can be appreciated by today's pagans, for whom such thematic music is more than mere entertainment. It can be regarded as music of praise to the divine that appears under many guises.

◆ **Gustav Holst,** *The Planets*   If you're into astrology, you'll probably enjoy this melodic suite of tone poems from a twentieth-century German composer. Each composition is based on the astrological meanings associated with each planet from Mercury to Neptune.

◆ **Igor Stravinsky,** *The Rite of Spring*
Stravinsky's masterpiece provides a brooding, chaotic soundtrack to what an ancient Beltane ritual must have been like. The composition is divided into two sections: "The Adoration of the Earth" and "The Sacrifice."

◆ **Sir Granville Bantock, various works**
Twentieth-century British composer Bantock's music is lyrical and accessible, and many of his works explore specifically pagan themes, including "The Cyprian Goddess," "Celtic Symphony," "Pagan Symphony," and "The Witch of Atlas."

Oracle

Remember that pagan and mythological themes aren't limited to classical music. From the time of the Renaissance onward, fine art also has featured many pagan images, often derived from Greek or Roman mythology. Renaissance masterpieces dealing with pagan subject matter include Botticelli's *Birth of Venus* or Titian's *Bacchanal.*

- **Vincenzo Bellini,** *Norma*   If you're a pagan and an opera lover, *Norma* is for you. This nineteenth-century work features the story of a tragic romance between a druid priestess and a Roman soldier in ancient Gaul.

- **Charles Tomlinson Griffes,** *The Kairn of Koridwen*   Griffes was an early-twentieth-century American composer of chamber and theater music; like *Norma*, this concert piece dramatizes the love between a druid priestess and a warrior of ancient times.

- **Wolfgang Amadeus Mozart,** *The Magic Flute*   Mozart's final opera is filled with esoteric and mythic imagery, much of which is drawn from the traditions of free-masonry.

- **George Whitefield Chadwick,** *Aphrodite*   This symphonic poem, by nineteenth-century American composer Chadwick, is dedicated to the Goddess of love in her lesser-known aspect as Goddess of the sea and of sailors.

- **George Lloyd,** *The Vigil of Venus*   Beautiful, sensuous nature imagery weaves together with the joy of love in this choral setting (for soprano, tenor, and chorus) of an ancient Roman hymn to the Goddess of love.

- **Lord Berners,** *The Triumph of Neptune*   This is an early-twentieth-century ballet by a minor English composer. The ballet is filled with fairies, sylphs, and Goddesses.

- **Richard Wagner,** *The Ring Cycle* (*Das Rheingold*, *Die Walküre*, *Siegfried*, and *Götterdmmerüng*)   The ultimate pagan-themed opera is actually a cycle of four complete works, in which the majestic tale of the twilight of the Norse Gods and Goddesses is movingly recounted. If you're not wild about opera, you might enjoy one of several available recordings of musical highlights from the Ring Cycle without out words.

The Pagan Music Scene

More and more musicians have begun to perform and record music specifically written for pagans, Wiccans, and others who love the Goddess and the earth. Some of these bands proudly call themselves pagan musicians. Others may prefer to be called Celtic musicians or folk troubadours, but anyone who listens closely to the words in their songs will recognize the obvious earth-spirit energy.

Some of the earliest musicians who specifically recorded pagan music followed in the tradition of British and Celtic folk music. This makes perfect sense because many of the ballads, songs, and rhymes out of the folklore of the British Isles are filled with ancient imagery that evokes fairies, elves, and the powers of the land.

Emerald Rose is a Celtic band whose Goddess-oriented songs place them at the fore-front of the pagan music scene.

(© 2001 Fox Gradin)

This doesn't mean, however, that all pagan-oriented music is filled with guitars, flutes, harps, and fiddles. Especially as the pagan scene began to grow rapidly in the 1990s, more and more musicians representing a wide variety of genres and styles began to incorporate pagan themes in their compositions and performances. In the list of musicians that follow, you'll see not only folk but rock and roll, techno, new age, and even jazz and blues, all done with a pagan twist.

If you love music and you find meaning in earth spirituality, check out recordings by these artists. You're sure to find music that is as spiritually meaningful as it is entertaining.

Oracle

The single best source for pagan music is www.serpentinemusic.com, a website devoted to music for the earth-spirit community. With few exceptions, if a tape or CD is currently in print, Serpentine will have it. Plus it's a pagan-owned business, so when you shop here, your money goes to support members of the community.

Here's a sampling of some of the most exciting recordings that explore pagan themes:

- **Todd Alan & Friends, *Carry Me Home: A Collection of New and Old Pagan Songs*** Ohio-based Alan blends traditional folk songs and modern pagan chants and songs into a soft-rock format.

- **Jennifer Berezon, *Returning*** Ethereal and dreamy, this "long-playing healing chant" celebrates Goddess spirituality in a universal and inclusive way. It was recorded at a sacred site in Malta, a land of ancient Goddess worship.

- **Francesca De Grandis,** *Pick the Apple from the Tree*   De Grandis is a well-known teacher of shamanic and Wiccan lore, but one of her true passions is music and not just folksy pagan acoustic tunes. Her eclectic CD includes blues, jazz, rock, and ceremonial chanting.

- **Emerald Rose,** *Bending Tradition*   Inspired by the Scottish folk group Silly Wizard, Emerald Rose plays both traditional Celtic tunes and original songs, many of which have a clear mythological or Goddess-oriented theme.

- **Beverly Frederick,** *Through the Darkness: Chants and Songs from the Reclaiming Community*   Pagan ceremony comes alive when participants perform chants and songs, and this recording features a number of tunes you can incorporate into your rituals. Reclaiming is a well-known Wiccan community based in California (the Wiccan author Starhawk was one of its founders), and this recording features music used in that community's rituals.

- **Gypsy,** *Enchantress*   First recorded on cassette in 1990 and rereleased on CD a decade later, this recording from a witch based in Salem, Massachusetts, has a classic-rock sound and lyrics filled with a romantic depiction of the old religion.

- **Anne Hill,** *Circle Round and Sing! Songs for Family Celebrations in the Goddess Traditions*   Here's a collection of pagan songs for kids. Based on the book *Circle Round* by Starhawk, Diane Baker, and Anne Hill, this anthology of chants and folksongs takes the listener through the pagan year through the eyes of a child. It's great for kids of all ages.

- **Kenny and Tziporah Klein,** *Fairy Queen*   Through most of the 1980s and early 1990s, Kenny and Tziporah Klein traveled throughout North America, appearing at pagan gatherings, Renaissance Faires, and various other venues. Their repertoire, a blend of traditional folk tunes and original pagan compositions, set a standard of musical excellence for the nature spirituality community. The Kleins split up in 1992; unfortunately, their recordings are now out of print, although some pagan merchants still have a few old cassettes in stock.

Drumbeats

One of the most popular ways of making music in the pagan community involves drum circles. Thanks to the connection between drumming and shamanism, many pagans find that a circle of people playing hand drums together can create a hypnotic atmosphere of pure percussion. What's wonderful about drum circles is that even beginners can participate—all it takes is a basic sense of rhythm and a willingness to be part of a group creating musical magic. Of course, a person doesn't need to be a pagan in order to participate in drum circles, but such drumming is very popular among pagans, and often impromptu drum circles will form at pagan gatherings.

◆ **Moonstruck,** *Witch of the Wildwood*   Pagan spirituality meets garage-band rock in this recording of chants and songs based on Wiccan folklore.

◆ **On Wings of Song & Robert Gass,** *From the Goddess/O Great Spirit*   This CD features two extended chants by Gass and his choir: one based on the American Indian concept of the Great Spirit and the other a weaving together of three Goddess chants. The music is beautiful and hypnotic—perfect for meditation.

◆ **Gwydion Pendderwen,** *The Music of Gwydion*   This two-CD set includes two albums originally released in 1979 and 1982 by the acknowledged father of pagan music. Pendderwen died in a car crash in the early 1980s, making these recordings true classics. They are not the most professionally produced recordings, but the spirit of these songs embodies the excitement of paganism from a time when it was more truly an underground movement.

◆ **Rumors of the Big Wave,** *Burning Times*   Another out-of-print classic that's well worth looking for in your favorite used CD shop. Under the leadership of Charlie Murphy and Jami Sieber, Rumors of the Big Wave created environmentally-conscious rock music. The title track of this disc is the ultimate pagan song, a stirring tale of the era when witches were burned in early modern Europe.

◆ **Wendy Rule,** *Deity*   This Australian vocalist's lush Gothic sound should appeal especially to younger witches, although pagans of all ages may enjoy the lyrical romanticism of her songs devoted to Artemis, the Triple Goddess, and other elements of the pagan path.

◆ **Suzanne Sterling,** *Bhakti*   This is sacred Goddess music with a sensuous beat. Priestess Sterling incorporates Middle Eastern and modern dance rhythms into a trancey blend of world spirituality, celebrating the love of God, Goddess, and Spirit beyond all names.

◆ **Lisa Thiel,** *Lady of the Lake*   Celtic mysticism meets the deep spirit of the American land in this collection of shamanistic songs and rounds. Thiel's music is easy to sing along to, making it perfect for use in ceremony and ritual.

◆ **Three Weird Sisters,** *Rite the First Time*   This trio of acoustic musicians combines harp, upright bass, acoustic guitar, and bodhran (Celtic drum) with gorgeous harmonies on a wide array of musical styles, from silly sing-alongs to moody excursions into faery spirituality.

◆ **Leah Wolfsong,** *Songs of the Circle*   Drumming and chanting coalesce in this tribally inspired collection of prayers and chants, many of which evoke the mysticism of Native American spirituality.

As fast as the pagan community is growing, new music with pagan or Goddess themes will be appearing all the time. Although it might take a bit of effort to find pagan music like the recordings listed here (you'll probably have to go online to locate many pagan CDs), you'll be rewarded for your efforts with music that truly captures the essence of the pagan spirituality.

The Least You Need to Know

- ◆ For many pagans, reading is almost a sacred duty. Pagan-oriented themes can be found in many different literary works.

- ◆ Numerous television shows and films portray various aspects of witchcraft and other forms of pagan spirituality. In recent years, the portrayal of paganism in the media has become more and more positive.

- ◆ Pagan lyrics and musical themes can be found in both popular and classical music.

- ◆ More and more musicians are creating music specifically written and performed for pagans.

Chapter 24

Everyday Paganism

In This Chapter

- ◆ The 24–7 nature mystic
- ◆ The care and feeding of patron and matron deities
- ◆ When to come out of the broom closet (and when not to)
- ◆ Jewitches, Christopagans, and other hybrids
- ◆ Cyberpaganism: The world of nature spirituality online

As a spirituality grounded in nature, one of paganism's strengths is how easily it meshes with the ordinary daily lives of its practitioners. Some pagans don't like to use the word "religion," preferring instead to see the pagan path as a lifestyle that shapes the experience of being alive, 24–7. Indeed, there are many ways to be pagan as part of your ordinary daily routine. This chapter wraps up this book's overview of nature spirituality by providing some helpful hints for your unique brand of paganism.

Remember that there's no single right way to be a pagan. You can participate in a pagan group and merge your spirituality with the group's chosen way of doing things, or you can be a solitary practitioner with a creative flair for honoring the Goddess, the God, and nature in ways uniquely suited for you. Every suggestion or bit of advice in the pages to come ultimately must feel good and right to you to be appropriate for your path. Hopefully, at least one or two of these hints will resonate with you.

How to Be a Pagan Each and Every Day

Let's start with a look at some of the simplest ways to incorporate the spirit of paganism into your life. What follows is pretty much a review of suggestions given throughout this book. Refer to this chapter as a handy summary of the practical application of the pagan way.

Perform Mini Rituals

When the Sabbats or the full or new moons roll around, you may want to devote an entire evening to enacting a ritual designed to honor the spirits that illuminate your spiritual life. This doesn't mean, however, that rituals are only appropriate on holidays and festival days. If you keep it simple enough to be practical, you might even enjoy doing a basic ritual every day.

It is important, however, to keep it practical. A 30-minute or hour-long ritual may be fun on the Moons and Sabbats, but do it every day and it will soon lose its luster. A better strategy would be to devise a 5- to 10-minute mini ritual that doesn't require a lot of tools (maybe just a candle and a stick of incense) and that involves either words you've memorized or a simple structure in which you use your own words, spoken from the heart.

Rituals don't have to be fancy affairs. Even an impromptu drum circle with your pagan friends can be spiritually meaningful.

(© 2001 Fox Gradin)

One option is to light the candles and incense on your altar every morning and evening and take a few minutes for silent meditation and prayers. If your schedule permits, time such rituals to occur at, or just after, sunrise and sundown. According to Celtic legend, such "in between" times are considered to have particular magical power, so they make especially appropriate times for calling on the Goddess and God.

> **Oracle**
>
> Mini rituals and meditation go together nicely. Experiment with ways in which you can honor Mother Nature and spend time in meditation on a daily basis in a unified personal ceremony.

Meditate

Although some people find meditating daily to be a challenge, it's just a matter of developing a habit. Once you get into the swing of daily devotion to silence and inner journeying, it will become one of the most important parts of your day. Whether you follow the practice of Zen-like contemplation or a more shamanic form of visualization and spiritual journeying, your time devoted to inner cultivation will deepen your connection to the Gods.

> **Taboo!**
>
> Don't waste time worrying about the "right way" to be a pagan. Instead, focus your attention on how you most enjoy honoring Mother Nature. The more true you are to yourself, the better a pagan you'll be.

Keep a Journal

You don't have to be a great writer to benefit from a spiritual journal. The words you write (or the pictures you draw) are for your own benefit; you don't need to share them with anyone if you don't want to. Record your dreams (both literal and metaphorical), your experiences with ritual or meditation, your thoughts about what you believe and why, and your decisions regarding taking care of the earth or working for healing. If writing prose isn't your thing, write poems, draw pictures, or even talk into a tape recorder. Do whatever feels right for you in terms of making a record of your spiritual journey. Years from now, it will be one of your most prized possessions.

Study, Read, Spend Time in the Woods

Reading and hanging out in the forest may seem to be an odd combination, but from a pagan perspective, both are ways to nurture your soul. When you read the ancient myths, magical fiction, or books devoted to pagan spirituality or psychic development, you are feeding both mind and soul. Meanwhile, a regular weekend afternoon spent among the trees will keep your spirituality from being too much of a "head trip." In addition to walks in the woods, roll up your sleeves and get your hands dirty with a garden or even houseplants (a convenient choice for urban pagans).

Patrons and Matrons: The Gods Who Are Just Right for You

Most pagans love the rich diversity of Gods and Goddesses from throughout the world, but it can be overwhelming to try to learn about all the various deities from Greek myth, Egyptian religion, Celtic spirituality, Norse tradition, and on and on. To keep things in perspective, many pagans focus on just one or two particular pantheons. For example, in my own spirituality, I work specifically with the Celtic pantheon—that is, the Gods and Goddesses from Ireland, Wales, and ancient Gaul. If you join a pagan group, you'll want to focus on the pantheon(s) chosen by the group; otherwise, work with the pantheons from whichever culture or cultures you feel most drawn to.

You can narrow down your spiritual work even further by picking just two or three Gods and Goddesses from your chosen pantheon and dedicating a significant portion of your spiritual work to them. These deities will become your *patron* and *matron* Gods. As a rule, it makes sense to choose one God and one Goddess as your patron and matron, but you can choose more than two (as long as you commit to showing devotion to each one; it is a spiritual commitment to adopt a patron or matron deity).

EarthWords

A **patron** is a father, and a **matron** is a mother. So a patron God and matron Goddess are particular deities that a pagan chooses to give special devotion to, just as a child has special love for Mommy and Daddy.

Oracle

Most pagans recommend picking your patron and matron deities from the same pantheon. When you mix and match Gods from different cultures, they may not always get along energetically. For that matter, try to avoid working with deities who, according to tradition, didn't like each other. That energy of conflict could sabotage your own spirituality.

Picking Your Special Deities

How do you decide if a God or Goddess should be your patron/matron? Try to match your interests and desires with the personality of the deity. For example, if you want to become a more compassionate person, the Chinese Goddess Kuan Yin may be a wise choice for you. If you're trying to develop artistic skill, the Celtic God Lugh of the Many Talents may be the one you'll want to revere. Choose to show particular devotion to deities who embody qualities or characteristics you wish to cultivate in your own life.

Once you've selected your patrons and/or matrons, you can honor them in a variety of ways. When you perform ritual, always be sure to include prayers or invocations addressed to your chosen deities. Try to learn all you can about your God and Goddess through myth, history, and any other background information you can find. You might want to purchase or make a statue, painting, or other image of your patron and matron to set on or above your altar. Finally, work with your chosen deities in your meditations.

For many pagans, patrons and matrons become similar to spirit guides—personalized contacts with the otherworld who can guide and direct us in living out our soul purpose.

Personal Gods, Family Gods, Community Gods

Patron and matron deities don't have to be just the Gods and Goddesses who speak to you personally. Your family can have chosen deities to watch over the family as a whole. Your pagan group may have special Gods and Goddesses whom the group as a whole honors. In each case, the chosen deities represent energies or qualities that the family or group wishes to manifest, so a mutual relationship develops between the deity and people through meditation, group ritual, and any other shared activity dedicated to the deities.

Relating to Nonpagans

Sooner or later, all pagans face the question of whether to share earth spirituality with others. Do you tell everyone you know that you're following the path of nature spirituality, or do you keep it a secret from anyone who isn't already a pagan?

Historically, pagans have preferred to keep their spirituality under wraps. In early modern Europe, tens of thousands of people were killed for the "crime" of witchcraft. Even though no one gets burned at the stake for being a witch in modern civilization, that doesn't mean discrimination and prejudice have gone away. Even in the twenty-first century, people have lost their jobs, custody of their children, or the lease to their apartment simply for practicing witchcraft. Although other forms of paganism may not have the same public image problems that plague witchcraft, many pagans don't want to risk discrimination from those who are ignorant or bigoted. So, for many pagans, silence is the best policy. This extends to work and school as well as family and friends.

These days, more and more pagans don't want to go through life pretending they're something they're not. Not only does that seem dishonest, it's also unfair. If Christians and Jews and Muslims can practice their religion openly, why can't druids and witches and shamans? So more and more, pagans are "coming out of the broom

CAUTION

Taboo!

Remember that labels (like "pagan" or "witch") often alienate people needlessly. Your mother might freak out if you tell her you're a witch but might surprise you with an open-minded response if you talk instead about reverence for the Goddess and nature. Don't go out of your way to avoid the labels, but don't use them needlessly around nonpagans.

closet" and expecting the same privileges that other faiths enjoy in the modern world, where freedom of religion is considered a hallmark of liberty.

It is ultimately your decision whether to keep your spirituality to yourself or to let others know that you follow a nature-based path. If you decide to keep it quiet, you may have to come up with polite ways of behaving in certain situations. What will you say when people ask you if you belong to a church? When visiting your relatives around the holidays, will you go to church with them to be polite, or will you have an excuse as to why you'd rather not? When it comes time for a major rite of passage like marriage or a funeral, what will your wishes be (especially keeping in mind that many family and friends will want to participate in these rituals)?

If you decide it's easier to be honest about your spirituality than to hide it, here are a few guidelines to help make your journey out of the broom closet as low stress as possible.

Remember: Pagans Don't Convert Others!

The most important rule to keep in mind is that it's never your job to convince people that paganism is the right path for them (or even for you). You're not responsible if other people disapprove of your spirituality. You have a right to be treated fairly and respectfully by others, even in terms of your religion, but they don't have to like it.

When telling others that you practice paganism, never argue to prove a point. You'll just come across as arrogant and mean spirited. That's hardly the face of paganism you'll want to show to others. Also, although it's okay to invite people to learn more about paganism or even to come to public pagan rituals, don't push it if they choose not to. Even if you think your boyfriend has all the makings of a great Wiccan priest, let him make up his own mind in his own time.

Sharing with Your Parents

Coming out of the broom closet to parents can be a very delicate matter. If your parents have strongly held religious views of their own, your decision to change religions will likely be upsetting to them. This would be true no matter what faith you chose, but in choosing paganism (especially Wicca), you may have a double whammy to contend with. Not only might they be upset that you've rejected their religion, they also could be additionally triggered by your embracing a spiritual path that they think is bad.

You may need to be prepared to emphasize that your spirituality is based on loving and revering nature and God (only you call God "the God and the Goddess"). You may have to remind them more than once that no, you don't worship the devil. You don't even need to tell them you don't believe in the devil; that could lead to an argument. Just emphasize that you don't worship him.

Know exactly what you want from your parents. Chances are, all you really want is for them to acknowledge that you've chosen a different spiritual path, whether or not they approve. You'll also want them to respect that decision (in other words, not constantly try to convert you back to their religion). Keep in mind that, no matter how imperfect your folks may be, in their hearts they love you and want what they think is best for you. They're only human, which is why they might take it personally when you reject their religion. So be gentle with them and assure them that you love them, even though your spirituality is different from theirs. Remember that they may not ever fully accept your spiritual path, but they could surprise you. I know several Wiccans whose Christian parents love to come to circle with them from time to time!

Sharing with Your Friends

Telling your friends about your spirituality is usually much easier. Since we choose our friends, we often choose people whose values and outlook are similar to ours to begin with. Many of your friends may enthusiastically support your spiritual path and may in fact be pagans themselves, wondering when to admit it to you! Others may not have heard of paganism but will have an open mind and will want to learn more.

Occasionally, one or more of your friends might have such strong religious biases against paganism that they'll react by getting deeply upset or, worse, trying to "save" you from paganism. In this situation, follow the pointers in the section on sharing with parents. Reassure your friends that you're still the same person they've known and loved all along.

> **Oracle**
>
> More than anything else, your parents want you to be happy and safe. When telling them about your spiritual choices, make a point of telling them that you are perfectly safe and entirely happy following in the footsteps of the Goddess. Even if they won't admit it, this reassurance will likely help them accept your path.

> **Taboo!**
>
> Fundamentalist Christians (or fundamentalists of any religion) rarely can accept people whose spiritual path is different from theirs. Remember that they have been indoctrinated to be intolerant. Save your blood pressure—consider keeping your spirituality discrete from any fundamentalists in your life, whether family, friend, or acquaintance. What they don't know won't hurt them—or you.

Sharing with Others

There's also the question of sharing your spiritual path with co-workers, teachers, employers, business associates, and others who may be part of your life. Think long and hard before making a big deal out of paganism with these associates. It's probably not worth all the explaining you may have to do, and unfortunately, it does leave you more open to facing some form of religious discrimination. Most people keep their spiritual lives private. As a pagan, it makes sense to follow that social custom.

Sharing with Your Children

Sooner or later, most pagans have families, just like most other people in society. If you have children in your life, how do you share paganism with them?

As a parent, it's your right to bring up your children in your faith. More and more pagan organizations offer classes for children where your kids can connect with other pagan kids. Pagan parenting can be as simple as teaching your children to love and respect nature; of course, you can take it much deeper, teaching your children about magic and mythology and ancient wisdom.

Here are two principles worth keeping in mind if and when you do raise children in the pagan path:

- ◆ **Teach them discretion.** Children can be just as prejudiced as grownups, and teachers can have misconceptions as well. Don't make a big deal out of having to keep paganism a secret; rather, emphasize that all spirituality ought to be kept private, ours included.

- ◆ **Let them make their own decision.** Paganism emphasizes freedom, which ultimately means you cannot force your children to embrace the pagan path. As unique people with their own needs, your children must decide for themselves which spiritual path (if any) to follow. Be gracious if your children decide that paganism is not for them.

To Know, to Will, to Dare, and to Keep Silent

Among Wiccans, the phrase "To know, to will, to dare, and to keep silent" expresses the qualities necessary to be a powerful magician. When it comes to relating to the nonpagan world, the quality of keeping silent may be the most important of all. This is not the silence of deceit or dishonesty. Rather, it is the silence of understanding when nothing needs to be said.

Can Mother Nature and God the Father Be Lovers?

One interesting new development in the pagan community involves people who grew up in a traditional religion, discovered paganism as an adult, and decided to blend the two spiritual paths together rather than switching religions. Although this is a minority position, more and more pagans (especially online) have chosen to identify themselves as *Jewitches*, *Christopagans*, or some other kind of hybrid nature mystics.

Although traditional religions historically have not supported this kind of spiritual interbreeding, to many pagans, it is a perfectly acceptable matter of personal preference. Trying to blend paganism and Christianity is no different than trying to blend druidism and South American shamanism, or Egyptian and Norse mythologies.

EarthWords

A **Jewitch** is a person who integrates both Judaism and paganism into his or her spiritual practice; a **Christopagan** creates a similar blend with Christianity and paganism.

Generally speaking, people with an interfaith approach to paganism keep some sort of ties to their childhood religion. Perhaps they still attend church or synagogue or enjoy reading the Torah or studying the Christian mystics. They usually supplement the monotheist religion with a strong emphasis on the sacredness of nature, the importance of the Goddess, and the value of earth-centered ritual. Some Jewitches and Christopagans may be more oriented toward monotheism, more oriented toward paganism, or may try to blend the two more or less equally.

If you feel comfortable blending paganism with another religion, keep in mind that you may not find many others who share your views. It may be important for you to connect with online communities with a similar outlook. Don't be surprised if some pagans are suspicious of your hybrid spirituality; after all, nearly all monotheistic people will be suspicious of it. Finally, you'll probably need to accept that hybrid spirituality will have its share of internal contradictions. If you try to blend paganism with Christianity or Judaism, it works best on a spiritual level. (It's okay to pray both to Jesus and Isis.) On the level of theology or beliefs, however, many core concepts of paganism are difficult, if not impossible, to reconcile with the Judeo-Christian tradition.

Drumbeats

If you're interested in blending paganism with Christianity, check out the writings of the ancient Celtic Christians who lived in Ireland and Scotland in the fifth to seventh centuries right after those countries converted to the new religion. Celtic Christianity incorporated many spiritual practices that were deeply pagan, and many of the Celtic Christian writings reveal a deep reverence for nature.

Online Paganism

It may seem ironic that a spiritual tradition based on reverence for nature and living in harmony with the earth's cycles would become so deeply entrenched in the high-tech world of the Internet. But then again, maybe it isn't such a stretch. Pagans often tend to be young, educated, visionary people, the same kind of people who embrace the positive potential of new technologies. Because pagans run the risk of facing discrimination in a world where minority spiritual paths are not always tolerated, for some, the relative anonymity of cyberspace makes it a welcome setting to connect with other nature mystics.

Also, pagans do not have the cultural advantages enjoyed by other religions; there are no pagan universities, relatively few pagan books and magazines, and no widespread organizations dedicated to pagan causes. Thus, for many people, the Internet represents the best—and perhaps only—way to reach out to others on a similar spiritual path.

How the Internet Has Helped the Pagan Movement ...

For many pagans and would-be pagans, the Internet has been a brilliant, safe, and effective tool for networking and education. In just a few years, literally thousands of pagan websites have appeared, from major sources of news and information like the Witches' Voice website to the endless number of homemade sites in which local covens or pagan solitaries express their own particular take on earth spirituality. Go to virtually any search engine online, type in the word "pagan" and the name of your city, and you are likely to find several websites related to the pagan community in your neighborhood.

A number of leaders in the pagan community, including Starhawk, Isaac Bonewits, Francesca De Grandis, and R. J. Stewart, have created websites that feature essays and articles by and about them. These sites serve as important sources of information for the ongoing developments in contemporary pagan thought. See Appendix B, "Resources," for a list of pagan and pagan-friendly websites.

> **Oracle** _____
>
> Remember to set limits when using the Internet. If you're looking for information on a particular topic, the Internet may be the best place to do your research. However, you also need to turn off the computer and go spend time outdoors with the trees, soil, and sky. Ultimately, that's the most important place to practice the pagan path.

...and How It Hasn't Really Helped

It's important to point out that cyberpaganism is not the be-all and end-all of the pagan community. It's easy to sign on to a dozen e-mail lists, participate in newsgroups, and surf website after website. Before you know it, your entire experience of being a pagan involves staring at a computer screen. Many of the websites and newsgroups offer valuable, thoughtful information on pagan spirituality, but others betray the biases of their creators. In other words, it's important to remember that the web is just another tool for communication. Like any other form of communication, it can transmit valuable information and erroneous material.

The Varieties of Pagan Websites

When it comes to exploring the online pagan world, you'll find a number of websites. Here are some basic categories of the kinds of online resources you'll discover:

◆ **Merchants** Some of the most enjoyable pagan websites involve stuff to buy. Be careful—you can spend lots of money on jewelry, incense, oils, books, and various other tools to support your spiritual path. You'll find artists who sell rare, one-of-a-kind objects, as well as pagans who travel from gathering to gathering selling their wares, with the website keeping them in business between events. Try www.theblessedbee.com and www.whisperedprayers.com.

◆ **Covens and groups** More and more pagan groups are making themselves known to the world at large through a website. These range from the delightfully homegrown to the truly professionally designed. Most pagan groups only serve a particular region, so if you stumble across a coven web page featuring a group that's more than 50 or so miles away, it probably won't have much to offer. Still, many coven websites feature teaching materials, sample rituals, and articles by coven members that you'll find interesting. You can always contact a coven if you like its website to see if it offers distance training or, better yet, can refer you to a similar group in your area. To see some excellent coven websites, surf to www.unicorntrad.org and www.draknet.com/proteus/.

> **Oracle**
>
> If you like to write or create graphics, consider setting up your own pagan website to feature your nature- and Goddess-oriented artistic creations. You'll connect with many people from all over the world who come to appreciate your contribution to the pagan community.

◆ **Training and educational** Although many coven sites are also educational in nature, some pagan websites don't offer much in the way of community or public rituals but have lots to offer to support your education in pagan ways. These include sites run by teachers in whose classes you can enroll (usually for a fee), but they also may just offer a collection of essays and articles for your own personal study. Try www.neopagan.net and www.well.com/user/zthirdrd/WiccanMiscellany.html.

◆ **Networking and search engines** The single best use of the Internet still involves finding information. For pagans, several search engines and websites specifically provide you with tools to connect with other pagans, both online and in the real world. Use these sites to learn about other pagans, to access information about different traditions and lineages, and to make connections with real human beings. Of course, all the common-sense rules about contacting people you meet online apply to pagans as much as to anyone else. Use caution when arranging to meet with someone you've contacted online. Don't give out your contact information online and be sure to arrange to meet others in safe, public settings. Two excellent networking/search engine sites for pagans are www.avatarsearch.com and www.ariadnespider.com.

E-Mail Lists and Discussion Groups

Websites are not the only way to connect with pagans online. Indeed, one of the best tools for interacting with other pagans is the e-mail discussion list. E-mail lists exist on virtually every topic imaginable, including a wide array of pagan subjects. Lists may include just a few members who send out messages infrequently, or they can have hundreds of participants who will fill your e-mail inbox with dozens of messages every day.

Pick a Topic, Any Topic

Pagan-oriented e-mail lists include regional lists where people from the same area can communicate (like the "Georgia Pagans" list), or they may be devoted to a particular tradition ("Traditionalist Witches"). Some lists are very scholarly and require you to post only messages of an academic nature. Others are more social, filled with conversational chitchat. Some lists are very collegial, and people support one another in their learning and spiritual development; others are like minefields where participants are forever arguing about this or that. When you sign up for an e-mail list, it's a good idea to simply read the messages that appear in your inbox for a few days to see if the tone of the list's discussions fits with what you're looking for.

Where to Find Pagan E-Mail Lists

If you want to sign up for pagan-oriented e-mail lists, the best place to start is www.yahoogroups.com. There you can search for lists with keywords like pagan or shaman. If you want specifically druid discussion, visit www.adf.com, which includes a number of druid-oriented e-mail lists. Pagan search engines such as Avatar Search or Ariadne Spider also list many pagan e-mail lists.

There Are No Trees in Cyberspace

The Internet has become a major tool for pagans to connect with one another, to learn about different forms of paganism, and to support the ongoing emergence of this spiritual revival. As a pagan, you'll want to have online access, and you'll enjoy the friends you'll make in cyberspace. Just remember that there are no trees in cyberspace. Keep your time online in perspective and don't let surfing the Internet become an excuse for not spending time outdoors, in meditation, or in ritual.

Summary: Getting to Know the Spirit of the Land

There are many, many things you can do to weave pagan spirituality into your daily life. From meditation to ritual to websites to crafts, no matter what your personal interests may be, you can fine ways to be a pagan every day.

As this book draws to a close, I'd like to leave you with one final thought. Spend some time every day relating to nature in some form or another. Learn to approach nature not only with the appreciation of your five physical senses but especially with your intuitive, meditative, and psychic "senses" wide open and alert. Try to feel the spirit of the land wherever you may be. Even beneath the concrete and asphalt of a major city, the land has a spirit (and the spirit of the land beneath a city especially needs to be listened to and acknowledged!). When all is said and done, the key to being a pagan is forming a spiritual relationship with nature, the land, the sky, and all the blessings and glories of the physical universe. It means working to heal the environment when it has been ravaged by the excesses of human waste. It also means making choices in you life so that your impact on the environment is one of healing rather than harm.

So finally, take time every day to get to know the spirit of nature and land better and better. This will teach you far more than a book ever could.

The Least You Need to Know

- Part of being a pagan means finding ways to express your spirituality each and every day.
- For many pagans, forming a special relationship with a patron God or matron Goddess is a way to deepen their sense of connection with the world of spirit.
- As a pagan, you may choose to "come out of the broom closet" to your nonpagan friends or family, but you can also opt for keeping silent about your spiritual choices.
- One of the best ways to connect with other pagans and to learn more about nature spirituality is through the Internet.
- No matter how you practice your pagan spirituality, always make an effort to remain connected to nature.

Appendix A

Recommended Reading

From ancient mythology to psychic development to the relationship between quantum physics and magic, many areas of human research and knowledge might appeal to pagans. A list like this is necessarily incomplete, but hopefully it will get you started exploring topics of interest to you. Remember that pagans have no scripture or list of required reading. Follow your own interests and intuition when choosing books to read. Happy exploring!

Adams, Cass, ed. *The Soul Unearthed: Celebrating Wildness and Personal Renewal Through Nature*. New York: Tarcher/Putnam, 1996.

Adler, Margot. *Drawing Down the Moon: Witches, Druids, Goddess-Worshippers, and Other Pagans in America Today*, rev. and enl. New York: Penguin/Arkana, 1997.

Anapol, Deborah. *Polyamory, The New Love Without Limits: Secrets of Sustainable Intimate Relationships*. San Rafael, Calif.: IntiNet Resource Center, 1997.

Anderson, William. *Green Man: The Archetype of Our Oneness With the Earth*. New York: Harper Collins, 1990.

Andrews, Ted. *Animal-Speak: The Spiritual & Magical Powers of Creatures Great & Small*. St. Paul, Minn.: Llewellyn Publications, 1993.

———. *How to Meet and Work with Spirit Guides*. St. Paul, Minn.: Llewellyn Publications, 1992.

Andruss, Van, and Christopher Plant, Judith Plant and Eleanor Wright, editors. *Home! A Bioregional Reader*. Philadelphia: New Society Publishers, 1990.

Ann, Martha, and Dorothy Myers Imel. *Goddesses in World Mythology: A Biographical Dictionary*. New York: Oxford University Press, 1993.

Ardinger, Barbara. *Goddess Meditations*. St. Paul, Minn.: Llewellyn Publications, 1998.

———. *Practicing the Presence of the Goddess*. Novato, Calif.: New World Library, 2000.

Arnold, Charles. *Ritual Body Art: Drawing the Spirit.* Custer, Wash.: Phoenix Publishing, 1996.

Aswynn, Freya. *Northern Mysteries and Magick: Runes, Gods, and Feminine Powers.* St. Paul, Minn.: Llewellyn Publications, 1998.

Beck, Renee, and Sydney Barbara Metrick. *The Art of Ritual: A Guide to Creating and Performing Your Own Ceremonies for Growth and Change.* Berkeley, Calif.: Celestial Arts, 1990.

Bentov, Itzhak. *Stalking the Wild Pendulum: On the Mechanics of Consciousness.* Rochester, Vt.: Destiny Books, 1977.

Bernstein, Frances. *Classical Living: Reconnecting With the Rituals of Ancient Rome.* San Francisco: Harper San Francisco, 2000.

Beyerl, Paul. *The Master Book of Herbalism.* Custer, Wash.: Phoenix Publishing, 1984.

Bonewits, Isaac. *Real Magic: An Introductory Treatise on the Basic Principles of Yellow Magic,* rev. ed. York Beach, Maine: Samuel Weiser, 1989.

Bord, Janet and Colin. *Earth Rites: Fertility Practices in Pre-Industrial Britain.* London: Granada Publishing, Limited, 1982.

Broch, Janice, and Veronica MacLer. *Seasonal Dance: How to Celebrate the Pagan Year.* York Beach, Maine: Samuel Weiser, Inc., 1993.

Brown, Joseph Epes. *The Sacred Pipe: Black Elk's Account of the Seven Rites of the Oglala Sioux.* Norman, Okla.: University of Oklahoma Press, 1953.

Budilovsky, Joan, and Eve Adamson. *The Complete Idiot's Guide to Meditation.* Indianapolis, Ind.: Alpha Books, 1998.

Bunning, Joan. *Learning the Tarot: A Tarot Book for Beginners.* York Beach, Maine: Samuel Weiser, Inc., 1998.

Carlyon, Richard. *A Guide to the Gods.* New York: William Morrow and Company, 1981.

Carr-Gomm, Philip, ed. *The Druid Renaissance: The Voice of Druidry Today.* London: Thorsons, 1996.

Christ, Carol P. *Laughter of Aphrodite: Reflections on a Journey to the Goddess.* New York: Harper Collins, 1987.

Conway, D. J. *The Ancient and Shining Ones: World Myth, Magick, and Religion.* St. Paul, Minn.: Llewellyn Publications, 1993.

Cowan, Tom. *Shamanism as a Spiritual Practice for Daily Life.* Freedom, Calif.: Crossing Press, 1996.

Crowley, Vivianne. *Phoenix from the Flame: Pagan Spirituality in the Western World.* London: Thorsons, 1994.

———. *Wicca: The Old Religion in the New Millennium.* London: Thorsons, 1996.

Curott, Phyllis. *Witchcrafting, A Spiritual Guide to Making Magic.* New York: Broadway Books, 2001.

Davidson, H. R. Ellis. *Myths and Symbols in Pagan Europe: Early Scandinavian and Celtic Religions.* Syracuse, N.Y.: Syracuse University Press, 1988.

De Grandis, Francesca. *Goddess Initiation: A Practical Celtic Program for Soul-Healing, Self-Fulfillment and Wild Wisdom*. San Francisco: Harper San Francisco Publishers, 2001.

Devereux, Paul, John Steele, and David Kubrin. *Earthmind: Tuning in to GAIA Theory with New Age Methods for Saving Our Planet*. San Francisco: Harper & Row, 1989.

Eliade, Mircea. *Shamanism: Archaic Techniques of Ecstasy*. Princeton, N.J.: Princeton University Press, 1964.

Evans-Wentz, W. Y. *The Fairy-Faith in Celtic Countries*. New Hyde Park, N.Y.: University Books, 1966.

Farrar, Janet and Stewart. *A Witches' Bible: The Complete Witches' Handbook*. Custer, Wash.: Phoenix Publishing, 1984.

———. *The Witches' God: Lord of the Dance*. London: Robert Hale, 1989.

———. *The Witches' Goddess: The Feminine Principle of Divinity*. London: Robert Hale, 1987.

Farrar, Janet and Stewart, and Gavin Bone. *The Healing Craft: Healing Practices for Witches and Pagans*. Custer, Wash.: Phoenix Publishing, 1999.

Fitch, Ed. *Magical Rites from the Crystal Well*. St. Paul, Minn.: Llewellyn Publications, 1984.

Ford, Patrick K., ed. *The Mabinogi and Other Medieval Welsh Tales*. Berkeley, Calif.: University of California Press, 1977.

Fox, Selena, et. al, eds. *Circle Guide to Pagan Groups: A Nature Spirituality Networking Sourcebook*. Mt. Horeb, Wis.: Circle, Annual edition, 2001.

Freeman, Mara. *Kindling the Celtic Spirit: Ancient Traditions to Illumine Your Life Throughout the Seasons*. San Francisco: Harper San Francisco, 2001.

Gadon, Elinor W. *The Once and Future Goddess: A Sweeping Visual Chronicle of the Sacred Female and Her Reemergence in the Cultural Mythology of Our Time*. San Francisco: Harper & Row, 1989.

Gardner, Gerald. *The Meaning of Witchcraft*. 1959. Reprint, Thame, England: I-H-O Books, 2000.

———. *Witchcraft Today*. 1954. Reprint, Thame, England: I-H-O Books, 1999.

Gawain, Shakti. *Creative Visualization: Use the Power of Your Imagination to Create What You Want in Life*, rev. ed. Novato, Calif.: New World Library, 1995.

Gimbutas, Marija. *The Language of the Goddess*. New York: Harper Collins, 1989.

Ginzburg, Carlo. *Ecstasies: Deciphering the Witches' Sabbath*. New York: Pantheon Books, 1991.

Goodwin, Matthew Oliver. *Numerology, the Complete Guide*. 2 vols. North Hollywood, Calif.: Newcastle Publishing, Inc., 1981.

Griffin, Susan. *Woman and Nature: The Roaring Inside Her*. New York: Harper & Row, 1978.

Guiley, Rosemary Ellen. *The Encyclopedia of Witches and Witchcraft*. New York: Facts on File, 1999.

Hammerman, David, and Lisa Lenard. *The Complete Idiot's Guide to Reincarnation*. Indianapolis, Ind: Alpha Books, 2000.

Harner, Michael. *The Way of the Shaman*, rev. ed. San Francisco: Harper San Francisco, 1990.

Harris, Eleanor and Philip. *The Crafting and Use of Ritual Tools: Step-by-Step Instructions for Woodcrafting Religious and Magical Implements*. St. Paul, Minn.: Llewellyn Publications, 1998.

Harrow, Judy. *Wicca Covens: How to Start and Organize Your Own*. Secaucus, N.J.: Citadel Press, 1999.

Harvey, Graham, and Charlotte Hardman. *Paganism Today: Wiccans, Druids, the Goddess and Ancient Earth Traditions for the Twenty-First Century*. London: Thorsons, 1996.

Hope, Murry. *The Psychology of Ritual*. Shaftesbury, Dorset: Element Books, 1988.

Hopman, Ellen Evert, and Lawrence Bond. *Being a Pagan: Druids, Wiccans and Witches Today*. Rochester, Vermont: Destiny Books, 1996.

Hutton, Ronald. *The Triumph of the Moon: A History of Modern Pagan Witchcraft*. New York: Oxford University Press, 1999.

Ingerman, Sandra. *Soul Retrieval: Mending the Fragmented Self*. San Francisco: Harper San Francisco, 1991.

Jackson, Nigel. *Masks of Misrule: The Horned God and His Cult in Europe*. Chieveley, Berkshire: Capall Bann Publishing, 1996.

Johnson, Kenneth. *Witchcraft and the Shamanic Journey: Pagan Folkways from the Burning Times*. St. Paul, Minn.: Llewellyn Publications, 1998.

Jones, Prudence, and Caitlín Matthews, eds. *Voices From the Circle: The Heritage of Western Paganism*. London: Aquarian Press, 1990.

Jones, Prudence, and Nigel Pennick. *A History of Pagan Europe*. London: Routledge, 1995.

Judith, Anodea. *Wheels of Life: A User's Guide to the Chakra System*. St. Paul, Minn.: Llewellyn Publications, 1987.

K. Amber. *Covencraft: Witchcraft for Three or More*. St. Paul, Minn.: Llewellyn Publications, 1998.

Kindred, Glennie. *Sacred Celebrations: A Sourcebook*. Glastonbury, Somerset: Gothic Image Publications, 2001.

Kondratiev, Alexei. *The Apple Branch: A Path to Celtic Ritual*. Cork, Ireland: The Collins Press, 1998.

LaChappelle, Dolores. *Sacred Land, Sacred Sex, Rapture of the Deep: Concerning Deep Ecology and Celebrating Life*. Durango, Colo.: Kivakí Press, 1988.

Leland, Charles G. *Aradia, or the Gospel of the Witches*. Custer, Wash.: Phoenix Publishing, 1998.

Lovelock, J. E. *Gaia: A New Look at Life On Earth*. New York: Oxford University Press, 1979.

Markale, Jean. *The Druids: Celtic Priests of Nature*. Rochester, Vt.: Inner Traditions International, 1999.

Matthews, Caitlín. *Celtic Wisdom Sticks: An Ogam Oracle*. London: Connections Book Publishing, 2001.

Matthews, Caitlín and John. *The Encyclopedia of Celtic Wisdom: A Celtic Shaman's Sourcebook.* Shaftesbury, Dorset: Element Books, 1994.

Matthews, John. *Taliesin: Shamanism and the Bardic Mysteries in Britain and Ireland.* London: The Aquarian Press, 1991.

McArthur, Margie. *Wisdom of the Elements: The Sacred Wheel of Earth, Air, Fire, and Water.* Freedom, Calif.: Crossing Press, 1998.

McColman, Carl. *Embracing Jesus and the Goddess: A Radical Call for Spiritual Sanity.* Gloucester, Mass.: Fair Winds Press, 2001.

———. *The Well-Read Witch: Essential Books for Your Magickal Library.* Franklin Lakes, N.J.: New Page Books, 2002.

McCoy, Edain. *The Sabbats: A New Approach to Living the Old Ways.* St. Paul, Minn.: Llewellyn Publications, 1998.

Miller, Hamish, and Paul Broadhurst. *The Sun and the Serpent: An Investigation into Earth Energies.* Launceston, Cornwall: Pendragon Press, 1989.

Ming-Dao, Deng. *Scholar Warrior: An Introduction to the Tao in Everyday Life.* New York: Harper Collins, 1990.

Monaghan, Patricia. *The New Book of Goddesses and Heroines.* St. Paul, Minn.: Llewellyn Publications, 1997.

Nicholson, Shirley, and Brenda Rosen, compilers. *Gaia's Hidden Life: The Unseen Intelligence of Nature.* Wheaton, Ill.: Quest Books, 1992.

Orion, Loretta. *Never Again the Burning Times: Paganism Revived.* Prospect Heights, Ill.: Waveland Press, 1995.

Osborn, Kevin, and Dana L. Burgess. *The Complete Idiot's Guide to Classical Mythology.* Indianapolis, Ind.: Alpha Books, 1998.

Pennick, Nigel. *The Complete Illustrated Guide to Runes: How to Interpret the Ancient Wisdom of the Runes.* Shaftesbury, Dorset: Element Books, 1999.

———. *Magical Alphabets.* York Beach, Maine: Samuel Weiser, Inc., 1992

Pollack, Rachel. *Seventy-Eight Degrees of Wisdom: A Book of Tarot.* London: Thorsons, 1997

Reed, Ellen Cannon. *The Heart of Wicca: Wise Words from a Crone on the Path.* York Beach, Maine: Samuel Weiser, Inc., 2000.

Rees, Alwyn and Brinley. *Celtic Heritage: Ancient Tradition in Ireland and Wales.* New York: Grove Press, Inc., 1961.

Regardie, Israel. *The Complete Golden Dawn System of Magic.* Scottsdale, Ariz.: New Falcon Publications, 1990.

Rhodes, J. Philip. *Wicca Unveiled: The Complete Rituals of Modern Witchcraft.* Glastonbury, Somerset: Speaking Tree Books, 2000.

Robbins, Trina. *Eternally Bad: Goddesses With Attitude.* Berkeley, Calif.: Conari Press, 2001.

Roberts, Elizabeth, and Elias Amidon, eds. *Earth Prayers From Around the World: 365 Prayers, Poems, and Invocations for Honoring the Earth.* New York: Harper Collins, 1991.

Rolleston, T. W. *Myths and Legends of the Celtic Race.* New York: Schocken Books, 1986.

Sjöö, Monica, and Barbara Mor. *The Great Cosmic Mother: Rediscovering the Religion of the Earth.* San Francisco: Harper Collins, 1987.

Squire, Charles. *Celtic Myth and Legend.* Franklin Lakes N.J.: New Page Books, 2001.

Starhawk. *The Spiral Dance, A Rebirth of the Ancient Religion of the Great Goddess: Rituals, Invocations, Exercises, Magic,* 20th ann. ed. San Francisco: Harper San Francisco, 1999.

———. *Truth or Dare, Encounters with Power, Authority, and Mystery.* San Francisco: Harper & Row, 1987.

Starhawk, Diane Baker, and Anne Hill. *Circle Round: Raising Children in Goddess Traditions.* New York: Bantam Books, 1998.

Stewart, R. J. *The Living World of Faery.* Glastonbury, Somerset: Gothic Image Publications, 1995.

———. *The Underworld Initiation: A Journey Toward Psychic Transformation.* Lake Toxaway, N.C.: Mercury Publishing, 1998.

Streep, Peg. *Altars Made Easy: A Complete Guide to Creating Your Own Sacred Space.* San Francisco: Harper San Francisco, 1997.

Sutton, Maya Magee, and Nicholas R. Mann. *Druid Magic: The Practice of Celtic Wisdom.* St. Paul, Minnesota: Llewellyn Publications, 2000.

Suzuki, David, and Peter Knudtson. *Wisdom of the Elders: Honoring Sacred Native Visions of Nature.* New York: Bantam Books, 1992.

Toben, Bob, and Fred Alan Wolf. *Space-Time and Beyond: Toward an Explanation of the Unexplainable.* New York: E.P. Dutton, Inc., 1982.

Thorsson, Edred. *The Book of Ogham: The Celtic Tree Oracle.* St. Paul, Minnesota: Llewellyn Publications, 1992.

Titchenell, Elsa-Brita. *The Masks of Odin: Wisdom of the Ancient Norse.* Pasadena, Calif.: Theosophical University Press, 1985.

Vale, V., and John Sulak. *Modern Pagans: An Investigation of Contemporary Pagan Practices.* San Francisco: RE/Search Publications, 2001.

Valiente, Doreen. *An ABC of Witchcraft Past and Present.* New York: St. Martin's Press, 1978.

Vitebsky, Piers. *Shaman: An Illustrated Guide.* Boston: Little, Brown and Company, 1996.

Weinstein, Marion. *Positive Magic: Occult Self-Help.* New York: Earth Magic Productions, Inc., 1994.

Welch, Lynda C. *Goddess of the North: A Comprehensive Study of the Norse Goddesses, From Antiquity to the Modern Age.* York Beach, Maine: Weiser Books, 2001.

Wood, Robin. *When, Why … If: An Ethics Workbook.* Dearborn, Mich.: Livingtree Books, 1996.

Zimmerman, Denise, and Katherine A. Gleason. *The Complete Idiot's Guide to Wicca and Witchcraft.* Indianapolis, Ind.: Alpha Books, 2000.

Resources

Pagans have embraced the Internet as a primary tool for networking, so traversing the corridors of cyberspace is almost essential for connecting with today's pagan community. Here is a list of websites dedicated to a variety of pagan and pagan-related themes. This is only a mere sampling of the many resources available online. If you don't have Internet access, check with your local library—many have computers you can use for little or no charge.

Given the impermanent nature of the Internet, many of these organizations may change their web address. If the URL given here doesn't work, visit one of the pagan-oriented search engines and check for an updated address.

American Federation of Astrologers

www.astrologers.com

This is the largest astrological membership and accreditation organization in the world, dedicated to the study of all scientific methods of astrology and the dissemination of astrological knowledge and understanding.

American Tarot Association

www.ata-tarot.com

ATA brings together qualified students, teachers, and masters of the Tarot to promote high standards of ethics and education.

American Vinland Association

www.freyasfolk.org

This organization is dedicated to reviving the pagan ways of northern Europe.

Barbara Ardinger

www.visionaryfiction.com/bawriting

Author of *Goddess Meditations, Practicing the Presence of the Goddess,* and *Finding New Goddesses,* Barbara also offers her services as an editor to pagan writers.

Ár nDraíocht Féin: A Druid Fellowship

www.adf.org

This is the beautiful and informative home page of a pagan community that began as a specifically druid organization but now encompasses all forms of Indo-European paganism.

Ariadne Spider

www.ariadnespider.com

This is a search engine of exclusively pagan URLs on the World Wide Web.

The Asatru Alliance

www.asatru.org

This organization is dedicated to honoring the old Norse Gods.

Asatru Folk Assembly

www.runestone.org

This community is committed to calling the sons and daughters of northern Europe back to their native ancestral spirituality.

Avatar Search

www.avatarsearch.com

The search engine of the occult Internet, this offers a large selection of pagan sites.

The Blessed Bee

www.theblessedbee.com

This large pagan website offers a variety of jewelry, ritual items, and other interesting things to buy.

Isaac Bonewits

www.neopagan.net

As the author of *Real Magic* and the founder of ADF, Bonewits's website is filled with useful information and essays.

The Cauldron and the Cross

www.thewhitemoon.com/c_n_c/

This site recommends books and information on Christopagan spirituality and contains links to other Christian-pagan hybrid websites.

Cherry Hill Seminary

www.cherryhillseminary.org

This seminary offers professional training for current and future pagan clergy.

Children of Artemis

www.witchcraft.org

This site promotes an ethical approach to Wicca and a truthful and accurate view of Wicca/witchcraft for the outside world.

Church of All Worlds

www.caw.org

This pagan community originally was based on the writings of science-fiction author Robert Heinlein.

Circle Sanctuary

www.circlesanctuary.org

This is the publisher of *Circle Magazine* and the *Circle Guide to Pagan Groups*.

Larry Cornett's Calendar of Pagan Events

members.aol.com/lcorncalen/
CALENDAR.htm

In the past, this website provided a detailed list of pagan gatherings and festivals. It no longer does so, but it now includes links to a variety of other pagan web pages that provide information on upcoming events.

Covenant of the Goddess

www.cog.org

COG is one of the largest and oldest associations of autonomous Wiccan covens and solitaries.

Francesca De Grandis

www.well.com/user/zthirdrd/

This is the home page for the author of *Be a Goddess!* and *Goddess Initiation*. It includes a variety of book reviews, poems, rituals, and other useful materials.

Dragon Hills

www.dragonhills.com

This large, privately owned pagan campground in west Georgia is the site of numerous pagan gatherings and festivals.

The Dream Tree

www.dreamtree.com

This is an online resource center for the psychology and spirituality of dreaming.

Dreamtrybe

www.dreamtrybe.com

Dreamtrybe (formerly Velvet Hammer) is a pagan/tribal musical collaboration based in Austin, Texas.

Druid.org

www.druid.org

Articles about Druid spirituality can be found here, including "Druidbooks," an extensive Druid bibliography.

Emerald Rose

www.emeraldrose.com

This Celtic acoustic band's repertoire includes traditional Irish and Scottish songs and pagan-flavored originals.

Encyclopedia Mythica

www.pantheon.org

This site contains a huge database of mythology and folklore from around the world.

Janet & Stewart Farrar and Gavin Bone

gofree.indigo.ie/~wicca/

These pagan elders wrote classic books such as *A Witches' Bible* and *What Witches Do*.

Foundation for Shamanic Studies

www.shamanism.org

This is one of the leading institutions dedicated to teaching and preserving traditional shamanic ways.

Goddess Moon Circles

www.goddessmoon.org

A website of pagan resources, featuring clergy listings, information on crisis counseling, a pagan-friendly charity, handfasting and wedding resources, and more.

The Grove of the Unicorn

www.unicorntrad.org

This eclectic Wiccan tradition has covens in Georgia, Texas, and Germany. The website is filled with useful information.

Guide to the Druids and Celtic Mysticism

www.wildideas.net/cathbad/druid.html

A Canadian druid assembled this useful collection of essays and articles on pagan druid ways.

Henge of Keltria

www.keltria.org

An offshoot of ADF, the Henge of Keltria has remained more specifically focussed on Celtic paganism.

Hermetic Order of the Golden Dawn

www.hermeticgoldendawn.org

One of the most important ceremonial magical fraternities, the Golden Dawn seeks to preserve and promote the Western Esoteric Tradition.

Fiona Horne

www.fionahorne.com

Fiona Horn is an Australian punk rocker turned celebrity witch.

Hemi-Sync Recordings

www.hemi-sync.com

This isn't a pagan website, but it features recordings designed to help foster meditative states of consciousness.

Imbas

www.imbas.org

Imbas promotes the spiritual path of *Senistrognata*, the ancestral customs of the Celtic peoples.

Information on Pagan Festivals (Especially for First-Timers)

www.witchvox.com/festivals/tt00_intro.html
www.silverravenwolf.com/festival.htm

These are excellent web pages about the do's and don'ts of attending a festival.

Jewitchery

www.jewitchery.org

This site is devoted to the integration of Judaism and paganism.

The Kemetic Orthodox Faith (Egyptian Paganism)

www.kemet.org

This organization is devoted to the revival of ancient Egyptian paganism.

The Magickal Cauldron

www.magickalcauldron.com

Articles, workshops, and the *Mystic Journeys* e-zine feature a broad selection of pagan information and lore.

Carl McColman

www.carlmccolman.com

This is the home page of this book's author.

Meditation and Creative Visualization

wuzzle.org/cave/s_medit.html

This site contains information on the magical use of meditation and visualization.

Nova Roma

www.novaroma.org

This community is devoted to the revival and reenactment of ancient Roman religion and culture.

Omphalos

www.omphalos.net

This is a directory and search engine for witchcraft and paganism.

Ord Brighideach—A Brigidine Order of Flamekeepers

www.ordbrighideach.org

This spiritual order is devoted to the Celtic Goddess Brighid. Members commit to tending a sacred flame once every 20 days, which is dedicated to Brighid.

Ord na Darach Gile—Order of the White Oak

www.technovate.org/web/whiteoak/

The Celtic pagan/druidic organization is particularly concerned about ethics and Celtic tribal values.

Order of Bards, Ovates, and Druids

www.druidry.org

This is the home page of the OBOD, a British-based organization that is one of the world's largest and oldest druid groups.

Ordo Templi Orientis U.S. Grand Lodge

www.otohq.org

This is a fraternal, initiatory, social, and educational organization dedicated to the branch of ceremonial magic known as Thelema.

Pagan Chant of the Month

www.dol.net/~panpipe/chant.html

This site contains a collection of pagan chants in RealAudio. Listen to pagan chanting right on your computer.

Pagan Federation

www.paganfederation.org

In this British-based international association of pagans, membership is based on three principles: reverence for nature, positive ethics, and understanding Spirit as including both Goddess and God.

PagaNet News

www.paganet.org

This pagan periodical is dedicated to fostering the growth and progress of polytheistic beliefs, practices, and organizations.

Pangaia Magazine

www.pangaia.com

This is the premier magazine devoted to pagan ("earthwise") issues.

Proteus Coven

www.draknet.com/proteus/

This is a "thealogically liberal" community within the tradition of Gardnerian Witchcraft.

Ravenwood Church and Seminary of the Old Religion

www.ravenwoodchurch.org

This large, traditional Wiccan coven based in Atlanta that had to fight for its rights back in the 1970s. The excellent newspaper archives section reveals how much prejudice still exists against witches.

Reclaiming

www.reclaiming.org

This Wiccan community features a high level of social and political consciousness.

Revival of Traditional Hellenic Religion

www.geocities.com/Athens/Aegean/7773/

This site is devoted to the renaissance of Greek paganism.

Romuva

www.romuva.lt/engl/

This Lithuanian pagan organization is dedicated to the revival of Baltic spirituality. This is of particular interest to the larger pagan community because Lithuania was the last country in Europe to convert to Christianity, and therefore its pagan heritage is relatively more intact than in most other areas.

The Runic Journey

www.tarahill.com/runes/

This site contains an exploration of the history and divinatory use of the Norse runes.

SageWoman Magazine

www.sagewoman.com

The sister magazine to Pangaia, it features articles written specifically for women of the Goddess.

Serpentine Music

www.serpentinemusic.com

A website with extensive listings of pagan music in all genres. It also includes information about the artists.

Society of Celtic Shamans

www.faeryshaman.org

This site offers a series of correspondence courses for learning a path of Celtic shamanism.

Solitary-Pagan.net

www.solitary-pagan.net

This educational site has two goals: to inform the public about paganism and to provide a curriculum for solitary pagans to follow in their studies.

Starhawk

www.starhawk.org

This is the website of the author of *The Spiral Dance* and many other pagan books.

The Starwood Festival

www.rosencomet.com/starwood.html
This festival is one of the largest and oldest of pagan gatherings.

R. J. Stewart

www.dreampower.com
Stewart is the author of numerous pagan and occult books, most notably *The UnderWorld Initiation* and *The Living World of Faery*.

Tangled Moon Coven

www.tangledmoon.org
This Tennessee-based coven's website contains useful resources for coven leaders.

Three Weird Sisters

www.threeweirdsisters.com
This trio of women play acoustic instruments and write original songs that range from satirical ditties to moody excursions into Celtic myth.

Tuatha De Brighid

www.tuathadebrighid.org
This clan of modern Druids seeks to find common ground amidst all nonharmful spiritual loyalties and believes in the interconnectedness of all faiths.

Doreen Valiente

www.doreenvaliente.com
This is the home page of the one of the founding mothers of modern Wicca.

The Voice of the Woods

www.pixelations.com/ogham
This site contains an online Ogham oracle. Ask it a question to consult the wisdom of the Celtic tree system of divination.

Whispered Prayers

www.whisperedprayers.com
This site features a wide variety of pagan merchandise along with essays and articles on the pagan path.

The Witches' Voice

www.witchvox.org
www.witchvox.net
This is one of the largest, most important, and most useful of pagan websites. It is a proactive educational network dedicated to correcting misinformation about pagans, heathens, witches, and Wiccans. Visit www.witchvox.net for pagan networking: websites, individuals, communities, stores, festivals, and musicians/groups.

Index